W9-AJQ-118

921
FO

Ford, Gerald R.

A time to heal

DATE			
MAR 26 1983			
OCT. 03 1983			
MAY 08 1984			
MY 12 '89			
AUG 04 '97			
JAN 13 98			
MAR 12 98			
SE 19 01			
NO 10 03			
JE 29 13			

EAU CLAIRE DISTRICT LIBRARY

© THE BAKER & TAYLOR CO.

A TIME
TO HEAL

A TIME TO HEAL

THE AUTOBIOGRAPHY OF

Gerald R. Ford

WITHDRAWN

EAU CLAIRE DISTRICT LIBRARY

71283

HARPER & ROW, PUBLISHERS

AND

THE READER'S DIGEST ASSOCIATION, INC.

2/7/83 Br T #1295

Portions of this work originally appeared in *Time* Magazine and *The Reader's Digest*.

A TIME TO HEAL. Copyright © 1979 by Gerald R. Ford. All rights reserved. Printed in the United States of America. No part of this book may be used or reproduced in any manner whatsoever without written permission except in the case of brief quotations embodied in critical articles and reviews. For information address Harper & Row, Publishers, Inc., 10 East 53rd Street, New York, N.Y. 10022. Published simultaneously in Canada by Fitzhenry & Whiteside Limited, Toronto.

Designed by Gloria Adelson

Library of Congress Cataloging in Publication Data

Ford, Gerald R.   1913–
   A time to heal.
   Includes index.
   1. Ford, Gerald R., 1913–   2. Presidents—
United States—Biography. I. Title.
E866.F67   1979   973.925′092′4[B]   78–20162
ISBN 0–06–011297–2

79 80 81 82 83 10 9 8 7 6 5 4 3 2

to
Betty

Contents

ACKNOWLEDGMENTS

Reviewing my life and long political career for this book proved to be an enormous undertaking, and one that was often emotionally moving. Only with the help of many people has it been possible to bring back fully and accurately years of memories. Above all, *A Time to Heal* would never have come to fruition had it not been for the assistance of Trevor Armbrister, a distinguished journalist and probing reporter.

Trevor interviewed me for hundreds of hours, then assisted me in the assembling and writing of these recollections. Throughout our labors, he demonstrated a remarkable ability to corral a massive amount of material and to help me convey my innermost feelings and beliefs. Trevor's writing skills and fierce devotion to excellence have made my association with him one of the highlights of my days since leaving the White House. *A Time to Heal* has been as much a part of his life as it is a portrayal of mine. And for that I am deeply indebted to him.

My gratitude also extends to many others. For ideas and guidance: Jack Marsh, Brent Scowcroft, Dean Burch, Robert Barrett, David Kennerly, Paul O'Neill and James Humes. For research and checking: Ann Dear Gavell, John Vardeman, Betty Williamson, Sandra Eisert and archivists of the Gerald R. Ford Presidential Library. For endless hours of typing transcripts and drafts: Gloria Hill, Linda Hill, Lillian Simasko, Pat Merchant, Pat Lawson, Mary Christie, Jill Burckmyer. For enthusiasm and encouragement: all my staff, past and present, my family and numerous friends—some of whom I write about, some of whom I do not.

Finally, for their help and counsel, Harper & Row Publisher Erwin Glikes, *Reader's Digest* Editor-in-Chief Edward Thompson, *Digest* Washington Editor William Schulz, and the editor of this book, *Digest* Managing Editor Kenneth Gilmore, who guided all of us with good judgment and skill every step of the way.

"To everything there is a season and a time to every purpose under the heaven. A time to be born and a time to die; a time to plant and a time to pluck up that which is planted. A time to kill and a time to heal; a time to break down and a time to build up. A time to weep and a time to laugh; a time to mourn and a time to dance."

Ecclesiastes 3: 1-4

I

Uncertain Days

"I know there is a God. I see the storm coming, and I know His hand is in it. If He has a place for me, and I think He has, I believe I am ready; with God's help I shall not fail."

— Abraham Lincoln to his friend
Newton Bateman before the
Presidential election of 1860

Shortly before nine o'clock on the warm, cloudy morning of August 1, 1974, I received a telephone call from General Alexander M. Haig, Jr. For the past fifteen months—ever since the resignations of H. R. Haldeman and John Ehrlichman—Haig had been serving as White House chief of staff, and he had done a magnificent job in an almost impossible situation.

"Mr. Vice President," he said, "it's urgent that I see you as soon as possible."

From the tone of his voice I could tell that something very important was happening and that he didn't want to discuss it on the telephone. "Well, sure," I replied. "Come on over now. We have some meetings on the schedule, but we can push them back."

Fifteen minutes later, Haig arrived at my office on the second floor of the Executive Office Building. Robert Hartmann, the brusque former newspaperman who was serving as my chief of staff, had been talking with me about routine business, and I'd asked him to stay for the session with Haig. This, too, was routine. Whenever I had a meeting on a matter of some importance, the staff always made sure that a witness was there. But Haig did not know Hartmann well. He seemed surprised by his presence, and I had the impression that he didn't feel he could be as forthright as he might normally have been. Still, what he did say was worrisome enough.

Eight days earlier, on July 24, the Supreme Court had ruled that President Richard M. Nixon had to turn over to U.S. District Court Judge John J. Sirica the recordings of sixty-four conversations that had been taped in the President's offices. The Court felt that they might contain evidence for the pending cover-up trial of six of Nixon's former aides. The President had already turned over transcripts of twenty of those tapes; others were scheduled to be delivered to Sirica on Monday, August 5. And those others were the ones that bothered Haig.

"I want to alert you that things are deteriorating," he said. "The whole ball game may be over. You'd better start thinking about a change in your life. I can't tell you what's going to happen, but I have to tell you what I know."

The new tapes, he said, contained evidence that would contradict Nixon's version of events in the Watergate scandal. The evidence would prove that Nixon knew about the cover-up six days after the break-in at Democratic National Committee headquarters and that he'd been deceiving the American people ever since. He hadn't seen the evidence himself, Haig said, but he'd been told about it by people who had. They had explained that it contained the so-called smoking gun, and he felt sure that they were telling the truth.

I asked for more details. He said that at the moment he couldn't tell me anything more. The tapes were being transcribed. Eventually he'd have copies, but he didn't have them yet. And if those transcripts contained the evidence that he'd been told they would, then the President's chances of escaping impeachment in the House of Representatives—and conviction in the Senate—would disappear. He hadn't even suspected the existence of this new evidence. Neither, he added, had the President's attorney, James St. Clair. Like so many other Americans, they had believed Nixon's repeated assertions of innocence. Unknowingly, St. Clair had misrepresented the President's case before the House Judiciary Committee. St. Clair, Haig said, was angry about that now. I understood that. I was angry too.

There was nothing more to be said. After forty-five minutes, Haig returned to the White House. I swore Hartmann to secrecy, then concentrated on catching up with my schedule. My heart wasn't in it. For the past eight months, ever since I had become Vice President, I had been hoping against hope that Watergate would go away, that Nixon would prove his innocence of involvement in the affair, that the basic civility of our political process would return. Now those hopes were evaporating fast.

Shortly after noon that day, I drove to Capitol Hill. No sooner had I entered my office off the Senate floor than Haig telephoned again. He wanted another meeting as soon as possible, and this time he didn't want Hartmann there.

When Haig appeared at three-thirty that afternoon, he looked even more beaten and harassed than he had earlier. Since our morning meeting, he had either read the transcripts or heard them discussed in great detail. The tapes made clear that Nixon knew the whole story on June 23, 1972. And when that evidence became public, Nixon's case would disintegrate. In moments of stress, Haig proceeds very deliberately, choosing his words with great care. Now he came to the point: "Are you ready, Mr. Vice President, to assume the Presidency in a short period of time?"

"If it happens, Al, I am prepared," I said. Our conversation that day had an unusual formality, both of us aware that we were speaking not only as friends but also for the record book.

"I can't tell you what's going to happen in the next forty-eight hours," he went on. "I just don't know what the President is going to do." Haig said he had discussed the new evidence with Nixon the afternoon before, and Nixon had brushed it off by saying that it was "manageable." Everyone else who knew about it disagreed. Carefully, Haig laid out the options that the "knowledgeable people" on the White House staff had agreed were still available to the President. The first was that he could try to "ride it out" by letting impeachment take its natural course through the House and the Senate trial, fighting against conviction all the way. His second option was to resign.

Here the number of alternatives increased. Under provisions of the 25th Amendment to the Constitution, he could step aside temporarily. He could delay his resignation until further along in the impeachment process. He could try to settle for a censure vote in Congress. He could pardon himself and everyone else involved in Watergate and *then* resign. Finally, Haig said that according to some on Nixon's White House staff, Nixon could agree to leave in return for an agreement that the new President—Gerald Ford—would pardon him. Haig emphasized that these weren't *his* suggestions. He didn't identify the staff members and he made it very clear that he wasn't recommending any one option over another. What he wanted to know was whether or not my overall assessment of the situation agreed with his.

I had no doubts about his basic assumptions. If Nixon tried to "ride it out," he'd be impeached in the House, and the odds were overwhelming that he'd be convicted in the Senate. These new tapes would cause a groundswell of demands for his immediate resignation. But that's where Nixon's peculiar personality came into play. He was not one to quit. If someone went to him and said, "You must resign tomorrow," that would inevitably tilt his decision to stay and fight it through. Pressure couldn't be applied directly.

Haig agreed completely with that. Next he asked if I had any suggestions as to courses of action for the President. I didn't think it would be proper for me to make any recommendations at all, and I told him so. Because of his references to pardon authority, I did ask Haig about the extent of a President's pardon power.

"It's my understanding from a White House lawyer," Haig replied, "that a President does have authority to grant a pardon even before criminal action has been taken against an individual." He didn't name the lawyer. Nor did he say whether or not that authority existed before the individual had been indicted. It was simply a general interpretation.

When Haig got up to leave, we put our arms around each other and then shook hands goodbye. "We've got to keep in contact," he said. "Don't hesitate to call me, and I won't hesitate to call you. Things could break so fast that we have to be accessible to each other."

"Well, Al," I replied, "I want some time to think. I want to talk to

St. Clair and to Betty. She deserves to be brought up to date and I want his legal assessment of Nixon's problems. In the meantime, I'll keep my cool. I'll be available."

For several minutes after Haig left, the implications of our conversation weighed heavily on me. Nixon was going to leave one way or the other. The only questions were when and how. And I was going to become President—a job to which I'd never aspired—at a tumultuous moment in the nation's history. I'm not the kind of person who is torn by self-doubt, and I had no doubts about my ability to function well in the office. What bothered me most was the nature of Nixon's departure. In the 198 years of the Republic, no President had ever resigned, and only one other Chief Executive—Andrew Johnson—had ever been the target of an impeachment effort in the Congress. But Nixon, I had to conclude, had brought his troubles upon himself.

Throughout my political life, I always believed what I was told. I was truthful to others; I expected others to be truthful with me. Repeatedly over the past several months, Nixon had assured me that he was not involved in Watergate, that the evidence would prove his innocence, that the matter would fade from view. He had said much the same thing to his Cabinet and staff, to his family and to the American people. I had chosen to believe him, and I had tried to give him the benefit of every doubt. One reason for my support was our long association together. We had been friends for twenty-five years. We had campaigned for each other, and there had never been a time when I felt he wasn't telling me the truth. A second reason, of course, was the office I held. I simply *had* to support him. If I did anything else, people would charge that I was undercutting him in order to acquire the Presidency myself.

My staff saw what was coming much earlier than I did. On several occasions during that spring and summer, Hartmann or Jack Marsh, a former Congressman from Virginia who was one of my closest aides, came into my office and said, "Well, it looks closer and closer, your becoming President." And I always brushed it off, partly because I didn't want to believe it and partly because I didn't want to say the slightest thing to anyone that might be construed as an effort to undermine Nixon. Indeed, until that moment, I had agreed with St.

Clair and others that as a matter of law, the President was not guilty of an impeachable offense. Bad judgment, yes, but not an impeachable offense.

And now this. I was angry that Nixon hadn't told me the truth. The hurt was very deep, and I wasn't sure that I could adequately express it in words to anyone, least of all to Nixon himself. I wanted time to think, and I wanted to be alone.

After several moments, Hartmann interrupted my reverie. I asked him to schedule an appointment with St. Clair first thing in the morning; then I told him about my latest conversation with Haig. As I repeated the options that Haig had listed for me, warning bells seemed to go off inside his head. "That's why you should have had a witness there," he said.

"What do you mean?"

"That last option Haig mentioned, that Nixon resign in return for an agreement that he receive a pardon from the new President. I don't like that at all."

"But, Bob," I replied, "Al wasn't suggesting that. It was just one of the ideas that he said were being kicked around by people at the White House."

"I know, I know. But Haig didn't come over here to go away empty-handed. And he didn't discuss this delicate matter without Nixon's knowing about it. And he mentioned the pardon option, and you sat there listening to him. Well, silence implies assent. He probably went back to the White House and told Nixon that he'd mentioned the idea and that you weren't uncomfortable with it. It was extremely improper for him to bring the subject up."

That reaction was typical of Bob. Because I'm not by nature suspicious of people or their motives, I thought it would be wise to have someone on my staff who was. And Bob was suspicious of everyone. Over the years, that Hartmann characteristic had saved me from many pitfalls. This time, however, I thought he was overreacting, making a mountain out of a molehill, and I told him so.

"Well," he replied, "I think you ought to get Jack Marsh's judgment on this."

I looked at my watch. It was five-thirty. Betty, I knew, was waiting for me in the limousine outside. The options discussion would have to be put off. "All right," I told Bob. "I'll talk to Jack, but I don't have time now. I've got to go."

Eight years earlier, in 1966, Congress had passed an authorization to build a house for the Vice President. Funds, however, had never been appropriated, and the men who'd held the office since then—Hubert H. Humphrey, Spiro T. Agnew and I—had continued to live in our private homes. A few months after I became Vice President, Michigan's Republican Senator Robert Griffin and several other friends on the Hill persuaded the Congress to approve an old Victorian mansion on the grounds of the U.S. Naval Observatory, just off Massachusetts Avenue, N.W., as a "temporary" residence for the VP. Traditionally, the mansion had housed the Chief of Naval Operations and his family, and the Navy didn't want to give it up. But the Congress insisted, and the timing was right. We were hoping to move in by the summer's end.

And so for the past several months, Betty had been meeting with officials of the Navy and the Secret Service in an effort to determine what changes would have to be made. It was quite a job, and soon it became obvious that the renovation was going to be far more expensive and time-consuming than anyone had expected. But Betty kept at it with her characteristic enthusiasm and drive. She was, in fact, planning to go to New York City the following week to select furnishings. This Thursday afternoon, she wanted me to approve the areas she'd selected for our living quarters and for entertaining guests. The exercise at this moment, I felt, was ridiculous. The possibility that we'd ever live in that house was slim, and getting slimmer all the time. Still, I had to make my appearance. To change plans at the last minute would invite reporters to ask questions. And that I didn't need.

The rush-hour traffic was heavy that afternoon, and it took us nearly twenty minutes to reach our destination. An interior designer and an official from the Navy Department proceeded to give us a tour. The CNO, they said, had preferred to use the entrance that fronted on Massachusetts Avenue. Perhaps we'd prefer the more secluded entrance on Observatory Circle. We agreed that we would. They talked about their plans to redecorate the master bedroom and each of the children's rooms, then discussed where they were planning to take Betty in New York the next week to purchase china, draperies and furniture. The conversation droned on endlessly, and I was growing more and more impatient. Yet I couldn't say anything to Betty in the presence of these people.

Finally, mercifully, our tour was over. The limousine dropped me off at the EOB and whisked Betty home. Back at the office, I talked to Hartmann about my schedule. For some time I'd been planning to fly to Mississippi to campaign for Republican Congressional candidates, then go on to New Orleans to speak at the annual convention of the Disabled American Veterans. I was due to leave Saturday morning, less than forty-eight hours away. Now the question arose: Because of what Haig had told me and the possibility that Nixon might have to resign, should I break the commitment and stay in Washington? It didn't take me long to decide to make the trip. If I canceled it, the reaction would have been: "Well, the game's over." And that would have been premature, perhaps complicating problems in the White House.

Initially, we had agreed that Jack Marsh would accompany me. Military affairs were his specialty. I was going to speak to a veterans' group, and he had already pulled together most of the information I needed for the speech. But now we agreed that Hartmann would go instead. My press secretary, Paul Miltich, didn't know the details of my conversations with Haig. Hartmann did. As a former reporter, he would be better equipped to deal with the press contingent that covered the Vice President. He would help to assure that I didn't get too far out on a limb in what I perceived to be my still necessary function of defending the President. Besides, Marsh got along well with Haig—far better than Hartmann did—and I had every confidence in his ability to mind the store in Washington.

Hartmann reminded me now that I still hadn't briefed Marsh about my meetings with Haig and the options he'd discussed. "Jack is standing by," he said, "and I think you ought to talk to him before this goes any further."

Time was the problem again. "Well, I've got to go," I said. "I'm going to talk to Betty tonight, and in the morning we'll discuss it some more. I promise you I'll talk to Jack."

By seven o'clock, I was back at our two-story brick and frame house in Alexandria. Betty and I had promised the George Graebers

(Washington *Star* society columnist Betty Beale and her husband) that we would join them for dinner that evening at their home. As we dressed in our bedroom, I told Betty that the situation had changed and that new evidence would be coming out which would deal a blow to the President. She was curious, of course, but she knew that we were running late. We couldn't talk about it then.

After dinner, we returned home, sat in the family room downstairs, and talked about what had happened that day. As I described my two meetings with Haig, her eyes widened in disbelief. She had long shared my view that everything we'd been told by the White House was the truth. Now the story was falling apart, and she was dumbfounded.

"My God," she replied, "this is going to change our whole life."

Betty is not the kind to be vehement and say, "Damn it, Nixon wasn't fair to you. He wasn't fair to the country." She's a soft-spoken, very compassionate woman, and her immediate reaction was one of sadness for the President and his family, friends of ours and people whom we'd admired for years. It was hard for us even to talk about what was going to happen to them.

Our conversation was all the more solemn when we considered the new experiences we were about to share. Both of us recognized the awesome responsibilities that would fall on my shoulders and to some degree on hers. And both of us were conscious of how tentative and uncertain everything was. "I just can't tell you what's going to happen," I said. "We could be going to the White House next week, maybe even sooner, or we could be dangling for the next six months while the impeachment process winds through the House and the trial concludes in the Senate. It all depends on what Nixon decides to do."

Next we discussed the options that Haig had said were still available to the President. Betty was very firm in her view that because of the peculiar position I was in, I shouldn't get involved in making any recommendations at all. Not to Haig, not to Nixon, not to anybody. I concurred fully. Finally, we talked about her pending trip to New York. Things were moving so fast, we agreed, that the proper thing to do would be to postpone it until we had a better idea of what was going to happen.

As we prepared to go upstairs, I received a phone call from Haig.

"Nothing has changed," he said. "The situation is as fluid as ever."

"Well," I replied, "I've talked with Betty, and we're prepared, but we can't get involved in the White House decision-making process."

"I understand," he said. "I'll be in touch with you tomorrow."

It was almost one-thirty and time to go to bed. We entered our bedroom, undressed and snapped off the light. As we lay there in the darkness, our hands reached out and touched simultaneously without either of us having said a word. Then we began to pray.

"God, give us strength, give us wisdom, give us guidance as the possibility of a new life confronts us.

"We promise to do our very best, whatever may take place.

"You have sustained us in the past.

"We have faith in Your guiding hand in the difficult and challenging days ahead.

"In Jesus' name we pray."

I concluded with a prayer from the fifth and sixth verses of chapter three of the Book of Proverbs: "Trust in the Lord with all thine heart, and lean not unto thine own understanding. In all thy ways acknowledge Him, and He shall direct thy paths."

Fifty years before, I had learned that prayer as a child in Sunday school. I can remember saying it the night I discovered that my stepfather was not my real father. I had repeated it often at sea during World War II. It was something I said whenever a crisis arose.

Shortly after eight o'clock the next morning, I met with James St. Clair, the Boston attorney who had been handling Nixon's impeachment defense for the past seven months. A soft-spoken, rather handsome man, St. Clair had a retiring, almost self-effacing manner that belied a first-rate legal mind.

Until our meeting that morning, I had assumed that St. Clair had been given access to all material relevant to the Watergate affair. Yet it was obvious to me that the three June 23 tapes of Nixon's conversations with Haldeman had caught him by surprise. He was shocked by them. "Until I found out about those tapes," he said, speaking very deliberately, "I was absolutely convinced that the President was not guilty of an impeachable offense, and I was preparing my defense based on that belief."

"What's your assessment now?"

"Probably the same as yours," he said. "Unquestionably, this will lead the House to impeach the President. It'll lead the Senate to convict him. The only question now is: What does he do? Resign or fight it through?"

Neither one of us could know his answer then. Quickly, I asked St. Clair, "Do you know of any other new or damaging evidence besides what's on the June 23 tapes?"

"No," he replied.

Then I told him about the options that Haig had mentioned to me the afternoon before. St. Clair listened quietly, commenting only that he had not been the source of any White House staff opinion about a President's power to issue pardons.

No sooner had St. Clair left than I called in Marsh. I briefed Jack on everything that had occurred in the past twenty-four hours. He seemed just as stunned by the news as I had been. That is not to say that he registered much emotion. Anyone who can make thirty-eight parachute jumps while serving as a Congressman has to be fairly calm and unflappable. And Jack was certainly that. But he was also a man of incredibly good judgment. He agreed with Bob that the mere mention of the pardon option constituted a potential time bomb for me. I explained that Haig was not suggesting a deal, that these options hadn't even originated with him, that I had said nothing to signal approval or disapproval of any of them. But like Hartmann, Marsh was adamant. "If you don't believe us," Jack said, "talk to someone else whose advice you value."

To whom could I turn? Almost instantly, Bryce Harlow came to mind. A short, solemn-faced Washington business executive who had served as adviser to six Presidents, he was a man of total integrity. Possessed of infinite tact—in 1972, when the late House Majority Leader Hale Boggs and I traveled to the People's Republic of China, Harlow was the man I asked to bridge the gap between our staffs— he also had more common sense and political perception than anyone I knew. I was sure I could rely upon him totally, and I told Hartmann to arrange a meeting as soon as possible.

Just before one o'clock, I drove to Capitol Hill to meet with the Senate's Republican and Democratic leaders, Hugh Scott of Pennsylvania and Mike Mansfield of Montana. Both had wanted to talk to me about the proper procedures to be followed in the event of a Senate trial of the President. Under the Constitution, the Vice President doesn't preside over the Senate when such a trial occurs. I could, of course, have exercised my tie-breaking responsibilities as the Senate's presiding officer during the debate about the rules governing the trial, but this would have put me in an awkward position, and I told Scott and Mansfield that I wouldn't do that.

We sat there puffing on our pipes, each of us conscious of the agony the country was going through, each of us aware of the responsibilities we would have to bear. Scott did most of the talking. I was sure he hadn't heard about the new evidence—and I didn't feel it was proper for me to tell him then—but on the basis of what he knew already, he seemed convinced that the case was lost. Impeachment in the House and conviction in the Senate were virtual certainties.

Mansfield raised the question of fairness. As the Majority Leader, he said, he had a responsibility to protect the President's constitutional rights. And he would honor that obligation. The constitutional process would be served, and there would be no railroading of the President.

After making that pledge, Mansfield left the room. Scott and I were alone. He told me that he had talked to Arizona Senator Barry Goldwater and that they had tried to determine how much support the President still had in the Senate. Nixon needed thirty-four votes to escape conviction; he had at least thirty-six now, but eleven of them were soft. Scott understood that I couldn't comment on that, that I was still obliged to support the President. His voice trembled, and he seemed deeply disturbed. "Continued support," he went on, "will make it hard later to unite the country. You're all we've got now, and I mean the country, not the party."

I thought I saw tears in his eyes and tried to comfort him, but I found it hard to keep my own emotions under control. Finally, I changed the subject and suggested that it might be a good idea for me to make a public statement within the next few days. In it I could say that since the executive and legislative branches of our government were now locked in an adversary relationship, it would no longer be proper for me to seem to be a participant in the process or to seek to affect the outcome. In sum, I'd be declaring my neutrality.

But where to make such a statement? I told him that I'd be traveling to Mississippi and Louisiana that weekend and suggested that I could issue it there.

Scott didn't like that idea at all. "A nationally important statement should be made in the nation's capital and nowhere else," he said. He was right. It was something I could do when I returned from the trip. As we left the room, he put his arm around me and gripped my shoulder hard. Neither of us had to say another word.

My schedule that afternoon was crowded as usual: an interview with James Reston of the New York *Times*, a session with representatives of the National League of Families of American Prisoners and Missing in Southeast Asia, individual meetings with Deputy Assistant Secretary of Defense Roger Shields, Office of Management and Budget Director Roy Ash and Secretary of the Treasury William Simon. Then there was that all-important get-together with Bryce Harlow. He came to my office late in the afternoon and, with Hartmann present, I told him everything I knew. He listened, his expression betraying no emotion at all. Only after I had finished did he let me know in no uncertain terms that he agreed with Bob and Jack, that the mere mention of the pardon option could cause a lot of trouble in the days ahead.

We agreed that the only thing I could do would be to call Haig in the presence of witnesses and button this thing down. Minutes later, Haig was on the line. I had written out in longhand what I wanted to say to him, and I read it slowly so that there could be no ambiguities. "I want you to understand," I said, "that I have no intention of recommending what the President should do about resigning or not resigning and that nothing we talked about yesterday afternoon should be given any consideration in whatever decision the President may wish to make."

"You're right," Haig said.

The aircraft provided for the Vice President's use that summer of 1974 was called *Air Force Two*, but it was hardly luxurious. It was a squat and aging Convair, a turboprop that creaked and groaned its way through the skies. The pilots, however, were superb. They had flown me through all sorts of terrible weather, and although we'd ex-

EAU CLAIRE DISTRICT LIBRARY

perienced one or two fairly close calls over the past few months, I
had every confidence in their ability. At eight o'clock on Saturday
morning, August 3, we lifted off from Andrews Air Force Base and
headed for Mississippi.

Normally, only a handful of Secret Service agents accompanied me
on my trips away from Washington. There were thirteen of them
aboard the plane that day. The same was true of the press. I was used
to being covered by the regulars: Maggie Hunter of the New York
Times, David Kennerly of *Time* magazine, Tom Joyce of *Newsweek*,
Ron Nessen of NBC and Phil Jones of CBS. But there were eleven additions for this trip.

They must have suspected that something special was going to
break, but I was determined not to give away the secret. To make
sure that he wouldn't fall into reporters' traps, I had not even told
Paul Miltich, my own press secretary, about the new evidence. The
only staffers who knew were Hartmann and Marsh.

Ever since my confirmation as Vice President, I had spent countless hours—and logged thousands of miles—away from Washington
in order to speak at Republican gatherings. I had been criticized severely for this. "The new Vice President," one editorial fumed,
"should stay home and mind the store." Yet it was imperative for me
to maintain my busy schedule out of town. Congressional elections
were just three months away. Because of Watergate and the Vietnam
War, Republicans everywhere were in trouble. Virtually no one was
speaking up for the GOP. To stave off crushing defeat at the polls
that fall, somebody who knew the party's accomplishments and goals
had to be willing and available to explain and answer questions about
them. And nowhere was that more important than in the states of the
Deep South. For nearly one hundred years Democrats had controlled
those states. Not until 1964 had the GOP gained any respectability
there—and that was in a losing cause. In 1968, however, Nixon had
done well in the South. In 1972, he'd swept every Southern state, and
I wanted to do everything I could to prevent the pendulum from
swinging the other way.

Shortly after ten that morning, we touched down at the Golden
Triangle Regional Airport in Starkville, Mississippi. I spoke at a rally
there for our House candidate, Ben Hilbun. Then we reboarded the

EAU CLAIRE DISTRICT LIBRARY

plane for the forty-minute flight to Jackson. Representative Thad Cochran (who in 1978 was elected Mississippi's first Republican Senator since Reconstruction) was among the notables who met me as I stepped onto the tarmac and he escorted me to a luncheon at the Jackson Hilton Hotel. There I repeated my assertion that the President was not guilty of an impeachable offense. Had I said otherwise at that moment, the whole house of cards might have collapsed.

That it was about to collapse was becoming clearer by the hour. As I was en route to Hattiesburg to speak at a rally for Representative Trent Lott, Senator Griffin telephoned me through the White House switchboard. He said he wanted to read me a letter he was sending to Nixon. "Dear Mr. President," it began, "there is no doubt in my mind that unless you choose to resign, the House will adopt articles of impeachment making necessary a trial in the Senate." The Senate, he predicted, would issue a subpoena for the Watergate tapes. And he concluded: "If you defy such a subpoena, I shall regard that as an impeachable offense and shall vote accordingly."

I appreciated Bob's decision to keep me informed. Just twenty-four hours before, after my meeting with Scott and Mansfield, I'd had lunch with him in Washington. He had tried to tone down my public defense of Nixon. "You don't have to act like the President's lawyer," he said. I knew he had thought hard about this, and I recognized that what he said in the letter was right. But now I knew something that he didn't know, which made his scenario irrelevant. Judge Sirica would receive the new evidence in another two days. It was bound to leak out. The time to "stonewall" or defy subpoenas had passed.

Given what was happening in Washington, the rest of my weekend was remarkably low-key: a press conference in New Orleans, followed by a cocktail party and a fund-raiser for Representative David Treen. Every night, of course, I called Betty at home in Alexandria. She was carrying an enormous burden, so I was concerned about how she was feeling and what the children were doing. Then, too, I wanted her impressions of the news. Had our friends told her anything I should know?

Although she'd never enjoyed politics, she had a good ear and a remarkable sensitivity for the nuances of what was happening. Everything was quiet, she said. She had heard that Nixon and a few trusted aides had gone to Camp David to plan their strategy, but she didn't know anything more. That morning's Washington *Post*, she said, had carried an article entitled "A Capitol in Agony"; the subtitle had been "The Impeachment Monster Is Unleashed."

On Monday morning, August 5, I arrived at the Marriott Hotel in New Orleans, where I delivered my speech to the Disabled American Veterans. I expected some applause. What I didn't expect was what happened next. No sooner had I sat down than the DAV's national commander, John Soave of Detroit, took the microphone and said, "Thank you, Mr. President." That was the first time I'd been called that by anyone, and it startled me.

Flying home from New Orleans that afternoon, I received word from Jack Marsh that the White House would make a significant announcement, adverse to the President, later that day. *Air Force Two* touched down at Andrews Air Force Base at 2:45 P.M. Half an hour later, I was in my office at the EOB. Marsh brought Hartmann and me up to date on what was happening, and we notified Haig that I was back in town. He came over at once. He looked more haggard than he had before, and I remember thinking that I'd never seen a man so physically and emotionally drained. He reported that the White House was releasing the documentation. Nixon, he explained, was wavering between resignation and attempting to ride it out. Almost all of his senior aides were urging the first course. Others—although he didn't mention any of them by name, I assumed he meant the members of the Nixon family—were telling him to stay and fight. And there was a strange cycle to his moods. In the morning, buttressed by late-night talks with his supporters, he appeared determined to hang in. By the end of the day, after listening to realistic reports from his senior aides, he seemed willing to step down. "I can't tell you with any certainty what's going to happen in the next seventy-two hours," Haig said. "I don't know myself. It could go either way."

Late that afternoon, the White House sent a copy of Nixon's statement to my office in the EOB. In it the President acknowledged that he had tried to use the Central Intelligence Agency to block the Federal Bureau of Investigation from discovering that his own reelection committee had financed and arranged the break-in at the Democratic National Committee office in the Watergate complex. Having admitted that, he concluded: "Whatever mistakes I made in the handling of Watergate, the basic truth remains that when all the facts were brought to my attention, I insisted on a full investigation and prosecution of those guilty. I am firmly convinced that the record, in its entirety, does not justify the extreme step of impeachment and removal of a President. I trust that as the constitutional process goes forward, this perception will prevail."

The reaction among Republicans was explosive. Senator Griffin called openly for Nixon's resignation "in the national interest." The ten GOP Congressmen who had supported him in the House Judiciary Committee vote on impeachment announced that they were switching sides or reassessing their stands. And in the midst of all this came reports that the President and his family were about to take an evening cruise down the Potomac. I hadn't listened to the tapes, nor had I read the transcripts of Nixon's conversations with Haldeman. Still, the President's own admissions required a statement from me, and with the help of Hartmann and Marsh, I prepared one for release at seven o'clock that night.

"I have come to the conclusion," I said, "that the public interest is no longer served by repetition of my previously expressed belief that on the basis of all the evidence known to me and to the American people, the President is not guilty of an impeachable offense. . . . When I was nominated by the President to be Vice President ten months ago, I promised the Congress . . . that I would do my very best to be a calm communicator and ready conciliator between the executive and legislative branches of our federal government. I have done so. But in the impeachment process, the President and Congress are now in an adversary relationship which as deeply divides the legislators as it does the people they represent. . . . The business of government must go on, and the genuine needs of the people must be served. I believe I can make a better contribution to this end by not involving myself daily in the impeachment debate, in which I have no constitutional role."

No longer was there the slightest doubt in my mind as to the outcome of the struggle. Nixon was finished. The only question now was when he'd realize this and what he'd do about it. I was tired, I hadn't seen Betty or the children for several days, and I was anxious to get home. The water in our backyard pool was cool and inviting. I swam a dozen laps, then had drinks with Betty on the patio. No sooner had Betty, Susan, Steve and I sat down to eat than the telephone rang. It was Major George Joulwan, Haig's assistant at the White House. A Cabinet meeting had just been scheduled for tomorrow morning, he said. Nixon, I assumed, would disclose his intentions then. The possibility of our moving to the White House suddenly seemed very real.

Initially, the Cabinet meeting had been scheduled to begin at ten o'clock, but it was pushed back an hour. I spent the time conferring with Hartmann and Marsh, both of whom felt very strongly that I had a moral obligation to tell the President to his face exactly where I stood. Marsh, in fact, prepared a list of talking points for me to follow. From time to time in our respective political careers, I had given Nixon advice that had conflicted with what he wanted to do. Never, however, had I spoken out as forcefully as these talking points suggested I do now.

I walked across West Executive Avenue, entered the West Wing of the White House and proceeded to the Cabinet Room. I was standing behind my heavy brown leather chair talking to Treasury Secretary Bill Simon when Nixon strode into the room. This was the first time I'd seen him in about ten days, and the change in his appearance was unmistakable. Although he wasn't a particularly vigorous-looking man, he had always taken care of himself. But since the Supreme Court's decision of July 24, he had been closeted with only his most trusted aides. It was obvious he hadn't been sleeping well. His complexion had turned sallow, and he seemed less energetic—both physically and mentally—than I had ever seen him before.

When Nixon took his seat at the center of the oblong table, the rest of us sat down too. The tension in that room was unbelievable. I was nervous, and so, I think, was everyone else. Yet Nixon appeared not to notice. He glanced first at a clock on the table in front of him, then at a leather-bound folder which contained his talking points.

"I would like to discuss the most important issue confronting the nation," he said, "and confronting us internationally too—inflation. Our economic situation could be the major issue in the world today."

My God! I had assumed that this was going to be a momentous occasion, that Nixon was going to come to grips with the threat to his Presidency, that he was going to tell us about his future plans. Instead, he started out with this dissertation on the economy. The more I listened to him, the more apprehensive I became. He was talking about something that was totally irrelevant to the circumstances that confronted him and the nation as well. I thought it was a ludicrous attempt to avoid the hard decisions he had to make.

But abruptly, Nixon shifted into Watergate and the new evidence that had just been released. "I want to say at the outset that major problems plagued us," he began. He mentioned the CIA and the FBI. He said his primary concern had been national security, but that "certain political interests" had also been discussed. "Under the circumstances," he went on, "I thought it was proper to make the tapes [of his June 23, 1972, conversations with Haldeman] available now." He didn't want the House, he said, to vote on impeachment without having all the facts. Some of the new material, he conceded, was damaging to him, but some was exculpatory. There was no "intentional breach of the law" and "no obstruction of justice." He simply hadn't wanted to let "national security matters [get] messed up in this asinine business [of Watergate]."

He sat with his back to the windows that look out onto the South Lawn. I was directly across the table from him, and I remember thinking how tired and drawn he seemed. "The consensus now is that we'll lose in the House," he said, referring to the impeachment debate that was scheduled to begin August 15. "But I want all the facts out. I'll take whatever lumps are involved. After consulting with people more knowledgeable than I about constitutional law, I am convinced that there is no evidence of an impeachable offense. If there were, I wouldn't stay in this office one more day."

He mentioned the Vietnam War and his Administration's new relationship with the People's Republic of China. He had been preoccupied with these weighty matters, he said, and hadn't been "tending the store on the political side. Those who were [tending the store] were overeager." Then he expressed his appreciation to the Cabinet: "You've been splendid in standing up. I've been very moved by it. It's easier to run away. [But] I don't want you to stand and fight without knowing the facts.

"Some, including some good friends," the President went on, "feel that the situation is so unmanageable that the best thing I can do is resign and not go through the ordeal of a Senate trial. I have considered that, as a matter of fact. It should be considered, but I had to make a decision. A President is really not in the position of an ordinary citizen in this kind of matter. I am of the view that I should not take the step that changes the Constitution and sets a precedent for future Presidents. It would be the parliamentary system with all of its weaknesses but none of its strengths. I will accept whatever verdict the Senate hands down, and I recognize the possibility that the outcome won't be favorable. A very important consideration here is my sworn promise to uphold the Constitution. And it provides the process."

He paused. His eyes flickered around the room as if he expected support. Seeing none, he continued: "I don't ask any of you to do anything that would be embarrassing to you, your personal interests. I do ask you to run your departments well.

"I vetoed $35 billion in appropriations during Watergate. I intend to fight the inflation battle with all the tools we can. Needless to say, it hasn't been a very easy year for me or an easy week. I want to do the right thing for the country. For me, too, but the country comes first. If I resign, it would change the Constitution. Some of you may disagree, and I respect that, but I have made the decision. I ask your support of this decision."

The President paused again and looked around the room. The silence was deafening. "You don't have to talk about Watergate," he went on. "I suggest you talk about the good things the Administration has done. Watergate will be brought to a conclusion by the constitutional process. Nothing will be withheld. I don't ask you to get involved with my problems, but it is time to do a bit extra in running your departments and selling our programs. If I thought there was one impeachable offense, I wouldn't put the Senate through the agony of trying to prove it."

He was about to shift to another subject. I had to speak up now or the moment would be lost. "Mr. President," I said, conscious that everyone was looking at me, "with your indulgence, I have something to say."

"Well, Jerry, go ahead."

"Everyone here recognizes the difficult position I'm in," I said. "No one regrets more than I do this whole tragic episode. I have deep personal sympathy for you, Mr. President, and your fine family. But I wish to emphasize that had I known what has been disclosed in reference to Watergate in the last twenty-four hours, I would not have made a number of the statements I made either as Minority Leader or as Vice President. I came to a decision yesterday and you may be aware that I informed the press that because of commitments to Congress and the public, I'll have no further comment on the issue because I'm a party in interest. I'm sure there will be impeachment in the House. I can't predict the Senate outcome. I will make no comment concerning this. You have given us the finest foreign policy this country has ever had. A super job, and the people appreciate it. Let me assure you that I expect to continue to support the Administration's foreign policy and the fight against inflation."

Nixon seemed taken aback by what I had to say and the fact that I'd interrupted him. "I think your position is exactly correct," he said, a sad smile on his face.

Then he turned once more to the economy, but after a few minutes of discussion George Bush, chairman of the Republican National Committee, tried to refocus on the major issue of the day. Watergate had to be handled expeditiously, he told us. The lack of public confidence was affecting the economy.

Nixon brushed him aside. He seemed to want to talk only about budget cuts and economic strategy. Perhaps the best thing to do, he said, would be to sponsor a summit meeting on the economy.

William Saxbe, the former Senator from Ohio who was serving as Attorney General, interrupted. "Mr. President," he said, "I don't think we ought to have a summit conference. We ought to be sure you have the ability to govern."

A stunned silence hung over the room. Finally, Nixon replied, his voice drained of emotion: "Bill, I have the ability just as I have had for the last five and a half years."

Sensing that the meeting could turn ugly and rancorous, Secretary of State Henry A. Kissinger intervened. "This is a very difficult period for the country in every way," he said. "We must show confidence. We must show that the country is strong enough to go through the constitutional process. It is imperative that in foreign policy we act with assurance and confidence and with total unity. If we can do that, we can vindicate the structure for peace."

Finally, after one hour and thirty-seven minutes, Nixon pushed back his chair from the table and signaled that the meeting was over. I picked up my papers and walked out as quickly as I could. Kissinger, I learned later, followed the President back to the Oval Office. Aware that telling him bluntly that he ought to resign would be a counterproductive way to proceed, Henry referred to the comments made by the participants in the Cabinet meeting. In a roundabout way, he told the President he ought to think about resigning. Nixon listened but didn't reply.

I had a long-scheduled luncheon on Capitol Hill with members of the GOP Senate Policy Committee, and they were curious, of course, about the Cabinet meeting. John Tower of Texas asked if I could tell them what had happened. I replied that Nixon had said he had no intention of resigning, and that he'd spent most of the time discussing the economy.

Maryland's J. Glenn Beall asked if there had been any mention of the impeachment question.

"The President believes he's not guilty of an impeachable offense," I said. "He concedes the House battle is lost and that the situation has to be resolved in the Senate."

Idaho's James McClure asked if any Cabinet members had spoken out against the President. Tower wondered whether Nixon had asked for anyone's advice. Then Barry Goldwater chimed in with a view that was characteristically blunt. "I've been defending Richard Nixon for years," he said. "While he may be right legally—and on that ground I've been one of his strongest backers—the situation now is totally out of hand. We can't support this any longer. We can be lied to only so many times. The best thing he can do for the country is to get the hell out of the White House, and get out this afternoon."

Colorado's Peter Dominick endorsed Barry's stand. So did Jacob Javits of New York. Javits said that although he recognized the difficult position I was in, I should tell Nixon what I was hearing from them. Trying to steer the conversation onto safer ground, I told the Senators what Kissinger had said about the need for unity.

Looking directly at me, Tennessee's Bill Brock said he was extremely concerned. "What more can we Senators do to transmit our feelings to the President?" he asked. "Senators have no impact on the White House even in this situation of extreme tension, and that bothers me a lot."

"I can't be a conduit either way," I replied. "I can't pass along any information."

Norris Cotton of New Hampshire, one of the oldest and most respected members of the Senate, picked up on Brock's theme. "I have suffered through this along with everybody else," he said. "I have great sympathy for Richard Nixon. We entered Congress and were sworn in on the same day, and we've been friends ever since. But we in the Senate are in an impossible situation, second only to that of the Vice President. The good of the nation, the people and the Constitution are involved. It's no use to sit here and merely talk to each other. It should be possible to have some group talk to the President and make him understand the danger of his position if he carries out his present intention. There must be some way that we as Republican Senators can officially warn the President that the decision he has apparently made can only lead into more serious difficulty for the country and himself."

Cotton and McClure then began to discuss who should pass the word to the President. "I don't think I should be part of this discussion any more," I said. "I'd like to excuse myself." The Senators understood. As I left the room, they gave me a round of applause.

The Capitol was awash with rumors that afternoon. The worst thing I could do would be to cancel my appointments and contribute to the formation of new rumors. So I told Hartmann, "Damn it, let's keep the schedule and just wait and see what happens in the White House."

Betty had invited Phil Buchen, an old friend now working on a White House Domestic Council assignment, to have dinner with us that night. Initially, we steered the conversation away from current events. It was far more enjoyable to talk about old friends, shared experiences, our children's summer plans. But after dinner we sat in the living room, and for the first time the conversation turned to the drama surrounding us. Phil seemed very upset by what he considered to

be my matter-of-fact attitude. "Look," he said, "you'd better tell me
what's going on."

I couldn't respond categorically. The only source I had was Haig,
and he had told me that afternoon: "Mr. Vice President, I can't tell
you what's going to happen. One moment I think there will be a resignation, the next I get the feeling that he's going to fight it through."
Obviously, Nixon's resignation seemed an increasingly likely possibility, and I told Phil that.

And that's when Phil hit me with a real surprise. The resignation,
he said, had seemed likely to him for the past several months. He'd
been so concerned about it, so mindful of all the things that would
have to be done, that early in May he'd formed a sub rosa "transition
team," and he had been meeting with them on a regular basis. The
co-chairman of the team was Clay T. Whitehead, director of the
White House Office of Telecommunications Policy. That surprised
me too. I didn't know Whitehead well at all and—other than having
read about a speech he gave which blasted the television industry—
knew next to nothing about him. Logistics, Phil explained, had dic-
tated Whitehead's selection. His office was very close to the one Phil
used as executive director of the Domestic Council's Committee on
the Right to Privacy. They could meet without anyone's finding out
about it.

And secrecy, Phil went on, had been a vital consideration. They realized that had I known of their activities, I would have demanded
that they stop. If Nixon or any one of his supporters found out, it
would have been construed as an act of disloyalty on my part, and
the results could have been disastrous. It was a dangerous and questionable undertaking. The transition team hadn't accomplished all
that much, but it did provide a good start and there was a great deal
that still needed to be done: arranging for the swearing in, drawing
up a list of potential Vice Presidents, considering appointments to the
new White House staff, schedule changes and an inaugural address—
all those matters that a new President normally has months to think
about. Unconsciously, even though I wasn't President, I began to
make "Presidential" decisions. The other members of the team—
Jonathan Moore, Brian Lamb and Larry Lynn—were competent

young men, but I felt we needed people with more stature and experience.

"Now look," Phil said, "tell me who I can call on immediately."

Bob Griffin came to mind. So did Secretary of the Interior Rogers Morton, former Wisconsin Representative John Byrnes, Bryce Harlow and Bill Whyte, another old friend, who was a vice president of U.S. Steel. Bill Scranton, the former governor of Pennsylvania, would be an ideal addition to the team. As we ticked off the names, Betty produced her address book and gave Phil the numbers to call.

"We'll get them together as soon as possible," Phil said. He was anxious to leave and begin making his calls. I reminded him that secrecy was absolutely imperative, that chaos would ensue if Nixon discovered what was being done. Standing by the front door, he kissed Betty and put his arm on my shoulder. It was an emotional goodbye. "It's happening," he said, "and I'm proud of you."

Next morning, August 7, I woke up early, swam my laps, then drove toward Capitol Hill for the weekly breakfast of the Chowder and Marching Society. I'd been a member of this social group ever since it was organized by a few young Republican House members in 1949. My car was halfway to the Hill when the Secret Service relayed a message from Haig. It said: "Forget the breakfast. Let's meet in your office as soon as possible."

Haig was there shortly before eight o'clock. The two of us sat on the davenport, looking at each other. "Mr. Vice President," he said, "I think it's time for you to prepare to assume the office of President."

But even then he qualified it. Nixon hadn't made a final decision yet. Haig simply thought he was about to accept the fact that he would have to go.

Originally, I was scheduled to leave the city at noon Thursday on a twelve-day speaking tour of the West. After our meeting, I decided to cancel it. Events were happening so quickly that the best thing I could do was stay in Washington. I called in Hartmann, Marsh and Buchen and authorized them to organize the new transition team as soon as possible. The afternoon before, I had asked Hartmann to prepare a draft of an acceptance speech. He'd gone to a movie, slept for several hours, then risen at 3 A.M. to start hitting his typewriter. He had been working ever since. Hartmann wrote all his speeches for me that way; he couldn't produce until the deadline was upon him and he was under the gun. His work habits often frustrated me, but the results were almost always first-class.

And that was certainly true this time. As I read his draft, tears came to my eyes. "I am indebted to no man," he had written, "and only to one woman, my dear wife." Hartmann understood my feelings perfectly. Then I came to the line "My fellow Americans, our long national nightmare is over." I wondered whether that was overly harsh on Nixon, and I asked Hartmann if we shouldn't say something else.

"No, no," he replied. "It's been a nightmare for everybody. For you, for me, for Nixon's friends and Nixon's enemies. For everybody in this country. It's something that has to be said, and you're the only one who can say it." He was absolutely right.

At eleven-thirty that morning, I went to my "ceremonial" office at the Capitol and then to the office of House Minority Leader John Rhodes for our regular Wednesday prayer session with Minnesota Representative Albert H. Quie and former Wisconsin Representative Melvin Laird. We'd been having these private sessions for some time, and the pattern was always the same. One of us started out with a simple prayer. Then we went around the room in no predetermined sequence. When the last person had finished, we said the Lord's Prayer in unison.

Even though Rhodes had announced publicly that he was planning to vote against the President, no one mentioned the political crisis gripping the capital. No one had to. The prayers the others offered were all in my behalf as the potential President. And mine were for their support—and God's—in meeting the new challenges that I'd face.

After talking with Bob Griffin and securing his agreement to participate in the transition group, I returned to my office in the EOB. There I received a briefing on foreign policy from Major General Brent Scowcroft, Henry Kissinger's deputy on the National Security Council, and a separate briefing on the status of pending legislation from Bill Timmons, the White House aide responsible for Congressional relations. Then Hartmann and I went over the acceptance speech again.

While I was doing that, I discovered later, Senators Goldwater and Scott and Representative Rhodes were meeting with the President. "You must not ask him to resign," Haig had cautioned them in advance. "He feels that this is a very difficult decision, and he's got to make it himself. He's been up and down several times today. So let him do the talking. But if he asks how many votes he's got, tell him the truth."

When they entered the Oval Office, the President stood up to shake hands with them, then motioned toward three chairs in front of his desk. "Well, I know why you gentlemen are here," he began. Then, looking at Rhodes, he said, "Johnny, I know how you feel."

"Yes, Mr. President," Rhodes replied.

Nixon turned to Goldwater: "Barry, how does it look?"

"Well, Mr. President, I'll give you my best judgment. You haven't got more than twelve people who will stand with you in the Senate. I've got to be frank: I don't know whether I would be one of them."

"Hugh," the President said, looking at Scott, "do you agree with that?"

"You know, Mr. President," Scott replied, "I'm used to counting votes. I would say it's between twelve and fifteen, but I think it looks very bad."

"It looks damn bad," Nixon agreed. Then: "You all agree that it looks bad?"

"Yes," the three of them replied.

"Well," the President said, "I'm going to make up my mind very shortly. It won't be long, and you'll know what that decision is. I wanted your advice, and I'm grateful to you for giving it." The meeting was over. The three left Nixon alone with his thoughts.

Shortly before ten o'clock Thursday morning, Marsh and I went to Blair House, across the street from the EOB, where I was to present Congressional Medals of Honor to the families of seven servicemen who had died in Vietnam. These ceremonies were usually very emotional—and hard for me to perform—and this one was no exception. No sooner had I returned to my office than I received a call from Haig. His voice was calm, but I also sensed a feeling of relief. "The

President wants to see you," Haig said. "I think you know what he's going to say."

Ten minutes later, I entered the White House. I stopped at Haig's office first. His eyes told me all I needed to know. I walked into the Oval Office alone.

Nixon was sitting behind his desk, but he stood up as soon as I entered the room. We shook hands; he said, "Sit down," and I took the chair to his right. The President leaned back in his chair with his hands clasped together in his lap. His face was solemn. He had been under tremendous strain; he was still very tense, but in control. Speaking slowly and deliberately, he came right to the point. "I have made the decision to resign," he said. "It's in the best interest of the country. I won't go into the details pro and con. I have made my decision." He paused for a moment, then added, "Jerry, I know you'll do a good job."

"Mr. President," I replied, "you know that I'm saddened by this circumstance. I would have wanted it to be otherwise, but I am ready to do the job and think I'm fully qualified to do it."

"I know you are too."

Once he'd said that, he relaxed and our conversation became much more informal and as pleasant as it could be under the circumstances. Now that he had relinquished the burdens of the world, he was offering an old friend the best advice he had for the days ahead. We talked about the timing of the transition and the way it would be accomplished. Nixon would announce his resignation on TV that night. It would be effective at noon the next day. On Friday morning he wanted to say goodbye to his loyal aides and their families in the East Room. He hoped I would understand his desire to do that. He would write a letter of resignation to Henry Kissinger. When Kissinger received it, Nixon would no longer be President. He would be on his way to San Clemente as a private citizen. Then I could take the oath of office.

He talked pragmatically about the problems I would face in both foreign and domestic affairs. He mentioned the need to strengthen the North Atlantic Treaty Organization, as well as his hope that I could reach agreement with the Soviet Union on strategic arms limitations. Leonid Brezhnev, the Soviets' top man, was bright and tough,

Nixon said, but he could also be flexible. He hoped I would continue a strong policy in South Vietnam and Cambodia, and he emphasized the role that Kissinger could play. "Henry is a genius," Nixon said, "but you don't have to accept everything he recommends. He can be invaluable, and he'll be very loyal, but you can't let him have a totally free hand."

Turning to domestic affairs, he noted that the economy was suffering. Inflation was horrendous, and there were some ominous signs of a general economic slowdown in the months ahead. He stressed the need to hold the lid on federal spending and said he hoped that I would work closely with Federal Reserve Board Chairman Arthur F. Burns. His own decision to impose wage and price controls in 1971, the President went on, had been more harmful than helpful, and he hoped that I wouldn't try to impose them. I told him that he didn't have to worry about that. I'd lived through wage and price controls during the Korean War and again in 1971, and I was convinced they didn't work.

He showed no vindictiveness toward anyone, no bitterness toward people he'd criticized in my presence before. He made no comments about the press and didn't even mention the name "Watergate." That was something he wanted to put out of his mind.

Then we talked about who my Vice President would be. He suggested that Nelson A. Rockefeller, the four-term governor of New York, would be a wise selection. He didn't identify anyone else by name. "There are a number of good people," he said. "It's your choice. I won't be talking to you again, but you'll want somebody who will add stature to the Administration, somebody who will generate national as well as international confidence."

I had heard rumors that the discussions among members of the Nixon family about resignation had been volatile, but in our meeting the President never brought it up. He had made his decision. It was over, as far as he was concerned, and his only interest now was to foster a smooth, orderly transition. After seventy minutes we had touched every base, and it was time for me to leave. As we walked toward the doors, Nixon put his arm around me. "Here's an old friend who's made a major decision changing both our lives," I said to myself. "Now he's wishing me the best not only for myself but for the country." I couldn't be very eloquent because my emotions were too strong. There was a choking in my throat.

"Well," I said, "I'll see you tomorrow. Give Pat and the family my best." Even those low-key words didn't come out easily.

"You and Betty will enjoy living in the mansion," the President replied. "We'll see you tomorrow."

We shook hands again, and I walked the forty yards to the limousine waiting in the driveway. I never once looked back. Nor did I glance at the Secret Service agents accompanying me because I was afraid my feelings might show. I stared ahead at the car, and I wanted the agents to open the door as soon as possible so I could climb inside. I needed to be alone.

But that, I knew, would be impossible, for there were still too many things to do. As soon as I returned to the EOB, I telephoned Kissinger. I thought it urgent to tell him right away how I felt about him. "Henry," I said when he came on the line, "I need you. The country needs you. I want you to stay. I'll do everything I can to work with you."

"There will be no problem," he replied in his deep, accented voice. "Sir, it is my job to get along with you and not yours to get along with me."

"We'll get along," I said. "I know we can get along." We talked about the two hats he wore, as Secretary of State and National Security Adviser to the President. "I don't want to make any change," I said. "I think it's worked out well, so let's keep it that way."

Hartmann, Buchen and Marsh came into my office with lists of other decisions that still had to be made: the selection of a site for the swearing in, the choice of a person to administer the oath, the compilation of a guest list for the ceremony, the naming of a new press secretary and final approval of the speech I'd have to give.

Traditionally, I knew, most Presidents were sworn in on the steps of the Capitol. As a former Congressman, I would have preferred the Capitol myself, yet I realized there simply was no time to arrange the site. Besides, that would have lent a festive air to the occasion, and the country was hardly in a festive mood. The East Room of the White House, I thought, would be far more subdued and appropriate.

"Whom do you want to swear you in?" Hartmann asked.

It was important to demonstrate that the three branches of our government were acting in unison, so I suggested Chief Justice Warren Burger, then attending a conference at The Hague in the Netherlands. Marsh telephoned him and, minutes later, signaled me that he was on the line. "Mr. Chief Justice," I said, "I guess you've heard the news. I hate to interrupt your trip, but I would like it very much if you could be here for the swearing in."

The Chief Justice broke in quickly. "Oh, I've got to be there. I *want* to be there," he said.

"It's going to be difficult," I explained, "because it's now evening your time, and the ceremony is at noon tomorrow. But we can get you an Air Force plane."

I asked Marsh to get on the extension and work out the details. Jack would have a long night ahead of him, I knew, because I'd also asked him to be responsible for inviting 275 guests and making sure that the list met all the protocol requirements. (One person I really wanted to attend was John McCormack, former Democratic Speaker of the House, who now lived in Boston. I offered to send a plane to pick him up, and even though he hated to fly, he agreed to come.)

The next item on the agenda was my new press secretary. Buchen recommended Jerald terHorst, the Washington bureau chief of the Detroit *News*. I'd known Jerry since 1948, when he had covered my first Congressional campaign. I had always been impressed by his sense of fairness and integrity, and over the years we'd become personal friends as well. The moment I heard he might be available, I told Phil to call and offer him the job. TerHorst said he wanted to talk to his wife and his editors. He called back soon and accepted.

It was amazing how all the small details were falling into place. Next I called Senate Minority Leader Scott. "As you know, Hugh, things have come to pass," I said. "Our relationship has been excellent, and I expect it to continue as it has between friends. Accessibility and openness will be the hallmarks of my Administration. There will be no filtering of leadership views through others. No, sir."

At two forty-five that afternoon, I placed a call to Thomas P. ("Tip") O'Neill, Democratic Majority Leader of the House. We had played together in a golf tournament near Worcester, Massachusetts, eight days before. *Newsweek* had run a photograph of the two of us strolling down a fairway with our arms around each other, and we opened by discussing that. "Well, we sure had a helluva time that day," the two of us agreed. Then we got down to business. Nixon was submitting his letter of resignation to Kissinger at 10 A.M. It would be effective at noon, and I wanted Tip to be at the swearing in.

"Are wives invited, Jerry?" Tip asked. "The reason I'm asking is that I've already told Millie to pack and get down here."

"Wives were not invited," I said, "but they are now."

"Now, Jerry," Tip went on, "I've got a statement prepared, and I want to read it to you." He paused, then began again: "While we are close personal friends and I have great respect for his honesty, integrity and ability, our political philosophies are diametrically opposed. I wish him every success in bringing our politically torn country together. He can expect cooperation from Congress, and I trust he will cooperate with Congress and the rest of America in the days ahead."

"That's fine, Tip," I said. "And I want to say that I'll be relying on you for your advice and assistance."

"I can tell you one thing, Jerry," he went on. "Don't think of a Democrat for Vice President. This country doesn't work that way."

"Thanks for the advice," I said.

For a moment neither of us spoke. Then he sighed. "Christ, Jerry, isn't this a wonderful country? Here we can talk like this and you and I can be friends, and eighteen months from now I'll be going around the country kicking your ass in."

That, I thought, was one hell of a way to speak to the next President of the United States. But it was vintage O'Neill, and it contained a large measure of truth. We *were* close personal friends. But we were also fierce political enemies, and I knew that he'd be doing what he promised to do in less than eighteen months. That, after all, was the essence of democracy.

Since Wednesday morning when he'd brought in the first draft of my acceptance speech, Hartmann had gone over it several times. I'd told him that I'd wanted it to be short and dignified and to have a healing theme. And I'd insisted that he say something thoughtful about Nixon and his family. Bob had an uncanny ability to craft a sentence or a phrase so that it expressed my sentiments, and now, as I read over his polished draft, I saw that he'd succeeded again.

Because I tend to be low-key, people have the impression that I'm unemotional. I *do* care very deeply about my family, close personal friends and intimate experiences I've shared with others, and I have a hard time with my voice. Tears well up in my eyes very easily. I don't hide it very well. I don't apologize for it, but a lot of people who know me casually probably have no idea of this. I knew that when I gave the acceptance speech, I couldn't afford to break down. I wanted to appear confident, to give the public the assurance that I was in charge and could do the job, so I decided to rehearse the speech again that night, with Betty as my judge.

Later that afternoon, I had a lengthy meeting with Henry Kissinger. Both of us were aware that some of our country's adversaries might misinterpret the transition as a time of chaos in America and might decide to probe militarily where we seemed vulnerable. It was essential, we agreed, that a message go out to all governments warning that such probes would be resisted by force, that although the country was switching Presidents, its foreign policy remained the same. Just to make sure that everyone got the word, he urged me to let him arrange meetings, after the swearing in, with ambassadors from all over the globe.

Quickly, I agreed.

Then our discussion touched on the world's trouble spots. Although the Communists had signed the Paris peace accords in 1973, they were still causing trouble in South Vietnam and Cambodia. The situation in both countries looked worrisome indeed. The Middle East remained a tinderbox. The Yom Kippur War had ended ten months before, but new hostilities could break out at any time. We would have to watch the area carefully. The one bright spot I remember in our session that day was the possible chance to reach agreement with the Soviets during strategic arms limitation talks. Nixon and Brezhnev had agreed to meet later in the fall. Kissinger asked me if I wanted him to push ahead with those plans.

"Yes, of course," I replied. Anything that would bring the arms race under control would be a plus for the entire world.

Mike, our oldest son, and his wife, Gayle, were due in from Massachusetts, but they hadn't arrived by the time I returned to our Alexandria home at eight twenty-five. Nor had Jack, our middle son, flying in from Yellowstone National Park. Susan and Steve were home; they had just finished dinner, and as we sat in the family room, they seemed unusually reserved. Although they didn't know the Nixons well at all, they were saddened by what was taking place and somewhat awe-stricken by the changes that were about to occur in all our lives.

Nixon was due to appear on TV at nine o'clock. As I waited for his speech to begin, I couldn't help but reflect on my long association with him. My political career had coincided roughly with his. His had begun two years earlier, in 1946, when he had answered an ad placed by Republicans in his California Congressional District who were seeking an opponent for an entrenched liberal Democrat. He volunteered and won as an idealistic believer in the American economic and political system. My own began in 1948 with a similar dedication to the American way and U.S. leadership abroad. In January 1949, after I had been sworn in as a member of the House, Nixon was one of the first colleagues I met. Over the next twenty-five years, our political paths crossed many times, and our friendship grew. His career was always more visible, more dramatic than mine, but that was fine with me.

In writing about a friend, one likes to consider the mutual bonds and good qualities on which the friendship is based. One of our strongest ties was the fact that we came from Middle America (economically if not geographically), and from families that had suffered much during the Depression years. We respected each other because each of us knew that the other had come up the hard way. Both of us were lawyers; both had served as naval officers during World War II. We had similar interests aside from politics: football, baseball and other sports. Each of us had a wonderful wife and fine children. We understood each other's ambitions in politics—his to become President of the United States, mine to be elected Speaker of the House. And all the while, our friendship was strengthened by our mutual adherence to the same basic policies, both at home and abroad.

Nixon had a brilliant mind, a great sensitivity to the public's political mood and a unique ability to analyze foreign policy issues and act decisively on them. Big decisions were his strength, and his batting average was excellent. But he abhorred details, and rather enjoyed pushing them off on subordinates. And that, it seemed to me, was one of the several reasons he had come to this point of having to resign.

With all his experience in giving speeches and press conferences, one might have assumed that he was an extrovert. In fact, the opposite was true. He was very shy, a loner in many respects, and he seemed to prefer dealing with paper work to dealing with people. His oratorical capabilities were the result of his recognition that in order to succeed in politics, he had to be able to speak convincingly before large audiences. His fierce determination and able mind propelled him toward the highest office in the land.

Most of us have hidden flaws or personality quirks that seldom come to the surface. We control them successfully and resist their exploitation by those around us. In Nixon's case, that flaw was pride. A terribly proud man, he detested weakness in other people. I'd often heard him speak disparagingly of those whom he felt to be soft and expedient. (Curiously, he didn't feel that the press was weak. Reporters, he sensed, were his adversaries. He knew they didn't like him, and he responded with reciprocal disdain.) He was very bitter about members of Congress who wanted to cut and run from our obligations in South Vietnam, and he detested those lawmakers who were trying to hamstring his efforts to settle the war from a position of strength. He felt that ever since the days of House Speakers Sam Rayburn and John McCormack and Senate Majority Leader Lyndon Johnson, the Democratic leadership of the Congress had been eroding. Because it had become increasingly weak, it was deserving of his contempt. That attitude was reflected in his selection of Bob Haldeman and John Ehrlichman as the White House aides through whom he wanted to deal with the Hill.

It was reflected, too, in his explanations of Watergate. His pride and personal contempt for weakness had overcome his ability to tell the difference between right and wrong. What some journalists called the "dark side" of his personality had prevailed over his judgment, which was normally sound. And once the course had been set, there was no turning back.

As I sat in our family room, I wondered whether he had known in advance about the break-in at the Watergate. I couldn't really believe that he had. The new tapes, however, revealed that he had found out about it soon afterward. And I could see why he felt trapped. Some of the people involved—John Mitchell, for example—were friends of his, and he didn't want to force them to pay the consequences. His pride was stronger than his recognition that he had made a mistake. He viewed admitting the truth in this matter as a sign of weakness, and that was another mistake.

There was irony in his predicament. Six years before to the day, August 8, 1968, Nixon had won the Republican nomination for President. In his acceptance speech he had claimed that America was in trouble because "her leaders have failed." Now this. Even more ironic was the fact that his enemies were not the only ones who were forcing his removal from office. That job was also being done by his most trusted advisers and friends.

Precisely at nine o'clock, the familiar face appeared on our TV screen. "Good evening," the President began.

> This is the thirty-seventh time I have spoken to you from this office where so many decisions have been made that shaped the history of this nation. . . . Throughout the long and difficult period of Watergate, I have felt it was my duty to persevere, to make every possible effort to complete the term of office to which you elected me. In the past few days, however, it has become evident to me that I no longer have a strong enough political base in the Congress to justify continuing that effort.
>
> As long as there was such a base, I felt strongly that it was necessary to see the constitutional process through to its conclusion; that to do otherwise would be unfaithful to the spirit of that deliberately difficult process and a dangerously destabilizing precedent for the future.
>
> But with the disappearance of that base, I now believe that the constitutional purpose has been served and there is no longer a need for the process to be prolonged.
>
> I would have preferred to carry through to the finish, whatever the personal agony it would have involved, and my family unanimously urged me to do so.
>
> But the interest of the nation must always come before any personal considerations. From the discussions I have had with Congressional and other leaders, I have concluded that because of the Water-

gate matter, I might not have the support of the Congress that I would consider necessary to back the very difficult decisions and carry out the duties of this office in the way the interests of the nation would require.

I have never been a quitter.

To leave office before my term is completed is abhorrent to every instinct in my body. But as President, I must put the interest of America first.

America needs a full-time President and a full-time Congress, particularly at this time, with problems we face at home and abroad.

To continue to fight through the months ahead for my personal vindication would almost totally absorb the time and attention of both the President and the Congress in a period when our entire focus should be on the great issues of peace abroad and prosperity without inflation at home.

Therefore, I shall resign the Presidency, effective at noon tomorrow.

Vice President Ford will be sworn in as President at that hour. . . .

I regret deeply any injuries that may have been done in the course of the events that led to this decision. I would say only that if some of my judgments were wrong—and some were wrong—they were made in what I believed at the time to be the best interest of the nation. . . .

The speech lasted fifteen minutes, and at the end I was convinced that Nixon was out of touch with reality. The fact that he was linking his resignation to the loss of his Congressional base shocked me then and disturbs me still. If he had been more contrite and asked the American people for forgiveness, he would have received a warmer response. Yet he couldn't take that final step. I'm convinced he thought what he said was enough.

A slight drizzle had begun to fall. Reporters were clustered outside our front door and they expected a statement from me. Determined to heal the divisiveness that had racked us so long, I stepped outside and said, "I think the President of the United States has made one of the greatest personal sacrifices for the country and one of the finest personal decisions on behalf of all of us as Americans by his decision to resign." Then, after promising to cooperate with the Congress during the difficult days ahead, I went back inside.

After a late dinner Betty and I discussed what we were going to wear the next day and how we were going to coordinate our arrival in the East Room of the White House. I rehearsed my speech and just before going to bed, we watched the eleven o'clock news. This was my last night as Vice President, and the prospects of the change in my life kept me awake longer than usual.

Early Friday morning, Phil Buchen and former Republican House member John Byrnes arrived at our Virginia home and had coffee with me. Then they joined me for the trip across the Potomac to Washington. Since Tuesday night they had worked around the clock to compile a list of the first decisions I'd have to make as President, and they had summarized their suggestions in a four-page memorandum. It was broken down into four sections: Transition Organization; The Business of Government; Old White House Staff; Vice Presidential Search Process. "We share your view," I read, "that there should be no Chief of Staff, especially at the outset. However, there should be someone who could rapidly and efficiently organize the new staff organization, but who will not be perceived [as being] nor be eager to be Chief of Staff." Under that they'd listed three names. One of them was Don Rumsfeld, a former Congressman from Illinois who was currently serving as our ambassador to NATO. I thought he'd be ideal for the job and wrote his name in the blank space provided for me.

Other candidates seemed equally ideal for the slots that had to be filled. Secretary of the Interior Rogers Morton would act as my liaison with the Cabinet and government agencies. Jack Marsh would perform the same function with the Congress, the governors, business and labor groups. Bill Scranton would serve as my chief of personnel. "For public confidence," the memorandum went on, "to keep the executive branch administration intact, and to assure the smoothest, most rapid assumption of the Presidential mantle, you should have a series of meetings the first few days to assert your personal direction and control over the executive branch of the government." I agreed with that idea and with the sequence of meetings they suggested. Then I turned to the section on the old White House staff.

"You must walk a delicate line," I read, "between compassion and consideration for the former President's staff and the rapid assertion of your personal control over the executive branch. The old White House staff will submit their resignations, but they should be asked to stay on for a time to help with the transition. It will be clear that most of the political types will be expected to leave within a reasonable time. The one exception we recommend is Al Haig. Al has done yeoman service for his country. You should meet with him personally as soon as possible and prevail upon him to help you and your transition team, thus completing the holding-together he has done for so long. He also will be needed for liaison with Mr. Nixon and his family. However, he should not be expected, asked, or be given the option to become *your* Chief of Staff." I knew we needed Haig, and I wanted him to stay as long as he possibly could. Yet I also knew that he had his own career to consider. He'd been away from active duty for a long time and I suspected that he'd want to get back to the Army soon.

At eight-fourteen, the limousine arrived at the EOB. I went over the speech once more and attended to last-minute details. Nixon, I knew, was saying farewell to his Cabinet and his White House staff. I did not attend, but learned soon after that his remarks had been philosophical. "Always remember," he had told his listeners, "others may hate you, but those who hate you don't win, unless you hate them, and then you destroy yourself." If he'd followed his own advice, I thought, this moment might never have come.

Shortly after nine-thirty, I received word that the Nixons were ready to leave. Betty and I joined them in the Diplomatic Reception Room on the ground floor of the White House. An olive-drab helicopter, *Army One*, was waiting on the South Lawn to fly the Nixons to Andrews Air Force Base. The four of us walked toward it. "My heavens," Pat Nixon said, "they've even rolled out the red carpet for us. Well, Betty, you'll see many of these red carpets, and you'll get so you hate 'em." The moment was terribly painful for all of us; we were trying to put up the bravest, strongest front. Standing by the helicopter's door, we wished the Nixons happiness and good health. The President grabbed my elbow and held it for a split second longer than necessary, as if to say "Good luck." The moment had come. Then he uttered the words. "Goodbye, Mr. President," he said, and put out his hand.

"Goodbye, Mr. President," I said. We shook hands, then stepped back. The pilot started the engines. The rotors spun around faster and faster now, and as the chopper lifted off, we gave a final wave. I grabbed Betty's hand. "We can do it. We're ready," I said. She did not reply, just looked me in the eye and smiled. As we walked hand in hand back inside the White House, guards rolled up the carpet behind us.

At eleven forty-five, I left my Vice Presidential office in the EOB and walked over to the Red Room of the White House, where Betty was waiting for me. Minutes later, we were escorted into the East Room, which was filled to overflowing. Three huge chandeliers glittered from the ceiling. In the front row, on my right, sat the members of the Cabinet and their wives. On my left I spotted our children. They were looking directly at me, their faces solemn yet proud. A military aide announced the arrival of Chief Justice Burger.

As I waited for the proceedings to begin, I felt a sense of awe. It was different from the feeling I'd had when I took my oath as a member of Congress in 1949 or even as Vice President in 1973. At this historic moment, I was aware of kinship with my predecessors. It was almost as if all of America's past Presidents were praying for me to succeed.

Chief Justice Burger cut into my reverie. "Mr. Vice President," he asked, "are you prepared to take the oath of office as President of the United States?"

Betty was holding the Bible. I placed my hand on it, repeated the oath and then walked over to the podium. Conscious that the world was watching me, I began to speak:

Mr. Chief Justice, my dear friends, my fellow Americans. The oath that I have taken is the same oath that was taken by George Washington and by every President under the Constitution.

But I assume the Presidency under extraordinary circumstances never before experienced by Americans. This is an hour of history that troubles our minds and hurts our hearts.

Therefore, I feel it is my first duty to make an unprecedented compact with my countrymen. Not an inaugural address, not a fireside chat, not a campaign speech, just a little straight talk among friends. And I intend it to be the first of many.

If you have not chosen me by secret ballot, neither have I gained office by any secret promises. I have not campaigned either for the Presidency or the Vice Presidency. I have not subscribed to any partisan platform. I am indebted to no man and only to one woman, my dear wife, as I begin this very difficult job.

I have not sought this enormous responsibility, but I will not shirk it. Those who nominated and confirmed me as Vice President were my friends and are my friends. They were of both parties, elected by all people and acting under the Constitution in their name. It is only fitting then that I should pledge to them and to you that I will be President of all the people. . . .

Even though this is late in an election year, there is no way we can go forward except together and no way anybody can win except by serving the people's urgent needs. We cannot stand still or slip backwards. We must go forward now together.

I believe that truth is the glue that holds government together, not only our government but civilization itself. That bond, though strained, is unbroken at home and abroad.

In all my public and private acts as your President, I expect to follow my instincts of openness and candor with full confidence that honesty is always the best policy in the end.

My fellow Americans, our long national nightmare is over. Our Constitution works. Our great Republic is a government of laws and not of men. Here, the people rule. . . .

In the beginning I asked you to pray for me. Before closing, I ask again your prayers for Richard Nixon and for his family. May our former President who brought peace to millions find it for himself. . . .

With all the strength and all the good sense I have gained from life, with all the confidence my family, my friends and dedicated staff impart to me and with the good will of countless Americans, I now solemnly reaffirm my promise I made to you last December 6, to uphold the Constitution, to do what is right as God gives me to see the right, and to do the very best I can for America.

God helping me, I will not let you down.

The uncertainty was over, but the real challenge was about to begin.

2

Boyhood—and Beyond

"To laugh often and love much; to win the respect of intelligent persons and the affection of children; to earn the approbation of honest critics and endure the betrayal of false friends; to appreciate beauty; to find the best in others; to give of one's self; to leave the world a bit better, whether by a healthy child, a garden patch or a redeemed social condition; to have played and laughed with enthusiasm and sung with exultation; to know even one life has breathed easier because you have lived—this is to have succeeded."

The friend who first showed me the lines quoted above didn't know who had written them. But he had found them inspiring and had kept them in his wallet for years. When, some time ago, he showed them to me, I thought immediately of my parents. Nothing I've ever read sums up better the credo by which they both lived. By that definition they "succeeded" indeed.

My mother, Dorothy Gardner, was born in 1892 in Harvard, Illinois. She attended high school there and a girls' finishing school, then spent one year at college. In 1912, when she was twenty years old, she met a wool trader named Leslie Lynch King, who lived in Omaha, Nebraska. After a whirlwind courtship they married, and on July 14, 1913, I was born. My parents christened me Leslie L. King, Jr.

Apparently, my parents quarreled all the time—later, I heard that he hit her frequently—and in 1915 they decided to divorce. Mother's parents were living in Grand Rapids at the time, so we left Omaha and stayed with them in their large, comfortable house near Garfield Park.

Following her divorce, mother fell in love with and married Gerald Rudolf Ford, a paint salesman for the Grand Rapids Wood Finishing Company. (Years later, he took out formal adoption papers and renamed me Gerald R. Ford, Jr.) For the first three years of Mother's marriage we lived in a rented two-family house on Madison Avenue, S.E. My recollections of that time are vague. I still have a faded photograph of myself as a youngster dressed like an early frontiersman, with a coonskin cap on my head. One of our neighbors was a salesman for the Franklin "air cooled" automobile. All the children in our neighborhood were fascinated by it. Another local attraction was Firehouse No. 7, several blocks away. It was the last in the city to rely on horse-drawn equipment. Whenever there was a fire, the bells would clang, the sirens would scream, the station house doors would swing open and the teams of horses would come charging out. The sight was spectacular.

I went to kindergarten at Madison Elementary School, a block and a half from home. It was an old three-story building with a gravel playground in the back. Even at that age I recall playing softball and football and coming home with a dirty face, torn clothes and skinned knees and elbows. In July 1918, my half-brother Tom was born. When he was still an infant, he came down with scarlet fever. In those days if someone had scarlet fever, the family was quarantined; a big sign on the door warned visitors away. Our family physician was Dr. John Wright, a friendly, heavy-set general practitioner who had scraggly white hair and drove a fancy car. He made house calls frequently and somehow Tom pulled through.

One day when I was five years old, I had a terrible stomach ache. My parents rushed me to Butterworth Hospital, where the doctors diagnosed my problem as appendicitis and decided to operate as quickly as possible. When it turned out that my appendix hadn't been infected, my parents were furious.

In 1919, shortly after the end of World War I, we moved to more prosperous East Grand Rapids and bought a home—the first my parents ever owned—on Rosewood Avenue; and I attended the East Grand Rapids Elementary School. My stepfather was making headway as a salesman at the Grand Rapids Wood Finishing Company, and soon he got into the coal business with his oldest sister's son, Harold Swain.

As a child I had a hot temper, which Mother taught me to control—most of the time. A strict disciplinarian, she would ridicule me and show me how foolish I looked when I got angry and said stupid things. She also used to twist my ear. Even more effective was her habit of sending me up to my room with orders to stay there until I was ready to come downstairs and discuss rationally whatever I'd done wrong. One time she gave me the poem "If" by Rudyard Kipling. "Read this and profit from it," she said. "It'll help you control that temper of yours."

Despite all the discipline, I never once doubted her love. A stout, big-boned woman with an attractive face, she was the most selfless person I have ever known. Because she made other people's problems *her* problems, she had thousands of friends. The Grace Episcopal Church Guild, the Grand Rapids Garden Club, the Daughters of the American Revolution—she was engaged in one church or civic activity after another. And when she wasn't attending meetings, she was busy baking bread or sewing clothes for needy families. Having the family together for major holidays like Thanksgiving or Christmas would fill her with joy and she wasn't shy about expressing it. And if a relative or neighbor suffered in any way, she would be reduced to tears.

Although my stepfather didn't display his emotions quite so openly, I know he felt them just as deeply. At six feet one, he was a handsome man with jet-black hair parted in the middle. He kept himself in excellent physical shape and had the straightest shoulders I have ever seen. Tragedy had entered his life at an early age. His own father had been killed in an accident when he and his three sisters were very young, leaving his mother without funds. As a result, he was forced to leave school after the eighth grade to support the family, working first for the local electric railroad, then for the Grand Rapids Wood Finishing Company. Although he knew that formal education opened the doors to success, he never felt sorry for himself. Instead, he did what he could to help others in need. He was a vestryman in

church, a devoted Mason, a Shriner, an active Elk, and a strong sup-
porter of the Boy Scouts.

As a disciplinarian, he was every bit as strict as Mother. A man of
impeccable integrity, he drilled into me and my three half-brothers
(Dick was born when I was eleven; Jim when I was fourteen) the importance of honesty. In fact, he and Mother had three rules: tell the
truth, work hard, and come to dinner on time—and woe unto any of
us who violated those rules.

This is not to say that my stepfather couldn't laugh or have a good
time. Even when I was a toddler, he'd toss baseballs and footballs
with me. In the summer, he and Mother would drive us to Ottawa
Beach on Lake Michigan, thirty miles away. Along with three other
men, he owned a cabin near Bitely, on the Little South Branch of the
Pere Marquette River. He'd take me there to fish and share in a wide
variety of outdoor activities. He was a marvelous family man. Neither of my parents could be described as "secure" economically; but
emotionally both were very secure, and if I retain that characteristic
today, I owe it to them.

At about this stage in my life, I developed a stuttering problem.
Some words gave me fits and it would take me forever to get them
out. I don't know what caused the problem—eventually, at the age of
about ten, it went away—but it may have been related to my ambi-
dexterity. For as long as I can remember, I have been left-handed
when I've been sitting down and right-handed standing up. As
strange as this may sound, I'd throw a football with my right hand
and write with my left. It seemed perfectly natural to me. My parents and early teachers, however, became quite concerned and tried
to make me use my right hand all the time. After a while, they gave
up and I continued switching hands as I'd done before.

In 1921, my stepfather suffered some financial setbacks. The bank
foreclosed on our Rosewood Avenue mortgage and we were forced to
move to a rented home on Union Avenue. The house was large and
clean and we boys all had chores to do. Between six and six-thirty every morning, I had to remove the ashes from the furnace and put in
the day's supply of coal. Every night, I banked the furnace before going to bed. During the summer I cut the lawn and often had to clean

out the garage. All of us had to make our own beds and take turns cleaning up the kitchen and washing the dishes after every meal. No one complained—chores were a matter-of-fact part of everyday life.

In the mid 1920s, Grand Rapids was known as a strait-laced, highly conservative town. The large number of Dutch immigrants and their descendants were hard-working and deeply religious. Almost everyone attended church and a strict moral code was scrupulously observed. Like many youngsters my age, I was tempted to defy convention. In the rear of our rented property on Union Avenue stood a two-story garage which resembled a barn. There, a group of us established a social club. We learned to play penny-ante poker and other games. It was a great hideaway because my parents wouldn't climb the ladder to get to the second floor—or so I thought. My stepfather, however, knew better. He caught us red-handed several times and reprimanded us severely.

By the time I entered seventh grade, I was becoming aware of the deep emotions that rivalries can stir. Sometimes the competition stemmed from an effort to win the attention of a girl; or it emanated from a natural desire to outperform others in sports. The fact of the matter was that several of my classmates hated each other. Because of this, I developed a philosophy that has sustained me ever since. Everyone, I decided, had more good qualities than bad. If I understood and tried to accentuate those good qualities in others, I could get along much better. Hating or even disliking people because of their bad qualities, it seemed to me, was a waste of time.

In my sophomore year at South High School, I played center on the city championship football team and was named to the all-city squad. Our coach, Cliff Gettings, used the double wing formation. He was a stern taskmaster, and I remember the hours I spent learning how to center the ball with speed and accuracy. The T-formation center today looks directly ahead and simply hands the ball to the quarterback. But with the single or double wing, the center was forced to view everything upside down. The opposing lineman had the jump on you and to carry out your blocking assignment you had to be very quick. You also had to perfect different types of snaps. If the fullback was coming into the line, you had to drop the ball softly in his hands as he was moving forward. The snap for a punt had to be on the kicker's right hip. If the tailback was running left or right, you had to lead him an arm's length in the right direction.

Athletics, my parents kept saying, built a boy's character. They were important, but not nearly as important as attaining good grades. My parents made sure I did my homework and pressed me to excel. In chemistry and other science courses, I received average grades. In Latin, which I disliked, it was a struggle to earn C's. Math was not too difficult. In the courses I really enjoyed, history and government, I did very well. At the end of my junior year, I made the National Honor Society and ranked in the top 5 percent of our 220-member class. My parents also insisted that I hold part-time jobs. I mowed lawns, handled concessions for Alex Demar at a local amusement park, and at lunchtime worked in Bill Skougis's restaurant, across the street from school. It was there, in the spring of 1930, that I received the first major shock of my life.

My job was to slap hamburgers on the grill, handle the cash register and wash dishes. One day at noon, I was behind the counter in my regular spot near the register when I noticed a man standing by the candy display case. He'd been there fifteen or twenty minutes without saying a word and he was staring at me. Finally, he came over. "I'm Leslie King, your father," he said. "Can I take you to lunch?"

I was stunned and didn't know what to say. When I was twelve or thirteen, Mother had told me that Gerald R. Ford, Sr., was not my real father, but we hadn't really discussed the situation at home. I knew that the court in Omaha had ordered my father to pay her between fifty and seventy-five dollars per month for child support. He hadn't paid what he owed. His own father, my grandfather, had assumed that obligation. But when Grandfather died, the checks stopped coming in. Until now, my father had made no attempt to get in touch with us.

I looked him in the eye. "I'm working," I said.

"Ask your boss if you can get off," he persisted.

Bill Skougis told me it was all right. My father took me outside to a new Lincoln. A woman was sitting inside; he introduced her as his wife. They had taken the train to Detroit from Wyoming, where they lived, had purchased the car, and now they were driving home through Grand Rapids.

"Where shall we go for lunch?" he asked.

"The Cherry Inn," I said.

As we drove to the restaurant, he told me how he had located me. There were five high schools and one parochial school in Grand Rapids at the time. He had gone to the principal's office at South High and asked, "You have a Leslie King, Jr., in school here?" The secretary had said no. "Well, do you have a Junior Ford here?" They told him they did and added that I worked part-time in the restaurant across the street.

Our talk over lunch was superficial. My father knew I was an athlete and he wanted to know how good the team at South High was. We didn't mention the divorce or anything else disagreeable. Leaving the restaurant, we drove back to South High, where my father handed me twenty-five dollars. "Now, you buy yourself something, something you want that you can't afford otherwise," he said. Then, with a wave, he and his wife were gone.

That night was one of the most difficult of my life. I don't recall the words I used to tell my parents what had happened, but I do remember that the conversation was a loving and consoling one. My stepfather loved me as much as he loved his own three sons. I knew how much he wanted to help me and how lacking in financial resources he was. Nothing could erase the image I gained of my real father that day: a carefree, well-to-do man who didn't really give a damn about the hopes and dreams of his firstborn son. When I went to bed that night, I broke down and cried.

During the summer of 1930, after my junior year, my parents scraped up enough money to buy an old house on Lake Drive in East Grand Rapids. The place was in terrible shape, and all of us spent nights and weekends trying to refurbish it. The house's location presented a problem of another kind. East Grand Rapids was four miles from where we'd lived previously. I'd been going to South High since the seventh grade. I was captain-elect of the football team, and I wanted to win my diploma from the school I'd attended for the last five years. Public transportation between Grand Rapids and East Grand Rapids was inadequate. That summer I had worked at the Ford Paint and Varnish Company—which my stepfather had founded two years before—and earned forty cents per hour cleaning smelly paint vats, mixing colors and filling thousands of cans. I had some cash in the bank. So I exhausted my savings and for the magnificent sum of seventy-five dollars, bought a 1924 Ford coupe with a rumble seat.

The car ran beautifully during the football season (we were undefeated that year and won the state championship), but then cold weather set in. One December day, the temperature fell below zero and there was snow on the ground. Because I didn't know much about cars, I hadn't bothered to pour antifreeze into the radiator. I parked the car at school, attended varsity basketball practice and drove home for dinner that night. As I pulled into the driveway, I noticed clouds of steam rising up from the engine. I lifted the hood, saw that the motor was a fiery red and decided—incredibly—that what I needed was something to keep the car warm all night. Some old blankets were lying in the garage. I laid them on top of the engine and went inside to eat. Just as we finished the family meal, we heard fire engine sirens loud and close. We looked out the window and my poor car was in flames. That was a serious loss economically (I didn't have any insurance), and the fact that my own stupidity had caused the fire made me feel even worse.

I wish I could say that experience taught me all I needed to know about cars. In my senior year, my parents bought a six-passenger Chandler sedan. At the time, I was on the South High track team. We had a meet at Grand Haven, thirty-five miles away. The team had no money to pay for traveling expenses, so the coach suggested that several of us borrow our parents' cars for the journey. My stepfather agreed. We got to Grand Haven on time and won the meet. That's when my troubles began. Leaving the parking area, I backed the Chandler into a tree. The impact broke the clamp that attached the spare tire to the back of the car. We couldn't put the tire inside because six of us from the track team were packed in the car. No problem, I thought; I would simply tie the tire on the back. Not until I returned home did I realize my mistake. The heat from the exhaust had burned a hole through the tire and my stepfather let me have it. "Why did you back up without looking?" he fumed. "Look at all the damage you caused." Insurance paid the bill to repair the car, but the policy didn't cover the ruined tire. I had to pay for that.

Although Arthur Krause, the principal of South High, was an alumnus of the University of Indiana, he was an ardent University of Michigan fan. The Wolverines, he pointed out, were one of the finest teams in the land. They had boasted stars like Bennie Oosterbaan and Benny Friedman. Their former coach and present athletic director, Fielding ("Hurry Up") Yost, was a living legend and their fabulous new stadium could accommodate crowds of nearly ninety thousand. I had captained the all-state squad that year and it seemed natural to him that a boy with my record would want to go to the best college in the area. And Michigan was not only tops athletically; it had a fine academic reputation. Again the problem was money. My stepfather was busy raising three other children; he had no funds to spare.

That's when Krause came to the rescue. Learning of our family's strapped financial situation, he arranged for me to receive a one-hundred-dollar South High "bookstore" scholarship—a full year's tuition in those days. Whatever other funds I needed I could earn myself by doing part-time jobs. Which is precisely what I did as soon as I entered the freshman class at Ann Arbor in the fall of 1931. I'd saved one hundred dollars that summer working at the paint factory. For three hours every day, during the lunch period, I waited tables in the interns' dining room at the university hospital, then helped clean up the nurses' cafeteria. A wonderful aunt and uncle, Roy and Ruah La Forge, sent me a two-dollar check every week. And once every two or three months, I received twenty-five dollars for donating blood at the university hospital.

If I had to go back to college again—knowing what I know today—I'd concentrate on two areas: learning to write and to speak before an audience. Nothing in life is more important than the ability to communicate effectively. As an athlete at South High, I'd attended a number of public functions and had had some experience speaking before large groups. But I was horribly unprepared for the challenge of my freshman English course. (South High hadn't taught me—or I hadn't bothered to learn—anything about basic composition.) Every weekend, I would labor over the one-thousand-word theme due on Monday morning. At the end of the year, I earned a C in the course—and I was glad to get it.

In the spring of my freshman year, I pledged Delta Kappa Epsilon fraternity. That fall, I moved into the Deke house, where I'd spend the next three years. In order to earn my board, I washed dishes after meals. Although these were Depression years, most of my fraternity brothers came from well-to-do families; only three or four of us had to work. Academically, the Deke house had a lousy reputation. Athletically, however, it ranked fairly high, and it was certainly no slouch as a party house. Because I divided my time between studies, sports and part-time jobs, I seldom had time for parties and I guess I was naïve about alcohol.

My parents didn't drink and never kept liquor in the house. I had never smoked and hadn't had a drink until the spring of my sophomore year. The previous fall, when Michigan was the undefeated national champion, I'd injured my knee playing football, and I was scheduled for an operation. The night before I was to go to the hospital, Jack Beckwith, a friend and roommate, took me to the Spanish Club in Ann Arbor, where we spent hours drinking tequila and smoking long cigars. I woke up the next morning with probably the worst hangover I have ever had. I got to the hospital on time, but the doctors and nurses took one look at me and decided to postpone the operation until the next day.

In the fall of my junior year, my need for funds became critical, despite all my jobs and blood donations. My bills for clothes, lodging, books and supplies totaled six hundred dollars and I didn't have anywhere near that amount. My stepfather wasn't able to help since his business was faltering in the wake of the Depression and other family costs were rising, so I wrote to my real father in Wyoming and asked him for a loan. I never received a reply. Then I thought of Mr. and Mrs. Ralph Conger, good friends of my parents in Grand Rapids. Mrs. Conger, I knew, had recently inherited a large sum. Perhaps she could help. I wrote the Congers and received a letter from them by return mail. Inside was a check for six hundred dollars.

In my first year at Michigan, I had won the Meyer Morton Trophy—a silver football—awarded to the outstanding freshman player in spring practice. But I saw limited action as a sophomore and junior, playing behind our All-America center, Chuck Bernard. I took solace from the fact that the team was undefeated and won the national championship two years in a row. "A punt, a pass and a prayer"—that was the way the sportswriters described the Wolverine offense and they had a point. The theory that Yost developed—and that coach Harry Kipke refined—was that if you had a good punter, a good passer and a strong defense, you would always win. If you won the toss of the coin, you always kicked off and gave the other team the ball. You counted on your defense to force them into mistakes. Inside your own 40-yard line, you always punted on second or third down. If you were near your own goal line, you punted on first down. If your punter did his job, you could pick up 10 or 15 yards with every exchange. Then, if your passer connected, you could score and score again.

Although we'd lost a number of first-string players through graduation, I felt confident as I headed into my senior year that our 1934 team would be on a par with its predecessors, perhaps even winning the national title again. Bill Renner was a fine passer, John Regeczi was an outstanding punter and our defense was strong. Then disaster struck. Renner broke his leg before the first game and was out for the season. Regeczi injured his knee. Our defense struggled mightily, but we just couldn't score. We lost to Michigan State 16–0 and then to the University of Chicago—the great Jay Berwanger team—by the lopsided score of 27–0.

Team morale was low. Then something happened to give us a needed lift. One of the best pass receivers on the team was a black track star named Willis Ward. He and I were close friends—we roomed together on trips out of town—and our friendship grew even closer during our senior year. Our next game was against Georgia Tech, an all-white school whose coach threatened to forfeit the contest if Willis played. Michigan tried to work out a compromise whereby both Willis and some Georgia Tech star would stay on the bench. Because I felt this was morally wrong, I called my stepfather and asked what I should do.

"I think you ought to do whatever the coaching staff decides is right," he said.

Still unsatisfied, I went to Willis himself. He urged me to play. "Look," he said, "the team's having a bad year. We've lost two games already and we probably won't win any more. You've got to play Saturday. You owe it to the team." I decided he was right. That

Saturday afternoon we hit like never before and beat Georgia Tech 9–2.

The rest of the season was disastrous. We lost to Illinois, Minnesota, Wisconsin, Ohio State and Northwestern and were outscored 98–12. For me, one of the toughest games was the 7–6 defeat we suffered at the hands of Illinois. It had been raining for days in Ann Arbor; the field was a quagmire and we must have punted fifteen or twenty times. On a number of those occasions, we were inside our own five-yard line and I had to make damn sure that I snapped the ball to the punter so he could kick it out of our backyard on time. Despite the slippery ball, I had a perfect day. Old "Hurry Up" Yost was not the sort to compliment anyone, particularly when the team lost. Yet at the end of that game, he came up to me in the locker room and said, "Ford, that was one of the finest exhibitions of centering I have ever seen."

If that wasn't enough to turn my head, my teammates selected me, at the end of the season, as the most valuable player on the squad and I was named to the East team for the annual Shrine Crippled Children's Hospital game in San Francisco. I played fifty-eight of the sixty minutes that New Year's Day, and although we lost by a 19–13 score, I was pleased because I had played well.

Looking back, I realize I was lucky to have competed in sports. As a football player, you have critics in the stands and critics in the press. Few of them have ever centered a ball, kicked a punt or thrown a touchdown pass with 100,000 people looking on, yet they assume they know all the answers. Their comments helped me to develop a thick hide, and in later years whenever critics assailed me, I just let their jibes roll off my back.

Although I ranked in the top quarter of my class—I was majoring in economics and political science—I still hadn't decided what I was going to do as graduation neared. Both the Detroit Lions and the Green Bay Packers offered me $2,800 to play for them that fall. That was big money, but pro football wouldn't lead me anywhere. What intrigued me most was the possibility of studying law. I never thought of myself as a great orator in the tradition of William Jennings Bryan or Clarence Darrow. Rather, I thought my talents would be those of the mediator and counselor. As Abraham Lincoln once wrote: "It is as a peacemaker that the lawyer has a superior opportunity." That appealed to me.

The trouble was that I had no money to attend law school. I spoke to Kipke about this one day in February and asked if he could hire me after graduation as a freshman football coach and pay me several hundred dollars a year. Kipke always thought that I was a good kid who worked hard and who didn't bitch even when I sat on the bench. "I can't promise you a thing," he said. "We'll know later this spring what our budget will be. Maybe we can hire you then. Meanwhile, if I hear of anything, I'll get in touch with you."

He was a man of his word. A month or so later, he called me to say that Ducky Pond, the head coach at Yale, was coming to Ann Arbor to recruit an assistant line coach. He arrived by train and huddled with Kipke, who recommended me. Over lunch at the Michigan Union, Pond offered me the chance to visit the campus in New Haven to see if I liked it there and if the Elis approved of me. Although I had gone to Washington, D.C., for several days in the summer of 1931, I had never been to New York or New England. As soon as the check for my ticket arrived in the mail, I was on my way to New Haven, with a brief, wide-eyed look at Grand Central station when I changed trains.

The Yale campus, an attractive place today, was even more beautiful then. The tall Gothic towers were inspiring, the long, sweeping lawns refreshing and clean. Everywhere I went, I discerned an atmosphere of scholarship, dignity and tradition. At the end of my second day, Pond offered me $2,400 a year if I would join him as an assistant and also coach the freshman boxing team. I knew nothing about boxing, but I promised to take instruction at the Grand Rapids YMCA before returning that fall. Then I raised the question of attending law school. Pond was dubious. The job I'd agreed to take would occupy all my time, he said, but he promised to relay my request to the law school deans. Once again, the answer was negative. The deans didn't feel that I could carry the dual load of full-time coach and law student. I decided to take the job, save as much as I could, then try again.

In the summer of 1935, I played in the College All-Star game against the Chicago Bears. With such stars as Jack Manders and

Bronko Nagurski on their roster, the Bears should have whipped us handily. Instead, we held them to a 5–0 win, which I considered a moral victory and a gratifying windup to my football career. The game had a fringe benefit for me. Each of the college players received one hundred dollars, and that was enough to pay for my trip to Yale.

On August 1, 1935, I arrived in New Haven. Quickly, I discovered that coaching was a full-time job. The team that year finished with a record of six and three, which gave me some satisfaction. Even more pleasing, for the first time in my life, I was able to save some money. By January 1, 1936, I had accumulated enough to repay, with interest, the six hundred dollars that the Congers had lent me two years before.

One of my roommates at Yale, Ken Loeffler, was the basketball coach. He kept telling me what a fine experience he'd had working summers in one of the national parks out West. So I filled out an application and with the help of Senator Arthur H. Vandenberg of Michigan I landed a job at Yellowstone National Park. We directed traffic, supervised the campgrounds and monitored the feeding of the bears at Canyon Station. At five-thirty every afternoon, we'd load metal containers filled with garbage onto the back of a flatbed truck, then dump them into an open pit a mile or so away. The smaller black bears would come out of the woods first. Then the grizzlies would saunter forth and drive them away. Tourists watched the feeding ritual in a fence-enclosed area from the banks of the pit and I stood on the flatbed truck, rifle in hand, to make sure that the bears kept away from their audience. Although I saw some bloody fights between the grizzlies, I never had to fire the rifle. (Years later, when our four children were growing up, I'd tell them bedtime stories about my summer in the park. My accounts grew richer and more dramatic, of course, with the passage of time and I have to admit that I embellished them a lot. Finally, one by one, each of the children said, "Dad, please don't tell me the story of the bears again.")

Yale's 1936 team was even better than the previous one. We won the Ivy League crown with a record of seven and one; halfback Clint Frank and end Larry Kelley made the All-America team and I received a six-hundred-dollar raise. (Among the players I coached that

fall were a tackle named Bob Taft and a thin but very gutsy end
named Bill Proxmire.) That encouraged me to think about law school
again. In the summer of 1937, I decided to return to Ann Arbor and
attend law classes at Michigan. If I received good grades, I could use
them as a wedge to try again at Yale.

Back in New Haven that fall, I showed Ducky Pond the grades I'd
received (B's in criminal law and civil procedure). "Would you
mind," I asked, "if I took some courses here if they'll accept me?"
Ducky relented on one condition. "You've got to do it in the spring
term," he said. "You can't let it interfere with your coaching responsibilities." At the end of the season, I approached the law school
deans. They were reluctant—98 of the 125 members of the freshman
class had made Phi Beta Kappa as undergraduates, they pointed
out—but they finally agreed to let me take two courses that spring. I
earned two more B's. Satisfied that I could do the work, they withdrew their objections and accepted me full time.

The competition was stiff. Among my fellow law students at Yale
were Cyrus Vance, Potter Stewart and Sargent Shriver, and none of
them took a back seat to anyone. Somehow I managed to rank in the
top 25 percent of our class. How that happened I can't explain. I was
taking a full load of courses; coaching was a full-time job and, to
complicate matters further, I had fallen deeply in love for the first
time in my life.

Her name was Phyllis Brown and she was a slim, gregarious blonde
who attended Connecticut College for Women in New London. I
met her in the most improbable way. The Yale boxing team was traveling to New London to compete against the U.S. Coast Guard Academy. I was going along as assistant coach. Friends of mine from
Grand Rapids were cadets there and suggested that I call Phyllis,
whom they described as beautiful. Several days later, I telephoned
and made a date. My friends were right. Phyllis *was* beautiful. The
only problem was that she wasn't going to stick around very long.

In her junior year, she left college to become a model in New York
City and soon her face appeared regularly on the covers of *Cosmo-
politan* and other magazines. But Phyllis didn't rely solely on her
good looks. She was one of the most all-round women I've ever
known. She loved to ski. I'd never skied before, but if I wanted to

stay in her league, I simply had to learn. Soon we were spending weekends together on the slopes. We went to the theater in New York, the first time I'd ever done that; we played bridge, tennis and golf; we visited each other's homes in Michigan and Maine. Everything, it seemed, was fitting together perfectly. I was in love with her; she—in her own way—was in love with me, and we talked about getting married as soon as I earned my law degree and found a decent job.

And that was the sticking point. Although I'd received tentative offers from law firms in Philadelphia and New York, I really wanted to practice in Grand Rapids. But Phyllis's modeling career was blossoming in New York and she didn't think she could afford to leave. We talked for hours but got nowhere. Reluctantly, we agreed to part. The end of our relationship caused me real anguish and I wondered if I'd ever meet anyone like her again.

In January 1941, I finished my courses at Yale, returned to Michigan and prepared to take the bar exam. Phil Buchen, a friend and fraternity brother at Ann Arbor, was doing the same thing. Normally, young attorneys sought positions with old, established firms. Phil and I were impatient and ambitious; we decided to strike out on our own. As soon as we passed the bar, we formed the firm of Ford and Buchen and waited anxiously for clients to appear. Our first "success" was hardly auspicious: a routine title search. We billed the client fifteen dollars; when he protested that it was too much, we cut it down to ten. Phil and I were glad to have any cash in the till.

Gradually, the firm began to break even and soon we had more than enough to do. Labor law, pension trusts, separations and divorces—we took on everything we could. I was working as hard as I'd ever worked before. Then, on December 7, 1941, Japanese planes attacked Pearl Harbor. I was in the office that Sunday afternoon and didn't hear the news until I flicked on the radio while driving home that night. There was no doubt in my mind that the United States would go to war, that the war would be long and that everything would change very quickly for me.

Early in 1942, I entered the Navy as an ensign. I was sent to the Naval Academy in Annapolis, Maryland, and then to the V-5 pre-flight school at Chapel Hill, North Carolina, as a physical fitness instructor. But there was a war going on; I wanted desperately to be part of it, so I wrote letters to everyone I knew, pleading for a billet on a ship. Finally, in the spring of 1943, I received orders to report to U.S.S. *Monterey,* a light aircraft carrier which was due to be commissioned soon at the Navy Yard in Philadelphia. I had a dual assignment on the ship: athletic director and gunnery division officer. After a shakedown cruise to the Caribbean, we passed through the Panama Canal, stopped at San Diego to put on extra planes and headed at flank speed toward Pearl Harbor.

In November 1943, we joined the aircraft carrier U.S.S. *Enterprise,* a light cruiser and six destroyers for our first taste of combat. Our planes blasted Makin Island in the Gilberts, then moved southwest to hit the Japanese base at Kavieng on New Ireland. We really clobbered Kavieng, waves of planes bombing the port on Christmas morning 1943 and sinking enemy ships. As a gunnery officer, my job was to stand on the fantail and direct the crew firing the 40-mm anti-aircraft gun. The Japanese planes came after us with a vengeance. We had many general quarters calls and it was as much action as I'd ever hoped to see. Still, I was a bit restless in the gunnery division and wanted to do something more challenging. At about that time, the assistant navigator was transferred to another ship. I asked for the job and got it. When general quarters was called, I moved up to the bridge, and now I felt that I knew what was going on.

After refueling and taking on supplies in New Guinea, we steamed north and east to support the landings on Kwajalein and Eniwetok and the thrusts against the island of Truk. We participated in the famous "Turkey Shoot" in the Marianas, during which we decimated the enemy's forces. Then we joined the task force gearing up for the battle of the Philippine Sea. One day in October 1944, our planes took off to hit targets on Taiwan, forty miles away. They returned at dusk, and when they'd been secured, we prepared to steam away. Just then, the Japanese planes attacked. The noise was deafening as our gunners opened up with everything they had. A torpedo from one of the planes nearly hit us and crashed into the side of the cruiser U.S.S. *Canberra* instead. Another torpedo smashed into the cruiser U.S.S. *Houston.* After a fierce few minutes, the attack was over. Both our cruisers were dead in the water. Other ships in the task force began towing them away, but they could only progress at a speed of about four knots. At dawn the next day, we were less than eighty miles off the coast of Taiwan, a sitting target for the Japanese. They attacked us all day long. Our guns blasted away and finally drove them off. We thought we had seen the worst of it, but our gravest crisis was still to come.

On December 18, we ran into a vicious typhoon in the Philippine Sea. Rain and hundred-knot winds whipped the ocean into a mountainous fury. That night was pure hell. I had the deck watch from midnight to four o'clock. In the pounding seas, three destroyers simply rolled over and capsized, with an enormous loss of life. At four o'clock, I left the bridge, stepped down to my cabin and tried to get some sleep before general quarters at five-fifteen.

The crew went through the predawn general quarters routine in the increasing fury of the typhoon. The wind and the rain were horrendous. I was glad when we secured, so I could hit the sack after a rough night.

I hadn't been back in my bunk many minutes before I heard the clang of general quarters again. Waking, I thought I could smell smoke. I went up the passageway and out to the catwalk on the starboard side which runs around the flight deck, where I started to climb the ladder. As I stepped on the flight deck, the ship suddenly rolled about 25 degrees. I lost my footing, fell to the deck flat on my face and started sliding toward the port side as if I were on a toboggan slide. Around the deck of every carrier is a steel ridge about two inches high. It's designed to keep the flight crews' tools from slipping overboard. Somehow, the ridge was enough to slow me. I rolled and twisted into the catwalk below. I was lucky; I could have easily gone overboard. Then, much more carefully this time, I made my way up to the bridge. That's when I realized the severity of the problems we faced. Fifteen or twenty fighters and torpedo bombers were tied down on the hangar deck below. At the height of the storm, one of the planes broke loose from its cables. Every time the ship rolled, it crashed into other planes. Soon, a number of planes were darting around down there like trapped, terrified birds. Gas tanks were punctured, the friction produced sparks and a fire broke out.

Because *Monterey* was a converted cruiser, the hangar deck air

vents were inadequate. They were supposed to funnel fresh air down
to the engine and boiler rooms, but now they were funneling smoke.
One sailor died of asphyxiation and 33 were injured. With no one to
tend them, three of the four boilers stopped functioning. The fire on
the hangar deck was raging out of control, and if we lost the last boiler, we'd lose the pressure in our fire hoses and have no way to fight
the blaze. We would have to abandon ship. Admiral William F. Hal-
sey, commander of the Third Fleet, authorized us to do just that and
he told two cruisers and three or four destroyers to stand by and try
to rescue survivors. But our skipper, Captain Stuart H. Ingersoll,
wasn't ready to quit. "Give us more time," I heard him radio from
the bridge. "I think we can solve the problem." The ship was still
dead in the water. The storm was raging. The fire was uncontrolled.
Ingersoll sent a rescue party wearing gas masks to the engine and
boiler rooms. They brought out the survivors, kept the one boiler
functioning and worked to repair the others. After seven hours of
battering by monstrous waves, all our boilers were working again; we
were able to extinguish the fire and steam toward the island of Saipan. Years later, when I became President, I remembered that fire at
the height of the typhoon and I considered it a marvelous metaphor
for the ship of state.

As soon as we reached Saipan, I flew home for a short leave, then
reported to the Naval Reserve Training Command in Glenview, Illinois. That's where I was destined to serve for the remainder of the
war. Ironically, I came closer to death at home than I ever did during
combat at sea.

As chief of the Naval Air Primary Training Command, Rear Admiral O. B. Hardison had some thirty bases under his jurisdiction.
One of them was the preflight school in Chapel Hill, North Carolina.
During the 1945 football season, Navy was scheduled to play North
Carolina at Chapel Hill. One of Hardison's top aides was an Annapolis graduate and ardent fan; he wanted to see the game. We timed
an inspection tour of bases in the South so we'd arrive in Chapel Hill
Friday night. As we approached our destination the weather was terrible. Rain was pelting down; it was getting dark outside and the air-
port didn't have runway lights. Our pilot had flown for TWA before
World War II. He knew how much the admiral and his aides wanted

to see the game and he was determined to land at Chapel Hill. Years earlier, while stationed there, I'd taken up flying myself in a Piper Cub, and I knew the airport well. But our pilot thought he was touching down on one runway when, in fact, he was landing on another, which was considerably shorter and had a different angle of approach. Suddenly, the plane pitched forward, plunged down an embankment and crashed into a clump of trees. Stunned, we searched for the exits and scrambled out as fast as we could. Seconds after we escaped, the plane burst into flames. I got out with only the shirt on my back.

In February 1946, I received my Navy discharge as a lieutenant commander and returned to Michigan. During the time I'd been away, Grand Rapids had changed significantly. Furniture was still the major industry, but General Motors and auto parts manufacturers had established plants there and the city's economy was beginning to diversify. Labor unions were attracting new members and becoming a potent force. There had been an influx of blacks from the South, and the once powerful grip that the early Dutch immigrants and their descendants had held over the community was weakening.

And I had changed. Before the war, I'd been an isolationist. Indeed, while at Yale, I had expressed the view that the U.S. ought to avoid "entangling alliances" abroad. But now I had become an ardent internationalist. My wartime experiences had given me an entirely new perspective. The U.S., I was convinced, could no longer stick its head in the sand like an ostrich. Our military unpreparedness before World War II had only encouraged the Germans and Japanese. In the future, I felt, the U.S. had to be strong. Never again could we allow our military to be anything but the best. And because a strong America would need strong allies to resist the growing Communist threat, we simply had to provide the money, muscle and manpower to help the nations of Western Europe rebuild their shattered economies.

At the moment, however, the only economy I had to worry about was my own. I was approaching my mid thirties and I had no job. During the war, the firm of Ford and Buchen had dissolved. Phil's childhood polio had left him ineligible for military service. After I'd gone off to war, he'd joined the prestigious firm of Butterfield,

Keeney & Amberg and become a partner there. We considered rees-
tablishing our own firm, but it seemed far more sensible for me to
join the Butterfield firm. The senior partners agreed, and in the early
spring of 1946, I began earning a living in the private sector again.

Incredibly, the harder I worked at the practice of law, the more
time I seemed to have for community activities. I was a compulsive
"joiner," but the truth is that I really enjoyed the challenges. I joined
the Kent County cancer drive and the county chapter of the American Red Cross. I became an active member of the American Legion
Furniture City Post and of the Veterans of Foreign Wars. I raised
money for the United Fund, served on the board of directors of the
Family Services Association and helped plan weekend outings for a
local Boy Scout troop. Since my days at South High, I had had a
number of black friends in athletics and school social events. I was
sympathetic to their economic and political plight and I hoped to
broaden my experience by joining the local chapter of the National
Association for the Advancement of Colored People.

My spartan social life was a matter of some concern to my family.
My three half-brothers had married; they were raising children of
their own and I was still ensconced in my parents' house. "When are
you going to start dating again?" Mother asked in her good-natured
but very persistent way. "You're thirty-four years old. When are you
going to settle down?"

One night I was at Frank and Peg Neuman's house, planning the
1947 Kent County cancer drive. "Gee," I said as I was leaving,
"who's around that a bachelor my age can date? You have any
ideas?"

"How about Betty Warren?" Peg suggested. "You know she's getting a divorce."

She was younger than I was; she'd gone to a different high school
and I didn't know her well. Still, I remembered how very attractive
she was and I knew that she was one of Peg's best friends. "Well, why
don't you call her?" I said. "I'll get on the phone and see if I can convince her to have a drink."

Easier said than done. Betty was a fashion coordinator for Herpolscheimer's, a large department store; she had scheduled a show the
next morning and had better things to do than have a drink with a

former football player whom she hardly knew. Besides, she reminded me, her divorce wasn't final yet. She didn't think she should date until the decree came through. As a lawyer, she said, I ought to understand that.

I did, but I didn't give up. "Just for an hour or so," I promised. "It'll be good for you."

Finally, she agreed. I picked her up at her apartment; we drove to an out-of-the-way bar on the corner of Hall Street and Division Avenue. I had no idea that someone special had just come into my life. In the weeks that followed, we saw each other frequently, but we weren't able to go out every night. She was busy with her job. I was spending long hours in the office. I had my extracurricular activities and then I was becoming interested in politics.

For the past several decades, "politics" in Grand Rapids—and indeed throughout the state—had been synonymous with the Republican Party; more specifically, with the well-oiled machine of a crusty old millionaire named Frank D. McKay. Central casting would have found him ideal in the role of a political boss; he was heavy-set, wore a pince-nez and his mouth turned down in what seemed to be a perpetual snarl. A strong believer in patronage, he was powerful, arrogant and dictatorial. Intimidation, not persuasion, was the secret of his success, and if he wasn't well liked, he was certainly feared. In the summer of 1940, just before I completed my courses at Yale, my stepfather had arranged for me to meet McKay. The Republicans had nominated Wendell Willkie for President that year. I thought I could help the Willkie campaign in Michigan and I wanted some marching instructions from McKay. He kept me waiting for four hours in his anteroom, finally giving me less than five minutes. He wasn't interested in my offer of help.

Over the years, McKay had treated young, idealistic Republicans with contempt. Inevitably, they decided to challenge him. In 1941, several of us formed an organization called the Home Front and took on McKay's county machine. When the war intervened I had to abandon the fight, but in 1942 the Home Front beat McKay in the battle for control of the county delegation. By 1946, he was finished as a political power. His hangers-on, however, were not. And one of them—first elected in 1940 with McKay's support—was the Fifth

District's Congressman, Bartel J. ("Barney") Jonkman. A fervent iso-lationist, Jonkman was a senior Republican on the House Committee on Foreign Affairs and was doing everything he could to torpedo constructive foreign aid legislation. To help the nations of Europe re-build, for example, President Harry S Truman had proposed the Marshall Plan. Michigan's senior Republican Senator, Arthur H. Van-denberg, was working with the President and trying to convince the Congress to cooperate. But Jonkman would have none of it. "No, no, no," he thundered.

Someone, I thought, should oppose him for renomination. Many of my Home Front colleagues agreed, but none of them seemed at all interested in the race. That was understandable. Jonkman was of strong Dutch heritage and there were many Dutch families living within the Fifth District's boundaries. Then, too, having amassed some seniority on Capitol Hill, he was able to grant the sort of politi-cal favors that earn IOUs from constituents. In 1946, he'd had no Re-publican opposition at all and he had swamped the Democrat. "Leave him be," I was advised. "He can't be defeated. He's too strong." And when I protested that nothing was impossible, the in-variable response was: "Well, if you feel that strongly, why don't you run yourself?"

My parents thought I should try. So did Phil Buchen, who said I should hire a campaign manager right away. We agreed to ask Jack Stiles, who had been a classmate of Phil's at Ann Arbor. For the time being, Phil counseled me, it was important to keep my efforts totally under wraps. Once Jonkman discovered that he had a challenger, he would counterattack fiercely. McKay's friends would help him as much as they could. My one advantage was surprise—and Jonkman's overconfidence. Until the moment came for me to declare my candi-dacy, I should tell no one what I was planning to do. "Even Betty?" I asked.

"Even Betty," he said.

Over the past six months, ever since our first date in August 1947, we had been seeing each other frequently. At first, neither of us had thought the relationship was "serious." She had been married for five years; she'd just received her divorce decree and wasn't about to plunge into matrimony again. And I was simply too busy with my legal career and community activities to think about shouldering more responsibility. We spent weekends with friends who owned a cottage on Lake Michigan; we drove to Ann Arbor during the football season. We played bridge together and attended dinners, dances and benefits, but that was it.

Or so I thought at the time. Right after Christmas that year, I flew out to Sun Valley, Idaho, for a two-week skiing vacation. While I was there, Betty traveled to New York City for Herpolscheimer's to attend fashion showings there. Suddenly, it dawned on me that I missed and needed her very much. I wrote to her every day. I bought her a hand-tooled leather belt with a silver buckle in Sun Valley. ("What?" a shocked friend asked when she found out about this. "Do you mean that Jerry Ford actually gave a present to a *girl?* This must be serious.") And when she returned from her trip it was obvious to me that she'd been sharing my emotions. One evening in February 1948, sitting with her on the couch in her apartment, I proposed. "I'd like to marry you," I said, "but we can't get married until next fall and I can't tell you why." She didn't press me for my reasons then. She just said in her soft-spoken way that she loved me too, and that a fall wedding would be fine.

Fortunately, Betty's first marriage had ended amicably. The experience had matured her and she knew what she wanted this time. Although I hadn't been married myself, my torrid four-year love affair with Phyllis Brown had matured me too. Betty and I had talked often about our values and goals. They were almost identical and I felt good about that.

In June 1948, just before the filing date, I announced my candidacy for the Republican Congressional nomination. To our surprise, Jonkman didn't seem concerned at all about having a primary opponent. Then luck intervened on my behalf. President Truman called the Congress back into session. While Jonkman had to remain in Washington, I had an open field to run all over the district, turning up at plant gates, picnics and county fairs, shaking hands and making speeches everywhere I went. The senior partner in our firm, Julius Amberg, was a Democrat. Because the Fifth District was overwhelmingly Republican, Amberg knew that no Democrat could hope to win the general election. The winner of the primary fight in the GOP would be the next Congressman. Amberg despised Jonkman's isolationist views. He wanted Jonkman out of there, so he told me to work one hour per day in the law office and campaign the rest of the time. And that's precisely what I did.

By that summer, I had pretty well formed the political philosophy I've maintained ever since. On economic policy, I was conservative— and very proud of it. I didn't believe that we could solve problems simply by throwing money at them. On social issues, I was a moderate; on questions of foreign policy, a liberal. The voters of the Fifth District didn't think the federal government had the answers to all the problems they faced. They tended to agree with Thomas Jefferson's axiom that the best government is the least government, and I was determined to reflect their views.

As it turned out, the major issue of that campaign was foreign policy. Jonkman and I were about as far apart as any two candidates could be. He was against the Marshall Plan and all other forms of foreign aid. I was convinced that they were not only necessary but also morally right, and I said so repeatedly. Even in the rural areas of the district, the voters seemed able to draw the distinction between our stands. My crowds were getting larger and more enthusiastic with every passing week.

In August, when the Eightieth Congress finally adjourned, Jonkman returned to Grand Rapids and found, to his dismay, that the tide was running against him. What upset him and Frank McKay the most was a red-white-and-blue Quonset hut that I had erected as my campaign headquarters in a parking lot of Wurzburg's department store. Wurzburg's was oblivious to any political ramifications when we made the deal to rent the space. But Frank McKay, whose office overlooked the parking lot, was furious that he had to see my campaign headquarters from his window. He called the Wurzburg officials. "Get Ford off that property," he said. Although Wurzburg's was a client of our firm, the store officials didn't want to alienate either an incumbent Congressman or Frank McKay, and they asked Julius Amberg for his advice. Amberg summoned me into his office, reminded me that Wurzburg's was a good client and asked me if I'd be willing to place the hut somewhere else. "Mr. Amberg," I replied, "we're *not* going to move that hut."

"Excellent." He smiled. "That's exactly what I hoped you'd say."

Not long afterward, I challenged Jonkman to a debate. He spurned the idea, and that was his first mistake. Then he alienated Leonard Woodcock, the United Auto Workers representative in western Michigan. Woodcock and his men decided to support me. Lee Woodruff, the editor of the Grand Rapids *Press*, abhorred Jonkman's isolationist views and deeply resented the attacks that he was making against Senator Vandenberg. Shortly before the primary on September 14, he wrote an editorial endorsing me. That's when Jonkman made his fatal mistake. Instead of attacking me, he blasted the Grand Rapids *Press*. They got into a bitter fight and I was the beneficiary. Jonkman was desperate now; he began to hurl ridiculous charges against me and my supporters. On election day, I won the primary by a margin of nearly two to one.

In an effort to gain support, I had told one area farm family that I would return after my victory and milk cows for two weeks, so at four-thirty the next morning, I got up and drove to a farm twenty miles away. That farmer sure was surprised to see me. "I said I'd come," I explained, "and I'm not going to break my campaign promises."

On Friday, October 15, 1948, just a little more than two weeks before the general election, Betty and I were married at Grace Episcopal Church in Grand Rapids. I had been campaigning until minutes before the ceremony and when I walked up to the altar, I had mud on my shoes. My mother was furious but Betty pretended not to notice, and friends still kid me about it to this day. Our honeymoon was brief, a fact that I've also not been allowed to forget. Jack Beckwith, my best man, gave a party for us in Ann Arbor on Saturday morning. It was so strenuous that Betty didn't accompany me to the Michigan-Northwestern game, but came at half time. That evening, we drove to Owosso, where the Republican Presidential candidate, Thomas E. Dewey, spoke at an outdoor rally. Then we headed for Detroit, arriving at 3 A.M. We had a quiet Sunday, and on Monday morning I attended some meetings in Ann Arbor. After we returned to Grand Rapids late that afternoon, I told Betty that I wouldn't be home for dinner that night. "Can you make me a sandwich?" I asked. "There's a meeting tonight that I just have to attend." That was her introduction to married life with a politician.

I was elected to Congress on November 2, with nearly 61 percent of the vote. I had a campaign debt of $7,000; a Congressman earned only $15,000 per year and my financial prospects weren't encouraging. Still, I had won a race that no one six months before had given me a chance to win. After the election, Betty and I had a chance to catch our breath and get to know each other as a married couple. We also began thinking of our new life in Washington. At the end of November, we flew to the nation's capital, found an apartment to rent on Q Street, N.W., then checked with party leaders in the Congress to determine on which committees I'd serve. My first assignment in 1949–1950 was the Committee on Public Works.

Freshman Congressmen seldom get the chance to sit on major committees, but midway through my first term, as has happened so often in my life, I received a break. Representative Albert Engel decided to leave the Congress to run for governor of Michigan, creating a Republican vacancy on the Appropriations Committee in the next session. Because I was from the same state and shared Engel's philosophical views, I was appointed to take his place. Initially, I sat on the Deficiencies and Civil Functions Subcommittee, which handled all the pork-barrel legislation; I also became a member of the subcommittee on General and Temporary Activities, which had just been created as a consequence of the Korean War.

Very early in my Congressional career, a senior member took me aside and said that as a representative, I could choose one of two alternatives. I could spend most of my time in my office attending to the problems of constituents and providing service to the district, or I could spend my time on the floor of the House listening to the debate, mastering parliamentary procedures and getting to know the other members personally. I could not do both. Since I had a good staff to handle constituent problems, I elected to spend time on the floor. That's how I got to know Richard Nixon. He was serving on the Education and Labor Committee and on the House Un-American Activities Committee as well. Both committees and the issues with which they dealt were highly controversial. Nixon and I would chat during floor debate and I made it a point to be present when he rose to speak. He wasn't a spellbinding orator, but he was convincing because he always knew his subject; he organized his remarks and argued logically. He was, I thought at the time, a very talented man.

In November 1950, he defeated Representative Helen Gahagan Douglas in the contest for a California Senate seat. I was reelected by Fifth District residents with 66 percent of the vote. One of my duties as their Congressman was to find a distinguished speaker for the annual Lincoln Day banquet in February 1951. Convinced that Nixon had a role to play in national politics, I invited him to come to Grand Rapids for the event. His reputation as a partisan must have preceded him, for we had a larger than usual crowd at the dinner that night. In the middle of his speech, a fuse blew and plunged the ballroom into darkness. Instead of losing his poise, Nixon handled the mishap with a joke. He was equally cool when, at a private gathering after the banquet, about twenty-five Republicans, some of them liberals, were waiting to question him on his role in the Alger Hiss case. Even though several of the questions were hostile, he was unruffled and for the next hour and a half responded fully to everyone. My parents had gone to Florida for a winter vacation, so at the end of the meeting, I took Nixon to their home. We had a drink or two and talked about how necessary it was for us to reverse Truman in domestic policies. Then I showed him Mother's old fourposter bed and said that was where she wanted him to spend the night. Later, she hung a sign on the bed: "The Vice President slept here."

In February 1952, eighteen of us in the House sent a message to Dwight D. Eisenhower asking him to run for President as a Republican. The leading candidate at the time was Senator Robert Taft of Ohio, but his foreign policy views were too isolationist for my taste. Furthermore, I was convinced that Ike could win in November and after nearly twenty years of Democratic Presidents the country needed a change. I was delighted, of course, when Ike won the nomination, but I was also pleased when he chose Nixon to be his running mate. During the fall campaign, the press made much of the fact that Nixon had a secret "slush fund." The furor over that fund really surprised me. Other members of Congress—myself included—had maintained reasonably similar funds. If, at the end of a campaign, I still had left-over contributions, I put the money in a separate "Fifth District" account at the bank and drew from it regularly to pay for my newsletters to constituents and my travels home. Under existing rules, those funds were both legal and appropriate. The fact that the press singled Nixon out as a special case and implied that he had done something wrong explains in part why he developed such hostility toward the media.

The 1952 campaign gave Republicans a much-needed shot in the arm. The Eisenhower-Nixon ticket helped our candidates everywhere and, for the first time since 1946, we won control of the House. Joe Martin of Massachusetts was elected Speaker and John Taber of New York became chairman of the Appropriations Committee. He named me chairman of the Army panel on the Defense Subcommittee. That surprised me, so I went to him and said, "I know something about the Navy. I have a lot of friends in the Navy."

"Jerry, that's why I put you on the Army panel," he said in his gruff way. Of course, he was right. Had I chaired the Navy panel, my old friends would have attempted to come in the back door and I would have had a difficult time resisting them.

Shortly after I came to Congress in 1949, I hired a stocky former Marine named John Milanowski as my administrative assistant. John turned out to be an excellent administrator; he functioned as my "conscience" as well. I recall one incident when a lobbyist came into my office and implied that he would hand over cash in return for my support on an important vote. John didn't even have to check with me; he simply threw the lobbyist out the door. Then in 1954, I told him that I was thinking of putting Betty on my office payroll. Other members had added wives and relatives to their office staffs. Betty was seeing my constituents and participating in other political activities, and I thought she deserved to be paid for her efforts. Furthermore, our family was growing. Mike had been born in 1950. Jack had come along two years later. Betty and I had decided to buy a home in Alexandria; we had a real need for the income she would deservedly earn.

"I know it's legal," John said, "and I know that other members are doing it. But you can't. First of all, it would be misunderstood in the district. But more importantly, it's contrary to your whole philosophy of public service." I had to agree that he was right. Betty never received a nickel for her activities.

By 1954, the Cold War was raging furiously and Wisconsin Senator Joseph McCarthy was peddling his charges of treason in high places. People who should have known better tolerated him because they felt that *someone* had to alert the nation to the Communist threat. They acknowledged that his tactics were deplorable but excused him because they thought he had a worthwhile goal. I thought he was a professional bully and I detested him personally, so I kept my distance from him. In retrospect, that was wrong. I should have taken him on. Others were equally silent in calling him to account, but that provides little consolation now. The fact that I didn't speak out against McCarthy is a real regret.

At the time, I had no other major regrets. My career was progressing nicely. I loved the legislative life, and in 1956, I was given additional responsibilities by being appointed to the special subcommittee that controlled funding for the CIA. My seat in the House seemed safe; every time I ran for reelection, the percentage of my winning margin was larger than in my first race, and I dreamed of becoming Speaker of the House. Personally, Betty and I were as happy as we could possibly be. In March 1955, we bought the house on Crown View Drive in Alexandria. Steve, our third son, came along in 1956 and Susan was born one year later. Betty had long since resigned herself to the fact that as a household maintenance man, I was a total incompetent, a truth she'd first recognized when I managed to hang a screen door upside down. My one contribution was to wash and dry the dishes after meals, and I mowed the lawn until the children were old enough to relieve me of that.

Shortly after Mike was born, a marvelous woman, Clara Powell, joined our family. I mean just that; for the next twenty years Clara was a mainstay in raising the children. She was as devoted to them as a parent and they responded with equal affection and respect. Often I said, "If Clara leaves us, I'll have to quit Congress." She was always there to help when a family crisis arose. All of us loved her as one of us because she *was* one of us.

As parents, Betty and I tried to give our four children both roots and wings: the roots of family, heritage and values so they'd know who they were and in what they believed; and wings, the courage to seek personal challenges and the capacity to make it on their own. Even as a junior member of the House, I was on the road constantly and it was difficult to establish a patterned presence at home. So no matter where I was, I made it a rule to fly back and spend Sunday with the family. That was *their* day and they could count on it. After going to church together, we'd sit down for a huge brunch of sausage and bacon, waffles with strawberries and sour cream; then for dinner, Betty would serve roast beef. I know that the children looked forward to those Sunday meals as much as I did.

In 1958, the Republicans took a terrible licking in the fall campaign. One reason was the recession that year. Another was the old and tired image that the party was projecting. Although the election results helped me personally—two senior members left and I went from third-ranking to senior Republican on the Defense Appropriations Subcommittee—I was convinced that we had to change our image soon. As Minority Leader, Joe Martin had lost his punch; he was pleasant but ineffective. Along with Representatives John Byrnes, Glenn Davis and Don Jackson, I tried to convince Joe that he should leave his post and become leader emeritus. When he refused to do that, we decided to support Indiana's gut-fighting Charles Halleck. In January 1959, Halleck became our party's leader in the House. Eighteen months later, in the summer of 1960, I was surprised to learn that a group of Grand Rapids supporters were organizing a campaign to boost me as Nixon's Vice Presidential nominee. I didn't take it seriously. Thruston Morton of Kentucky was my candidate. He was a moderate; he'd served in both houses of Congress, and in the State Department as an Assistant Secretary under Ike, and he would, I felt, give the ticket a nice balance geographically.

Betty and I flew to Chicago the day before the convention began. When some state delegations invited me to address them as a potential nominee, I used those appearances to boost Morton as effectively as I could. But Morton, it turned out, didn't have a chance. Twenty-four hours before the Presidential balloting was to begin, a member of Nixon's staff got in touch with me to say that there would be a meeting immediately after Nixon won to help him decide on his choice. When I explained that I was backing Morton, the staffer let me know in no uncertain terms that Nixon had already made up his mind, that he had decided to select United Nations Ambassador Henry Cabot Lodge. "Morton is a fine person," the staffer went on, "but the nominee is Lodge and we hope there won't be much of a dispute."

I didn't want to believe what he was telling me. If Nixon had made up his mind, why would he go through the sham of asking for our advice? That wasn't the way to play the game. The staffer's assertion was true. At midnight, after he'd won the Presidential nomination, Nixon gathered some twenty of us in his hotel suite. He didn't indicate whom he favored himself, but it was obvious to me that he had chosen Lodge. When it came my turn to speak, I endorsed Morton, adding, "It looks like the die is cast for Lodge but I can support him." I didn't go away bitter, but I was very disappointed. Making up his mind and then pretending that his options were still open—that was a Nixon trait that I'd have occasion to witness again.

Because I knew my own seat was safe, I traveled all over the country in the fall campaign. For a while I thought Nixon would defeat John F. Kennedy. When he came to Grand Rapids, we held a rally in Campau Square in front of the Pantlind Hotel and we must have had 100,000 people there. Kent County supported him enthusiastically. The problem was the first Nixon-Kennedy debate. On TV Nixon appeared unsure of himself, and he looked terrible. If you listened to the radio, you could have concluded that he had won, but on TV, Kennedy was clearly the winner. Most Americans saw it on TV.

The Nixon-Lodge ticket, of course, went down to narrow defeat in November. Traditionally, the party that loses the White House manages to pick up many Congressional seats in the next off-year elections. That didn't happen in 1962. Republicans gained only two seats in the House and lost four in the Senate. One reason for this dismal showing was the cool way that President Kennedy had handled the Cuban missile crisis several weeks before. A second was the fact that Americans genuinely admired the President's personal style. I could understand that because I thought he was an enormously attractive man. We had served together in the House. Our offices had been nearby and we often walked over together to the floor to vote. As President, he had asked for my legislative support—especially on questions of foreign policy—and I was glad to help.

The Democrats' success, however, further convinced the House Republicans that we needed to do more to reverse our negative public image. We had to bring younger men into the leadership. In January 1963, four of the party's "Young Turks"—Mel Laird of Wisconsin, Charles Goodell of New York, Bob Griffin of Michigan and Don

Rumsfeld of Illinois—approached me about running for the Conference chairmanship, the third-ranking post in the House Republican leadership. The incumbent was Charles Hoeven of Iowa. He was a nice man and we'd always been friends, but he was sixty-seven years old. Under his stewardship, the Republican Conference had been dormant for years. It didn't take me long to agree to make the race, and when the ballots were counted I had edged him out in a narrow vote. "You'd better be careful," Hoeven warned Minority Leader Halleck after his defeat. "He's just taken my job and the next thing you know, he'll be after yours."

Most of us have vivid recollections of where we were and what we were doing at moments of national tragedy. I will never forget hearing that the Japanese had attacked Pearl Harbor as I was driving home from my small law office on December 7, 1941. Nor will I forget November 22, 1963. Our son Jack was having some trouble in school. His IQ was high, but his grades didn't reflect that at all. One of his teachers had suggested that he take a special test at George Washington University. After seeing the results, the counselor wanted to talk with Betty and me. We were driving back from the conference when we heard the news on the car radio that President Kennedy had been shot in Texas. I just couldn't believe it; I sped to the office to find out more details.

That same afternoon, Lyndon B. Johnson was sworn in as President. As Senate Majority Leader until 1961, he had been extraordinarily effective; as Vice President he had done well too, and I was confident that he could lead the nation through this difficult time. One evening in late November, I was sitting at home when the President called. "Jerry, I want to appoint a bipartisan blue-ribbon commission to investigate the assassination of President Kennedy," he said. "I've asked [Supreme Court Chief Justice] Earl Warren to be the chairman and he's accepted." Quickly, he ticked off the names of the other members: former CIA Director Allen Dulles, former chairman of the board of the Chase Manhattan Bank John McCloy, Georgia Democratic Senator Richard Russell and Kentucky Republican Senator John Sherman Cooper. Then he came to the point: "I want to have two members from the House. Hale Boggs is going to be one and I want you to be the other."

I told him I'd be honored to serve. The problem then became one of time. The Appropriations Committee was a full-time job; the Republican Conference chairmanship demanded another hour or two every day, and I didn't see how I could handle new responsibilities without obtaining additional help. Luckily, Jack Stiles, who had managed my first Congressional campaign, agreed to assist me. So did former Representative John Ray, who had left Congress several years before. They made a good team. Jack was a writer, John a lawyer. They prepared questions for me to ask at commission hearings, then analyzed the transcripts, looking for discrepancies.

Over the next several months, we heard testimony from Lee Harvey Oswald's widow, from his mother, and from dozens of other witnesses. Initially, Warren and I argued pretty strenuously over the direction the probe was taking. I thought he was making too many staff appointments himself and that the rest of us should have more of a say in the selection process. Our differences persisted until we got to know each other better when we had to fly to Dallas to interview Oswald's assailant, Jack Ruby, for two or three hours in the Dallas jail. Ruby was an unstable person and although willing to talk, he spoke in a rambling fashion and didn't contribute much. Then we drove to the Texas School Book Depository Building and stood where Oswald had stood when he'd fired the shots. We had a rifle similar to the one he'd used; we picked it up and through the scope sighted the cars passing by on the expressway below. Kennedy had been my friend. The thought that we were reconstructing his assassination sent a chill down my spine.

In the summer of 1964, the commission staff began work on our final report. Although we'd heard rumors that linked the FBI and the CIA to the President's death, we hadn't found any connection between those agencies and Oswald himself. As regards the possibility that the Soviets or the Cubans might have been involved, we checked every allegation to the best of our ability and came up with nothing tangible. We knew about Oswald's trips to Mexico and his meetings with representatives of the Cuban and Soviet embassies there, but because of the manner in which our intelligence agents had obtained the information (subsequently it was revealed that we had bugging devices in the Soviet embassy in Mexico City), we decided not to publish the details, and that was a judgment in which I concurred.

In the course of our investigation, we also heard testimony from a broad range of key witnesses. There was Howard Brennan, who saw the gunman take aim and fire the last shot from the southeast corner window of the sixth floor of the Texas School Book Depository Building. There were the people who found the cartridge cases by that window and Oswald's rifle by the back stairway on that floor. There were the scientific experts who testified that Oswald's rifle—to the exclusion of all other weapons in the world—was the assassination weapon, and that Oswald's revolver killed Dallas Police Officer J. D. Tippitt forty-five minutes after the assassination. There were the eyewitnesses who identified Oswald as the gunman they saw at the Tippitt murder scene. Beyond a reasonable doubt, I felt Oswald killed both President Kennedy and Officer Tippitt.

Warren and most of the staff had recommended that we say Oswald committed the crime. No one disagreed. Then we addressed the issue of a conspiracy and became entangled in a dispute that almost resulted in the issuance of a split report. The staff wanted us to say that there was no conspiracy, either foreign or domestic. Russell, Boggs and I thought that was too strong, so we prevailed on the other members to change the wording in a small but extremely significant way. The final report read that the commission "has found no evidence of a conspiracy." That, in my opinion, was far more accurate. When the report came out, critics charged that it was a whitewash, that we had covered up government complicity in the President's death. They make the same charges today. Nonsense! There was no complicity on the part of the CIA, FBI, Secret Service, Dallas police or any other state or federal agency. So far as foreign conspiracy is concerned, nothing I have learned in the years since then would prompt me to change any of the major conclusions we reached. I believe that the report—while not perfect—is a document of which the American people can be proud.

During my service on the Warren Commission, Republicans were choosing up sides and deciding whom to support for the 1964 Presidential nomination. Unfortunately, the battle was fought along ideological lines. Liberals and moderates boosted New York Governor Nelson A. Rockefeller; conservatives rallied behind Barry Goldwater. Because I was committed to support the favorite-son candidacy of Michigan Governor George Romney, I was able to stay out of that bitter struggle. Since 1960, the party had swung to the right. Zealots had taken over key positions and they seemed to believe that it was more important to nominate a candidate who was ideologically pure than to find someone who could win an election.

Predictably, the results that fall were disastrous for us. In every region except the South, President Johnson gave Goldwater a terrible thrashing and his landslide threatened to transform Republicans into an endangered species. We lost two Senate seats and thirty-eight in the House, and we knew that when the new Congress convened in January 1965, we'd have only 140 of the 435 House votes. The implications were troubling. President Johnson was going to "prove" to the country that despite his Texas roots he was just as progressive as Kennedy had been. Furthermore, he wanted to show that he could push landmark legislation through the Congress, something his predecessor hadn't really been able to do. I wondered how we could best restrain the flood of Great Society legislation that would be coming our way soon.

During the 1964 campaign, I'd heard rumors that some Young Turks—Laird, Goodell, Griffin and Rumsfeld—were seeking someone to take the place of Charlie Halleck, who as Minority Leader had simply failed to project the progressive, affirmative image that we needed to turn things around for our party. When I returned to Washington after the November elections, they sounded me out on my availability. I told them I was interested, but I didn't want to make a big pitch for the job because, due to GOP election losses, I had just become senior Republican on the Appropriations Committee. Later, I talked it over with Betty and the children. If I became Minority Leader, I'd have a real chance to become Speaker someday—a personal goal ever since I came to Washington. On the other hand, the post would require a lot of traveling; I wouldn't be able to spend as much time with the family. Our son Jack, then twelve, settled the issue once and for all. "Go for it, Dad," he said.

By mid December, Halleck sensed that a revolt was imminent. He invited members of the House Republican leadership into his private Capitol office for lunch. After the meal, he said, "Now, I assume everybody is going to run for the same office again." That meant he'd campaign for Minority Leader, Les Arends of Illinois would run again for Whip and I'd try for another term as Conference chairman.

"Charlie," I said, "I'm not going to make a commitment here. You know there's a group that's talking about finding somebody else for your job. They haven't selected a candidate yet, but the possibility does exist that I might run." Charlie recoiled at that and for several minutes the meeting was fairly tense. Then he relaxed and became friendly again. He seemed to feel that if he didn't attack, it might be easier for me to stay where I was; the challenge might go away.

Several days later, just before Congress reconvened, the Young Turks came to me and made the offer definite. I said I'd talked it over with the family and had decided to run. But I also said that I had a long-standing commitment to take the family on a skiing vacation to Boyne Mountain, Michigan. I wasn't going to stay in Washington and campaign from Christmas through New Year's Day.

The Eighty-ninth Congress was due to convene on January 4, 1965. Two days after Christmas, Griffin and Rumsfeld called me in Michigan and pleaded with me to fly back to Washington. The vote was going to be very close, they said. My presence in the Capitol—if only for two days—would signal House Republicans that my challenge was serious. Reluctantly, I returned to Washington. Halleck may have been slow to recognize the threat, but now he was doing everything he could to save his job.

"We're going to beat you badly," said Les Arends, grinning, as we entered the House chamber to vote on January 4.

"Well," I replied, "let's wait until the votes are counted."

Actually, the balloting was far closer than we had expected. John Lindsay of New York came down on Halleck's side and that was a surprise because I thought he viewed me as the more liberal of the two candidates. In the end, my approach to Kansas Representative Bob Dole probably saved the day. Kansas had a five-member delegation, and after talking with me, Dole persuaded three other Republicans to vote in a bloc. The final tally was 73–67 in my favor.

Six years earlier, when Halleck had defeated Joe Martin for the Minority Leadership, Martin had sulked for weeks and refused to speak to him. But Charlie took his defeat graciously and displayed no personal animosity. I offered him his choice of committee assignments, and over the next few months, he was very helpful in providing me with advice in my new leadership responsibilities.

Not all Republicans were so charitable. Some continued to resent my narrow victory, and my hold on the leadership was very shaky at first. LBJ, who had been a friend of Halleck's, tried to exploit this. On the afternoon of August 1, 1965, he told reporters at the LBJ Ranch that a Republican leader had "broken" his confidence and "distorted" the President's true position by leaking a story to the effect that only the opposition of influential Democratic Senators had made him decide against calling up the reserves for the war in Vietnam. The Republican, he went on, had spread this story during an off-the-record luncheon with newsmen who covered the House. It was "untrue and perhaps malicious," and furthermore, the leader's carelessness was endangering the lives of our troops in Vietnam. He didn't mention any names, but there was no doubt in anyone's mind that he was referring to me.

Next morning, the Washington *Post* carried the story on page one. So did the New York *Times*. And I was innocent. I knew the information, but I hadn't leaked it to anyone and now the President was questioning my integrity. He was blaming me for combat deaths in Vietnam. Senator Everett McKinley Dirksen and I were due to appear at an "Ev and Jerry" press conference on August 5 and I didn't know how to rebut the President's accusations convincingly. Then, on the morning of August 5, I received a letter from Sam Shaffer of *Newsweek*. He was on vacation in New Hampshire; he'd heard the news on the radio and he wanted to set the record straight. "I was at the background luncheon," he wrote. "You talked only about your goals as Republican leader in the House. The subject of Vietnam never even came up. The President's allegation is untrue." As soon as the session began, I read the letter aloud and distributed copies of it. The reporters there had so much respect for Sam that they never mentioned it again.

Ever since Kennedy had become President in 1961, House Republicans had been on the defensive. Almost automatically, we had allied ourselves with Southern Democrats to vote against Administration bills, amending a few of them but seldom developing programs of our own. This, I felt, was an abdication of our responsibilities. We simply had no right to shout "No, no, no" unless we had come up with better solutions to the problems at hand. And none of us doubted that those problems were real. In the richest nation on earth, millions of Americans lived in poverty. Despite a decade of effort and progress, racial discrimination was pervasive in many sections of the country. Our economy was expanding, yet millions of Americans were unemployed. Environmental hazards were becoming a matter of national concern.

LBJ, I knew, would be addressing these problems with a flood of Great Society legislation. And at the same time, he'd be trying to fight the war in Vietnam. I didn't believe that the nation could afford both guns and butter without a tax increase. The President had vowed not to submit a tax increase in 1965, so it was up to us in Congress to scrutinize his proposals very carefully and cut back wherever we could. A government big enough to give us everything we wanted, I felt, would also be big enough to take away from us everything we had. That's why I asked Goodell to chair a new GOP Planning and Research Committee. Under it, we established thirteen different task forces to study issues from federal aid to education to national health insurance to Congressional reform, and asked them to draft bills that we could support. Initially, we called the results Constructive Republican Alternative Proposals. Then we looked at the acronym—CRAP—and decided to find a different name.

In almost every case, we came up with better, less costly, more practical ideas than the Administration proposed. Take, for example, civil rights. The President had submitted a massive package of legislation aimed at ending racial discrimination once and for all. The problem was that it addressed itself to abuses only in seven Southern states and ignored similar conditions in the rest of the country. I thought that was unfair and declared that an antidiscrimination bill ought to be national in scope. Ohio Representative Bill McCulloch, a gentle man with a fervent belief in equal rights, was the ranking Republican on the House Judiciary Committee. Working together, we fashioned a new proposal that retained the thrust of protecting voters' rights but eliminated some of the more drastic provisions of the Administration's bill. It was not accepted by the House because of heavy White House pressure, but Bill McCulloch and I were proud of our alternative effort to ensure voting rights for all minorities nationwide.

The same was true when we tried to replace the War on Poverty with an Opportunity Crusade. Charlie Goodell and I felt that the federal government shouldn't bear sole responsibility for eliminating poverty. The private sector could play an important role, and if offered incentives, it would. Similarly, I worked with Mel Laird to develop a program that would lead, in time, to federal revenue sharing that funneled money directly to cities, counties and states. These initiatives upset members at both extremes of the GOP. Conservatives said we should denounce the Administration more vigorously; liberals were far more inclined to swallow whatever budget figure the Administration submitted. The opposition we were getting from both wings of the party convinced me that our approach was sound. Our strategy angered LBJ, but I considered his objections a compliment.

When I first came to the Congress in 1949, Sam Rayburn of Texas was Speaker of the House. An able parliamentarian, he was also a stern taskmaster who kept his troops in line. But he was a patriot first; he would support a Republican President when he thought that it was in the national interest. In 1961, after Rayburn's death, John Mc-Cormack of Massachusetts took his place. A tall, rail-thin man with a gaunt face and scraggly white hair which flopped over the side of his head, he tried to offer effective leadership. Slowly, however, the Speaker's power began to erode. McCormack wasn't as successful as Rayburn in cracking the whip over independent Democrats. He was just too decent a man to stifle those who disagreed with him. This is not to say that he couldn't be partisan. As the leaders of our parties, we'd clash frequently on the floor. "Now, I want my very good friend the Minority Leader to listen to what I have to say," he'd begin, pointing a bony finger at me as I stood at the Republican leadership desk. "He's one of my best friends, but on this issue he's wrong." When he finished his speech, I would walk down to the well of the House and kid him about his remarks. He'd wrap an arm around me and we'd step off the floor for a private chat.

Personally, McCormack lived a life of spartan simplicity. A devout Catholic, he was married to a wonderful woman whom he idolized, and I've been told that they had dinner together every evening for a period of some thirty-five years. Our own relationship was one of the most memorable I've had in public life. I always knew that I could go to him on a personal basis and request his help. "Now, Jerry," he'd reply, "if I can do it, I will." He always kept his word.

The same was true of my relationship with Everett Dirksen. He'd been Senate Minority Leader since 1959 and, as spokesmen for the party in the two houses of Congress, we would meet frequently to coordinate strategy on pending legislation. Then, once a week, we'd appear on the televised "Ev and Jerry" news conference. Initially, I was apprehensive about how he would treat me. We were not intimate friends and he had been very close to Halleck. Because he was my senior by many years and had a national reputation, I deferred to him and sought his advice. Instead of being bitter because I'd beaten an old friend, he responded graciously and brought me into his confidence.

"Minority Leader Ford is the sword," he used to tell the press, "and I'm the oil can." And that was true. I've never known anyone who could calm troubled waters faster than Ev Dirksen. He didn't tackle problems head-on; rather, he'd maneuver behind the scenes, recruit allies and let them fight battles for him. His command of the language was extraordinary and his manner of speaking unique. He'd obfuscate with such flair and weave his tales with such gusto that reporters soon forgot the questions they had asked.

On one occasion, he came to Grand Rapids at my request and spoke. He went on for forty minutes, his voice rising and falling dramatically, and when he finished, he received a standing ovation. People told me that his was the greatest political speech they'd ever heard. Later that evening, I took out a sheet of paper and tried to list the points he'd made. After an hour or so, the piece of paper was blank; I had to abandon the effort. Dirksen may not have "said" anything, but he had enchanted his audience, and months afterward, Fifth District Republicans were still talking about that speech.

Not everyone admired him. My staff felt that he was using me as "straight man" for his gags. "Dirksen's getting all the headlines; he's squeezing you out," they'd say, and urge me to demand equal time at our press conferences. But I decided to bide my time and the strategy worked; soon our press conferences became joint in fact as well as name. About the only issue on which we disagreed was the war in Vietnam. I thought we should use our Air Force more effectively and

I opposed the periodic bombing halts that LBJ announced. LBJ, I said in a speech, was guilty of "shocking mismanagement" of the war. Dirksen supported the President. They had been in the Senate "club" for many years and he was loath to criticize such an old friend.

At the time, my stand on the war was drawing fire from within the family. Mike and Jack were living at home and attending public school in Alexandria. They shared the antiwar views that most young people had, but they didn't change my mind and I didn't change theirs. Betty and I encouraged them to develop opinions of their own and to speak out when they thought they were right.

But now, as a family, we had a new problem to face. Two years earlier, in 1964, Betty had raised a window in the kitchen one afternoon. She didn't feel any discomfort at the time. That night, however, she developed an excruciating pain. Because she didn't want to bother me, she went downstairs and tried to sleep on the couch. In the morning, I took her to the hospital emergency room. Doctors said she had a pinched nerve in her neck. They put her in a soft collar, gave her some Darvon and told her to go home and relax. When the pain refused to go away, she returned to the hospital and spent several weeks in traction. Doctors didn't think they could operate because the nerve was too close to the spinal cord. To relieve her almost constant agony, they prescribed increasing doses of pain-killing drugs. Clara Powell, our housekeeper, was indispensable, the children were very supportive, and I tried to help out in every way I could.

The problem was that my hands were full. As Minority Leader, I was making about two hundred speeches a year, most of them out of town. Still, I thought they were in a worthy cause. Many of the Great Society programs were foundering; LBJ was in deep trouble over his conduct of the war and the GOP had a real chance to win control of the House for the first time since 1952. That would elevate me to the Speakership. The performance of the Eighty-ninth Congress, I felt, had been disgraceful. It had enacted irresponsible legislation that gave the federal bureaucracy unprecedented control over the lives of private citizens. It had passed spending bills without imposing restraints. "Congress now is a pawn in the hands of the White House," I charged in a speech in Cincinnati in October 1966, "and 50 percent of the members are puppets who dance when the President pulls the strings." On election day that November, voters showed that they agreed. Although we didn't win control of the House, we wound up with a net gain of forty-seven seats.

Our victory was marred only by my increasing concern for my family's health. Betty's pinched nerve and arthritis were a painful burden for her and my mother's ailments were worrisome as well. My stepfather had passed away in 1962. Mother moved into an apartment in Grand Rapids and tried to maintain her busy schedule of activities. But it was difficult. She had high blood pressure and diabetes. Cataracts clouded her vision in both eyes. She had a splenectomy, a double mastectomy and she survived two heart attacks. Still, her spirits remained high. "I want to drop dead with my boots on," she said. (Mercifully, she did, succumbing in church one Sunday morning in September 1967, just before the service began. She was seventy-four years old, and yet when Betty and I checked her date book, we found that she had scheduled appointments every day for the next month.)

Returning to Washington after the 1966 elections, I found that LBJ was furious—not only because of the Republican gains in the House but also because of my attacks on White House policies. He tended to take criticism personally and lashed out at me. He jibed that I'd played football without wearing a helmet, that I couldn't walk a straight line and chew gum at the same time. I realized how frustrated he was and brushed off his attacks. Then, preparing my speech for the annual dinner of the Gridiron Club in March 1968, I decided to confront them directly. Someone found an old leather helmet that I had worn at the All-Star game in Chicago in 1935 and, dressed in white tie and tails, I tried to put it on. When the flaps didn't fit easily over my ears, I grinned and said it was because "heads tend to swell in Washington." That brought down the house.

The speech I gave that night was probably the most humorous I'd made up to that point in my life. For that I had two people to thank. One was Bob Orben, a mild-mannered gag writer who worked for comedian Red Skelton. The second was Bob Hartmann, who, since joining the staff of the House Republican Conference in 1966, had made increasingly valuable contributions to me. Once Washington bureau chief for the Los Angeles *Times*, he was a Republican and was forthright about it. Most Washington reporters insist they're "independents" when, in fact, they're liberal Democrats. Bob stood out in that crowd and I admired him for sticking to his convictions. In the early days of the Kennedy Administration, he fell out of favor at the White House and the *Times* shifted him to Rome. His old friends, however, didn't forget him. Shortly after I became House Minority Leader, several of them came to me and said I needed an "idea man" to develop sound approaches to the nation's legislative needs. Bob, they said, would be perfect.

True, he didn't know how to get along with others on the staff. He was always snapping at people and he was a terrible administrator himself. But I could—and did—overlook these faults because Bob was shrewd and he possessed good political judgment, a rare commodity in Washington. In addition, he could write an excellent speech, one that suited my style.

In March 1968, LBJ announced that he would not run for President again. Stung by criticism of his policies in Vietnam, he had become isolated in the White House. He wanted to retire and hunker down in peace on his Texas ranch. In August, Republicans met in Miami Beach to adopt the party platform and nominate our Presidential candidate. Rockefeller was a possibility; so was Ronald Reagan, but Nixon clearly had the most support and he won a first-ballot victory. Later that evening, he invited about a dozen of us to meet with him in his hotel suite to discuss a possible running mate. Turning to me, he said, "I know that in the past, Jerry, you have thought about being Vice President. Would you take it this year?"

At that moment we had 187 Republicans in the House—and we had won forty-seven of those seats two years earlier. The Democrats were terribly divided by the Vietnam War and another big Republican win seemed a strong possibility. If we captured just thirty-one more seats, I'd be Speaker of the House. I thanked Nixon for his compliment but said I wasn't interested.

"Well, whom do you favor?" he asked.

I replied that I'd found strong support in the House for New York City Mayor John V. Lindsay. As a Congressman, he'd been far to the left of most Republicans. I wasn't concerned about that. He was an able attorney, a very articulate and attractive man. Lindsay, I told Nixon, would provide a nice balance to the ticket in 1968. California Representative Bob Wilson seconded my recommendation. Lindsay, he said, would be a superb nominee.

But Nixon wasn't interested. Other names were bandied about, and the meeting broke up without an apparent decision being made. Next morning, Betty and I and four or five members of my staff were relaxing by the pool at the Fontainebleau Hotel when I received a telephone call from a Nixon aide. Nixon had selected Spiro T. Agnew, the governor of Maryland, as his running mate. I couldn't believe it. Here was a man who had risen from total obscurity a few years earlier to become governor of a border state. I remembered meeting him two years before at a Republican dinner in Annapolis. He'd come up to me, a well-groomed but somehow diffident man who seemed to talk out of the corners of his mouth. "Hi, I'm Ted Agnew, Baltimore County executive, and I'm running for governor," he'd said, sticking out his hand. He seemed like a nice enough person, but he lacked national experience or recognition. And now, after just two years as governor, he was going to run for Vice President. I shook my head in disbelief. This was the reaction of many of my House colleagues.

Several weeks later, in Chicago, the Democrats gathered to nominate Vice President Humphrey as their Presidential candidate. Over the years I'd gotten to know Hubert well; we'd come to Washington together as members of the Eighty-first Congress; our wives had become good friends, and we enjoyed the good-natured ribbings that each of us gave the other. On questions of foreign policy our views tended to coincide. Domestically, however, we disagreed frequently. He seemed to have more solutions than there were problems to solve; all of them involved an expanding government role in the lives of private citizens, and the concept of fiscal restraint was totally foreign to him. Still, I thought he was a very decent man and I was glad that he had won his party's nomination. It meant that we could do battle on the issues instead of resorting to attacks on personalities.

That's why I was angry when Agnew charged that Humphrey was "soft" on communism. The allegation was ridiculous and it was poor politics as well. I got word to Agnew and urged him not to make that kind of mistake again. During the rest of the campaign, I had no contact at all with either Agnew or Nixon. For a while it seemed that a landslide victory was within our grasp. Then the Democrats got their act together. Humphrey and his running mate, Senator Edmund Muskie of Maine, narrowed the gap in the polls. On election day, the Nixon-Agnew ticket won by a hairline margin and we picked up a mere five seats in the House. That was a severe disappointment to me.

Several weeks after the 1968 election, I received a call from the White House. LBJ wanted to see me privately. Suddenly, images of my past associations with him flashed through my mind: the opening day of baseball season in Washington, D.C., when he had invited Dirksen and me to sit in the Presidential box and he had held four hot dogs in one massive hand; the time that our son Steve had smashed his finger in the door of our station wagon and he had reached me in the hospital emergency room to convey his sympathy; the warm personal note that he had sent to thank me for serving on the Warren Commission.

We talked for more than an hour in the Oval Office that day and LBJ was very philosophical. He felt that Nixon had run a shrewd race and that his selection of Agnew had been wise. The Democrats, for their part, had deserved to lose. The President was very proud of his accomplishments in the field of civil rights. He felt that he had achieved more liberal objectives than any President in history and he couldn't understand why the liberals had never welcomed him into their circle of friends. He was puzzled by their lack of gratitude. The mandate he'd won so overwhelmingly in 1964 hadn't given him anywhere near the satisfaction that he'd thought it would. As he talked, pouring out revelations that he said he'd wanted to tell me for a long time, I couldn't help but feel a great sympathy for him. "Jerry, you and I have had a lot of head-to-head confrontations," he said toward the close of our conversation, "but I never doubted your integrity."

"Mr. President," I replied, "I never doubted yours, either. I didn't like some of the things you said about me, but I never questioned your patriotism."

He walked me to the door, and draped an arm around my shoulder. "When I leave here," he said, "I want you to know that we are

friends and we always will be, and if I can ever help you, I want you
to let me know."

   In general, I was pleased with the men Nixon chose to serve in his
Cabinet. I knew Mel Laird would be an excellent Secretary of Defense, that George Romney would perform with zeal and credit at
the Department of Housing and Urban Development, and that Bill
Rogers would provide quiet leadership at the Department of State.
The appointment of Henry Kissinger as National Security Adviser to
the President was, I thought, a master stroke. He had invited me to
speak at his Harvard graduate school seminars on several occasions in
the past and I'd been enormously impressed by his grasp of the nuances of foreign policy. I barely knew John Mitchell, Nixon's selection to be his Attorney General, but soon I had the chance to see a lot
of both him and his wife.

   One occasion was an embassy dinner where I had the misfortune
to sit next to Martha. Here was this overdressed, robust blonde boast-
ing that she was the wife of the Attorney General. The White House
and the Cabinet were the real power centers, she said repeatedly, and
they would run the country for the next eight years. Congress, she insisted, was irrelevant.

   Unfortunately, she wasn't the only person to hold that attitude.
Haldeman, Ehrlichman and a few of their associates on the White
House staff viewed Congress in much the same way that the chairman of the board of a large corporation regards his regional sales
managers. We existed, they seemed to believe, only to follow their
instructions and we had no right to behave as if we were a coequal
branch of government. And this from former advance men whose
only political experience had been to hold Nixon's raincoat and organize his crowds. Haldeman seldom came to Capitol Hill. Ehrlichman
did, however, and I remember one occasion when he met with the
Republican leaders of the House in my Capitol office. A controversial
bill was about to come up for consideration in the Congress. We expected him, as head of the Domestic Council, to tell us how the
White House viewed the measure. Instead, he never said a word; he
sat there in the corner, his disdainful expression revealing that he

thought he was wasting his time. I was so mad at him that it was hard for me to contain my anger.

As Minority Leader under a Democratic Administration, my responsibility had been to propose Republican alternatives. With Nixon in the Oval Office, those responsibilities changed. Now I had to push *his* programs through the House. Ev Dirksen had to do the same thing on the Senate floor. Incredibly, we had trouble finding anyone on the White House staff dealing with policy who was interested in consulting with us on domestic legislative priorities. The legislative liaison people from the White House were helpful, but not Ehrlichman and his staff. Every ten days or so, the Republican leadership met with Nixon in the Cabinet Room. We told him and his people that we wanted to help. We recognized we had a lot of work to do to untangle many of the Great Society programs. Still, we had some real experts in the House—Al Quie on education and labor, Bill Ayres on veterans' affairs, Bill Widnall on housing and urban affairs—and we thought they constituted a valuable resource that the new Administration ought to use. Nixon and his policy aides promised to work with us, but they never did. In contrast, most of his Cabinet members were helpful on legislative matters.

In November 1969, Agnew flew to Des Moines, Iowa, and delivered a speech blasting the network newscasts. I suspected that Haldeman and Ehrlichman had orchestrated his attack and that Nixon had approved it. Although many Republicans cheered, I thought the speech was a serious mistake. Nixon may have had some valid complaints about the way the media had treated him in the past. Since his election, however, the press had been fair to him, and it was stupid to reopen old wounds. But this was only a harbinger of things to come.

Increasingly, among senior White House aides, an "us versus them" attitude began to emerge. If you even questioned their policies, you became "the enemy" and retribution was swift. A case in point was Don Riegle, then the Republican Representative from the Seventh District of Michigan. An intense, enormously likable young man, Riegle had won an upset victory in a solid Democratic district, and I had campaigned for him. He had shown an ability rare among

Republicans to attract support from both organized labor and minority groups. I liked him and respected his drive. As our involvement in Vietnam increased, so did Riegle's sincere doubts about our policies there. He wanted to talk to someone in the Nixon White House and he asked me on several occasions to help arrange a meeting for him. We were stonewalled; Riegle was a nonperson there. With nowhere else to turn, Riegle took out his frustrations on the floor of the House and criticized the White House attitude. As a result, Haldeman, Ehrlichman and other Nixon aides tried to "discipline" him. They wouldn't invite him to state dinners or Sunday prayer breakfasts. They made sure he had no input legislatively and even refused to let him be photographed with the President and the poster child of the National March of Dimes (who came from his district in Michigan).

"Disagree without being disagreeable," Sam Rayburn used to tell freshman Congressmen, and throughout my career in the House I tried to follow his advice. If I wanted a colleague's vote on an important bill, I'd offer my most persuasive arguments and ask him straight out for support. I certainly wouldn't threaten him with retaliation if he decided to vote the other way. I didn't always win, but I left the colleague with a feeling that I'd been fair and the next time I needed help, I'd have a chance to secure his cooperation. Nixon's aides never understood that, and it developed into one of the worst failings of his Administration.

Because they knew that I wouldn't tolerate vindictiveness toward my colleagues, White House aides never urged me to discipline their Republican "enemies" in the Congress. Instead, they tried to persuade others to do their dirty work. And Riegle wasn't their only target. They were also out to "get" Pete McCloskey, a liberal Republican from California, and Charles Goodell, then a Senator from New York. On several occasions in 1969 and 1970, meeting with Nixon and his entourage, I defended all three men even though they had disappointed me at times. The Nixon "experts" discounted my comments as hopelessly naïve.

In May 1969, in the wake of charges that he had received questionable payments from financier Louis Wolfson, Abe Fortas resigned his seat on the U.S. Supreme Court. At about the same time, I received information that Associate Justice William O. Douglas was collecting an annual retainer of $12,000 for serving as the only paid officer of something called the Albert Parvin Foundation. I also heard that he'd received $4,000 from the Center for the Study of Democratic Institutions. If these allegations were true, I thought, then Douglas should also resign. The statutes were clear that members of the federal judiciary could not earn income from sources outside the government. Representatives H. R. Gross of Iowa and John R. Rarick of Louisiana called for his resignation. When Douglas ignored them, I decided to launch an investigation myself and asked Bob Hartmann—now my legislative assistant—to undertake research on Douglas's conduct during his years on the bench.

What concerned me were his possible conflicts of interest. In 1964, *Fact* magazine had published "A Special Issue on the Mind of Barry Goldwater." The thrust was that Goldwater was psychologically unfit to be President. Goldwater filed suit. A federal court in New York City found *Fact*'s publisher, Ralph Ginzburg, guilty of libel and the U.S. Court of Appeals sustained the judgment against him. Ginzburg promptly appealed to the U.S. Supreme Court, which declined to review the case. Douglas dissented from that opinion and supported Ginzburg. Interestingly, several months before, Douglas had received $350 from Ginzburg for an article he'd written in *Avant Garde* magazine. (The piece followed one entitled "The Decline and Fall of the Female Breast.") At the very least, given the financial relationship between the two men, I thought Douglas should have disqualified himself from passing judgment in the Ginzburg case.

Then there was the question of his association with the Parvin Foundation, which had been paying him for the past nine years. Albert Parvin claimed that Douglas had assisted him in establishing the foundation. There was also the possibility that in the process he had provided legal counsel to the foundation on how to obtain tax exempt status. While Hartmann and I were pursuing these leads, we heard that the Justice Department possessed additional information about Douglas which would be helpful to us. Bob called Will Wilson, chief of the Criminal Division, who agreed to meet with us in my office on Capitol Hill. "Yes," Wilson confirmed, "we have the information and we'll make it available soon." Weeks passed and he didn't fulfill the promise. What material he did supply wasn't helpful at all. Feeling that we'd been misled, Hartmann and I met with Attorney General Mitchell at the Justice Department and asked why we weren't receiving any assistance. Mitchell gave us some double-talk. He, too, promised cooperation and then went back on his word.

In August 1969, Nixon nominated Clement F. Haynsworth, Jr., a respected federal judge from South Carolina, to fill the Fortas vacancy on the Supreme Court. Throughout that summer and fall, I did everything I could to keep my probe of Douglas under wraps. Somehow, in November, Haynes Johnson of the Washington *Post* found out about it and asked me if the story he'd heard was true. When I replied that it was, the press concluded—inaccurately—that I was trying to hold Douglas hostage for Haynsworth and blasted me editorially. And none of that publicity did Haynsworth any good. On November 21, the Senate rejected his nomination by a 55–45 roll call vote.

Nearly two months later, on January 19, 1970, Nixon tried again and submitted the name of G. Harrold Carswell to the Senate. Liberals discovered that Carswell had made a speech in praise of racial segregation some twenty-odd years before and they attacked his "mediocre" record as a federal judge in Florida. That nomination, too, was rejected, by a vote of 51 to 45 on April 8. Conservatives in both houses of the Congress were furious. The President, they felt, had the right to nominate a "strict constructionist" to the Court. Many liberal Democrats in the Senate were voting against his nominees solely because they came from the South. These Senators, the conservatives went on, were hypocrites because they simply blinked and looked the other way when somebody questioned what Douglas had done.

Most people believe that federal judges are appointed for life. Actually, the Constitution says that they shall serve only during periods of "good behavior." Convinced that Douglas's behavior had failed that test, his opponents in the House wanted to launch impeachment proceedings against him. The most ardent of them were Louis Wyman of New Hampshire and William Scott, an inflexible, very disagreeable Republican from Virginia. Under the rules of the House, a motion to impeach is of the highest parliamentary order. A member can rise on the floor and shout, "Mr. Speaker, I have a motion of impeachment," and the Speaker has to recognize him. The member can demand a roll call vote right there, and that's what Wyman and Scott were threatening to do.

Such an effort would fail, but what really mattered was the harm it would do to the GOP. A motion to impeach would widen the gulf between conservatives, moderates and liberals, and I had a duty to try to prevent that from happening. At that moment, however, the April issue of *Evergreen Review* appeared, carrying an excerpt from Douglas's recent book, *Points of Rebellion*. "Where grievances pile high and most of the elected spokesmen represent the establishment," he had written, "violence may be the only effective response." The magazine also contained a full-page caricature of Nixon made out to look like King George III of England, and pages of sexually explicit photographs. Outraged conservatives howled "pornography" and gave me an ultimatum: unless I did something about Douglas, they'd take matters into their own hands.

On the evening of April 15, I made a speech on the floor in which I laid out the information that our probe had uncovered. I didn't call for Douglas's impeachment. Instead, I asked the House to appoint a select committee that would have ninety days to determine whether or not grounds for impeachment even existed. I didn't want the matter referred to the House Committee on the Judiciary because that panel was stacked with liberal Democrats. But Representative Andrew Jacobs, Jr., of Indiana beat me to the punch. In the middle of my speech, he marched up to the well of the House and dropped into the hopper a resolution to impeach Douglas. His action transferred the probe to the Judiciary Committee, which, as I had feared, recommended that the House take no action at all. The committee's "investigation" was a travesty. Members didn't hold public hearings, examine witnesses under oath or make public the pertinent documents they obtained. They simply decided that grounds for impeachment didn't exist. Yet, as a result of my involvement in the matter, I received a terrible press. Ignoring the fact that Douglas gave up his retainer as soon as its existence was publicized and that he had promised to disqualify himself from ruling in cases where conflict of interest was involved, reporters accused me of pursuing a witch hunt and urged me to cease my "partisan" attacks. What I did at the time may have been politically ill advised, but it was not irresponsible.

During the Christmas holidays in 1970, Betty and I took the children to our condominium in Vail, Colorado, where, for the past three years, we'd skied together as a family. By then the children were skiing faster and faster and I was skiing slower and slower. Forgetting that I'd picked them out of countless snowbanks when they were seven or eight years old, they were zooming down the slopes and shouting gleefully, "Hi, Dad. We'll see you later." Toward the end of our vacation, Nixon was interviewed by four television correspondents in the White House library. When I called to congratulate him, he invited Betty and me to fly to San Clemente for dinner before returning to Washington. Bob and Dolores Hope were there; so were Henry Kissinger and Arnold Palmer, who was playing in a golf tournament in Los Angeles. The Nixons gave us a tour of La Casa Pacifica and the grounds, and our stay was delightful. Seldom in all the years that I'd known the President had I seen him so relaxed.

On June 17, 1972, five men broke into the Democratic National Committee headquarters in Washington's Watergate complex. An alert security guard notified police, who promptly arrested them. When I heard about the incident on the radio the next day, I was flabbergasted. Who, I wondered, could have been so dumb? What was there to gain? Ron Ziegler, the President's press secretary, called the incident "a third-rate burglary" and that seemed to sum it up perfectly. Then I heard that G. Gordon Liddy had been involved and the case took on a new dimension for me.

In 1968, Hamilton Fish, Jr., had run for Congress in New York State. He'd asked me to speak at a rally for him in Dutchess County one Saturday afternoon. Ham had just beaten Liddy in a bitter Republican primary fight and he was very concerned because Liddy was possibly going to run for Congress as a Conservative that fall. Republicans, he feared, would split their votes and a Democrat would win. Ham said the only way to keep Liddy from waging an active campaign would be to recommend him for a federal appointment of some kind.

I found Liddy cocky and demanding; I formed a bad impression of him the first time we met. "Gordon," I said, "I can't offer you a job. What you'll have to do is to get the local party organization to endorse you, plus the state organization. After you've received both endorsements, if Ham will come to me as a member of Congress and ask for my help on your behalf, I'll do whatever I can to find a place for you."

Liddy seemed satisfied with that. Although his name remained on the ballot as the Conservative nominee, he endorsed Fish. Ham was elected to Congress and came to Washington in January 1969. Some months later, he got in touch with me on Liddy's behalf. Liddy was making noises about running in 1970, he said, and would probably do so unless we produced for him. Having heard about an opening at Treasury, he had secured the necessary endorsements. I made a pro forma telephone call to Eugene Rossides, then Assistant Secretary of the Treasury for Enforcement and Operations, and recommended that Gene hire him. I didn't like the man, but rationalized that it was only for the purpose of helping Hamilton Fish.

Liddy's career at Treasury was curious indeed. The Nixon Administration was supporting a bill to bar the manufacture and sale of cheap handguns called Saturday Night Specials. The National Rifle Association, one of the most effective lobbies in Washington, opposed the measure because it thought passage of the bill would lead to further government restrictions on the right to bear arms. As a member of the Administration, Liddy might have been expected to push for adoption of the bill. Instead, he did his best to sabotage it, speaking out in favor of the position taken by the NRA. And now, somehow, he had wound up at the Committee to Reelect the President (CRP).

On the Monday morning after the Watergate break-in, I learned another reason for concern. Jack Marsh, now retired from Congress, was practicing law in an office in downtown Washington. The CRP—which many called CREEP—had offices on the third and fourth floors of the same building. One of John Mitchell's aides had come into Jack's office frequently to use the telephone. The aide had talked about "security precautions" that he was undertaking for the Nixon campaign. The aide's name was James McCord. And McCord had been one of the men arrested at the Watergate.

The link was tenuous, but it had to be explored. "Do you think anybody in the White House was involved in this?" I asked Jack that Monday morning.

"I don't know who's involved," he replied, "but I do know McCord. He's a former employee of the CIA and he works for Mitchell now. I think there'd have to be some involvement there."

"You know, Jack, I don't give a damn who's involved or how high it goes," I said. "Nixon ought to get to the bottom of this and get rid of anybody who's involved in it."

At the time, Republican chances in the fall campaign looked promising indeed. My ambition to become Speaker of the House seemed attainable. The Republican leadership in the Congress and the chairmen of the House and Senate campaign committees had, in fact, scheduled a meeting at CRP headquarters that Monday afternoon with Mitchell and Jeb Magruder, his top assistant, to see how we could mesh our joint efforts with the President's. I arrived at the meeting several minutes early and saw Mitchell in his office alone as we waited for the others. Remembering what Marsh had told me just hours before, I asked Mitchell directly whether he or anyone else in CRP or anyone in the White House had had anything to do with the break-in at the Watergate.

He looked me right in the eye. "Absolutely not," he said.

"Well, did the President have anything to do with it?"

Mitchell shook his head emphatically. "Absolutely not," he said again. At that moment, the others came into the room and the conversation shifted to the fall campaign. The CRP, Mitchell said, wanted to work closely with us and to help us financially; 1972 would be the year of the New Majority in the Congress as well.

But first it was necessary for me to be off the political scene for a while. Nearly four months earlier, in February 1972, Nixon had traveled to the People's Republic of China and, in doing so, had taken giant strides to advance the cause of peace. It was important, he'd told Chinese leaders, to increase the flow of travelers between the two countries. The Chinese agreed and had invited me and Democratic

Majority Leader Hale Boggs to visit in June with our wives and several members of our staffs. As a youngster, I used to dig in the sand on the beaches of Lake Michigan. If I dug deep enough, my mother told me, I'd wind up in China. Now I was actually going to make the trip. As a member of Congress, I'd made many journeys overseas—to Vietnam, Japan, Taiwan and Korea in 1953, to Western Europe in 1954, 1956 and again in 1965; to Eastern Europe and the Soviet Union in 1959—but the chance to visit China was a rare opportunity indeed.

Arriving in Shanghai on June 26, we toured the city and flew on to Peking. At the end of World War II, China had been prostrate economically and her population demoralized. The change since then was remarkable. The cities we visited were clean; we saw no litter, no flies, no dogs. The people were friendly and hard-working. They appeared to be well fed, clothed and housed and if they lacked political liberty and social mobility, it was impossible to get them to discuss that.

During our third day in Peking, we received word that Premier Chou En-lai would have dinner with us. We sat in a banquet room in the Great Hall of the People and enjoyed a fabulous meal of Peking duck. Our conversation was friendly although somewhat superficial, and we didn't leave the table until after midnight. But that was just the beginning. Saying he understood that our wives must be tired, Chou excused them graciously, then met with Boggs and me and our aides for a discussion that lasted until after three o'clock in the morning. He impressed me immediately as a man of steel will, high intelligence and super sophistication.

"Well, a small Ping-Pong ball has brought us together," he began. And then he was off on a wide-ranging discussion of the snub he'd been given by John Foster Dulles at Geneva in 1954, the manner in which Charles de Gaulle had extricated the French from Algeria, the U.S. role in Asia after the Vietnam War and the question of the future of Taiwan. He was conversant to a surprising degree with what was happening politically and otherwise in the United States. He talked to Boggs, for example, about efforts to solve the pollution problem in New Orleans; he knew the dates of the forthcoming Republican and Democratic conventions and he even suggested to us that we go back and read a speech that Nixon had given in Kansas City a year before. Again and again, he returned to what he perceived as a growing Soviet threat and he was troubled by Senator George McGovern's suggestion that the Pentagon's budget could be slashed by as much as $30 billion. "We don't believe you can reduce your military spending," he said. "With the Soviet Union increasing their own defenses, how can you reduce yours?"

"You don't believe the Soviet Union is going to reduce its defense budget, do you?" Boggs asked.

Premier Chou didn't wait for the translator to finish. "Never, never, never," he replied in perfect English.

Leaving China on July 5, we returned home to find Republican political fortunes significantly improved. Liberal activists had taken over the Democratic Party. They were set to nominate McGovern as their candidate to oppose Nixon and that, I felt, would ensure enormous gains by the GOP. The opportunity was there, but it was ignored. On July 1, claiming he was spending too much time away from his family, Mitchell resigned as director of the CRP and his subordinates failed to honor the promises he'd made. Ten days before the election, leaders of the Republican Congressional Campaign Committee came to me and asked for last-minute assistance. Half a dozen of our candidates in the Western states were involved in close races. Could I fly to their districts and campaign for them? Certainly, I replied, but it was like pulling teeth to get money from officials at CRP to lease an executive jet. At the last minute they relented, supplying only enough money to let me campaign for two or three of our candidates. They wanted to reelect Nixon and didn't much care about helping anyone else.

On election day, November 7, Republicans gained only thirteen seats in the House and even lost two in the Senate. But Nixon won with the second-largest plurality ever awarded an American President. Instead of accepting his victory magnanimously and thanking the team that had worked so hard for him, he promptly demanded the resignation of all non-career employees in the Executive Branch. I thought his action strange and unwise. His whole life had been spent in a drive to acquire power, and now that he had that power he seemed to be veering off on a tangent.

Early in 1973, the Senate established a special committee to look into charges arising from Watergate and named North Carolina Democrat Sam Ervin as the chairman. The press paid a lot of attention to this, but as an issue Watergate didn't really seem to concern many Americans then. In March, however, that began to change. At the sentencing of Watergate defendants, Judge John Sirica read a letter he had received from McCord in which he said that witnesses at the trial had committed perjury and that "higher-ups" were attempting to prevent the truth from coming out. Reporters dug harder and the competition for "scoops" began.

It was about this time that Betty and I first discussed my retirement plans. Reluctantly, I had to conclude that I would never become Speaker of the House. The opportunity that Republicans had had in 1972 wasn't likely to repeat itself in the foreseeable future. We agreed that I would run one more time in 1974, then announce my retirement from public life in early 1975. Betty's pinched nerve and arthritis kept her in pain a good deal of the time, and it was hard on the whole family to have me away so much. (In one year, I had logged 138,000 miles, the same as flying around the world five and a half times.) If I left the Congress in January 1977, I'd be sixty-three years old—still active enough to practice law or enter into a business partnership with friends. I wasn't sure exactly what I'd do, but the opportunity to earn additional income as a private citizen seemed very attractive to me. If I won again in 1974, I thought, I might even forgo my position in the leadership and pass those responsibilities to a younger man. That would give me two years to wind down.

During the Easter break in 1973, Betty and I flew to Palm Springs, California, to relax. While there, I heard that former Treasury Secretary John Connally was staying for several days at the nearby El Dorado Country Club. Connally, I thought, was one of the ablest men in America. As Navy Secretary in the early sixties, he'd testified many times before the Defense Appropriations Subcommittee, and I'd always been impressed with him. He was bright, decisive and poised and he could deliver an excellent speech. Over breakfast one morning, we discussed the possibility that he might run for President in 1976. I told him what I had decided to do and added that I saw no chance of changing my mind. I felt sure at the time that both Nixon and Agnew would serve out their terms. Agnew might try for the Presidential nomination in 1976, but Connally would be a far more effective candidate and potential President. I told him so and said he'd have my support, whatever he decided to do. Connally was noncommittal, but I had the impression he would make a bid.

Back in Washington, the Watergate boil was festering. Rumors abounded that Administration officials were scrambling to save their own skins by telling prosecutors all they knew in hopes of receiving immunity. On April 30, Nixon announced the resignations of Haldeman and Ehrlichman and the outright dismissal of White House Counsel John Dean. The departure of Dean didn't upset me at all. I'd gotten to know him several years earlier when he'd served as minority counsel on the House Judiciary Committee staff and had spent considerable time on the floor. At first I considered him very capable. The longer I watched him, however, the less enthusiastic I became. He was always trying to score "brownie" points and ingratiate himself with senior Republicans. I concluded, finally, that he was a young man on the make. I never did find out how he'd promoted himself into his White House job, but I was confident that he wouldn't be missed on Capitol Hill.

The departures of Haldeman and Ehrlichman presented problems of another kind. Despite their alleged involvement in Watergate, they had kept the West Wing functioning effectively according to their standards. Al Haig, then deputy to National Security Adviser Henry Kissinger, had agreed to serve as chief of staff in the new setup and to coordinate the paper flow, but he couldn't do everything himself. Nixon would need other men of stature and integrity to help him restore public confidence in the office of the President. Mel Laird and Bryce Harlow came to mind immediately and I appealed to their patriotism in asking them to return to the government and help their President. Neither man wanted to go back to what Laird called "that jungle"; each had business opportunities he wanted to pursue. Fortunately, the President, Haig and many of us from both parties were able to convince them that the country needed their services; they agreed to come back in the summer of 1973.

In a way, their return seemed further "proof" of Nixon's innocence. I knew both men well and realized how much they valued their reputation for integrity. Neither man, I was sure, would have gone back to the White House without first having received a personal assurance from Nixon that he wasn't involved in Watergate.

Since he first became Vice President in January 1969, Spiro Agnew and I had remained pretty much at arms' length. We simply didn't have much in common. But in the summer of 1973, Agnew suddenly became very friendly. On several occasions he called and invited me to play golf with him at the Burning Tree Club. As a golfer, he was strong but inconsistent; he would par one hole and then double-bogey the next four in a row. I sensed that he had something other than golf on his mind. Then, on August 4, in Groton, Connecticut, the Navy launched the U.S.S. *Glenard P. Lipscomb*, a new nuclear submarine. Because Lipscomb, a long-time Republican member of the House, had been a good friend until his death in 1969, I attended the ceremony. On the flight back to Washington, Mel Laird and I began talking about all the troubles the Administration was having. Agnew's name came up during our conversation and Mel frowned. "You think things are bad now," he said. "Well, they're going to get worse."

"Tell me about it."

"I can't," Mel said. "I would if I could, but I can't."

Three days later, the *Wall Street Journal* reported that Agnew was in serious trouble indeed. Federal prosecutors in Baltimore were investigating allegations that as governor of Maryland he had accepted kickbacks from architectural and engineering firms in return for the awarding of state contracts. There were even rumors that he had taken bribes while serving as Vice President. Agnew blasted the accusations as "damned lies."

But by September 15, it seemed clear that the noose around Agnew's neck was tightening. In the third week of September, Harlow, White House counsel Leonard Garment and I met in the office of House Republican Whip Les Arends. They asked me to approach the Democratic leadership and request a meeting on Agnew's behalf. During that meeting, the Vice President would ask the Democrats for their help in persuading the House Judiciary Committee to begin an impeachment probe. That way, he could avoid criminal prosecution. I replied that I wanted Agnew to write me officially, requesting a meeting with the leadership. He did; the Democrats agreed and the session was held in Speaker Carl Albert's office on September 25.

"The Vice President wanted to consult with you," I said as the meeting began. "You have agreed and now I'm going to let him carry the ball."

Agnew was very matter-of-fact. He said that there were forces in the press, in the Congress, and in the Executive Branch as well, that wanted to get rid of him. His attorneys had advised him that the Constitution barred any kind of criminal proceeding against a sitting President or Vice President. He would have to be impeached by Congress first. He was willing to take the risk.

House Judiciary Committee Chairman Peter Rodino of New Jersey was cautious and noncommittal. Speaker Albert asked some questions, and their tone suggested to me that he was sympathetic to Agnew's predicament. Tip O'Neill, however, was skeptical. After an hour or so, the meeting broke up. The Democrats said they'd think it over before reaching a decision, but I had the distinct impression that Tip would prevail. Agnew was very dispirited; he hadn't made headway at all and I began to suspect that he knew the game was over for him.

Still, he continued to fight. Late in September, he flew to Los Angeles and spoke to the National Federation of Republican Women. He accused Justice Department aides of "outrageous" attempts to smear him through leaks to the press. "I will not resign if indicted," he vowed.

On the afternoon of October 10, while the House was in session, I received a call from Haig. The President wondered if I could join him in his private office in the EOB. I arrived to find Nixon by himself, sitting in a big leather chair in the corner of the room. He was dressed casually—a sports jacket and a pair of slacks—and he was about as relaxed as I'd ever seen him. He put his feet up on an ottoman and began puffing on a pipe. "Mr. President," I said, "I've never seen you smoke a pipe."

"Well, I do it when I'm alone," he said, "or when I'm with an old friend like you."

We talked for the next hour and a half. It was one of the few times while he was President that the two of us just sat and talked by ourselves. "Jerry, we've got a terrible problem," he said. "The Vice President is in serious difficulty. He's acted like many public officials in Maryland. That's the way things are done there. Nevertheless, that sort of behavior isn't acceptable under the law. If I'd known about this before 1972, I wouldn't have had him on the ticket, but I only found out about it subsequently."

I listened in utter astonishment as Nixon described the cash payments that Agnew had allegedly received. When I asked for details, he said he had been told one of the transactions had taken place in the West Wing of the White House. He'd talked to Agnew on several occasions. The Vice President denied everything, but the evidence was irrefutable. Nixon didn't say that he had been betrayed but—to the extent that he could display emotion—he was disappointed. Attorney General Elliot Richardson, the President went on, was trying to work out an arrangement with Agnew, his attorneys and the court. He didn't know what would happen, but none of the options looked good.

That was the first time I'd heard the charges spelled out in any detail. I wondered why an adequate examination of Agnew's finances hadn't been made in 1968 or in 1972, and I had to conclude that the President and his staff had been derelict. Agnew had certainly not been honest with me at a time when he was asking me to go out on a limb for him. I was disgusted.

At the end of that meeting, I returned to Capitol Hill and sat in the Minority Leader's chair on the Republican side of the chamber. I hadn't been there ten minutes when Michigan Representative Elford A. Cederberg rushed out from the Republican cloakroom, ran down the aisle, slapped me on the back and asked, "Have you heard?"

"What?"

"Agnew has resigned."

Wire service stories spelled out the details of the "arrangement" that Nixon had mentioned to me half an hour before. In return for a plea of nolo contendere to a single charge of income tax evasion, the government had agreed not to put Agnew on trial. He was fined $10,000 and placed on probation for three years.

That night Betty and I had dinner at home. Mel Laird called me there about ten o'clock. Characteristically, he opened with small talk.

Then he got to the point: "Jerry, if you were asked, would you accept the Vice Presidential nomination?"

I knew Mel well enough to realize that his question hadn't come just like that. Someone had told him to call. I asked him to let us think about it and promised to call him back. For the next hour or so, Betty and I sat in the family room and debated the pluses and minuses. And there *were* minuses. Traditionally, the Vice President didn't have much to do. His job was chiefly ceremonial and his impact on legislation was minimal. I wasn't sure that I'd be happy working at a slower pace. Then, too, if I became Vice President, I had to consider how it would affect the children. They'd be more exposed to the press; their lives would be more regulated in almost every respect.

On the other hand, the Vice Presidency would be a splendid cap to my career—not the office I'd sought, but one that would also constitute recognition of my long service in Washington. Because I had many friends in the Congress, I could push Nixon's programs on Capitol Hill and try to improve his relations there. Best of all, I could accept the offer without violating my commitment to Betty that I'd leave public life in January 1977. I called Mel and said, "We've talked about it and agreed that, if I were asked, I'd accept. I'll do whatever the President wants me to do, but we won't do anything to stimulate any campaign. I'm not promoting myself. We have made our plans and we're happy with what we've decided to do."

"I understand," Mel said. "I don't know what's going to happen. I just wanted to check."

Even at that point, neither Betty nor I thought it was likely that Nixon would choose me. I was too valuable to him on Capitol Hill. Besides, other Republicans—Connally, Rockefeller and Reagan—had national reputations and ambitions to match. I thought Nixon would select one of them.

On Thursday morning, October 11, Nixon met with the Congressional leadership to discuss the procedures that he wanted to follow in making his nomination. "I'd like to be in the shape with the American public that Jerry Ford is," he joshed, but I didn't take him seriously. Next morning, however, Haig asked me to come to the Oval Office at eleven o'clock. Hugh Scott accompanied me. He had also received a call, so I assumed that Nixon had some legislative matter that he wanted to discuss. Usually, Scott and I saw the President together, so I was surprised when Haig ushered Scott into the Oval Office alone and asked me to wait outside the door. Minutes later, Scott left; I entered and took the chair to the President's right.

Nixon came directly to the point. Because of the Agnew tragedy, he said, there was an urgent need to restore public confidence in the office of Vice President. He wanted me to be his nominee. Then he asked if I'd made any political plans. I told him about my promise to Betty and said that I had no ambitions to hold office after January 1977. Just because I'd be serving as Vice President for the remainder of his term didn't mean I'd expect to be the Presidential nominee in 1976.

"Well, that's good," Nixon replied, "because John Connally is my choice for 1976. He'd be excellent."

"That's no problem as far as I'm concerned," I said, and told him about my discussions with Connally in Palm Springs several months before.

The Constitution gives the Vice President two functions to perform: to preside over the Senate and to replace the President should he die or leave office during his elected term. Recent Chief Executives had used their Vice Presidents in different ways. Eisenhower had sent Nixon overseas extensively. Kennedy had done the same with Johnson. Johnson had involved Humphrey more in domestic politics, and this, Nixon told me, was what he wanted from me. I'd attend all meetings of the Cabinet, the National Security Council, the Domestic Council and the Emergency Energy Action Group. I would chair the new Commission on the Right of Privacy and make recommendations to preserve that right. Additionally, I'd appear at political functions, speak up for the Administration and help in dealing with the Congress. I told the President that his plans sounded fine to me.

Press Secretary Ron Ziegler had told reporters that the President would telephone his nominee at seven o'clock that night. Nixon wanted to make sure that I'd be near my phone and that I'd be able to appear with him in the East Room of the White House for the announcement at 9 P.M. And there was one other caveat: I couldn't tell anyone—even Betty—before he made the call. We had covered everything and I was ready to leave. Nixon pressed a buzzer on his desk and summoned Ollie Atkins, the White House photographer. "Come on in, Ollie. Take the picture and make history," he said.

I'm sure Betty suspected that something was up when I arrived home at six-thirty that night. Both she and Susan asked what was happening. Did I know the name of Nixon's nominee? The only thing I knew, I said, side-stepping gingerly, was that the President would telephone his man soon. I swam my laps in the pool, changed clothes, then checked the time. It was almost seven o'clock. In our bedroom upstairs was an unlisted phone with no extensions. The downstairs phone was listed in the directory and had a number of extensions so several people could use it simultaneously. Betty was using the downstairs phone talking to our son Mike, who was at the Gordon-Conwell Theological Seminary in Massachusetts. Susan was upstairs when the phone rang there. "Dad, the White House is calling," she shouted down.

I dashed upstairs, grabbed the receiver and heard Haig say, "The President wants to talk to you."

Nixon came on the line and said, "Jerry, I want you to be Vice President and I think Betty ought to hear what I'm telling you."

"Mr. President," I replied, "I'm on a line that has no extensions. Can you hang up and call back on the other number?"

"Betty, get off the line," I said as I ran downstairs. "The President wants to call." She did. Seconds later, Nixon was on the phone and repeated what he had just said. As soon as we hung up I told Betty about my earlier conversation with the President. I had no plans to run for the White House in 1976, I said; this was going to climax my political career.

Two hours later, Nixon appeared before TV cameras in the East Room. A large group of people—myself included—had been gathered there for the announcement. "Let me tell you what the criteria were that I had in mind," he said. "First and above all, the individual who serves as Vice President must be qualified to be President. Second, [he] must be one who shares the views of the President on the critical issues of foreign policy and national defense . . . Third, at this particular time when we have the Executive in the hands of one party and the Congress controlled by another party, it is vital that the Vice President be an individual who can work with members of both parties in the Congress. . . . The man I have selected meets those criteria. First, he is a man who has served for twenty-five years in the House of Representatives . . ."

The audience began to applaud. Everyone looked at me, but Nixon wanted to prolong the suspense. "Ladies and gentlemen, please don't be premature," he said. "There are several here who served twenty-five years in the House." Finally, he named me and I stepped to the podium to acknowledge the cheers.

Considering what had precipitated it, the ceremony that night was oddly exuberant. It had all the trappings and the hoopla of a political convention. The President didn't even mention Agnew's name and he certainly didn't refer to the reasons why he had had to select another Vice President. Later that evening, relaxing with friends at home, I received a call from Agnew. "I just wanted to offer you my congratulations," he said. "You'll do a fine job and I want you and Betty to know that Judy and I are behind you 100 percent." I thanked him and said how sorry I was that events had worked out this way. Our conversation was brief. His call was a nice gesture, undoubtedly hard for him, and one Betty and I appreciated.

On Saturday morning, October 13, after Nixon submitted my nomination to Congress, I received a foreign policy briefing from Henry Kissinger. Then I flew to Michigan to march—for the twenty-fifth time—in the annual Red Flannel Day parade in Cedar Springs, which bills itself as the "red flannel manufacturing capital of the world." The weather was perfect on that fall afternoon; the crowds that lined Main Street were large and enthusiastic. This small, friendly community had always been one of my favorite places. Tears filled my eyes and it was difficult to maintain my composure.

Nixon nominated me, I was convinced, because he wanted to pick someone who could win speedy confirmation in the Congress.° He also wanted someone who could help repair his frayed relations with

----

°Later I discovered the background maneuvering that made me Vice President. Connally had been Nixon's first choice, but Laird and others convinced the President that it would be difficult for him to be confirmed. Rockefeller and Reagan were the next two men Nixon considered, but he was persuaded that the selection of either one would split the party ideologically. That left me as the "safest" choice.

Capitol Hill and the media. With me as his nominee, those relations did improve temporarily. Then came the "Saturday Night Massacre," and any new amity between the Executive and Legislative branches disappeared.

Five months earlier, with Nixon's approval, Attorney General Richardson had named Archibald Cox, his former law professor at Harvard, as special prosecutor and said he would have jurisdiction over all offenses arising out of the Watergate break-in. On July 18, Cox wrote Nixon's lawyer, J. Fred Buzhardt, requesting tapes of eight Presidential conversations. The White House refused to yield and the issue went to court. On August 29, Judge Sirica ordered the President to make the subpoenaed tapes available to him. On October 12—the same day that Nixon announced my nomination as Vice President—the U.S. Circuit Court of Appeals upheld Sirica. Nixon then suggested a compromise. He would let Mississippi Senator John Stennis, one of the most respected members of Congress, listen to them and verify that they contained no evidence of impropriety. Cox rejected that idea.

On Saturday, October 20, Cox held a nationally televised press conference in which he defended his position, demanded the tapes, and maintained that he could be fired only by the Attorney General. That was waving a red flag in front of an angry bull. Nixon told Haig to order Richardson to fire the special prosecutor. Richardson refused the order and resigned as Attorney General. Haig then asked Richardson's deputy, William Ruckelshaus, to get rid of Cox. Ruckelshaus, too, refused and resigned instead. The third-ranking official at the Justice Department was Solicitor General Robert H. Bork. Although he had misgivings about Nixon's decision, Bork concluded that he couldn't defy an order from the President. He fired Cox. At a press conference that evening, Ziegler announced the day's developments and said that the President was abolishing the office of special prosecutor. Even as he spoke, the FBI was guarding that office and making sure that no one removed any files.

The fire storm that followed swept across the entire country. Nothing that Nixon had ever done had so enraged ordinary citizens, and by Tuesday of the following week, dozens of bills reflecting their anger had been introduced in the House of Representatives. Twenty-two of them called either for Nixon's impeachment or for an investigation of possible impeachment proceedings. That day, surprised by the intensity of the feeling against him, Nixon relented and agreed to give Sirica the contested tapes.

At the time, I still believed that Nixon was innocent. What he had done was politically dumb, but he had acted within his rights as Chief Executive in firing a subordinate. House Republicans were frustrated by his conduct. They didn't know what to make of it and I didn't know how to respond to them. In my meetings with Nixon, I kept telling him, "Damn it, why don't we get the records out that prove your innocence? Why don't you release the documentation?" But he wouldn't give me a direct reply. He'd say that important constitutional principles were involved, that he was convinced that his decision was right and that "if you ever occupied this office, you'd have the same feelings about protecting the Presidency." Then our meetings would end.

For me, this period was very difficult. No Vice President had ever taken office before under the provisions of the 25th Amendment. My confirmation hearings were due to begin before the Senate Rules Committee on November 1, and before the House Judiciary Committee on November 15. I asked all public officials—federal, state and local—and all persons or agencies dealing with normally private records to make those documents regarding me available. I wanted to be fully prepared for the grilling I knew I'd receive, so I also asked some old friends to help me prepare for my appearances. Robert McBain, my accountant in Grand Rapids, pored over my financial records for the past twenty-five years, which he had scrupulously kept in the course of preparing my federal income tax returns. Phil Buchen and Benton Becker, a Washington attorney, put together a loose-leaf notebook with questions that committee members might ask and suggesting the appropriate replies.

The FBI's investigation of me was the largest, most intensive probe that the Bureau had ever conducted into the background of a candidate for public office. Since October 13, some 350 special agents from 33 of the Bureau's field offices had interviewed more than 1,000 witnesses and compiled 1,700 pages of reports. (So thorough was this probe, I discovered later, that agents even interviewed a former football player from Union High School in Grand Rapids. More than forty years before, during a game between Union and South High, I had tackled the man after the whistle had blown and, as a consequence, had been ejected from the contest. The agents' question: had I been a "dirty" player?) The IRS looked into my tax returns; other government agencies conducted checks of their own, and it was a tough ordeal for everyone. The process was like undergoing an annual physical exam in public view. Still, the American people wound up knowing more about me than any other nominee in history.

The hearings themselves, in both chambers of the Congress, proceeded uneventfully. Aware that they might be confirming a future President, the lawmakers probed into my political philosophy, my views on the issue of executive privilege and my opinion as to whether or not the President was obligated to obey orders from a court. They asked me about the impeachment process, the President's impoundment of appropriated funds, campaign financing laws and how I'd handled my finances personally. What they really wanted to know was: "What makes you, Jerry Ford, qualified to be Vice President of the United States?" And secondly, "What kind of Vice President do you hope to be?"

I couldn't help but notice the irony, and replied that life certainly played some funny tricks on people. Here I'd spent twenty-five years trying to become Speaker of the House. Suddenly, I was a candidate for president of the Senate, where I could hardly ever vote and where I'd never get a chance to speak. Then I returned to the question at hand. "I believe I can be a ready conciliator and calm communicator between the White House and Capitol Hill," I said. "I believe I can do this not because I know much about the Vice Presidency but because I know both the Congress and the President as well and as intimately as anyone who has known both for a quarter century."

In a 1972 book entitled *The Washington Pay-Off* and in a later affidavit that he had submitted to columnist Les Whitten, a lobbyist named Robert N. Winter-Berger had leveled a number of serious allegations against me. He had charged, for example, that he had lent me $15,000 between 1966 and 1969 and that I'd never repaid the loan; that I had attempted to obtain an ambassadorship for one Francis L. Kellogg in return for a sizable financial contribution and that I'd tried to pressure Winter-Berger into paying the cost of a private jet that I needed to fulfill a speaking engagement in Iowa. All these allegations, of course, were lies, as was his claim that after talking to him, I had decided to become the patient of a prominent psychiatrist in New York City. I had met Winter-Berger—I didn't dispute that—but it didn't take me long to determine that I didn't want anything to do with him. I had told my staff that and they made sure that he was kept out of my way.

Still, because I knew that questions would be raised about my relationship with him, I assembled documents proving that each of his charges was false. Meeting in executive session, members of the Senate Rules Committee asked Winter-Berger to produce supporting evidence. He could provide none. And when the House Judiciary Committee looked into his allegations, its members grilled him extensively. Quickly, they concluded that his claims were unfounded.

From time to time, Nixon would ask me how the hearings were progressing and when they would conclude. If he died or resigned before my nomination came up for vote, House Speaker Carl Albert would succeed him as President. That made Nixon nervous because he wasn't sure Albert could handle the Presidency. Finally, both committees approved my nomination and sent their recommendations to the Senate and House floors. On November 27, the Senate confirmed me by a vote of 92 to 3. On December 6, the House followed suit by a vote of 387 to 35.

As soon as we realized that my confirmation was probable, we began to discuss a site for my swearing in. Nixon, I was told, wanted the ceremony in the East Room of the White House. I felt the Capitol would be far more appropriate. That was where I'd served for twenty-five years and where I'd been confirmed. Speaker Albert agreed with me. White House aides resisted that idea because they would not be in control unless the ceremony was held in the East Room. If it was in the Capitol, the legislative leadership would call the shots and White House aides weren't sure what sort of reception Nixon would receive. When we saw that we weren't making any headway, I went to Nixon myself. "Mr. President," I said, "the place to have it is in the Capitol. That would be a much better place for my relations with the Congress and for yours as well." Quickly, he agreed.

As I entered the House chamber on the evening of December 6, members slapped me on the back. This was going to be my farewell to the House and it was bound to be an emotional experience. In one of his typical performances, Hartmann had stayed up until four o'clock that morning to prepare my speech. His eyes were puffy, he was exhausted, but he had done another fine job.

Wearing his flowing black robes, Chief Justice Burger stepped forward to face me. If he hadn't decided to practice law, he would have been a perfect candidate for Hollywood. His white hair, deep-blue eyes and chiseled features seemed to come straight from central casting. Earlier, Betty and I had talked to our son Mike about the Jerusalem Bible he had purchased for this occasion. Where, we wondered, should it be open to when I took the oath? We agreed on Psalm 20: "May [God] answer you in time of trouble . . ." Now, as Betty held the Bible, I raised my right hand and repeated the oath of office.

The members gave me a standing ovation and I stepped forward to the microphone. "Together, we have made history here today," I began. "For the first time, we have carried out the command of the 25th Amendment. In exactly eight weeks, we have demonstrated to the world that our great Republic stands solid, stands strong upon the bedrock of the Constitution.

"I am a Ford, not a Lincoln. My addresses will never be as eloquent as Mr. Lincoln's. But I will do my very best to equal his brevity and his plain speaking . . . As a man of the Congress, let me reaffirm my conviction that the collective wisdom of our two great legislative bodies, while not infallible, will in the end serve the people faithfully and very well . . . Before I go from this House, which has been my home for a quarter century, I must say I am forever in its debt . . . To you, Mr. Speaker, and to all of my friends here . . . I say a very fond goodbye."

At six twenty-one that evening, it was over. I had entered the chamber as a Congressman from one of nineteen districts in Michigan; I was stepping out as the new Vice President of the United States. Leaving the Capitol, I rode to the White House and met with

Nixon alone. "Congratulations," he said, smiling broadly. "It's good to have a teammate at last."

During that meeting, he assured me once again that when all the facts came out about Watergate, he would be proved innocent of any involvement at all. The allegations, he said, were just partisan attacks and people would grow tired of them. Then he'd be able to concentrate on fulfilling his Administration's goals. Neither then nor at any other time did I ask him categorically: "Mr. President, were you involved in Watergate or the cover-up?" His constant, although indirect, assurances, coupled with what John Mitchell had told me, made that seem unnecessary. In retrospect, it would have been proper for me to have confronted him with the question. Yet I'm certain that had I asked him as directly as I'd asked John Mitchell in June 1972, I would have received just as firm a denial.

As Minority Leader, I had received between forty and fifty social invitations every week. Now, as Vice President, the number shot up to five hundred. Betty and I moved up a notch on the social scale and for the first time we had round-the-clock protection from the Secret Service. Some of that protection was inconvenient—and expensive. The Secret Service had to install a command post in the two-stall garage of our home. They tore out plaster to put in new wiring and smoke detectors. They excavated the driveway and reinforced it to bear the weight of an armored limousine. They installed bulletproof glass in the windows of our house. In the process, we wound up paying more than $4,300 out of our own pocket just to make the house as livable as it had been before.

There were "fringe benefits" to the agents' presence which took on humorous overtones. They kept a daily log tracing the arrival and departure times for every member of the family. As an attractive teenager, Susan had a busy social life. She knew that Betty and I didn't want her staying out after eleven on school nights, but she also knew that we'd usually gone to bed by that time and weren't likely to keep close tabs on her. "What time did you get home last night?" I would ask her in the morning. "Oh, early," she'd reply, and normally, that would have been the end of it. But now, with the agents' logs at my disposal, I could say, "Well, I think I'll check on that." And Susan would respond, "Uh-oh, I guess I'm grounded for a week." I didn't actually ground her and our talks were in good fun. Still, the fact that those logs were there made the younger children more responsible.

From my perspective, I felt that recent Vice Presidents had not been used at all well by the men they had served. They'd been given minor—occasionally dirty—little chores that Presidents themselves didn't want to do. During the three years that I expected to be Vice President, I hoped to participate in major decisions, and Nixon had promised that I would have far greater responsibilities than my predecessors. I hoped I could get the Administration over its Watergate problems with Congress and the press. Then, too, Nixon's legislative programs were stalled on Capitol Hill and I thought I could be helpful there.

An opportunity to act as a conciliator arose almost immediately. On December 19, three Senate Watergate Committee subpoenas were served on the White House, demanding nearly five hundred Presidential documents and tapes. On January 3, just before being sworn in as Attorney General, Ohio Senator William Saxbe criticized the committee's requests as a "fishing expedition." The next day, Nixon wrote Chairman Sam Ervin and refused to comply with his demands because to do so "would unquestionably destroy any vestige of confidentiality of Presidential communications." It seemed to me that the relevant material on those tapes ought to be released, that stonewalling or hoping the issue would fade away was an exercise in futility. Appearing on *Meet the Press* on January 6, I said a compromise was possible.

Obviously, Nixon didn't agree, and there was a chill in my relations with the White House after that. There was also conflict between our respective staffs. The middle-echelon people who worked under Haig seemed to resent the fact that I had gone through the confirmation process so easily, and they were determined to make life as difficult as possible for me and my assistants. We had trouble securing office space in the EOB, procuring desks and furniture and hiring sufficient staff. Inevitably, personalities clashed. Dewey Clower of the White House staff was assigned to us as an advance man and he set out to program what he wanted me to do. I didn't like him. Hartmann hated him and the atmosphere became ugly indeed.

For the past several years, the Nixon Administration had closed the door to minorities, particularly to blacks. I wanted these groups to know that I could be—and really wanted to be—point man for them in their dealings with the government; that there was at least one man in the Administration who would listen to them and try to solve their problems. On January 9, I held the first of two hour-long sessions with black leaders, The meetings, I thought, helped to clear the air and I submitted a report with my recommendations for follow-through action to officials in the West Wing of the White House. Unfortunately, there was no follow-through; the people there didn't care.

At the outset, I had no full-time speechwriters at all on my limited staff. The White House staff, however, contained several talented writers. Because Nixon was making few speeches at the time, I requested their help in preparing drafts of the speeches I had agreed to make. The drafts tended to be hard-line and vehement in their defense of the President, but Hartmann and I usually saw them far enough in advance to have time to tone them down. On January 15, however, we fumbled the ball. I was scheduled to address the American Farm Bureau Federation at its convention in Atlantic City. Under the press of events, neither of us took the time to review the speech and I delivered it pretty much as it had been submitted to me. In it, I lashed out at "a few extreme partisans . . . bent on stretching out the ordeal of Watergate for their own purposes. Powerful organizations," I went on, "the AFL-CIO and the Americans for Democratic Action, [want] to crush the President and his philosophy." There *were* people in those groups who felt that way, but I overstated the case and subjected myself to considerable embarrassment.

Only an hour or so after making the speech, I heard a news report from Washington. A panel of six technical experts had examined the June 20, 1972, tape of a conversation between Nixon and Haldeman. In focusing on the mysterious eighteen-and-a-half-minute gap, they concluded that it had been caused by five separate manual erasures. "Mechanical problems" had not been involved. I didn't believe Nixon had erased the tape, because I knew he wasn't adroit mechanically. Still, it was obvious that *someone* had and this constituted a clear obstruction of justice. Had I known that this was going to happen, I would have been far more restrained in my Atlantic City speech, no matter what the time pressures.

The overwhelmingly negative reaction to the speech caused me to face the fact that Nixon's speechwriters would continue to use me to say what they wanted said about the President and his problems. My credibility would erode overnight. I couldn't allow myself to operate as a White House appendage any more. Quickly, I brought in my own speechwriters, Milton Friedman (no relation to the well-known economist) and Bob Orben, and told them to consult with Hartmann and fashion drafts that would reflect my own style.

On January 21, for the first time in several weeks, I met with Nixon in the Oval Office. Haig sat in a corner and took notes on a legal pad. What I remember most about this session was its length; it droned on for an hour and forty-five minutes. The President had called the meeting and he did 90 percent of the talking. He said there was material that would clear him of involvement in the Watergate mess and he volunteered to show me some of it. He also claimed that he'd had absolutely nothing to do with the eighteen-and-a-half-minute erasure on the tape. Then he began to ramble about the political history of our time and the things we'd done together in Congress years before. It was embarrassing. I had a lot of appointments on my agenda that day; I knew that he had work to do and I felt I ought to leave. But you just don't get up and walk out on the President while he's still talking. I kept looking at my watch, but he didn't seem to notice and he continued to give me his impressions of world affairs and his reactions to what was happening on Capitol Hill. He touched on a number of irrelevancies.

In retrospect, it's clear that he needed me as an escape valve. He had been reelected by an overwhelming majority of Americans just fourteen months before; he had achieved great success in foreign policy, yet he was a prisoner in the Oval Office. He couldn't go to college campuses; he couldn't make public appearances; he couldn't speak before groups of any kind without harassment.

Leaving the White House, I returned to my office in the EOB and mentioned to Hartmann and Marsh (who had recently joined my staff) that Nixon had offered to let me see some exculpatory evidence. They felt—and I agreed—that because of my sensitive position I should stay away from it. I didn't want to look at the evidence and have to pass judgment either exonerating or convicting him. Once I listened to the tapes or read the transcripts, I'd be sucked into the whirlpool of claims and counterclaims, and that was something I had to avoid.

As it turned out, Senator Hugh Scott plunged—inadvertently, to be sure—into that whirlpool. Over the past several months he had become very uneasy about Nixon's role in Watergate and had made public statements increasingly critical of the President. In December, just before Congress had adjourned for the Christmas holidays, Haig had shown him a transcript of Nixon's still-secret March 21, 1973, conversation with John Dean. At the time, White House officials believed this to be the tape most damaging to the President. Yet even this tape, they felt, contained no evidence that Nixon had committed an impeachable offense. After he went through the transcript, Scott agreed. He said publicly on January 20 that the White House had information that cleared Nixon. He had seen it himself.

Scott's willingness to take this position was enormously reassuring to me. Perhaps Nixon had been leveling with us all along. Perhaps he really did feel strongly about the need to protect the office of the President.

On February 18, a special election took place in the Fifth District of Michigan to fill the Congressional seat I had occupied since 1949. The Republicans had held the seat for sixty-two years and I was confident that our party's nominee, a respected state senator named Bob Vander Laan, would win. On election night, I was shocked to learn that the Democratic candidate, Richard Vander Veen, had won with 51 percent of the vote. The results told me that Watergate was an issue nationally, that the public was fed up with the Nixon Administration and that Republicans everywhere would be in real trouble that fall.

Not long after, I met with Nixon again. We talked about the Fifth District race and he said that inflation had brought about Vander Laan's defeat.

"No, Mr. President," I replied. "It's Watergate that's responsible. In 1960, you know, you were very popular in that district. You generated the largest rally ever held in Grand Rapids. You've been to

Grand Rapids on several occasions and you've always been well received. I want you to know that this election reflects the district's verdict now and it's not good."

"Yes, Jerry, I know things look bad," the President replied. "I know it's discouraging. But we've got a big job to do and we're not going to let the voter pendulum deter us from our responsibilities."

I urged him to release "as quickly as possible" any evidence that would clear him from involvement in Watergate. "The election result," I said, "is a signal that if you don't clear up Watergate soon, we're going to face disaster in November."

Cooperation, he replied, would be forthcoming soon. He had the documents that his supporters were urging him to release. He would make them available at the proper time and they would help his cause. I left the Oval Office with the sinking feeling that I had heard the story before.

When I became Vice President, I had put Bob Hartmann in charge of my office and named him chief of staff. By March 1974, I realized that I had made a dreadful mistake. Hartmann didn't cause trouble deliberately; he just didn't know how to manage an office staff. Now, all of a sudden, I desperately needed a first-class manager. At Phil Buchen's suggestion, I asked Bill Seidman to come down from Grand Rapids and organize my office.

A trim, energetic physical-fitness buff, Seidman was a graduate of Dartmouth and the Harvard Law School, and managing partner of an international accounting firm. His involvement with George Romney's Citizens for Michigan crusade had left him with a taste for politics and an abiding interest in effective government. Although Hartmann bristled about Seidman's appointment, the office was soon functioning more efficiently.

After my January speech and the information about the gap in the tapes, I had to put some distance between me and the White House on the issue of Watergate. On March 30, I was scheduled to address the Midwest Republican Leadership Conference in Chicago. Hartmann and I tried to point up the lessons that Republicans should learn from the scandal. "Never again must Americans allow an arrogant elite guard of political adolescents like CRP to by-pass the regular party organizations and dictate the terms of a national election," I said. "The fatal defect of CRP was that it made its own rules and thus made its own ruin. It violated the historic concept of the two-party system in America and ran roughshod over the seasoned political judgment and experience of the party organization in the fifty states. . . . If there are any more cliques of ambitious amateurs who want to run political campaigns, let the Democrats have them next time."

Throughout my political career I have always believed that a sense of humor and an ability to laugh at your own mistakes are essential ingredients for success. The trouble with Washington in the spring of 1974 was that nobody was laughing any more. The atmosphere was vindictive and mean. I understood the reasons, of course, but I was convinced that the country—and especially the members of the Washington press corps—needed some relief. So I was delighted to appear at the annual dinner of the Gridiron Club on April 6. Traditionally, speakers at this off-the-record affair poke fun at themselves, kid leaders of the other party and endeavor to wind up on a semi-serious note. Bob Orben, the resident humorist on my staff, came up with some fine quips that enabled me to get off to a decent start.

I reminded the guests that I'd spoken at the Gridiron dinner six years before and had shared the platform with Hubert Humphrey. I quoted what I'd said at the time: "Let me assure the distinguished Vice President of the United States that I have absolutely no designs on his job." The crowd roared. "I'm not at all interested in the Vice Presidency. I love the House of Representatives despite the long, irregular hours. Sometimes, though, when it's late and I'm tired and hungry on that long drive home to Alexandria, as I go past 1600 Pennsylvania Avenue, I do seem to hear a little voice say, 'If you lived here, you'd be home now.'" That brought down the house.

Some time after the Gridiron dinner, Maggie Hunter of the New York *Times* told me she had a book that I ought to read. Its title was *The Twilight of the Presidency* and its author was George E. Reedy, a press secretary to former President Johnson. Reedy's thesis was disturbing. The current structure of the Presidency, he said, virtually ensures that a President is cut off from the country he leads, from the problems he must solve and from any checks upon what is weakest in his personality. "Below the President," he wrote, "is a mass of intrigue, posturing, strutting, cringing and pious 'commitment' to irrelevant windbaggery—that all too frequently successful collection of the untalented, the unpassionate and the insincere seeking to con-

vince the public that it is brilliant, compassionate and dedicated."
Reedy was convinced that Presidents shouldn't hire any assistants
who were under forty years of age and who hadn't suffered any major disappointments in life. When young amateurs find themselves in
the West Wing of the White House, he concluded, they start thinking
that they're little tin gods. Reedy was right, I thought. He had left the
White House staff several years before, but he was predicting the climate that had led to Watergate. I read his book, read it again, then
gave it to Hartmann to read. "I don't operate that way and I don't
want anyone on my staff operating that way," I said. "Make sure everyone gets the message."

By the end of April Watergate was on the front pages of newspapers every day. And in the back of my mind I realized that my becoming President was an increasing possibility. The odds were fifty-
fifty that Nixon would have to step down eventually. Yet this was
something I couldn't address publicly. I had to be very careful not to
let it affect my behavior in any way and I couldn't afford to mention
it to anyone—my family, my staff and certainly the press. Despite
my best efforts, I slipped several times. On one occasion I gave a
backgrounder for reporters aboard *Air Force Two*. During the session
I said that Kissinger and I were gravely concerned about the impact
Watergate was having on our foreign policy. I assumed my remarks
would be off the record, so I was distressed to find out that several reporters intended to file the story. I called them myself to plead for restraint, but it was too late. Nixon, I heard later, was angry about that.
Then there was the time that I was about to return to the capital after
an Easter vacation at Palm Springs. Reporters were waiting at the
airport and—before I could stop myself—I said something like,
"Well, I'm looking forward to seeing you all back at the White
House . . . er . . . and on Capitol Hill."

On May 4, I traveled to Ann Arbor to address the graduating class
at the University of Michigan and to receive an honorary doctor of
laws degree. A crowd of about twelve thousand was packed into
Crisler Arena and several hundred of them tried to disrupt the ceremony. "Jerry Ford is a Neofascist," one placard announced, and
demonstrators hanged both Nixon and me in effigy. I was dismayed,
but I didn't believe their hostility was aimed primarily at me. They
were associating me with the President.

At least once a week, at Nixon's request, Henry Kissinger or his deputy, Air Force Major General Brent Scowcroft, would brief me on foreign policy. Henry *was* concerned that domestic politics would impede his ability to achieve his foreign policy goals. And there was still so much that he wanted to do: further improve U.S. relations with the People's Republic of China, defuse the potential conflict in the Middle East, reach agreement with the Soviets on a new strategic arms limitation treaty. Watergate, he concluded, was undermining his efforts in all these areas.

Kissinger, who shared my belief that Nixon hadn't been involved in the Watergate cover-up, felt that the President had many admirable traits, but he, too, was concerned about his recent habit of calling aides into the Oval Office and then rambling on. ("We were always hoping that a nuclear war would start somewhere," he said jokingly, "so we could leave the Oval Office and get back to work.") Kissinger simply didn't have time for aimless chatter; he knew that Haig didn't, either, and he worried that decisions which had to be made might fall through the cracks.

On May 15, the House Judiciary Committee issued new subpoenas for additional Watergate tapes and other evidence. One week later, the President announced that he would not comply with these demands. The battle lines had hardened. Committee Chairman Peter Rodino called Nixon's decision "a very grave matter" and implied that his refusal to release additional evidence constituted in and of itself sufficient grounds for impeachment. All this took place while I was on a speaking trip to Hawaii and the state of Washington. As soon as I returned to the capital, I met with Nixon and told him that I couldn't support his stonewalling committee requests any more. Unless he supplied the relevant information, I said, there would be a confrontation between the White House and the Congress, which the President would almost certainly lose.

"We're handling it this way because we think we're right," the President replied. "I know you and others would do it differently, but we think we're right and we're going to continue to do it this way."

I brought up another problem that had caused me some personal dismay. According to *Newsweek*, Nixon had invited Nelson Rockefeller to the Oval Office for a ninety-minute chat and he had allegedly asked, his voice dripping with scorn, "Can you see Gerald Ford sitting in this chair?" I felt damn mad when the story appeared and I decided to ask Nixon about it personally. "Of course I never said anything like that," he replied. "It's just another story that our enemies made up. The press is always exaggerating. Don't pay any attention to it." Although I wanted to believe him, I wasn't completely convinced.

On June 5, I spoke at a Republican dinner in Columbus, Ohio. "The preponderance of the evidence," I said, "is that [the President] is innocent of any involvement in any cover-up." No sooner had I finished the speech than word flashed over the wires that the federal grand jury in Washington had voted 19–0 to name Nixon as an unindicted co-conspirator in the cover-up. It seemed that every time I went out on a limb to support the President, a bombshell would explode. I damn near blew my stack.

Nixon must have sensed my predicament. Two days later, I received a handwritten note from him. "Dear Gerry," he began, misspelling my first name. "This is to tell you how much I have appreciated your superb and courageous support over these past difficult months. How much easier it would have been for you to try to pander to the press and others who desperately are trying to drive a wedge between the President and Vice President. It's tough going now, but history, I am sure, will record you as one of the most capable, courageous and honorable Vice Presidents we have ever had." Although I appreciated his gesture, it didn't relieve my concern about the way he was handling his own defense.

Critics charged that in my speeches and press conferences I was "zigzagging" all over the lot and taking positions that seemed contradictory. There was some truth to that. On the one hand, I was chiding Nixon for failing to turn over all the evidence; on the other, I was saying that his attitude was proper. By the nature of the office I held, I was in an impossible situation. I couldn't abandon Nixon, because that would make it appear that I was trying to position myself to become President. Nor could I get too close to him, because if I did I'd risk being sucked into the whirlpool myself. It was a day-by-day balancing act and I detested the whole thing. Generally, based on the information I had, I was consistent on four positions. They were: (1)

Nixon was innocent of any impeachable offense; (2) his tactics were wrong; (3) the House Judiciary Committee was trying to do a good job; and (4) constant leaks to the press by a few irresponsible members were reprehensible. And those were the positions I maintained until the very end, when new information emerged which changed everything.

On July 8, Nixon called me to the White House and we conferred for seventy-five minutes about domestic issues and the summit talks he had held with Brezhnev the last week in June. I gathered those sessions had not gone well. He was in one of his rambling moods and I didn't feel that our discussion was at all productive. Five days later, I saw him again, in San Clemente, and we focused on the deteriorating economy. I cannot pick out a date and say, "This is when he started to lose his grip," but it was clear to me that he wasn't as strong either mentally or physically as he had been before. I had a growing sense of his frustration, his resentment and his lack of a calm, deliberate approach to the problems of government. He complained bitterly how he was being mistreated by Congress and the press. His resolve to stay and fight seemed to be weakening.

On Wednesday, July 30, the House Judiciary Committee passed the third and final article of impeachment. That morning I returned to the Capitol—after having made speeches in California and Nevada—and I stayed there just long enough to pick up House Majority Leader Tip O'Neill and several other members of Congress and fly with them to Massachusetts, where we were scheduled to play in a pro-am golf tournament near Worcester that afternoon. A marvelous raconteur, Tip is also a shrewd vote counter, and he was explaining on the plane why the President's position looked precarious. I didn't want to talk about it, and tried to steer the conversation onto safer ground. I kidded him about his golf game—which was no model of consistency—and we reminisced about the good times we'd had serving together in the House. That evening, I flew back to Washington. No sooner had I arrived home in Alexandria than Bob Hartmann called. He had just talked with Haig, who wanted to see me as soon as possible. Haig would call me himself first thing in the morning. It was important, he said.

3

Brief Honeymoon

"Get all the facts and all the good counsel you can and then do
what's best for America."

— Dwight D. Eisenhower

W hen John F. Kennedy became President in 1961, he invoked
the New Frontier and vowed to lead us away from the "pas-
sivity" of the Eisenhower years. Lyndon Johnson's vision was even
more grandiose: the federal government could do *anything* once it
provided funds. Richard Nixon promised to "bring us together," but
his Presidency achieved the opposite result. In the years since JFK,
the country had been buffeted by riots in our major cities, political
assassinations, a bloody and divisive war and the tawdry spectacle of
Watergate. What we needed now was a time to heal, and I was reminded of a story I'd heard from Peter Lisagor of the Chicago *Daily
News*. In 1948, during the civil war in Greece, a villager was making
plans to emigrate to the United States. "What should I send back
when I reach America?" he asked his weary neighbors. "Should I
send money? Should I send food? Should I send clothes?" "No," one
of his neighbors replied, "you should send us a ton of tranquillity."

But in August 1974, tranquillity was in short supply. The years of
suspicion and scandal that had culminated in Nixon's resignation had
demoralized our people. They had lost faith in their elected leaders
and in their institutions. I knew that unless I did something to restore

124

their trust, I couldn't win their consent to do anything else. And rhetoric alone would not suffice. The New Frontier and Great Society promises of the 1960s had been partly responsible for the national disillusionment. The country didn't need more promises. It yearned for performance instead. When I was growing up, my parents told me about an old tradition of the American West. A pioneer family would struggle for years to pay off the mortgage on their home. Once the final payment was made, they'd place a special stone above the fireplace or in the newel post of the stairs. They'd call it a "peacestone" and its presence would signify that the home was theirs at last. In August 1974, my ambition was to put the peacestone back in the foundation of America.

We needed calm solutions to many problems. The nation's economy was in terrible shape. Inflation had soared out of control and was accelerating at an annual rate of more than 12 percent. (Indeed, the wholesale price index figure for the month of July—released the day before I became President—rose 3.7 percent, the second biggest monthly jump since 1946.) The stock market was jittery. The Dow Jones industrial averages had plummeted below 780 and there were ominous signs of an increase in the number of unemployed.

In the area of foreign policy, the Nixon Administration had ended U.S. involvement in the Vietnam War, but tensions in that part of the world remained high, and renewed conflict could shatter the Paris peace accords. The same was true of the Middle East. The Yom Kippur War of October 1973 had ended in an uneasy truce. Progress had been made through disengagement in the Sinai and on the Golan Heights, but unless that process could be continued, another war could explode at any time. Relations with the Soviet Union were strained; we had moved from the more glamorous phase of détente into a time of testing. And then there was the conflict that had just broken out on Cyprus and the explosive situation it had created between Greece and Turkey. I knew that events there could threaten the security of the Western Alliance.

These challenges were sufficient to test the mettle of any Chief Executive, but I think it's fair to say that I took office with a set of unique disadvantages. Normally, Presidents have about seventy-five days of grace between their election and their inauguration. They use this "shakedown" period to recruit the members of their Cabinet and staff and to decide their legislative priorities. I didn't have that luxury, and the lack of a normal transition time caused problems right away. Many of the Nixon holdovers on the White House staff were saying, "Here comes Jerry Ford and his minor leaguers. Once we settle them down and show them how this game is played, everything will be all right." And my own people were saying, "As soon as we get rid of these Nixon appointees, the government will be legitimate again."

Moreover, there's a seasonal cycle to a Presidency. The first year the President lays out his programs. During his second and third years, he tries to push them through Congress. The fourth and final year, he mends his fences politically and runs for reelection. I had to do all that in 895 days—*if* I decided to be a candidate. Most Vice Presidents who become President have buried their predecessors and then gone on to reassure the people by wrapping themselves in the mantle of the men they followed. ("Let us continue," LBJ said after Kennedy's death.) At the time of *his* departure, Nixon had no mantle left. Then, too, I'd been a Congressman for a long time. The White House press corps doesn't take members of Congress very seriously. To many of those reporters, my Vice Presidency had seemed disorganized, so they harbored a natural skepticism about my talents and skills. Finally, I had no mandate from the people, and the Congress understood that.

But if I had some handicaps, I also had advantages. Nixon, by nature, was a recluse who preferred to deal with problems through paperwork rather than through people. I don't do business that way. From the first, I sought an "open" Administration. One thing I wanted to do right away was to eliminate the trappings of an "imperial" Presidency, so even before being sworn in, I asked Al Haig to tell the Marine band that I didn't want to hear "Hail to the Chief" or "Ruffles and Flourishes"; the "Michigan Fight Song" would suffice. I asked Haig to make sure that the Oval Office was swept clean of all electronic listening devices—there would be no bugging or taping during my Administration. I also expressed reservations about holding religious services inside the White House. In the Nixon years, those observances had become social occasions. I didn't feel comfortable with them.

Walking back from the East Room after I was sworn in, Hartmann and I entered the Cabinet Room. Traditionally, a President selects the portraits of the three former Presidents that hang there. Nixon had chosen Eisenhower, Lincoln and Woodrow Wilson. Wilson was not among my favorites, so I suggested that we replace his portrait with Harry Truman's. The former haberdasher from Missouri had been the first President under whom I had served. He had been a People's President, and it seemed only right that his portrait should hang prominently in the People's House.

Bryce Harlow has said that my most fervent hope in those early days was to replace a national frown with a national smile, and I would have to agree. Some of the changes I made were cosmetic, of course, but I felt it important that the new President signal the change in Washington by gesture as well as by deed. For example, Nixon and his aides had always referred to the living quarters in the White House as the executive mansion. The residence, I decided, was a better term. Similarly, he had renamed the Presidential aircraft the *Spirit of '76.* Everyone knew it as *Air Force One,* and I decided that was the name it should have. Then there was the matter of the Secret Service detail that protects the President. Nixon's agents had done their job with a grim determination. I passed word that I didn't want my agents to push people around. I said that it was all right if they smiled once in a while.

Another gesture I made was toward members of the press. In my eight months as Vice President, I'd held fifty-two press conferences, given eighty-five formal interviews and talked with reporters informally on dozens of occasions. I wanted them to know that I would continue to be as open and candid as possible, and soon after the swearing in, I walked over to the press room and introduced Jerry terHorst as the chief spokesman for the new Administration. Jerry, in fact, needed no introduction. He knew every member of the White House press corps and they all respected him as a true professional. With press relations in his able hands, I was confident that my Administration would be off to a good start.

Historians reading of the first twenty years of Richard Nixon's political career will find few foreshadowings of the dramatic foreign policy moves he initiated as President. Until 1970, he had maintained a hard line against the Soviet Union and the People's Republic of China. The clipping file will contain accounts of the famous "kitchen debate" with Nikita Khrushchev and the many speeches he made chastising Mao Tse-tung. But those clips will be footnotes in the pages of history. The headlines will record his grand strategy to move from the Cold War to a policy of détente with the Soviets. That policy was best exemplified by the Strategic Arms Limitation Agreement of 1972, the joint space effort and the numerous cultural and technical exchanges between the two countries. Historians will wonder how this Cold Warrior of the 1950s and 1960s could move so successfully to a policy of accord with the Soviets. The consensus will be that Nixon saw the big picture.

Our new ties with the Soviets were possible, I believed, only because the Soviet leaders were becoming concerned about developments within the People's Republic of China. Both Mao Tse-tung and Chou En-lai were making increasingly antagonistic speeches toward the Kremlin. Nixon sensed that the Chinese leaders feared and distrusted the Soviets. Their long-standing border dispute was a festering sore. Mao had never forgiven the Soviets for mistreating him in the 1950s, and he was concerned about Soviet intentions in the Pacific. Skillfully, Nixon moved to take advantage of the split.

The result was a recognition in world capitals that the United States was once again the master of the international scene. American involvement in Vietnam had undercut our worldwide leadership role and many old friends and neutrals were moving away from us. After the overtures to Moscow and Peking, U.S. prestige began to rise again. Nixon's initiatives defused the trend against us and created a new foundation for peace.

And now with Nixon gone, nations around the world wondered whether I would keep that foundation strong. The prevailing wisdom in Washington at that time was that I knew very little about foreign policy. Like so much of the wisdom in the capital, it was totally inaccurate. Since 1953, as a member of the House Defense Appropriations Subcommittee—and later as a member of the subcommittee that had a watchdog responsibility for the CIA—I'd had ample opportunity to listen to Administration experts testify about all aspects of our relationships with other countries. In addition, from 1956 through 1964 I had served on the Foreign Operations Appropriations Subcommittee. I had questioned Secretaries of Defense and State and directors of the CIA. I'd traveled to Europe and Southeast Asia, and I was confident that I knew as much about foreign policy as any member of Congress. And for the past eight months, I'd had the benefit of weekly briefings from Henry Kissinger or his deputy, Brent Scowcroft.

It would be hard for me to overstate the admiration and affection I had for Henry. Our relationship began on solid, unshakable ground and grew even better with the passage of time. He had gone through hell during the final days of the Nixon Administration and he had agreed to stay on only because I said I needed him. People who don't know Kissinger view him as solemn, gruff and pedantic. The truth is that he has an engaging sense of humor. Sure, he had an ego—most people who achieve international stature do—and it's also true that he had a penchant for secrecy. But that, I felt, was a necessary ingredient of successful diplomacy, and of Kissinger's success there could be no doubt. Our personalities meshed. I respected his expertise in foreign policy and he respected my judgment in domestic politics. He was a total pragmatist who thought in terms of power and national interest instead of ideology. He had a global view of international relationships and tried to rearrange them in a way that would be beneficial to the United States. I think we worked together as well as any President and Secretary of State have worked throughout our history.

The Nixon resignation, of course, had been just as profound a shock internationally as it had been in the United States. Henry impressed upon me how essential it was that I become identified in the minds of the diplomatic corps as someone knowledgeable about and involved with the conduct of American foreign policy. Thus, on my first day as President, I met with some sixty envoys from nations all over the world—some privately, such as representatives of the Soviet Union, the People's Republic of China, Israel, several of the Arab nations and South Vietnam. Others—the envoys from our NATO allies—we received as a group.

In the Oval Office that evening, I conferred with the members of the transition team who had been devising ways to facilitate the change in Administrations. Able, hard-driving Don Rumsfeld was the coordinator of the team's efforts and, in my opinion, he was a perfect choice. I'd been disappointed when he'd left the Congress in 1969 to run the Office of Economic Opportunity for Richard Nixon, though I felt confident that if anyone could take that mess and straighten it out, Rumsfeld was the man. In 1971, when Nixon adopted wage and price controls, he named Rumsfeld to administer them. Don had achieved great success in everything he'd done, and so I wasn't surprised when he left Washington in 1973 to become Ambassador to NATO. Both of us had athletic backgrounds—his was in wrestling— and both of us were straightforward. Above all, he was a superior administrator and a demon when it came to working long hours, organizing an office and making sure that everything functioned efficiently. The fact that he was in the Nixon White House from the earliest days and didn't get involved in Watergate said much about his personal integrity. He wouldn't tolerate political shenanigans and the men around Nixon knew he wouldn't, so to protect themselves, they kept him out of the loop.

The transition team member responsible for liaison with the federal agencies and departments was Rogers Morton, the Secretary of Interior. I had been in the House with his brother, Thruston, so when Rog came to Congress as the Representative from the Eastern Shore of Maryland, we became friends right away. We shared the same philosophy and political beliefs. He was a hulking bear of a man, six feet eight, but he was also one of the gentlest people I have ever known. No one ever got mad at him. Most important, both Don and Rog had no qualms about telling me when I was wrong.

The third member of the team—responsible for personnel—was Bill Scranton. He and I had overlapped at Yale. I'd gotten to know him better when he served in the House, and I'd been saddened by his decision—after one splendid term as his state's governor—to retire from politics. But our relationship was such that I knew I could count on him to help when I needed him. Jack Marsh was the fourth and final member of the group, and as a former Congressman, the obvious choice to handle my liaison with Capitol Hill.

During that initial meeting, the transition team sought and received my agreement on four general operating principles. They wanted to organize the Ford White House to give me control over the major functions of my office and to make sure that key people had ample access to me. Secondly, they wanted to guarantee that the organization reflected my personal style by assuring openness and the free movement of people and ideas. A third goal was to reduce the overall size of the White House staff. Finally, they wanted to make the structure as flexible as possible.

Rumsfeld and the others were acutely aware of the dangers inherent in the role they played. They didn't want the transition team to "take over" the government, and Don said it should go out of business within thirty days. If it didn't, chaos could ensue. People anxious to appeal decisions that the Nixon Administration had made would turn to the transition team, and there was a possibility that we'd wind up with two "White House staffs" and two Administrations. "So let us get in and help out," Don said, "and let's understand that, barring some major catastrophe, we'll be out of here in a month." (The group did its job in less than two weeks.)

On Saturday, my second day as President, I convened the Cabinet. Nixon had always behaved rather formally with his Cabinet, seldom shaking hands or engaging in banter; he got down to business very quickly. It's pretty hard to change your style at the age of sixty-one, and I had no intentions of changing mine. I strode into the room, shook hands all around and asked the Cabinet members to take their seats. I told them that I didn't want—indeed, that I wouldn't accept—any resignations. The country needed stability and continuity. I urged the Secretaries to be more "affirmative" in their relations with the press, and I also asked them to "come and see me with your problems. I think we have a fine team here," I concluded, "and I'm looking forward to working with each and every one of you."

What I wanted in my Cabinet were strong managers who would control the career bureaucrats and not become their captives; people who knew how to build support in the Congress and the media. I would leave the details of administration to them and concentrate on determining national priorities and directions myself. I wanted men and women who would give me unvarnished truth, then lay out the options for decisions that I would have to make. If several of them disagreed with each other before the decision was made, well, that was all to the good. I'd be the beneficiary of their arguments.

And as I glanced around the room during that first Cabinet meeting, I had to admit that Nixon—whatever his shortcomings—had recruited a Cabinet of fine quality. Kissinger was superb as Secretary of State. As Secretary of the Treasury, Bill Simon stood for a fiscal responsibility that I thought was mandatory for the Cabinet. I liked his drive, his obvious intelligence and his desire to work with others. As Secretary of HUD, Jim Lynn was excellent. So was Agriculture Secretary Earl Butz. Former Ohio Senator William Saxbe was Attorney General. Some members of my staff found him garrulous, and he tended to shoot from the hip, but his independence made him credible, and I was delighted when he agreed to stay. As for Secretary of Defense James Schlesinger, I respected his intellect, but I wasn't sure how effective he would be in dealing with the Congress. People on Capitol Hill often found him patronizing or arrogant. Some of the other Cabinet members—Casper Weinberger at the Department of Health, Education and Welfare and Claude Brinegar at the Department of Transportation, for example—were exhausted by the turmoil of the Nixon years and really wanted to leave. In the spirit of unity, they, too, agreed to stay.

In the Nixon years, the Cabinet departments and agencies had lost power and influence to such White House appendages as the Domestic Council, the Office of Management and Budget, and the Council on International Economic Policy. That tended to destroy one of the foundations of our form of government. A Watergate was made possible by a strong chief of staff and ambitious White House aides who were more powerful than members of the Cabinet but who had little or no practical political experience or judgment. I wanted to reverse the trend and restore authority to my Cabinet. White House aides with authority are necessary, but I didn't think they had the right to browbeat the departments and agencies. Nor did they have the right to make policy decisions. I decided to give my Cabinet members a lot more control.

To a large degree, any Administration's success depends on the ability of the President to work harmoniously with his Cabinet, and from the beginning I imposed a set of rules for myself in order to do just that. They were: (1) have no special confidants within the Cabinet; (2) listen, don't confide; (3) don't get involved in any jurisdictional rivalries; (4) have confidants outside the Cabinet from whom advice can be solicited; (5) don't get mired down in detail—handle the broad policy decisions and leave management and program implementation to the department heads; (6) move aggressively on all fronts toward resolution and decision; (7) look at all proposals as if you're going to have to be the advocate who sells them to the public at large; and (8) finally, encourage dissent before a final decision is made.

People probably expected me to move cautiously, even tentatively, in picking up the reins, but it was important to set an activist pace from the start. There had been a hiatus in the capital for the past few months; the government seemed to be standing still. Nixon hadn't talked to reporters; he hadn't dealt with the Congress; he hadn't reached out to the people of the country. I had to do all three. My actions had already signaled to the press that my Administration would be very different from his. Soon it would be time for me to address a joint session of Congress, and over that first weekend I worked with Hartmann and Milton Friedman on the text of my speech.

Shortly after eight-thirty on Monday evening, August 12, Betty and I drove from our home in Alexandria—we weren't set to move into the White House until the following week—to the Capitol. Kenneth R. Harding, the Sergeant at Arms of the House, and George M. White, the Architect of the Capitol, met us at a side door on the House side of the building. While aides led Betty to the family gallery in the House chamber, Harding and White escorted me toward the Speaker's office on the second floor. The corridors were packed with Congressional employees whom I'd known for years. They were smiling and clapping. The members of the Cabinet were gathered in the Speaker's office, waiting for me to arrive. So were the House and Senate leadership, and I shook hands warmly with each of them. These were my friends. They were cordial in their welcome. Everyone was patting me on the back.

"Mr. President," boomed the voice of William M. ("Fishbait") Miller, the crusty old doorkeeper of the House, "line up. We've got to move." Speaker Albert and Senate President Pro-tem James Eastland of Mississippi entered the chamber first. Then came the Justices of the Supreme Court, the diplomatic corps and the members of the Cabinet. After all the members had taken their seats, Fishbait led me and an escort group around the corridors so that we could enter the center aisle. "Ladies and gentlemen," he bellowed, "the President of the United States." And I walked down the aisle with Democrats on my left and Republicans on my right, and all of them were reaching over to shake hands and say encouraging things.

Standing at the podium, I acknowledged the cheers and tried to spot familiar faces in the audience. The Justices of the Supreme Court were seated to my left, the members of the Cabinet to my right, and I could see Betty and the children in the gallery. "My fellow Americans," I began, "we have a lot of work to do. My former colleagues, you and I have a lot of work to do. Let's get on with it . . . As President, within the limits of basic principles, my motto toward the Congress is communication, conciliation, compromise and cooperation. This Congress, unless it has changed, will be my working partner as well as my most constructive critic. I am not asking for conformity . . . I do not want a honeymoon with you. I want a good marriage . . . My office door has always been open, and that is how it is going to be at the White House. Yes, Congressmen will be welcomed—if you don't overdo it."

Then I expressed my concern about the state of the economy, urged Congressional spending restraint and accepted Mike Mansfield's suggestion for a domestic summit meeting to discuss ways to bring inflation under control. I assured allies and adversaries alike that our foreign policy wouldn't change, and I called for a strong national defense. Turning to the sort of abuse that had concerned so many citizens during Nixon's term, I promised that "there will be no illegal tapings, eavesdropping, buggings or break-ins by my Administration. There will be hot pursuit of tough laws to prevent illegal invasion of privacy. . . ." Then I concluded:

"Frequently, along the tortuous road of recent months from this chamber to the President's house, I protested that I was my own man. Now I realize that I was wrong. I am *your* man, for it was your carefully weighed confirmation that changed my occupation. The truth is, I am the people's man, for you acted in their name, and I accepted and began my new and solemn trust with a promise to serve all the people and do the best that I can for America."

So much for rhetoric. During my first weeks as President, I was confronted by half a dozen separate challenges which demanded a response. One of them came from the largest manufacturer in the country, the second from the Soviet Union, the third from a member of my Cabinet and the rest from Congress itself. On August 9, the day that I became President, General Motors announced an average price increase of 9.5 percent on its 1975 model cars, and company officials said their decision was not subject to negotiation. I knew the hikes would stimulate other industries to raise prices, pushing the inflation rate even higher. So I called Dick Gerstenberg, the chairman of GM's board of directors, and pleaded for restraint. GM's image in the past had been one of noncooperation with Presidential appeals, and I wasn't sure that my personal request for a rollback would have any effect. Gerstenberg told me that GM's facts and figures justified the hikes, yet he promised to reconsider them. Some days later, the corporation agreed to cut its increase by a full one percent—or an average of fifty-four dollars per vehicle. Hardly a major victory, but it was significant psychologically.

The challenge from the Soviets posed a possible confrontation in the northern Pacific. Six and a half years earlier, a Soviet "Golf" class diesel submarine had sunk several hundred miles southeast of its base at Vladivostok. (American subs—the U.S.S. *Thresher*, for example— had met the same fate and we had no way of retrieving them. We needed to have that capability.) Although the sub lay at a depth of more than 16,000 feet, U.S. intelligence experts thought it might be possible to recover her. The CIA let a contract to build a vessel that would hover over the sub and drop an ingenious, powerful grappling machine. The giant claws would lift the sub and bring her up inside the hull of the ship. Then the hull would be closed and the ship would return to the United States. The name of the vessel was *Glomar Explorer*, and as Vice President I'd been briefed about her mission. The cost of the attempt was high—some $300 million—but the money would be well spent if we could recover the sub's advanced weapons and codes.

On the second morning of my Presidency, Kissinger, Scowcroft,

Schlesinger and CIA Director William Colby came to the Oval Office to advise me that *Glomar Explorer* was on station and ready to drop the claws. But now there was a serious complication. A Soviet trawler, which had been trailing the *Glomar* for days, was hovering around her, and we had to talk about contingency plans in case the Soviets tried to board. *Glomar Explorer* had been designed as an oceanographic research vessel, and she was unarmed. Moreover, she was operating alone. To lend credence to the cover that she was engaged in underwater research, the Navy had kept supporting ships far away from her. If an incident similar to the 1968 seizure of U.S.S. *Pueblo* occurred, we couldn't come to her rescue in time.

The decision I had to make was whether or not to continue the operation even though there was the possibility that the trawler might attempt to stop it. I decided that having progressed as far as we had, we should gamble and proceed. Twenty-four hours later, *Glomar* lowered its claws and succeeded in pulling sections of the sub into the ship. Then, tragically, the claws broke, and part of the sub fell back to the ocean floor. We managed to retrieve a significant amount of information and the circling Soviet trawler never interfered.

In the wake of Nixon's resignation, the newspapers were full of bizarre stories about his conduct in the final days. Some of them indicated that Schlesinger was so concerned about Nixon's mental stability that he had taken steps to make sure the President couldn't give orders to the Armed Services unilaterally. The story made me furious because I was assured no such measures had been taken. I talked to Haig about it, and we concluded that it had been leaked deliberately from the highest level of the Pentagon. That made me madder still. Haig was present when Schlesinger walked into the Oval Office. "Jim," I said, "I'm damn disturbed by these rumors about what was done in the Pentagon during the last days of the Nixon Administration. Obviously, they come from the top, and I want the situation straightened out right away." Schlesinger didn't admit that he had been the source of the leak, but the significant thing was that the leaks did stop, at least for a while. As President, that was the first run-in I had with Schlesinger. I hoped it would be the last, but I suspected otherwise.

The challenges I received from the Congress were more significant and, in the long run, more damaging to the nation than an erroneous leak. In my August 12 speech to the joint session, I had said, "To our allies and friends in Asia, I pledge a continuity in our support for their security, independence and economic development." One day after I'd made that promise, a Senate subcommittee cut $5.1 billion from the defense budget for fiscal year 1975. Congress had been asked for approximately $2 billion in military and economic aid to South Vietnam. Congress later slashed $1 billion from that and, in my opinion, gravely impaired the ability of our ally to forestall further aggression from the North. Its action diminished the prospects for lasting peace.

Equally disturbing was the Congressional response to the Turkish invasion of the island of Cyprus. In July, when I was still Vice President, the military junta in Greece instigated a coup on Cyprus. Their purpose was twofold: to assassinate the country's leader, Archbishop Makarios, and to strengthen the Greek Cypriot National Guard. The Turks responded by sending forty thousand troops to Cyprus and soon occupied some 40 percent of the island, even though the Turkish Cypriots constituted only 18 percent of the island's population. That caused the downfall of the Greek junta and its replacement by a democratic government led by Prime Minister Constantine Karamanlis. Instead of blaming the former Greek government for starting the incident, Congress moved to embargo delivery of American arms to Turkey. The lawmakers' argument was that the Turks had used American arms—in violation of U.S. law—to invade the island. It didn't matter to them that the Greek Cypriot National Guard had also used weapons of U.S. origin. Nor did it seem to concern them that a Turkish withdrawal from the NATO Alliance—something the Turks were threatening at the time—would imperil the security of the entire eastern Mediterranean. They didn't want to know the facts; they simply wanted to punish the Turks.

The leaders of this effort in the House were three Democrats, Ben Rosenthal of New York, Paul Sarbanes of Maryland and John Brademas of Indiana. In the Senate, Missouri's Thomas Eagleton was spearheading a similar drive. I tried to persuade them that if we stopped delivery of arms—which the Turks had paid for already—they would probably respond by closing vital intelligence facilities we had been using for years near their border with the Soviets. I tried to convince Rosenthal in particular that a weakened Turkey would imperil the future security of Israel. None of my arguments made any headway. Congress was determined to interfere with the President's traditional right to manage foreign policy, and if this interference had dire consequences for the country as a whole, well, that was just too bad.

The final Congressional challenge came from opponents of legislation designed to improve our relationships with the Soviet Union. For years the Soviets had wanted us to grant them most-favored-nation status for purposes of trade. This didn't mean that they would receive preferential treatment, only that they'd fare as well as any other country. That is, their exports would be subject to the lowest tariff rates we applied to any third country. We had already granted most-favored-nation status to other Communist nations—Poland and Yugoslavia—so ideology didn't pose a problem. Nixon had wanted to extend it to the Soviets because he thought that it would advance the cause of détente. The House had passed the Administration's Trade Reform bill, but it had been stalled in the Senate for nearly a year. The argument centered on the degree of control that the Congress would exert over decisions made by the President. In return for giving trade concessions to the Soviets, Senator Henry M. ("Scoop") Jackson, a Democrat from Washington, wanted a written commitment from the Soviets that they would agree to allow at least fifty thousand Jews to emigrate every year, and when he had such a commitment, he intended to hold a press conference to claim that it was his tough stand that had made the Russians capitulate.

I fully agreed that the Soviet anti-emigration policy was deplorable and contrary to my long-held belief that people should be free from oppression. Yet by pursuing quiet but firm diplomacy, Nixon and Kissinger had persuaded the Soviets to ease their restrictions. Jewish emigration from the U.S.S.R. jumped from four hundred a year in 1968 to about 35,000 in 1973. When I became President, I sought to assure the Soviets that I was going to pursue the same kind of quiet diplomacy.

On Wednesday, August 14, I welcomed Ambassador Anatoly Dobrynin to the Oval Office with Henry Kissinger. I told him that I would consider it a personal favor if his government would agree to release Simas Kudirka, a Lithuanian seaman who had jumped aboard a U.S. Coast Guard vessel, only to be turned back to the Soviets by the American captain. Dobrynin said he would see what he could do. (Three months later, Kudirka was given permission to leave the Soviet Union.) Then our conversation turned to the emigration of Soviet Jews. The Kremlin, Dobrynin said, would give us an oral guarantee that it would allow 55,000 to leave every year, but it wouldn't put that guarantee on paper and let Jackson use it for his own political purposes.

Next morning I met for breakfast in the White House with Jackson, Senator Abraham Ribicoff of Connecticut and Senator Jacob Javits of New York. I reported Brezhnev's promise and warned that if they insisted upon a written guarantee, the agreement would come unstuck. In fact, I said, the Soviets would probably cut back on the number of Jews they allowed to emigrate. Ribicoff and Javits were understanding and cooperative. But Jackson was adamant. He kept saying that we were being too soft on the Russians. I left the breakfast hoping that we would be able to agree on a compromise, but I wasn't optimistic. Jackson had a strong constituency among American Jews. He was about to launch his Presidential campaign, and he was playing politics to the hilt.

While all this was going on, the Senate was considering the Export-Import Bank bill. Adlai Stevenson, a Democrat from Illinois, was shepherding the measure. Soviet trade with the U.S. had never reached its full potential, and we wanted to see it expand to billions of dollars per year. Export-Import Bank credits for the expansion of U.S. exports had seldom been restricted by Congress, but Stevenson amended the bill so as to limit the credits available to the U.S.S.R. to a paltry $300 million per year. No such limitation had ever been imposed upon other Communist nations. Poland and Yugoslavia, for example, had used billions of dollars of these credits. But Stevenson was insistent about his amendment and wouldn't listen to our predictions that its passage would have grave consequences.

During my first two weeks in office, I made a strenuous attempt to show critics that an "open" White House meant exactly that. George Meany of the AFL-CIO hadn't been invited to the Oval Office in more than a year. On August 13, I asked him over for a forty-five-minute chat. Blacks and other minorities felt—with some justification—that Nixon hadn't cared about their problems at all. I telephoned Representative Charles Rangel, a Democrat from New York, who was chairman of the Congressional Black Caucus, and invited him to bring his colleagues by. (Our meeting, he said later, was "absolutely, fantastically good.") I held a similar session with thirteen Congresswomen who were endorsing the Equal Rights Amendment. When I signed a proclamation backing the measure myself, even Bella Abzug smiled.

In dealing with the Congress, Nixon and some of his aides had tended to work with individual Senators and Representatives who they felt were loyal to him instead of working with the elected leadership. That strategy didn't help the legislation that Nixon was trying to push, and it infuriated Hugh Scott and John Rhodes because it undercut their authority as party leaders. I assured both men that I considered them leaders in fact as well as in name, and I promised to pull no end runs. Indeed, from the moment I became President, I set aside several hours a week for any member of Congress who wanted to come and see me privately.

For some time before Nixon resigned, King Hussein of Jordan had planned to visit the U.S. beginning August 15. In view of the change in Administrations, I was asked whether I wanted him to postpone the trip. Of course not, I replied. I had met Hussein on several occasions in the past; in fact, the previous spring, in President Nixon's absence, I had hosted a state dinner for him. I admired his personal courage—he has probably survived more assassination attempts than any head of state—and leadership. The state dinner we were planning for him and Queen Alia on August 16 would also give Betty and me an opportunity to put our personal imprint on White House social occasions. During the Nixon years, those occasions had been formal and rather dull. After dinner the guests sat in stiff-backed chairs to listen to the "entertainment." The Nixons usually left as soon as the show was over. Betty and I wanted our dinners more relaxed. To honor Hussein and his queen, we invited a cross section of people who hadn't been to the White House for years. Among them: three reporters who had covered me as Vice President, not always favorably. Eric Sevareid was also on the list. So was Bob McNamara (Defense Secretary under Kennedy and president of the World Bank) and his wife Margaret, who were old friends of ours from Michigan. We danced after dinner—I remember stomping to "Bad, Bad LeRoy Brown." Betty and I stayed up until 1 A.M., and we had a thoroughly enjoyable time. As they were leaving, the McNamaras came up to us and said, "Boy, what a change."

On August 19, I was scheduled to fly to Chicago to address the seventy-fifth annual convention of the Veterans of Foreign Wars. A week or so earlier, Secretary Schlesinger had suggested that one way to hasten the healing process and draw a real distinction between the Nixon and Ford Administrations would be to do something about the fifty thousand draft evaders and deserters from the Vietnam War. Mel Laird, a former Secretary of Defense, agreed with him; so did my three sons, and I was leaning that way myself. The question then became what sort of program to espouse.

After the Civil War, Lincoln had offered deserters restoration of their rights if they withdrew support from the enemy and swore allegiance to the Union. He was criticized for being too lenient, but his was probably the right decision at the time. Nixon had maintained a tough approach. Because draft evaders and deserters had broken the law, he felt, they should be punished before being allowed to return to society. After Schlesinger's suggestion, I talked to Hartmann, Marsh, Haig and Buchen. All of us agreed that any proposal I made should be conditional and that the draft evaders and deserters should have to "earn" the amnesty I would be offering. Because the process was highly technical, I asked Marsh to work with the Veterans Administration, the Justice Department and the Pentagon in putting the package together. Then we talked about an appropriate forum for me to announce the plan. A liberal audience—Americans for Democratic Action, for example—would be pleased by the change of approach. The more conservative VFW would be very disturbed, but announcing it to them would indicate strength on my part. The Chicago address was the right occasion.

I am sure the VFW expected me to talk about the importance of a strong national defense and the necessity of meeting our responsibilities overseas. So did reporters aboard *Air Force One*. (To preclude the possibility of an organized demonstration, we hadn't included the

earned-amnesty proposal in the prepared text.) The weather in Chicago that Monday morning was glorious. Mayor Richard J. Daley
made sure that Betty and I received a tumultuous State Street welcome, and the reception in the VFW convention hall at the Conrad
Hilton Hotel was equally enthusiastic.

In my speech I announced that I was going to nominate former
Representative Dick Roudebush to be the VA's new administrator. I
pledged that I would do everything I could to upgrade veterans' hospitals. Then I came to the crucial paragraphs: "In my first week at
the White House," I said, "I requested the Attorney General and the
Secretary of Defense to report to me personally, before September 1,
on the status of some fifty thousand of our countrymen [who have
been charged with] offenses loosely described as desertion and draft-
dodging. . . . All, in a sense, are casualties, still abroad and absent
without leave from the real America. I want them to come home if
they want to *work* their way back. . . . In my judgment, these young
Americans should have a second chance to contribute their fair share
to the rebuilding of peace among ourselves and with all nations. So I
am throwing the weight of my Presidency into the scales of justice on
the side of leniency. I foresee their earned reentry—*earned*
reentry*—into a new atmosphere of hope, hard work and mutual
trust."

While I hadn't yet worked out the details of my plan, I knew it
would dismay conservatives. My next Presidential act, however,
seemed certain to leave them sputtering. For the past ten days, I'd
been giving a lot of thought to the selection of the nation's next Vice
President. There was one overriding criterion: he had to be a man
fully qualified to step into my shoes should something happen to me.

By the end of my first week as President, the list of candidates had
been narrowed from sixteen to five. Bryce Harlow considered their
national stature, executive experience and ability to broaden my political base, assigned them points and ranked them numerically.
George Bush, a former Congressman from Texas who had been our
ambassador to the United Nations and was now serving as chairman
of the Republican National Committee, led all contenders in the Harlow evaluation with a total of 42 points. He was described as "strongest across the board," and his only weakness seemed to be that some

of my advisers regarded him—unfairly, I thought—as not yet ready to handle the rough challenges of the Oval Office. In second place was Rog Morton, another former chairman of the GOP, but there were some doubts about his age and the state of his health. Minority Leader Rhodes ranked third, but if I selected him, a divisive leadership fight would break out in the House. Moreover, his background was too similar to mine. Next was Tennessee Senator Bill Brock, who, as Harlow noted, was "generally strong and especially useful and attractive to youth." But he wasn't well known nationally, and although he had served with distinction in the Congress, he didn't have much executive experience.

The fifth name on the list—with a total of 35 points—was Nelson Rockefeller. He was, Harlow pointed out, "professionally the best qualified by far with the added strengths of (a) proving the President's self-confidence by bringing in a towering number two, (b) making available superb manpower resources to staff the Administration and (c) broadening the Ford political base." But he had drawbacks too. One was his age; he was sixty-six. A second was the fact that his name was anathema to conservatives. A third was the acute discomfort that I was sure he'd feel to find himself functioning as the number two man for someone else.

"In sum," Harlow continued, "it would appear that the choice narrows to Bush and Rockefeller. For party harmony, plainly it should be Bush. But this would be construed primarily as a partisan act, foretelling a Presidential hesitancy to move boldly in the face of known controversy. The Rockefeller choice would be hailed by the media normally most hostile to Republicans. It would encourage estranged groups to return to the party and would signal that the new President will not be the captive of any political faction. As for 1976, a Ford-Rockefeller ticket should be an extremely formidable combination against any opponents the Democrats could offer. Therefore, the best choice is Rockefeller."

Although the two of us had been in politics for most of our adult lives, we had had very different careers and had never become close political friends. He had always been very generous with his contributions to Republican candidates, but I had neither sought nor received any financial assistance from him. I knew that he had a sound

knowledge of foreign affairs. He had served as Assistant Secretary of
State toward the end of World War II, and he had been chairman of
Truman's Point Four Advisory Board in 1950 and 1951. During his
fifteen years as governor of New York State, he had displayed enormous drive, shrewd intelligence and an uncanny ability to get things
done. If his record was far more liberal than mine, that was only because he was reflecting his constituency, and it was obvious that in
his final term, he had begun to moderate his views. After stepping
down as governor in 1973, he came to Washington and talked to me
as Minority Leader about the Commission on Critical Choices for
America which he wanted to start. I helped to arrange sessions for
him with Senators Mansfield and Scott. When I became Vice President, he asked me to serve on his commission's board.

Some of my staff felt that Rockefeller was too strong, that he'd try
to dominate the Administration. That didn't worry me because I was
determined to heed the advice Laird had given me shortly after I'd
assumed the Presidency. "I have an idea that Nixon picked Agnew
because he was insecure and didn't want anyone who would overshadow him," Mel said. "Don't you do anything like that. When
you're President, you don't have to worry about being overshadowed
by anyone." If Rockefeller was strong, that was all to the good. What
the country needed was not just the image but the substance of
strength, and Rockefeller could contribute more to that strength than
anyone else. Adding up the pros and cons, I concluded that he would
be a fine partner.

But would he take the job? He had declined Nixon's offer in 1960
to be his running mate. I also knew that Humphrey had urged him to
switch parties and run on the Democratic ticket in 1968. He had rejected that offer as well. But this was a perilous time. The nation was
caught up in a crisis of confidence, and the addition of Rockefeller to
the Administration would go a long way toward helping me bind up
the wounds.

On Saturday, August 17, I called Haig into the Oval Office and
asked him to telephone Rockefeller at his summer home in Seal Harbor, Maine. When Nelson came on the line, I told him that I was
leaning toward nominating him as Vice President and that I was
wondering if he'd accept. He replied that he would have to talk to his

wife and family and call me back. Then I probed gently into his finances and health and asked if there were any "skeletons" that would
make his confirmation difficult. He said he didn't think there were. I
told him that I wanted to announce my decision the first part of the
following week and that if he was receptive to the idea, he should be
prepared to come to Washington.

The next day, he telephoned me to say that he would accept the
nomination if it was offered. The following evening, I called again
and made the offer definite. "Nelson," I said, "I've looked over all
the possibilities, and I'm convinced you're the man who can best do
the job as Vice President."

"Gee, Mr. President," he replied, as if he were taken by surprise,
"I'm honored. This is a great thrill."

Then our conversation turned to specifics. I said I wasn't going to
ask him merely to carry out the routine functions of his office, which
involve presiding over the Senate and traveling all over the world. I
wanted him to participate in all meetings of the Cabinet and the National Security Council. Additionally, I wanted him to head the Domestic Council and to help put together my domestic legislative
package. "You've been studying these issues," I said. "You've had a
lot of experience with them, and I think this is one area where you
can be very helpful to me." But I warned him that he would probably have a difficult time dealing with the Congressional committees
that would consider his nomination. There would be some members
of Congress, I said, who would attempt to delve into the Rockefeller
fortune and other aspects of his family's life that hadn't been made
public before. He assured me he was willing to take the risk. "Mr.
President," he went on, "I am going to do whatever I can to help you
and the country."

On Tuesday morning, August 20, he flew down from Maine and
met me in the Oval Office. Again we discussed my concept of what
his duties were to be, and he seemed very satisfied. Then I added a
caveat. "Nelson," I said, "there's one thing you'll have to do which
may present a problem for you. Congress has finally decided to give
the Vice President a home in Washington. It's up on Admiral's Hill,
and you'll have to live in it." I knew that he already owned a beautiful home on Foxhall Road, so I wasn't surprised by the pained expres-

sion that crossed his face. He looked at me quizzically as if to say, "Do you really mean that?" Then he nodded.

Minutes before I announced his nomination publicly, I telephoned Nixon as a courtesy and he seemed very pleased. It was my first conversation with him since his resignation. He said Nelson's name and experience in foreign policy would help me internationally and that he was fully qualified to be President should something happen to me. The extreme right wing, he continued, would be very upset, but I shouldn't worry because I couldn't please them anyway.

At about the same time that I was changing Nelson's future political plans, I was also altering my own. Bearing in mind my promise to Betty that I would retire in January 1977, as well as the statements I'd made during my confirmation hearings on Capitol Hill, I was giving serious thought to announcing once again that I would not be a candidate in 1976. If I did that, I thought, my credibility would be enhanced in both Congress and the country at large, and none of the tough decisions that I had to make could be challenged on political grounds. This very logical scenario dismayed Henry Kissinger. "Mr. President," he said, "you can't do that. It would be disastrous from a foreign policy point of view. For the next two and a half years foreign governments would know that they were dealing with a lame duck President. All our initiatives would be dead in the water, and I wouldn't be able to implement your foreign policy. It would probably have the same consequences in dealing with the Congress on domestic issues. You can't reassert the authority of the Presidency if you leave yourself hanging out on a dead limb. You've got to be an affirmative President. You've got to hold off on any announcement like that."

Henry was right. The moment I said I wasn't going to run, the succession struggle would start. That would be divisive in and of itself, and what the country needed was a period of stability. Besides, I relished the challenge of the Presidency, and both Betty and I found that we enjoyed living in the White House more than we ever thought we would. So on August 21, I authorized Jerry terHorst to tell reporters that I probably would run in 1976. The decision wasn't final then—I still had Betty to convince—but the statement enabled me to shed the image of a caretaker Chief Executive and to act more persuasively on my own.

Initially, when I became President, I did not want to have a powerful chief of staff. Wilson had had his Colonel House, Eisenhower his
Sherman Adams, Nixon his Haldeman, and I was aware of the trouble those top assistants had caused my predecessors. I was determined
to be my own chief of staff and Al Haig was agreeable to this change.
I would have five or six senior assistants with different areas of responsibility—legal matters, press and public information, Congressional liaison, personnel and White House administration—and they
would be able to see me at regular intervals during the day. In a report to me on August 20, the transition team concurred with this
"spokes of the wheel" approach. But as I was to discover soon
enough, it simply didn't work. Because power in Washington is measured by how much access a person has to the President, almost everyone wanted more access than I had access to give. I wanted to
have an "open" door, but it was very difficult; my working days
grew longer and longer, and the demands on my time were hinder-
ing my effectiveness. Someone, I decided, had to be responsible for
scheduling appointments, coordinating the paper flow, following up
on decisions I had made and giving me status reports on projects and
policy development. I didn't like the idea of calling this person chief
of staff, but that in fact was the role he would fill.

And Haig was the obvious choice. A very well-organized person
who had pushed himself unbelievably hard to keep the government
running during Nixon's final months, he had adjusted very easily
during the transition. Although he never talked about Nixon, I knew
that the changeover had taken a big load off his shoulders. The sun
had finally risen for him after a pretty dark night. He would come
into the Oval Office twice a day, early in the morning and then late
every afternoon. He'd always have a stack of papers in his hand.
He'd raise an issue; we'd discuss it, and I'd give him a decision. When
he was through, he would leave. He recognized that small talk was a
waste of my time, and he never tried to make our relationship into
something other than a professional one. Al was tired and really
wanted to return to the military as soon as possible, but I had asked
him to stay on for as long as he felt he could; he had agreed, and I
was very grateful.

My decision to retain Haig raised one of the thorniest issues of all:
what to do about the Nixon White House staff. In their report the

members of the transition team said that it was vital that I put *my* people in the top jobs as soon as I could. The Nixon staffers, they pointed out, had been recruited, hired and directed by a personnel system that Haldeman had controlled. It was not at all the kind of system that meshed with my approach to government. Then, too, they were worn out, and there was always the possibility that some of them might have had previously undisclosed links to Watergate that could embarrass me if I kept them on my team.

Many of my political advisers argued the same way. Hartmann was characteristically blunt: Fire every Nixon appointee—no matter how loyal, honest or competent the person might be—and clean house right away. "You don't suspect ill motives of anyone until you're kicked in the balls three times," he would say to me. "As a human being, that's a virtue. But as a President, it's a weakness." And then he would go on to use an analogy from the military: "In the Navy, when you have a change of command, you transfer your allegiance to the new skipper. You pipe the old guy over the side; you might be sad to see him go because he was a good skipper, or you might be happy because he was a son of a bitch, but that doesn't matter because you have a new chief now, and you're totally loyal to him." Then Hartmann would add, "Mr. President, that's not the way it works in the White House." The Nixon appointees were loyal only to Nixon. Therefore, they should be cast aside quickly. And Hartmann himself had shown the way. No sooner had I put him in charge of the White House speechwriters than he'd fired every one of them—and done it disagreeably.

Although I wanted people to perceive that there was a big difference between the Nixon and Ford Administrations, I didn't think that a Stalin-like purge was the way to go about it. Besides, there were people on the White House staff who had nothing to do with Watergate. For me to have fired them all would have tarred them with the Nixon brush. If I kept them on for a while, they could return to private life and be identified with the new President. That was the only fair thing to do, so I made the decision to proceed gradually. Some of the people I didn't want on the White House staff had already left of their own accord. The others, I told Haig, would have to be gone by January 1.

By the end of my second week as President, I had pretty well settled into the routine that I would observe for the rest of my term. I set my alarm clock to wake me up at five-fifteen every morning. The New York *Times* and the Washington *Post* were delivered to me on the second floor of the residence. I also received the written intelligence briefs and the daily news summary that Jerry terHorst's shop prepared. It would take me more than an hour to read those papers and documents thoroughly. Then I did my exercises, showered, dressed, ate breakfast and got to the Oval Office about seven-thirty. The first person to see me was usually Brent Scowcroft, Kissinger's deputy at the NSC, who came in either alone or with David Peterson of the CIA. Haig would come in next with his agenda for the day and a list of decisions for me to make. Then Jack Marsh would normally stop by. Jack seemed to know everything about the internal workings of the White House. He would tell me who was feuding with whom and what the problems were, and he would give me his recommendations for smoothing everything out. More than anyone else, he was the man who bridged the gap between the Nixon and Ford staffs. He had a knack for getting along well with everyone, his suggestions were almost always good and I could give him the worst conceivable problem to solve. He'd wander out of the office and after a while I'd forget about it because I never heard back. He'd taken care of it in his quiet, old-shoe way.

When Marsh became the head of my office of Congressional Liaison, succeeding Bill Timmons, who would be leaving soon to set up his own government relations firm, Jack selected a former reporter named Max Friedersdorf to assist him. A tall redhead with a Hoosier twang, Friedersdorf had also served as a Congressional assistant. He knew the people and the system, and he had excellent judgment in handling the different interest groups. He'd see me four or five mornings a week, and I soon discovered that he was a storehouse of information as to where specific legislation stood and how the Administration could swing a vote or two. Given the fact that little of substance had happened legislatively during the last few months, Friedersdorf's calendar was full. The Congress hadn't yet passed many major appropriations bills. Nor had it done anything about developing an energy policy, reforming the nation's chaotic welfare laws or even agreeing which approach to take to a national health insurance plan. Administration efforts to push land use legislation and the vital foreign trade bill had been languishing for some time; Friedersdorf had a big job to do. I was reminded of a comment that Ev Dirksen had made to me once: "Congress," he said, "is like a waterlogged scow. It doesn't go fast, but it doesn't sink."

When I was in the Congress myself, I thought it fulfilled its constitutional obligations in a very responsible way, but after I became President, my perspective changed. It seemed to me that Congress was beginning to disintegrate as an organized legislative body. It wasn't answering the nation's challenges domestically because it was too fragmented. It responded too often to single-issue special interest groups and it therefore wound up dealing with minutiae instead of attacking serious problems in a coherent way. Moreover, Congress was determined to get its oar deeply into the conduct of foreign affairs. This not only undermined the Chief Executive's ability to act, but also eroded the separation of powers concept in the Constitution.

Henry Kissinger and I would worry about such matters when we met in the Oval Office every day. He'd come in between nine and ten o'clock and stay for an hour or more. He knew he couldn't function effectively as Secretary of State unless it was known that he had the total backing of the President, and he would never make a move without first talking it through with me in great detail. We'd discuss pressing issues first—Cyprus, the Middle East, SALT—then we'd move on to questions of philosophical or theoretical import: How could we reassert the President's moral and legal authority to act decisively in foreign policy? How could we resist the "ethnic awareness" that tended to influence Congressional decisions affecting the Middle East, the eastern Mediterranean and the nations of black Africa? In the wake of Vietnam, should the U.S. retreat from its role as world policeman, and if so, how fast?

Later in the morning, after Kissinger left, I would sit down with Jerry terHorst and discuss questions reporters were likely to ask during his news briefing that day. My afternoon schedule would vary, depending on the groups I had to see and the decisions I had to make, but in those early weeks I found I was spending more time discussing the economy than almost anything else. And with reason.

This was taken when I was two, soon after my mother and father were separated. The bangs wouldn't last long, but I'd always have those bowlegs.

Our pioneer wagon train, with me holding the reins, heads for the neighborhood parade in Grand Rapids.

My stepfather and his four boys, after church. Tom is on my right, Dick on my left, and Jim is in Dad's lap.

Wide World Photos

My final year at Michigan, 1934. It was a losing season, but I learned a lot—most importantly, that there are things you can win even in defeat.

Skiing at Lake Placid, New York, in January 1941. This was just before I got my law degree from Yale and returned to Michigan.

In the Pacific, 1943. Between air strikes we played ball on the hangar deck of the U.S.S. *Monterey.* That's me on the left going for the tip-off.

On the primary campaign trail for Congress, 1948. I promised to milk their cows if I won—and I did.

The luckiest day of my life: October 15, 1948.

Wide World Photos

Richard Nixon, at top, LBJ and I listen as President Harry Truman delivers a State of the Union Address in 1950. Each of us would take his turn on that podium one day.

August 8, 1974. This photo was taken for the record. Minutes later, when we were alone, President Nixon said, "I have made the decision to resign." It was a moment of strange calm in the eye of the hurricane swirling about us both.

Wide World Photos

Wide World Photos

August 9, 1974. "I do solemnly swear…"

My first day on the job. The desk wouldn't be clean nor the shelves empty for long.

White House photo by David Hume Kennerly

White House photo by David Hume Kennerly

The morning I pardoned Richard Nixon. No decision of my Presidency would be so widely attacked.

Some House Judiciary Committee members had questions about the pardon. I decided the best course was to answer them face to face.

Wide World Photos

Wide World Photos

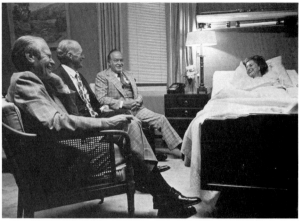
White House photo by David Hume Kennerly

Rocky has just been sworn in as my Vice President. What a fine team player he was.

Bob Hope, a friend and I visit Betty after her mastectomy. Who could better boost her spirits than Bob?

Late-night review of briefing papers at the Akasaka Palace in Tokyo, November 1974; the first step of my trip to Asia and the Soviet Union.

White House photo by David Hume Kennerly

Getting a GI's story near the DMZ in Korea.

White House photo by David Hume Kennerly

My first meeting with Brezhnev near Vladivostok, November 23, 1974. Our talks went better than expected.

White House photo by David Hume Kenner

Relaxing with Henry Kissinger and my staff on a Russian railroad car after the summit conference.

With French President Valéry Giscard d'Estaing (left), Henry Kissinger and French Foreign Minister Jean Sauvagnargues at Martinique, December 14, 1974. We got along . . . swimmingly.

White House photo by David Hume Kenner

Wide World Photos

Vail, December 1974. I'm off to the slopes—still on my feet.

Inflation was galloping ahead at an annual rate of more than 12 percent. Wholesale prices had spurted up 20.4 percent in the last year alone. The U.S. trade deficit in August had hit a record $1.1 billion and private housing starts had declined to their lowest level in five years. The unemployment rate was down to 5.4 percent, but that provided little comfort to the 5.5 million people seeking jobs. Over the past ten years, American productivity had been decreasing steadily, and it showed no signs of improving soon. What I had inherited, the New York *Times* pointed out, was "the worst inflation in the country's peacetime history, the highest interest rates in a century, the consequent severe slump in housing, sinking and utterly demoralized securities markets, a stagnant economy with large-scale unemployment in prospect and a worsening international trade and payments position."

The reasons we were in this terrible position were fairly clear. One was LBJ's attempt to provide guns and butter simultaneously in the mid sixties. His Administration had accelerated spending for both domestic and military purposes but hadn't imposed any new taxes to provide the revenue until it was too late. Result: a $25 billion deficit in 1968. A second reason was Nixon's decision to adopt wage and price controls in August 1971. There may have been some political justification for the move but its consequences had been disastrous economically, and the business community was concerned that it could happen again. The third reason was the staggering increase in energy costs that followed the 1973 Yom Kippur War. Oil-producing states in the Arab world slapped an embargo on exports to the U.S., then quadrupled the price they charged for a barrel of oil. The final factor was the rise in the cost of food. Drought had scorched the Middle West in the summer of 1974. There had been a poor corn crop and a disappointing wheat harvest. Demand exceeded supply, and that caused supermarket prices to soar.

But if the reasons for the crisis were clear, the solutions were not. The economy had been mismanaged so badly and for such a long time that it couldn't be cured without pain. And painful policies would cause divisions at a time when divisions were what I wanted to avoid. Some people believe that all a President has to do to end inflation and unemployment is to flick a switch. The realities are that you

can't do that in either case. You must have a sound economic plan—
and the guts to stick with it. We had the choice of being dramatic or
being cool. There wasn't much we could do that was dramatic anyway, and if we failed, we would have made the situation worse. We
tried to show leadership by projecting a calm and steady hand. Some
people misinterpreted this by concluding we were stodgy and
unimaginative, but that didn't bother me.

Since the days of FDR, the Democratic Party's philosophy has
been that unemployment is a more serious problem than inflation.
Traditionally, they've wanted to stimulate employment, increase the
federal budget—and the federal budget deficit as well—and then
gamble with the impact that their actions will have on the inflation
rate. In one sense that's understandable. Democrats had controlled
the Congress for all but four of the last forty-two years and Congress
has always contended that it could "do something" about unemployment much more easily—and with greater public relations impact—
than it could remedy inflation. Republicans, for their part, have always considered inflation to be public enemy number one. We have
denied the charge that if you tackle inflation you're going to increase
unemployment. Our position has been that you can reduce inflation
and unemployment at the same time. The more progress you make
in winning the battle against inflation, the more confidence the private sector acquires, and the more it expands; and expansion means
the creation of new jobs.

In deciding what specific steps to take to bolster the economy, I
was extremely fortunate to be receiving advice from such brilliant
figures as Alan Greenspan and Arthur Burns. A bespectacled, soft-
spoken bachelor, Greenspan had come to Washington to replace Herbert Stein as Chairman of the Council of Economic Advisers. As a
youth in New York City—he'd attended the same high school as
Henry Kissinger—he had wanted to be a musician, and he had
played the clarinet for a traveling dance band. Then he'd gone to
New York University, become fascinated by economics and launched
an enormously successful consulting firm. Reluctant to join the Administration, he agreed (at a considerable personal sacrifice) only because Haig had convinced him that the nation needed him. It didn't
take me long to appreciate the contributions he could make. No one

had a better ability to sit in a meeting, summarize the points that people around the table had made, and then lay out all the options for me.

For someone who'd spent most of his life sitting in an ivory tower, weighing tables and statistics and predicting economic trends, Greenspan had an uncanny grasp of public opinion. He was convinced that inflation was of far more concern than unemployment to the vast majority of Americans, and he was sure that people in the heartland weren't buying all that Capitol Hill propaganda about the need for more federal programs for which they'd have to pay. Whenever I was under pressure to add funds to a program and he thought I might be influenced by the political aspects of the decision, he would caution me to hold the line. Usually, he won because he was right.

If Greenspan was a newcomer to Washington, Arthur Burns was a veteran of the wars. A rumpled, gray-haired man who was seldom without his pipe, he was responsible as Chairman of the Federal Reserve Board for setting the nation's monetary policy. A master at appearing to be flexible, he never lost sight of his fundamental goals. He'd give a little here and there, but when the chips were down, he would make his point and stick with it and usually prevail. No economist I ever knew was more skilled in dealing with the Congress than Burns, and no one was more respected on Capitol Hill.

Traditionally, the relationship between the President and the Chairman of the Federal Reserve Board is a distant one—the Fed is set up as an autonomous group, and the President is not supposed to have any control over its decisions—so I was delighted when we developed an excellent rapport. He would be very frank and blunt with me, and I would reciprocate, but we seldom disagreed on any matters of substance because our economic philosophies were in tune. In the early days of my Presidency, he was being criticized by people who thought the Fed was restricting the money supply too much. Because of his concern about inflation, he was determined to hold fast to his policies, and I encouraged him as often as I could.

Even before Nixon resigned, Senator Mike Mansfield had suggested convening an economic "summit meeting" in Washington to discuss the causes of the runaway inflation and to recommend ways to bring it under control. Before we held that meeting—tentatively scheduled for late September—I thought it would be worthwhile to sponsor a series of regional "mini-summits" around the country, where businessmen, labor leaders and economists of all persuasions could articulate their views.

Prior to these "mini-summits," my advisers and I had discussed a three-pronged strategy to reduce inflation: spending cuts, the maintenance of a prudent monetary policy and, finally, a counseling process whereby Administration officials would try to anticipate wage and price increases and urge restraint. During the Johnson Administration, reporters called this process "jawboning." I thought "counseling" was a better word.

"The country needs two things for its long-term economic health," Nobel Prize-winning economist Milton Friedman once wrote. "First, a steady course on the part of government which can be known in advance by the people in the marketplace, and second, a course that is directed toward reducing the role that government plays in controlling our affairs." I agreed with him wholeheartedly. While we were preparing for the summit meeting, I asked my economic advisers to conduct a study aimed at identifying government policies or programs that might be contributing to inflation by promoting the inefficient operation of the private sector. The Interstate Commerce Commission, I knew, had rules that prohibited truckers from taking the shortest available routes between any two points. Such needless regulations added millions of dollars to the cost of doing business and hit consumers in their pocketbooks. Other agencies maintained similar rules, and I wanted to do everything I could to eliminate them.

Finally, I turned my attention to the $305 billion budget for fiscal year 1975 which I had inherited from Nixon. Burns and Simon thought I could slash between $5 billion and $10 billion from that amount, and although I wasn't so optimistic, I was determined to try. A cut of $5 billion wouldn't have any real effect on the inflation rate, but its impact would be beneficial psychologically.

And the importance of that kind of benefit couldn't be underestimated. I was the first President since Herbert Hoover to take office at a time of declining expectations about personal well-being. From 1933 through the summer of 1974, according to the public opinion polls, the American people either thought things were improving for them economically or that they would improve soon. Now those same polls showed that most people expected their own situations to get worse before they got better again. When people are optimistic, it's reflected in the economy. Pessimism is reflected the same way, and I was convinced that this national mood of apprehension and concern—of waiting for the other shoe to drop—was a major factor contributing to inflation.

It's discouraging how hard it is for a President to slice away large chunks from a $305 billion budget. He might want to, but the truth is he can't. Traditionally, Presidents have had the authority to impound funds earmarked for projects they didn't like. Johnson and Nixon had abused this privilege, so the Congress just took it away by passing the Budget Reform Act of 1974. This law stipulated that the President no longer had any independent control over spending once an appropriation had been approved. Under the act, a President can ask the Congress to defer or rescind its spending decisions, but he isn't likely to succeed, and that tells a lot about how the role of government in our economic system has changed.

In fiscal year 1965, total federal spending topped $100 billion for the first time in history. In fiscal year 1971, it exceeded $200 billion, and in the Nixon budget for fiscal year 1975 it climbed above $300 billion. Some pundits attributed this dizzy spiral to the war in Vietnam and the hearty appetites of the "big spenders" in the Pentagon. Nothing could have been further from the truth. In 1959, we were spending 40 percent of the budget for national defense. By 1974, that figure had declined to 24 percent, and the sums we were allocating for research and development, the procurement of new weapons systems and the restoration of mobilization capability had fallen to alarmingly low levels. At the same time, another trend was developing. In 1959, federal payments to individuals—either direct or indirect—accounted for 24 percent of the budget. By 1974, that figure had climbed to 44 percent. All these entitlement programs—social security, food stamps, military retirement and railroad retirement—had cost-of-living escalators built into them, and the result was that by 1974 they were mushrooming faster than the rate of growth of the economy.

And that was changing the nature of the government's role. In the

early days of the Republic, the government's function was to promote domestic order and to maintain national security. By 1974, its
main function seemed to be the redistribution of income on a massive
scale. More and more people who worked were transferring more
and more money to people who didn't work. This trend posed a real
threat to the survival of our free society. What worried me most was
that we could reach a point of no return, where the number of recipients was greater than the number of contributors. Those recipients
would have a vested interest in the perpetuation—and enlarge-
ment—of their benefits, and Congress wouldn't be able to stand up to
them. I couldn't abolish those entitlement programs, but I could try
to put the brakes on their rate of growth. I decided to ask Congress to
impose a 5 percent ceiling on any increases in these various programs
in the next fiscal year.

The economic proposals that I submitted to Congress in the early
weeks of my Administration were fairly similar to the ones that Nixon had proposed. But while his relations with Capitol Hill had been
terrible, mine were excellent and I hoped this good will might help
get those proposals through. How the tables had turned in just twenty-five years. In 1949, when I arrived in Washington, President Truman was a moderate-to-liberal Democrat who had struggled with a
conservative Republican Eightieth Congress. He wanted to spend,
and we Republicans wanted to save. Here I was in 1974, a conserva-
tive-to-moderate Republican about to struggle with a liberal Democratic Congress. The President wanted to save, and the Congress
wanted to spend. Well, Truman had won a good share of his battles
on Capitol Hill. With any luck, I would too.

Throughout my political career, my relations with reporters had
been excellent, and I was really looking forward to my first press conference on August 28. Nixon's press conferences—when he'd had
them—had often turned into surly, belligerent confrontations which,
in my opinion, had demeaned both the President and the press. I was
determined to get off to a different start. Jerry terHorst suggested
some changes in the format that the Nixon Administration had used.
One was to move reporters' chairs closer to the podium so as to reduce the sense of "distance" between the President and the press. Another was to discard the blue curtain that Nixon had always stood in

front of—it looked stagy and imperial—and to position me on the other side of the East Room before open doors that led to the red-carpeted Grand Entrance Hall. That, terHorst predicted, would create a much friendlier atmosphere.

Reporters wouldn't attend the session to be "friendly," of course, and I knew that I was in for a grilling. For several days prior to the press conference, I met with key members of my staff—terHorst and his deputy, Paul Miltich (who had been my press secretary when I was Vice President), Hartmann, Haig and Marsh—and tried to anticipate tough questions. I assumed that the reporters would zero in on the economy. Then there was the reorganization of the White House staff. Surely, they'd want to know what personnel changes I intended to make. Finally, there were the Cyprus issue, the pending SALT talks and the omnipresent possibility of renewed warfare in the Middle East. The press would want to know what initiatives I planned to take in foreign policy.

Hartmann and Miltich disagreed. The press corps was only interested in one issue, they warned—Richard Nixon. What was I going to do about him? How was I going to handle the disposition of his papers and tapes? I simply couldn't believe that the press would focus entirely on these matters. In the nineteen days since I'd become President, I had spent considerable time getting legal advice on what to do about those papers and tapes. (If they were sent to San Clemente as Nixon and his lawyer demanded, could they be saved from destruction? And how could they then be made available for the court orders and subpoenas that were already being issued to the government in a number of cases?) But I hadn't given any thought to Nixon's legal status. That was in the hands of responsible authorities, and it seemed to me that it would be inappropriate for the press to ask questions about a man whose fate was up to the Special Prosecutor and the courts. There were too many other things of vital importance to the country at home and abroad, and I was sure reporters would ask about them.

I was totally wrong. The first question—from Helen Thomas of United Press International—dealt with whether or not I thought Nixon should have immunity from prosecution. Others that followed were variations on the theme. Was I considering pardoning Nixon?

Did I think that the Special Prosecutor could pursue his cases against Nixon's aides as long as there was a possibility that the former President might escape having to go to trial? Had there been any communications between Jaworski's office and members of my staff regarding Nixon's fate? If Nixon was indicted, would I pardon him before his trial began?

The press conference gave me a chance to make a point that I wanted to underline. When a reporter asked if I planned to set up a code of ethics for the Executive Branch, I responded, "The code of ethics that will be followed will be the example that I set." But in general I was disappointed by the questions that were raised. The White House press corps didn't seem interested in finding out how I planned to deal with the substantive issues that confronted me. They just wanted to know what I was going to do about Nixon, and I thought they had wasted my time.

At the conclusion of the press conference, I walked back to the Oval Office and asked my advisers how long they thought this would go on. Was I going to be asked about Nixon's fate every time I met with the press? Each of them said it would continue as long as Nixon's legal status and the disposition of his papers and tapes remained unclarified. Their scenario was discouraging. I'd been hoping to have press conferences every two or three weeks. I realized now that I'd be questioned repeatedly about him and his many legal problems.

Worse, I recognized that the responses I'd already given could—and probably would—be variously interpreted. It would also seem to some in the press that I'd made statements that were contradictory. In response to Helen Thomas's question as to whether or not I agreed with Nelson Rockefeller that Nixon should have immunity from prosecution, I had said that I did, adding that "in the last ten days or two weeks I have asked for prayers for guidance on this very important point." But then, in response to another question, I had said that I thought the Special Prosecutor had "an obligation to take whatever action he sees fit and that should include any and all individuals." I realized those two answers seemed at variance with each other, yet I didn't know how to avoid the apparent contradiction. For me to have said that Special Prosecutor Leon Jaworski shouldn't do his duty would have been for me to tell a law enforcement officer to forget about his oath of office, and I didn't want to make it appear that I was signaling him to treat one potential defendant differently from any other.

Then, too, some of my replies seemed to commit me to waiting until after Nixon's trial and possible conviction before deciding what to do about his case. "In this situation," I had said, "I am the final authority. There have been no charges made, there has been no action by the courts, there has been no action by any jury. And until any legal process has been undertaken, I think it is unwise and untimely for me to make any commitment." And again: "I make the final decision. And until it gets to me, I make no commitment one way or another." Clearly, the implication was that if Nixon was convicted, I was going to wait until just minutes before he went to jail before—maybe—granting him a pardon.

All this forced me to address the issue squarely for the first time. I had to get the monkey off my back. I was already struggling with the question of who had jurisdiction over the papers and tapes, and that was cutting into my work schedule more and more every day. It intruded into time that I urgently needed to deal with a faltering economy and mounting foreign policy problems all over the world. With these critical issues pressing upon me—and the nation—I simply couldn't listen to lawyers' endless arguments about Nixon's tapes and documents or answer constant questions about his legal status. But just what should—and could—I do?

Several hours after that first press conference, I talked with Buchen. "Phil, I don't know what I'll decide, but I've got to have some information," I said. Did I, as President, have the legal right to pardon someone who had not been indicted, or convicted, yet? Although I remembered what Haig had told me about this during our meeting on August 1, I didn't consider his a definitive legal opinion, and I had to be absolutely sure. Could I issue a pardon that didn't contain a reference to a specific crime? Could it be a general pardon? Then I asked Phil to check with Jaworski, find out what possible criminal charges might be brought against Nixon and get an estimate as to how much time the Special Prosecutor thought would have to elapse between Nixon's indictment and the start of his trial. Here Phil would have to be very discreet. A prosecutor is not supposed to reveal whether or not a person is going to be indicted. Communicating with Jaworski publicly would embarrass him and prevent his giving us the best analysis. Phil would have to approach him in such a way as to afford him protection.

Phil was not a criminal lawyer, and I was throwing him into a situation different from any he'd confronted before. "Okay, I'll try to find the answers for you," he said, "but I'm going to need some help. I can't take the responsibility for the research and get everything done that I have to do. And I'm not sure I have anyone in my office who can handle it." Phil was silent for a minute. Then he said: "Well, there is one person I know you can trust. He'd be helpful to us. How about my approaching Benton Becker?"

As an attorney for the Department of Justice in the mid 1960s, Becker had helped to direct the case against former Representative Adam Clayton Powell. Moving over into private practice, he had assisted me in my probe of Justice Douglas, and he had been extraordinarily helpful in preparing the material I needed during the confirmation hearings that preceded my becoming Vice President. A prodigious worker, he was shrewd and tough. He was also discreet, and I thought he would be ideal.

Over the next few days, I agonized over the idea of a pardon, and eventually several key conclusions solidified in my mind. First of all, I simply was not convinced that the country wanted to see an ex-President behind bars. We are not a vengeful people; forgiveness is one of the roots of the American tradition. And Nixon, in my opinion, had already suffered enormously. His resignation was an implicit admission of guilt, and he would have to carry forever the burden of his disgrace. But I wasn't motivated primarily by sympathy for his plight or by concern over the state of his health. It was the state of the *country's* health at home and around the world that worried me. As Army Major Bob Barrett, one of my military aides, said: "We're all Watergate junkies. Some of us are mainlining, some are sniffing, some are lacing it with something else, but all of us are addicted. This will go on and on unless someone steps in and says that we, as a nation, must go cold turkey. Otherwise, we'll die of an overdose."

"Among the deficiencies of hindsight," Winston Churchill once wrote, "is that while we know the consequences of what was done, we do not know the consequences of some other course that was not followed." Yet I was very sure of what would happen if I let the charges against Nixon run their legal course. Months were sure to elapse between an indictment and trial. The entire process would no doubt require years: a minimum of two, a maximum of six. And Nixon would not spend time quietly in San Clemente. He would be fighting for his freedom, taking his cause to the people, and his constant struggle would have dominated the news. The story would overshadow everything else. No other issue could compete with the drama of a former President trying to stay out of jail. It would be virtually impossible for me to direct public attention to anything else. Passions on both sides would be aroused. A period of such prolonged vituperation and recrimination would be disastrous for the nation. America needed recovery, not revenge. The hate had to be drained and the healing begun.

Keeping all these thoughts to myself, I broached the possibility of a pardon with five key aides: Buchen, Haig, Kissinger, Hartmann and Marsh. I swore each of them to secrecy, emphasizing that there simply could not be any leaks until I had reached a decision. I urged them to give me their most candid feelings. Buchen, I knew already, was inclined to favor the idea. Haig was for it too, although he never flatly said as much. He laid out the pros and cons, then stepped back and said, "It's your decision, sir." When I talked to Kissinger at one of our private morning meetings, he said he thought it was the right thing to do. It was the quickest, really the only, way to clear the center stage. The spectacle of a former President on trial would damage our country's image internationally. It was a very impressive argument.

Hartmann and Marsh, however, had reservations. Neither argued the idea's equity, or disputed my view that this was the only way to get the matter behind us once and for all. Both simply considered it their job to present alternatives. "Mr. President," Hartmann said, "you'll have to expect a lot of flak. No one can predict just how deep the resentment will go, but there will be strong editorial condemnation, for sure. There will be all hell to pay with the news media, and the White House press corps will go up the wall."

"I know that," I replied, "but the press is going to react that way whenever I announce the decision, so it might as well be now."

Hartmann shifted to another tack. Mentioning a recent survey which showed that 56 percent of people interviewed thought Nixon ought to be tried, he warned that the pardon would damage me politically. "Your popularity in the opinion polls will suffer because the public won't understand. I know why you want to do it, but you should be cognizant of the down side."

"I'm aware of that," I said. "It could easily cost me the next election if I run again. But damn it, I don't need the polls to tell me whether I'm right or wrong."

For Marsh the important question was the timing. He felt the country wasn't ready for it yet and urged me to delay the announcement for several weeks. When he saw he wasn't making headway, he suggested that I lay the groundwork by notifying the key leaders on Capitol Hill and asking them to keep the secret until I decided to act. But that, I was certain, would increase the possibility of a leak to the press, and a leak would be calamitous. Then Marsh mentioned something else. "Look," he said, "both of us know about the meeting with Haig that took place on Thursday, August 1—the meeting where he discussed a pardon as one of several options available at the time. Although you and I understand the two are not related, will people try to connect them?"

"Maybe they will, but we both know the facts," I replied.

Usually, after dinner, Betty and I would be together in the former Nixon bedroom, which we had redesigned as our private sitting room. She would sit on my right; there was a small table between us, and I would go through an hour or two of paperwork every night. I told her I was thinking about pardoning Nixon, and I listed my reasons. She didn't get into the technical aspects of it but she did say she thought that Nixon had suffered enough. And she felt enormous sympathy for his family. "I'll support whatever you decide," she said, her typical response whenever I had a tough decision to make.

On Tuesday, September 3, I met with Phil Buchen again to discuss the Nixon pardon. He told me Benton Becker had spent that Labor Day weekend in law libraries seeking answers to my questions. His conclusion: as President, I had the authority to grant a pardon before an indictment was returned. Phil was very precise and deliberate in discussing that authority, and I knew from more than thirty years of dealing with him that if he made a categorical statement of the law, then I could be sure he was accurate.

The pardon power entrusted to the President, Phil pointed out, had a long history, and rested on precedents dating back long before the Founding Fathers drafted and adopted the Constitution. In fact, this precise point was raised at the Constitutional Convention and it was decided to give to the President the power of the pardon prior to indictment. "In seasons of insurrection . . ." Alexander Hamilton had written in *The Federalist*, "a well-timed offer of pardon to the insurgents or rebels may restore the tranquillity of the commonwealth." And again, from the same source: "Oftentimes a pardon can be issued to maintain public order and confidence." In 1833, Chief Justice Marshall referred to the power's application as "an act of grace . . . which exempts the individual, on whom it is bestowed, from the punishment the law inflicts for a crime he has committed." And in 1927, the Supreme Court declared that the granting of a pardon represented "the determination of the ultimate authority that the public welfare will be better served by inflicting less than what the judgment fixed."

But to me the most important precedent was a 1915 case involving an editor named George Burdick, whose newspaper, the New York *Tribune*, had run a series of articles about customs frauds committed by U.S. Treasury Department employees. An investigation was launched; a federal grand jury began taking testimony from witnesses. But when Burdick appeared, he refused to divulge his sources or answer the panel's questions. Such answers, he claimed, might tend to incriminate him. One month later, he was subpoenaed again. Asked the same questions, he refused to testify again. Whereupon the U.S. Attorney reached into his pocket and pulled out a piece of paper signed by President Woodrow Wilson which granted Burdick "a full and unconditional pardon for all offenses against the United States which he . . . has committed or may have committed or taken part in." The legal effect of Wilson's pardon was to remove any possibility that Burdick might incriminate himself in his answers to the grand jury. Accordingly, Burdick couldn't claim the protection of the Fifth Amendment.

But Burdick, still believing that he had done nothing wrong, declined the pardon. When he still refused to testify, he was thrown into jail for contempt of court. (Ultimately, the Supreme Court reversed his conviction and set him free.) All this legal maneuvering brought forth two crucially important findings by our highest judicial body. In their opinion, the Justices of the Supreme Court reaffirmed that "the President has power to pardon for a crime of which the individual has not been convicted and which he does not admit." Second, and most important, the Justices found that a pardon "carries an imputation of guilt, acceptance, a confession of it." These opinions were clear and unambiguous and had remained the law of the land for nearly sixty years.

So I had the legal authority to move ahead. I hadn't made a final decision, but it must have been obvious to Phil that I was leaning toward a pardon. "Look," he said, "if you're going to do this to put Watergate behind you, I think you also ought to let me see how far we can go to get an agreement on the papers and tapes and have that in place at the same time."

"Well," I said, "if you can get the papers and tapes question settled prior to the pardon, that's fine. Let's get it behind us. But I don't want to condition the pardon on his making an agreement on the papers and tapes, and I don't want you to insist on any particular terms."

"I won't condition it," Phil replied, "but I can work it out so by his agreement it'll come out at the same time."

The issue was far more complex than it appeared. Stored in the White House and the EOB were some 950 reels of tape and roughly 46 million pieces of paper. By both tradition and rulings by various Attorneys General those tapes and papers were the property of the former President. (On August 22, to make doubly sure of this, I had asked Attorney General Saxbe to give me a legal opinion. "To conclude that such materials are not the property of [Nixon] would be to reverse what has apparently been the almost unvaried understanding of all three branches of the government since the beginning of the Republic," he wrote, "and to call into question the practices of our Presidents since the earliest times." He recommended that I send everything out to Nixon; the members of the transition team concurred.) And Nixon wanted them desperately. He had already been served with a subpoena to appear as a witness in the trial of Mitchell, Haldeman, Ehrlichman and the other Watergate defendants. That trial was due to begin September 30. He had a legitimate need to review his records and tapes in order to prepare his testimony.

But Jaworski also had an interest in seeing the materials. So did the various Watergate defendants. Additionally, attorneys involved in a number of civil suits had issued subpoenas to the White House asking us to produce tapes and records relating to the matters under litigation in each of these separate suits. Somehow, we had to satisfy these competing claims and do so in such a way as to reassure the public—in light of the eighteen-and-a-half-minute gap on one of the crucial tapes—that nothing would be altered or destroyed.

The problem appeared to defy a solution. And, in a literally physical sense, it was getting worse. The packaging, boxing and storing of the materials was taking place on the fourth floor of the EOB. As the process continued, the Secret Service, in a confidential memorandum, expressed worry over the floor's ability to withstand the extra weight. But early in the week of August 26, the possibility of a solution emerged when Nixon retained Herbert J. ("Jack") Miller as his attorney. That at least opened an avenue of communication between Buchen and the former President that had not existed before.

After discussing the problem with Miller, Buchen and Becker came up with the concept of a Presidential deed of gift of the papers and tapes to the United States. Under this proposal, the documents would be stored at a federal facility near San Clemente. Nixon and the government would share formal ownership and the materials would be available for court subpoenas for between three and five years. To ensure their security, two keys would be needed to open the vault. Nixon would have one, the General Services Administration the other. After five years had elapsed, Nixon could order the tapes destroyed. Miller didn't know if Nixon would accept the plan, but he would prepare a draft of a letter from the former President to GSA Administrator Arthur Sampson which would express agreement with the concept. He hoped Nixon would okay the draft.

On Wednesday, September 4, Buchen and Becker met with Miller to discuss the wording of that letter. At one point, Buchen said: "President Ford is giving some consideration to pardoning your client. It's just in the consideration stage, and by no means do I want you or your client to get excited, because it's not a final decision yet." Then Phil added: "Look, I think it's important that there be a statement of true contrition from the former President. The President tells me we can't dictate that statement, but in the interests of both your client and the President, I hope you would persuade your client to develop something that would tell the world, 'Yes, he did it, and he's accepting the pardon because he's guilty.'"

Miller said he understood and volunteered his belief that if the pardon were granted, Nixon should issue a statement admitting his involvement in Watergate. But he wasn't optimistic about getting such a statement. His few meetings with his client had shown him that the former President's ability to discuss Watergate objectively was almost nonexistent. Buchen and Becker then said that if and when the pardon was issued, it would be without preconditions, that while we'd welcome a statement of contrition, we were not demanding one.

For the past several days, Buchen had also been meeting with Jaworski. Their contacts had been facilitated by the fact that both men were staying at the Jefferson Hotel. They could shuttle between floors without attracting undue attention. Jaworski never said so, but it became obvious to Phil that he thought the grand jury would indict Nixon soon. (After all, Phil realized, the grand jury had named Nixon as an unindicted co-conspirator in the Watergate cover-up several months before.) Then, on the afternoon of September 4, Jaworski gave Phil several crucial pieces of information. The first was a letter in which he expressed his opinion as to how long it would take—assuming Nixon was indicted—before a trial could begin.

> The factual situation regarding a trial of Richard M. Nixon within constitutional bounds is unprecedented. It is especially unique in view of the recent House Judiciary Committee inquiry on impeachment, resulting in a unanimous adverse finding to Richard M. Nixon on the Article involving obstruction of justice. The massive publicity given the hearings and the findings that ensued, the reversal of judgment of a number of the members of the Republican Party following release of the June 23 tape recording and their statements carried nationwide, and finally, the resignation of Richard M. Nixon require a delay, before selection of a jury is begun, of a period from nine months to a year and perhaps even longer. This judgment is predicated on a review of the decisions of the United States courts involving prejudicial pretrial publicity.
>
> The Government's decision to pursue impeachment proceedings and the tremendous volume of television, radio and newspaper coverage given thereto are factors emphasized by the courts in weighing

the time [until] a trial can be had. The complexities involved in the process of selecting a jury and the time it will take to complete the process I find it difficult to estimate at this time.

The situation regarding Richard M. Nixon is readily distinguishable from the facts involved in the case of *United States v. Mitchell, et al.* The defendants in the Mitchell case were indicted by a grand jury operating in secret session. They will be called to trial, unlike Richard M. Nixon, if indicted, without any adverse finding by an investigatory body holding public hearings on its conclusions. It is precisely the condemnation of Richard M. Nixon already made in the impeachment process that would make it unfair to the defendants in the case of *United States v. Mitchell, et al.*, for Richard M. Nixon now to be joined as a co-conspirator should it be concluded that an indictment of him was proper.

The *United States v. Mitchell, et al.*, trial will within itself generate new publicity, some undoubtedly prejudicial to Richard M. Nixon. I bear this in mind when I estimate the earliest time of trial of Richard M. Nixon, under his constitutional guarantees, in the event of indictment, to be as indicated above.

Shortly after four o'clock on the afternoon on September 5, Buchen and Becker came into the Oval Office and showed me Jaworski's opinion. It was worrisome. Even if a full year elapsed before a trial could begin, there was no telling how long it would last. And if the verdict was "guilty," one had to assume that Nixon would appeal. That process would take years. Of equal concern to me was a memorandum which the Special Prosecutor had attached. It was from Henry S. Ruth, Jr., Jaworski's deputy, and it listed ten areas of investigation that prosecutors were pursuing. (Among them: tax deductions relating to the gift of Nixon's Vice Presidential papers, misuse of the IRS through attempted initiation of audits of Nixon's "enemies," and the handling of campaign contributions by Bebe Rebozo for Nixon's personal benefit.)

"None of these matters at the moment rises to the level of our ability to prove even a probable criminal violation by Mr. Nixon," Ruth's memo continued, "but I thought you ought to know which of the pending investigations were even remotely connected to Mr. Nixon. Of course, the Watergate cover-up is the subject of a separate memorandum."

Ruth's recommendations to Jaworski stated: "If you decide to recommend indictment, I think it fair and proper to notify Jack Miller and the White House sufficiently in advance so that pardon action could be taken before indictment." He went on to say: "One can make a strong argument for leniency, and if President Ford is so inclined, I think he ought to do it early rather than late." That influenced me, because Ruth knew as much about Watergate as anyone. He was simply putting the nation's interests first. Which was precisely what I would have to do.

The conversation shifted to the papers and tapes. In order to button down an agreement, Miller wanted to go to San Clemente, and he thought someone from my legal staff should accompany him. Phil couldn't do it. His physical handicap made it difficult for him to move around. But more importantly, as White House counsel he was too well known. His going to San Clemente—and being recognized there—would have tipped off my plans, and with a matter as delicate as this, a premature leak would have been disastrous.

Becker was the obvious choice. I had full confidence in his judgment, his legal expertise and his loyalty to me. Haig arranged for an Air Force jet to fly Becker and Miller to California. Now Phil and I discussed Becker's mission with him. He was to negotiate an agreement covering the papers and tapes and to review any response Nixon might give in the event I decided to pardon him. He was authorized to say, "It's not final, but in all probability, a pardon will be forthcoming." He stood up to leave, and I walked with him to the Oval Office door. I put my arm around his shoulder. "Be very firm out there and tell me what you see."

The story Becker told me upon his return to Washington on Saturday was poignant. No sooner had he arrived in San Clemente very late Thursday night than Ron Ziegler had delivered a short, blunt warning. "Let's get one thing straight immediately," Ziegler said. "President Nixon is not issuing any statement whatsoever regarding Watergate, whether Jerry Ford pardons him or not." There it was, the same defiant attitude he had expressed so often during his years as press secretary, the reference to Nixon as if he still were President and the familiar, condescending use of my first name. As soon as he heard that, Becker threatened to turn around and leave; in fact, he asked Ziegler how to contact the pilot of the plane that had flown him to California. But Miller succeeded in calming both men down, and they agreed to meet the next morning.

Negotiations that day centered mainly on the papers and tapes. By midafternoon a compromise had been reached. It gave both Nixon and the government access to the materials but stipulated that only he could authorize the Special Prosecutor or anyone else to examine them. Becker telephoned Buchen, who informed me of the details. Both of them seemed convinced that it was the best arrangement we could obtain. On their recommendations, I decided to accept it. The discussions in San Clemente then turned to the response Nixon would make if he received a pardon. The first draft that Ziegler prepared for Becker was disastrous. It spoke of the pressures of the office of the President, the necessity for reliance upon the judgment and the honesty of the White House staff and the President's preoccupation with international affairs. It concluded by acknowledging that Nixon should have delegated less authority to—and placed less reliance on—the members of his staff. That was all. When Ziegler asked Becker what he thought of it, Becker replied that *no* statement would be better than that. He stressed that although a satisfactory statement was not a precondition for a pardon, he thought that Ziegler could do a better job.

Ziegler went through three more drafts. In the final one, the former President said:

> I have been informed that President Ford has granted me a full and absolute pardon for any charges which might be brought against me for actions taken during the time I was President of the United States. In accepting this pardon, I hope that his compassionate act will contribute to lifting the burden of Watergate from our country.
>
> Here in California, my perspective on Watergate is quite different than it was while I was embattled in the midst of the controversy and while I was still subject to the unrelenting daily demands of the Presidency itself.
>
> Looking back on what is still in my mind a complex and confusing maze of events, decisions, pressures and personalities, one thing I can see clearly now is that I was wrong in not acting more decisively and more forthrightly in dealing with Watergate, particularly when it reached the stage of judicial proceedings and grew from a political scandal into a national tragedy.

No words can describe the depth of my regret and pain at the anguish my mistakes over Watergate have caused the nation and the Presidency—a nation I so deeply love and an institution I so greatly respect.

I know that many fair-minded people believe that my motivations and actions in the Watergate affair were intentionally self-serving and illegal. I now understand how my own mistakes and misjudgments have contributed to that belief and seemed to support it. This burden is the heaviest one of all to bear.

That the way I tried to deal with Watergate was the wrong way is a burden I shall bear for every day of the life that is left to me.

Becker wasn't satisfied. It wasn't the "full confession" he'd been hoping the former President would make, and he suspected that it would fall far short of what I wanted Nixon to say. Still, reasoning that Nixon had said about as much as he was going to say, he told Ziegler that he'd take the draft back to Washington and see if it would pass muster there. Then, remembering my instructions, he asked to see Nixon personally. Ziegler refused, but Miller intervened and said he saw no harm in the meeting. "All right," Ziegler said finally, "you can go on in."

The office was very small and looked as though someone had just moved in. There were no pictures on the walls. There was just a desk, flanked by the U.S. and Presidential flags. Nixon sat behind that desk and, Becker told me later, he looked terrible. He appeared to have aged and shrunken in the month since his resignation. His jowls were loose and flabby, and his shirt seemed to be too big for his neck. Nixon didn't smoke, but his fingernails had a yellowish tint. His handshake was very weak, and Becker noticed that he wasn't wearing the customary American flag pin in the lapel of his suit. "Mr. President," Becker began, "your aides and I have accomplished some very good objectives for the nation and for you today with respect to your papers. President Ford doesn't wish to deny you your papers, nor does President Ford wish to deny access to other people."

Nixon made no response. Becker noticed that he was slouched in his chair, that the expression on his face seemed to be saying, "Leave me alone," and that he didn't seem to be following the conversation. It was almost as if he had lost the will to live. Then Becker turned to the pardon: "I'm sure that Mr. Miller and Mr. Ziegler have told you that President Ford is considering a pardon, and I know they've showed you a draft of the document. Now, there are certain things you should know about pardons, and I should satisfy myself that you do know them."

What Becker wanted to do was to explain the Burdick case of 1915 and restate the White House view that acceptance of a pardon was an acknowledgment of guilt. But Nixon didn't seem to want to talk about that. He asked Becker where he lived and was surprised to learn that he was from Washington. When Becker told him that, the former President asked, "How are the Redskins going to do this year?"

"I really don't know, Mr. President," Becker replied. "We have some important things to talk about. Let's talk about them." Once again he made the point that an acceptance of the pardon constituted an admission of guilt.

"Uh-huh," Nixon replied.

His attention span was short. What few remarks he made were left incomplete, in midsentence. After twenty minutes or so, Becker was finished with what had turned out to be a monologue. He left the office and, with Miller, waited for the car that would drive them away from San Clemente. Just then, Ziegler called him back and said that Nixon wanted to see him again.

Nixon seemed exhausted. "You've been a fine young man," he told Becker. "You've been a gentleman. We've had enough bullies." His voice faltered, and for a moment he looked away. "I want to give you something. But look around the office. I don't have anything any more. They took it all away from me."

Becker felt very uncomfortable. "That's all right, Mr. President," he began.

"No, no, no," Nixon went on. "I asked Pat to get these for me." He opened a desk drawer and pulled out two little boxes containing cuff links and a tie pin. "She got these out of my own jewelry box," Nixon continued. "There aren't any more in the whole world. I want you to have them."

Becker took the boxes, shook Nixon's hand again and left the room as quickly as he could. Any more, he told me when he returned to

Washington, and he would have broken down and started to cry himself. "I'm not a medical doctor," he said, "but I really have serious questions in my mind whether that man is going to be alive at the time of the election."

"Well," I replied, "1976 is a long time away."

"I don't mean 1976," Becker said. "I mean 1974."

By Saturday afternoon, September 7, I had pretty well decided to pardon the former President. But once again I wanted to weigh the pros and cons. And there were a number of arguments to be made against it. Critics, I knew, would charge that I was establishing a dual system of justice. They would ask whether it was fair to let Nixon's aides spend time in jail while the former President, the man who had told them what to do, went free. But I could justify the difference in the treatment of Nixon and his aides. Being forced to resign the Presidency and live with that humiliation the rest of his life was a severe punishment in itself, the equivalent to serving a jail term.

The second argument against the pardon was that it would probably prevent the American people from learning the whole truth about Watergate. I believed they deserved to know the entire story. The man in the best position to tell that story was the former President. If I pardoned him, I might preclude that possibility. On the other hand, if Nixon was brought to court as a defendant in a criminal trial, he would not have to take the witness stand. Surely, I felt, most of the story would come out during the trials of Mitchell, Haldeman, Ehrlichman and the other defendants. Nixon himself wouldn't have that much to add. The turmoil of putting a former President on trial didn't seem to me to be worth the possible revelation of a few more details. All the bad feelings that people had about Watergate and the cover-up would have boiled over again and the healing process would have been destroyed.

Then there was the fact that Nixon's statement was inadequate. I had thought he'd be very receptive to the idea of clearing the decks, but he hadn't been as forthcoming as I had hoped. He didn't admit guilt and it was a good deal less than a full confession. I was disappointed because I'd expected more. I was taking one hell of a risk, and he didn't seem to be responsive at all.

And, finally, there were a number of arguments that turned more on the timing than on the substance of the decision. Jaworski, I knew, would want the decision delayed until a jury could be chosen and sequestered for the defendants in the Watergate cover-up trial. He'd say that he would have a hard time going to trial with the jury aware that a principal in the alleged conspiracy had already received a pardon from the President. Although I recognized his concern, I didn't think a pardon would have that much effect on the trial of the others—and indeed, Mitchell, Haldeman and Ehrlichman were later convicted. Finally, I had to consider the impact that a pardon would have on GOP chances in the fall campaign. Republicans would howl, I knew, but I concluded that the national interest overrode any political considerations. That was the easiest objection to confront.

Above all, I wanted it understood that my fundamental decision to grant a pardon had nothing to do with any sympathy I might feel for Nixon personally or any concern I might have for the state of his health. Years before, at Yale Law School, I'd learned that public policy often took precedence over a rule of law. Although I respected the tenet that no man should be above the law, public policy demanded that I put Nixon—and Watergate—behind us as quickly as possible. The successful conclusion of the agreement concerning the papers and tapes together with the statement Becker had secured from Nixon persuaded me to act as soon as possible. You can't pull a bandage off slowly, and I was convinced that the sooner I issued the pardon, the better it would be for the country. I decided to make the announcement Sunday morning. But complications developed almost immediately. Becker telephoned San Clemente and discovered that Ziegler was watering down the Nixon statement accepting the pardon. "I'm afraid if this continues, we'll be back to square one," he told me.

"We can't tolerate any weakened statement," I said. "Call Ziegler back and tell him that."

The tactic worked. Ziegler stopped his attempts to change Nixon's words.

Up to this point on Saturday afternoon, only a few top aides knew what I was planning to do. One who didn't was Jerry terHorst. Buchen and I had discussed whether or not to bring him into the circle and had decided not to tell him until the afternoon before the announcement. This did not reflect any lack of confidence in his integrity. If anything, the reverse was true. I had known him for more than twenty-five years. I recognized that he would never knowingly tell a lie. But if I informed him of the decision and reporters asked him whether or not a pardon was in the works, he would either have had to lie and violate the pledge of openness and honesty he'd given his former colleagues, or have had to tell the truth. And public revelation of the truth—before the proper groundwork had been laid—could have been disastrous. Even if he'd said, "No comment," reporters would have assumed that I was about to move. By not telling terHorst, I thought I was protecting him and his relations with the press.

All in all, that first week of September had been a frustrating period for him. He felt—with some justification—that he wasn't being informed of major developments. Reporters, for example, had asked him whether or not Haig would be leaving the White House soon to take another job. TerHorst said no. Actually, Haig and I had talked about the possibilities of his becoming commander-in-chief of NATO, but this depended upon the concurrence of other nations and that would take time. That's why terHorst hadn't been informed. A similar case involved Republican National Committee Chairman George Bush. When he visited the White House September 3, we told terHorst to describe our meeting as a routine political discussion. I thought that George would be excellent as our representative to the People's Republic of China, and he had agreed to serve. But once again, we couldn't announce the appointment until we'd received formal approval from Peking. (Suppose we had admitted that these appointments were being considered, and then the host nations had rejected them. We would have looked foolish.) And that didn't happen until several days after terHorst—on my instructions—had termed stories about pending appointments inaccurate. And then there was a delicate situation involving the Cox newspaper group. On Friday morning, September 6, David Kraslow, the Cox Washington bureau chief, learned that Becker and Miller were meeting at the San Clemente Inn. That afternoon, Kraslow, believing he had evidence that these two were discussing the possibility of a pardon for Nixon, asked terHorst if that was true. After checking with Buchen, terHorst replied that the two men were just negotiating the transfer of Nixon's papers and tapes. Kraslow accepted the explanation and didn't report their presence in California. In retrospect I can understand why ter-Horst felt he was being misled.

Once I determine to move, I seldom, if ever, fret. I have confidence that my lifetime batting average is high, and I'm prepared to live with the consequences. Still, I wanted to go to church and pray for guidance and understanding before making the announcement. So at eight o'clock Sunday morning, I attended services at St. John's Episcopal Church on Lafayette Square. I sat alone in the Presidential pew, took Holy Communion and then returned to the Oval Office. Hartmann had drafted the pardon announcement. I read it aloud twice, wrote in a line about Nixon's health, then telephoned Congressional leaders to tell them what I was going to do.

Of the leaders I talked to personally—Senators Mansfield, Scott and Goldwater; Representatives Albert, Rhodes, O'Neill and John J. McFall—none expressed outright opposition. They may have been surprised, but they didn't try to argue with me. Tip's reaction was fairly typical. "Jesus," he said, "don't you think it's kind of early?"

"Well, there's doubt he could get a fair trial," I replied, "and it would take a year to a year and a half to try him. I just can't run the office of the President and have this thing running on day after day when there are so many important things for me to spend my time on. It's for the good of the country."

"Okay, Mr. President," Tip said, and that was the end of the conversation.

About an hour before the telecast, terHorst came into the Oval Office to see me. After some small talk about arrangements for the telecast, I sensed that something was bothering him. "Mr. President," he continued, "I have something here that you need to see." With that he opened a Manila envelope and handed me a single sheet of typed White House stationery:

> . . . It is with great regret, after long soul-searching, that I must inform you that I cannot in good conscience support your decision to pardon former President Richard Nixon even before he has been charged with the commission of any crime. As your spokesman I do not know how I could credibly defend that action in the absence of a

like decision to grant absolute pardons to the young men who evaded Vietnam military service as a matter of conscience and the absence of pardons for former aides and associates of Mr. Nixon who have been charged with crimes—and imprisoned—stemming from the same Watergate situation. . . . Try as I can, it is impossible to conclude that the former President is more deserving of mercy than persons of lesser station in life whose offenses have had less effect on our national well-being.

Thus it is with a heavy heart that I hereby tender my resignation as Press Secretary to the President, effective today. My prayers, nonetheless, remain with you, sir.

I put the letter down on my desk and turned my chair so that I was looking to the left of terHorst, out toward the South Lawn and the Rose Garden. "Jerry," I said, finally, turning again to face him, "I regret this. I think you've made a mistake. But I respect your views, and I'm sorry if there was any misunderstanding. As to the pardon, it was a decision I felt I had to make. I've made it and I'm going to stick with it. I hope that you will reconsider and change your mind."

"My decision is final," he replied. "I've expressed my views in the letter."

I knew that there was absolutely nothing I could do to change his mind. Rising from behind my desk, I shook hands with him, hung an arm around his shoulder and said I hoped our long personal friendship would continue. Then I turned back to the announcement I had to make.

Just before eleven o'clock, the TV cameramen and sound technicians entered the Oval Office. Soon after I saw the red light just below the camera flash on, I began to read:

Ladies and gentlemen, I have come to a decision which I felt I should tell you and all of my fellow American citizens as soon as I was certain in my own mind and in my own conscience that it is the right thing to do.

I have learned already in this office that the difficult decisions always come to this desk. I must admit that many of them do not look at all the same as the hypothetical questions that I have answered freely and perhaps too fast on previous occasions.

My customary policy is to try and get all the facts and to consider the opinions of my countrymen and to take counsel with my most valued friends. But these seldom agree and, in the end, the decision is mine. To procrastinate, to agonize, and to wait for a more favorable turn of events that may never come or more compelling external pressures that may as well be wrong as right, is itself a decision of sorts and a weak and potentially dangerous course for a President to follow.

. . . As we are a nation under God, so I am sworn to uphold our laws with the help of God. And I have sought such guidance and searched my own conscience with special diligence to determine the right thing for me to do with respect to my predecessor in this place, Richard Nixon, and his loyal wife and family.

Theirs is an American tragedy in which we all have played a part. It could go on and on and on, or someone must write the end to it. I have concluded that only I can do that, and if I can I must.

There are no historic or legal precedents to which I can turn in this matter, none that precisely fit the circumstances of a private citizen who has resigned the Presidency of the United States. But it is common knowledge that serious allegations and accusations hang like a sword over our former President's head, threatening his health as he tries to reshape his life, a great part of which was spent in the service of this country and by the mandate of its people.

After years of bitter controversy and divisive national debate, I have been advised and I am compelled to conclude that many months and perhaps more years will have to pass before Richard Nixon could obtain a fair trial by jury in any jurisdiction of the United States under governing decisions of the Supreme Court.

During this long period of delay and protracted litigation, ugly passions would again be aroused. And our people would again be polarized in their opinions. And the credibility of our free institutions of government would again be challenged at home and abroad.

. . . As President, my primary concern must always be the greatest good of all the people of the United States whose servant I am. As a man my first consideration is to be true to my own convictions and my own conscience.

My conscience tells me clearly and certainly that I cannot prolong the bad dreams that continue to reopen a chapter that is closed. My conscience tells me that only I, as President, have the constitutional

power to firmly shut and seal this book. My conscience tells me it is
my duty not merely to proclaim domestic tranquility but to use every means that I have to ensure it. . . .

Then I began to read from the pardon proclamation itself: "Now,
therefore, I, Gerald R. Ford, President of the United States, pursuant
to the pardon power conferred upon me by Article II, Section 2, of
the Constitution, have granted and by these presents do grant a full,
free and absolute pardon unto Richard Nixon for all offenses against
the United States which he, Richard Nixon, has committed or may
have committed or taken part in during the period from January 20,
1969, through August 9, 1974." I signed the proclamation.

Finally, it was done. It was an unbelievable lifting of a burden
from my shoulders. I felt very certain that I had made the right decision, and I was confident that I could now proceed without being
harassed by Nixon or his problems any more. I thought I could concentrate 100 percent of my time on the overwhelming problems that
faced both me and the country. It didn't take me long, however, to
discover I was wrong. Immediately after the announcement, I
walked down the hall to Bill Timmons's office, where Haig, Hartmann and Marsh were sampling Congressional reaction on the telephone. The initial responses were good. Then I drove to the Burning
Tree Club to play golf in a foursome that included Mel Laird. Convinced that I would hear further encouraging words, I asked Mel
what he thought. "We're still in this tournament and we have a pretty good chance of doing well," Mel said somberly. "I don't want to
talk to you about the pardon now. We'll play golf, and then we'll talk
about it later."

Mel's reaction was a harbinger of the public outcry that was developing. In the first month of my Presidency, I had received the kind
of press coverage that every politician loves but almost never gets. I'd
been in politics long enough to realize that popularity of this magnitude wouldn't continue forever. But what I had failed to anticipate
was the vehemence of the hostile reaction to my decision. Some of
Nixon's critics apparently wanted to see him drawn and quartered
publicly. They wanted a body, some broken bones or at least some
blood on the floor, and their mood was mean. I thought people would
consider his resignation from the Presidency as sufficient punishment

and shame. I thought there would be greater forgiveness. It was one of the greatest disappointments of my Presidency that everyone focused on the individual instead of on the problems the nation faced.

I knew when I became President that hard decisions would produce some bitter reactions. Still, I wasn't prepared for the allegations that the Nixon pardon prompted. What I had intended to convince my fellow citizens was necessary surgery—essential if we were to heal our wounded nation—was being attacked as a "secret deal" that I had worked out with Nixon before he had resigned. And the timing of the announcement—eleven o'clock on Sunday morning—was being touted as "proof" of the conspiracy.

Any doubts I might have had about this were dispelled Monday morning. I flew to Pittsburgh, where I was scheduled to speak before eight hundred delegates to a conference on urban transportation. "Jail Ford, jail Ford," some demonstrators shouted, and a workman standing by the airport fence told reporters, "Oh, it was all fixed. He said to Nixon, 'You give me the job, I'll give you the pardon.' " I began to wonder whether, instead of healing the wounds, my decision had only rubbed salt in them.

What made the situation worse was that even some members of my staff failed to understand my motives. Talking to reporters after his resignation, terHorst referred to the pardon as an "act of mercy." Similarly, Phil Buchen, asked by reporters why I hadn't demanded a confession of guilt by Nixon as a condition of the pardon, replied, "You do not put conditions on an act of mercy." Phil's personal reaction was one of compassion, which was fine and good. But compassion for Nixon as an individual hadn't prompted my decision at all. And I have to confess that my televised talk failed to emphasize adequately that I wanted to give my full attention to grave economic and foreign policy matters. Nor did I explain as fully as I should have the strong judicial underpinnings, in particular, the Supreme Court's ruling that acceptance of a pardon means admission of guilt.

Another misunderstanding erupted early in the week when reporters asked Acting Press Secretary Jack Hushen if I was planning to grant a blanket pardon to Nixon's former aides. "I am authorized to say that this entire matter is now under study," he replied. The truth is that I hadn't authorized him to say anything of the sort. I wasn't considering further pardons; I didn't know where he'd got that information. I was very upset, and I tried to shoot the notion down. If people were mad before, Hushen's statement made them angrier still, and on September 11, the Senate, by a vote of 55 to 24, passed a resolution opposing any more Watergate pardons until the defendants had been tried and found guilty and had exhausted all appeals. This struck me as unnecessary, but in view of the confusion that still swirled around the pardon, it was probably inevitable.

By the end of the first week after the pardon, the extent of the political damage it had caused was becoming clear. Of the nearly four thousand letters the White House had received, fewer than seven hundred approved of my decision, and my standing in the Gallup poll plummeted from a favorable rating of 71 percent all the way to 49.

On September 16, I held my second news conference, hoping to explain the pardon rationale more clearly. Of the twenty-two questions asked, fifteen concerned either the pardon or the agreement on Nixon's papers and tapes. And the tone of those questions was suspicious. Had I had a "secret reason" for granting the pardon? Why had I decided "on Sunday morning, abruptly" to announce the decision? Did I believe that the pardon "really served" to bind up the nation's wounds? Was there "some sort of arrangement, a deal" between me and the former President? Then Clark Mollenhoff of the Des Moines *Register and Tribune* asked: "Mr. President, at the last press conference you said, 'The code of ethics that will be followed will be the example that I set.' Do you find any conflicts of interest in the decision to grant a sweeping pardon to your lifelong friend and financial benefactor with no consultation for advice and judgment for the legal fallout?"

I had known and respected Clark for years, but that question seemed a pretty low blow. "Financial benefactor" indeed. Nixon had never contributed so much as a dime to any of my campaigns or to me in any other way, and here was a respected reporter, on nationwide TV, implying that some kind of cash consideration had been involved. I had all I could do to keep my temper under control. Sadly, I recognized after the press conference that I had not yet managed to get the story across and that I would have to find another way.

About a week or ten days after I granted the pardon, Nixon telephoned me. "Jerry," he said, "I know this is causing you great political difficulty and embarrassment, but I also want you to know that I'm appreciative and grateful."

"Mr. President," I replied, "I did it for reasons I've given publicly. I expected an adverse reaction. It's been worse than I thought, but I've done it, and I'm convinced it was the right decision, and I think history will prove my point."

But meanwhile, I had other things to worry about. Overriding almost everything else was the precipitous decline in the faith that Americans traditionally placed in their nation, their institutions and their leaders. In the fall of 1974 they even seemed to have lost faith in themselves. Not long after I became President, the London *Daily Telegraph* commented upon this in an editorial:

> For too long you have been beating your breasts in self-flagellation in the traumas over Watergate and Vietnam. Too many sections of the press and the Congress think there's a dollar to be made out of denigrating their country's institutions and leaders. The United States should know that its European cousins and allies are appalled and disgusted. The self-criticism and self-destructive tendencies are running mad.

In an interview with the Associated Press, I talked about "a self-destruct attitude which we've got to lick." It upset me deeply that people were so down on their country. It tore at my own convictions, because I felt just the opposite. We had gone through hell; we were on our way back up, and I thought there was cause for optimism again. We didn't need newer goals or nobler ones. What we did need was a renewed sense of purpose and a strengthening of our national will to pursue those goals.

There was no magic wand that I could wave to restore people's trust, but there *were* some specific steps I could take to nudge the process along. On September 16, I unveiled our program for the return to society of Vietnam-era draft evaders and deserters. In the same proclamation I announced the establishment of a Presidential Clemency Board which would review the records of the men involved. Draft dodgers, I said, could escape punishment for their offenses if they would agree to three conditions. First, they'd have to present themselves to a United States Attorney before January 31, 1975. They'd have to pledge allegiance to the country and agree to fulfill a two-year period of alternative service. Finally, they'd have to complete that obligation satisfactorily.

Deserters, for their part, could escape punishment once they pledged allegiance to the United States and agreed to spend two years in the branch of the military to which they had once belonged. At the end of this period they would receive a clemency discharge, which would not entitle them to normal VA benefits. The details of this plan, I knew, wouldn't satisfy liberals, who wanted me to give general amnesty. Nor would it please conservatives, who demanded harsher punishment. Still, I thought it was fair, and I was hopeful that the Clemency Board—which I'd asked former Senator Charles Goodell to head—would get off to a quick start in processing the thousands of applications that I expected it to receive.

I also concentrated on eliminating, once and for all, the sort of abuses of power by some at the top that had flourished during the Nixon years. I discovered to my disbelief that both tradition and existing law gave the President access to individual income tax returns. I didn't want to see anyone else's return. I certainly didn't think my staff should have that right, and in an executive order I placed severe restrictions on access to such files. Then, on September 20, in a memo to the heads of all departments and agencies, I talked about the need to keep the civil service—the more than two million government bureaucrats—out of politics. "I call upon you to see to it that the merit principles contained in the Civil Service Act and the personnel laws and regulations are fully and effectively carried out," I said. "Appointments and promotions in the civil service must not be made on the basis of either politics, race, creed or sex."

One of the first decisions I'd made as President was to ban any "bugs" or secret electronic recording devices either in the Oval Office or anywhere else in the building. The idea that anyone on my staff would tape another person without that person's knowledge or consent was unconscionable, and I made sure that everyone knew my feelings about it. Additionally, late in September, I asked senior aides to draft and implement a new code of ethics for the White House staff. We didn't put out a press release about this—we didn't want a lot of fanfare or publicity—but the word got around and caused an improvement in the atmosphere.

On the foreign policy front, one of my chief concerns was the situation in the Middle East. On September 10, Israeli Prime Minister Yitzhak Rabin and his wife arrived in Washington. I had known Rabin when he was Israel's ambassador to the U.S. A dour, very serious man who dressed conservatively and spoke in a soft, almost inaudible voice, he was nonetheless a tough negotiator. But toughness, I was convinced, was not the only ingredient needed to resolve the Middle East impasse. Flexibility—on both sides—was essential as well, and I wasn't sure how flexible Rabin could be. "We have taken risks for peace," he said, but he didn't spell out what those risks had been, and in toasting me at a state dinner on September 12, he indicated that he wasn't going to make concessions readily. Unfortunately, at the end of our two days of talks, we hadn't made much progress toward solving the issues that still divided us, and I asked Kissinger to plan an October trip to the Middle East to see what he could do.

The long-standing conflict in that part of the world was also on the mind of Soviet Foreign Minister Andrei Gromyko when he came to Washington for two days of talks on September 20. Even before I became President, Kissinger had achieved significant success in easing the Soviets out of the Middle East. I thought they didn't want a bona fide settlement there and that their only aim was to promote instability, so I wanted to keep them out. Gromyko, of course, complained about this. The U.S. and the U.S.S.R., he said, were cochairmen of the dormant Geneva Conference on the Middle East. Our two countries should work together in the interests of all parties. But Kissinger and I decided that we could accomplish more unilaterally by working with Israel and each of its Arab neighbors. Whenever Gromyko asked us about our plans, we would be as vague as possible. "We will keep you informed," we'd say. That made him very upset.

I had better luck with Gromyko in discussing bilateral relations. I told him I thought Congress would listen to reason and strike out irksome amendments to the Trade Reform bill and the Export-Import Bank bill. This was reassuring. Then we talked about SALT. Nixon and Kissinger had been to Moscow that summer and had made minimal progress in their talks with Soviet leaders. But now Gromyko hinted that his colleagues might be more "responsive" to the Ford Administration, just might be willing to make the sort of concessions that would enable us to agree on a new arms limitation pact. Kissinger and I decided that after his trip in early October to the Middle East, he would journey to Moscow to probe the Soviets' intent.

Next I turned my attention to reshaping the White House staff. Obviously, the first priority was to find a press secretary to replace terHorst. Although I knew that terHorst's deputies—Paul Miltich, Jack Hushen and Bill Roberts—were hard-working and competent, I didn't feel that any of them was up to so major a responsibility. Then Hartmann heard a rumor that Ron Nessen of NBC-TV might be interested. I asked him to double-check; it was true, and as it turned out, Nessen was the only person to whom I offered the post.

On the afternoon of September 19, Hartmann brought Nessen into the Oval Office. I told him I was surprised that he was interested in the job (which paid $42,500), because it would mean a cut in salary for him. He didn't care about that, Nessen replied. The challenge was what mattered most. He knew the job would be rough, but he thought he could handle it. In order to function effectively, he'd have to have as much information about all matters as quickly as possible. I raised a question: suppose a repeat of the terHorst-Nixon pardon situation occurred. If he knew everything and was asked about a sensitive issue, would that embarrass or compromise him before his former colleagues? No problem, he said. He recognized the potential conflict, but he would trust our judgment. I told him I would give him direct access to all staff members and allow him to sit in on all meetings except my private talks with individuals and the secret sessions of the NSC. As our meeting concluded, Hartmann turned to me: "You'd better tell him, Mr. President, that I have a lot of expertise in the field and that I'm going to be looking over his shoulder a lot."

I didn't think that was any way to welcome Ron to the staff. "Yes, it's true," I said, "Bob's had a lot of experience writing my speeches." There was a brief silence. Hartmann recoiled a bit. I had made the point.

Throughout my political career, nothing upset me more than bickering among members of my staff. It was time-consuming, terribly distracting and unnecessary. I had told my aides that I wouldn't tolerate it. But it continued, even accelerated, when I entered the White House, and—given the ambitions and personalities of the people involved—there didn't seem to be any way to put an immediate stop to it.

Hartmann was the worst offender, and to a degree it was understandable. Because he had been working for me since 1966 and had functioned effectively and loyally as one of my top aides since 1969, he expected to retain his position of primacy. Yet when we moved into the White House, he found that his direct access to me was blocked by Haig. He didn't like the idea of requesting an appointment to see me and Haig didn't want to let him waste my time. Inevitably, they clashed. Accounts of vicious infighting among members of the White House staff began to appear in the press. Hartmann seemed to be a likely source.

"You've got to get this guy under control," Haig told me on more than one occasion during my first month as President. "Otherwise, I can't serve you."

"Al, I want you to stay for at least a while longer," I replied.

I concluded that I'd have to handle Hartmann myself. Hartmann, to be sure, was a person who stirred the pot. He made us all mad at one time or another, but he also kept us from becoming complacent or self-satisfied. And, in his own way, he was extremely valuable. I talked to Hartmann, told him that I didn't want to see any more stories injurious to Haig. But when the squabbling intensified, I began to look at the broader picture. There was no doubt in my mind that Haig was 100 percent loyal to me. Still, he did possess a "Nixon image." Then, too, he was weary of White House intrigue, so we resumed our discussions about other opportunities.

General Creighton Abrams, the Army Chief of Staff, had died on September 4. I considered Haig as Abrams's replacement and he wanted the job, but in order to get it, he'd have to be confirmed by the Senate. Because of his ties to the former President, we thought it possible that the Senators might attempt to reopen the Watergate affair at a time when I was doing everything I could to put Watergate and Nixon behind us. We concluded that the best alternative was for Haig to take the NATO job. If I sent him there, I could bring him back to active duty without having to submit his nomination to the Senate. He agreed to leave the White House staff in late September.

Haig's departure, I knew, would create an enormous vacancy in the top echelon of my staff. Aware that Hartmann did not fit the prescription for the post, I began to consider other candidates. Foremost among them was Don Rumsfeld, a member of my transition team who had returned to his post as our NATO ambassador.

Rummy's father had just died; he had flown back from Brussels to attend the funeral in Illinois, and on September 21 I telephoned him there. He came to Washington the next day, and we talked for an hour and a half in the Oval Office that Sunday afternoon. Initially, Rummy was very reluctant to become my chief of staff. "I'm not the guy to do it, and I don't have any desire to do it," he said. "You'd be much better off with someone who does." One reason was personal. He enjoyed the NATO post. It was not only challenging; he was also able to spend more time with his wife, Joyce, and their children than he ever had in Washington. That was very important to him. The second reason was professional. He didn't think the job could be done the way I wanted it done. "Mr. President," he said, "as I understand it, you're still running this place on the concept of the spokes of the wheel. You're the hub of the wheel; each member of your senior staff is a single spoke, and each is supposed to have equal access to you. In theory, that sounds fine. It projects the openness you want. In practice, however, it won't work. You don't have the time to run the administrative machinery of the White House yourself. I know you don't want a Haldeman-type chief of staff, but someone has to fill that role, and unless I can have that authority, I won't be able to serve you effectively."

I concluded he was right. Everyone wanted a portion of my time, my accessibility was making me fair game for ridiculous requests, and the "spokes of the wheel" structure wasn't working well. Without a strong decision-maker who could help me set my priorities, I'd be hounded to death by gnats and fleas. I wouldn't have time to reflect on basic strategy or the fundamental directions of my Presidency. I told Rummy that I recognized this and that with his help, I could begin to do something about it. He would be performing a real service for the country if he joined my staff. When he still seemed hesitant, I asked Bryce Harlow to talk to him as well. Finally, Rummy agreed and came on board by the end of September. I was relieved and grateful.

One of Rumsfeld's first priorities was to help me streamline the White House staff. When Nixon took office in January 1969, that staff numbered 250. By the time of his departure, it had ballooned to 540. We had to cut it back. Rummy compiled a list of the personnel in a dozen or so departments and proposed a cut of roughly 10 percent. That would bring the staff down to 480 before January 1, 1975. One problem involved cuts of East Wing employees. That was Betty's area—traditionally the First Lady's domain. Rummy would enter the Oval Office, show me a list of people we could trim from her staff and ask me to talk to her about the changes. But that was one of the "perks" of being President. "Oh, no," I'd reply. "I'm not going to do that. You are chief of staff. This is *your* plan. You go up and settle it with her." Predictably, the size of the East Wing staff hardly changed at all.

Toward the end of the Civil War, the Confederates mounted a cavalry charge against Washington. It was more a desperation maneuver than a serious attack. President Lincoln rode out from the White House to watch the skirmish, which took place near what is now Walter Reed Army Hospital. As the six-feet-four-inch Chief Executive surveyed the scene, a young Union Army lieutenant shouted, "Get down, you damn fool." (The next day Lincoln wrote to thank the officer, future Supreme Court Justice Oliver Wendell Holmes.)

Few people, with the possible exception of his wife, will ever tell a President that he is a fool. There's a majesty to the office that inhibits even your closest friends from saying what is really on their minds. They won't tell you that you just made a lousy speech or bungled a chance to get your point across. Instead, they'll say they liked the speech you gave last week a little better or that an even finer opportunity to get your point across will come along very soon. You can tell them you want the blunt truth; you can leave instructions on every bulletin board, but the guarded response you get never varies.

And yet the President—any President—needs to hear straight talk. He needs to be needled once in a while, if only to be brought down from the false pedestal that the office provides. He needs to be told that he is, after all, only another human being with the same virtues and weaknesses as anyone else. And he needs to be reminded of this constantly if he's going to keep his perspective. Of the members of my immediate staff, Marsh, Hartmann and Rumsfeld probably understood that best. But so, too, in a marvelous way did David Kennerly, the official White House photographer. Initially, his brash manner and seeming irreverence for the office I held took me by surprise. Soon I began to depend on and draw strength from it.

Winner of the Pulitzer Prize at the age of twenty-five, for his pictures of the war in Vietnam, Kennerly began covering me for *Time* magazine when I became Vice President. As a group, news photographers are no fashion plates, but even among his peers Kennerly stood out. A thin young man with a balding pate and a reddish-brown beard, he wore tennis shoes with holes in them and the oldest Levi's imaginable. On the few occasions when he donned a sports coat, it looked like a hand-me-down from a garage sale. But his spontaneous humor and refreshing manner commanded my attention.

Returning to the capital aboard the Vice President's aircraft after making a speech somewhere, I would have a drink with members of the press. Inevitably, I'd repeat the story about the phone call Nixon had made asking me to be Vice President and how I'd had to ask him to call me again on the other line. From the back of the plane, Kennerly's voice would boom: "After the twelfth time we've heard that story, we wish the President hadn't called you back." Then one night in September after I became President, I made a speech in Philadelphia on the two hundredth anniversary of the convening of the First Continental Congress. The event would kick off preparations for our national Bicentennial in 1976, so I thought the speech was particularly important. I'd worked hard on it and I'd tried to deliver it well. Aboard *Air Force One* flying back to Washington, I asked aides to rate my performance. Hartmann said it was a plus. So did Marsh. Then I heard Kennerly's unsolicited view: "Too damn long—and dull."

One of the suggestions the transition team had made was that I convene a "kitchen cabinet" whose members would feel free to give me the same sort of blunt advice that a Kennerly could provide. I agreed, and met with this group informally at least once a month. Mel Laird was a member; so were Bryce Harlow and Bill Scranton. And in one sense at least, their concerns meshed with those of my White House staff. Time was running out, they warned; I had to do something to reverse the decline of the economy.

Nothing, in my opinion, was more important than holding the line on federal spending and keeping the budget for fiscal year 1975 at or under $300 billion. Accordingly, I told members of the Cabinet to scrutinize their own departments' budgets once more and recommend possible cuts. No department was sacrosanct. I also asked Congress to reduce projected federal civilian employment by forty thousand over the next fiscal year and to postpone a 5.5 percent pay hike for federal employees from October until next January. Together, those two steps would slice $1 billion from the budget.

Under the Congressional Budget Reform Act of 1974, I could trim federal spending either by asking the Congress to defer specific spending proposals or, by what is called a recision action, asking Congress to withdraw previously mandated spending authority and hoping it would go along within a forty-five-day time limit. Neither procedure was likely to win much support on Capitol Hill. Still, on September 20, I proposed deferrals and recisions totaling more than $20 billion. Then I waited for Congress to respond.

Back on September 5, I had presided at the opening session of the "mini-summit" conference on inflation in Washington. That was the first of eleven such meetings held around the country, which were to culminate on September 27 and 28 with a final "summit" conference on the problem. The mini-summits had gone well, and I was looking forward to addressing the final session. Then on Thursday, September 26, a family crisis intervened.

That afternoon one of Betty's aides, Nancy Howe, was scheduled to go to Bethesda Naval Medical Center for a physical examination. Nancy persuaded Betty to accompany her and get a checkup herself. When he examined her, the Navy doctor discovered a marble-sized lump in her right breast. He called the White House physician, Rear Admiral William Lukash, who examined her and called in a civilian specialist. Shortly after seven o'clock that night, Lukash telephoned to ask if I could stop by his office on the ground floor before I went upstairs to the residence. His request was unusual, so I knew something had to be very wrong. Still, because I hadn't known about Betty's afternoon trip to the hospital, I wasn't prepared for the report I received.

Lukash and a colleague, Dr. William Fouty, told me about the lump and recommended immediate surgery to determine whether or not it was malignant. Betty had said she couldn't go into the hospital right away because we had agreed to participate in ground-breaking ceremonies for the LBJ Memorial Grove on the banks of the Potomac at noon the next day. She had also promised to entertain Lady Bird Johnson and her daughters at a White House tea later that afternoon. I asked if twenty-four hours would make a difference. When both doctors said no, I told them I'd talk to Betty and recommend she enter the hospital early Friday evening, after she'd fulfilled her commitments. I would go with her. During the next twenty-four hours we wouldn't breathe a word about her condition to anyone. The doctors said they would perform the exploratory operation early Saturday morning. If they found that the lump was cancerous, they'd proceed with the full operation and remove the breast.

I took the elevator from the ground floor to the second floor, where Betty was resting in our bedroom. It had been a rough day for her. I kissed her, put my arms around her and said I was sure everything was going to turn out all right. We were lucky she'd had the examination, I said, and now we were luckier still that she was going to receive the very best care. I was deeply concerned and I knew that she was too, but we didn't let ourselves break down; we had to deal with reality. Neither of us is the kind who gets panicky in a crisis. If anything, we try to appear *un*emotional, to straighten up and put on a strong front. But later that evening, when we went to bed, we held hands and prayed.

Early next evening, after completing her schedule, Betty entered the hospital. Our eldest son, Mike, and his wife, Gayle, had come down from Massachusetts, and Susan and I had dinner with Betty in her suite. The doctors were going to operate at eight the next morning. We didn't talk about that. Betty was tense but very strong. She showed no apprehension. As we prepared to leave, I held her for a long moment and then squeezed her hand. She gave me a loving smile and squeezed my hand right back.

That night was the loneliest of my life. Lukash had told Susan, Mike and Gayle, "Make him laugh tonight. Say anything, but make him laugh." They tried. And tried again. They talked about everything under the sun, but it didn't work. The thought that the woman I loved might be taken away from me was almost too much to endure. Before I went to bed, I asked the florist to send three dozen red roses—Betty's favorite—to the hospital.

Saturday, September 28, was a dismal day in Washington. Sheets of rain poured down from a leaden sky. I was in the Oval Office with Bob Hartmann, working on the speech I was scheduled to give early that afternoon at the final session of the summit conference on the economy, when the telephone rang. Lukash was on the line. The lump had been removed, examined and found to be malignant, he said. He was proceeding with the full mastectomy. Until he received the pathologists' report—which would take several days—he wouldn't be able to say whether or not the cancer had spread beyond the lump. He promised to keep me informed. I put down the phone, and tried ineffectually to focus on the speech again. But too many emotions were churning inside me. Excusing myself, I stepped into a small bathroom adjacent to the office and attempted to wrestle those emotions under control. After a minute or so I returned to my desk. Hartmann looked at the expression on my face and understood immediately. "Go ahead and cry," he said. "Do cry." All my tensions and fears poured out in a brief flood of tears.

Lukash hadn't wanted me there for the operation, and I wasn't planning to visit Betty until after the speech; but now that I knew the diagnosis, I simply had to go. Mike and Gayle accompanied me on the short helicopter ride to Bethesda. During the flight, the three of us prayed and read passages from the Bible. Betty was in the recovery room by then. She tried to smile and gave my hand a gentle squeeze, but she was too tired and sedated to talk. I reassured her that with God's help she would have a full recovery.

My speech to the economic summit meeting that afternoon was no spellbinder, but the delegates, who knew Betty was in the hospital, seemed sympathetic to the strain I'd been under, and they gave me a warm round of applause. I thanked them for their contributions toward a solution to our increasingly serious economic problems, promised that I'd try to restrain federal spending and told them I would soon propose a national energy program aimed at assuring adequate domestic supplies while reducing our dependence on foreign sources. Within the next ten days, I added, I would submit specific legislative proposals to the Congress. Then I reminded my audience how Winston Churchill had rallied his embattled countrymen from almost certain defeat by a promise of blood, toil, tears and sweat. "I trust we can avoid blood and tears," I said, "and we will. But I do offer you plenty of toil and plenty of sweat. I will roll up my sleeves and work every bit as hard as you . . . until the job is done."

Gradually over the next week or ten days, Betty's condition improved. I tried to visit her twice a day, and her spirits got better all the time. Her adjustment to the diagnosis and to the mastectomy was superb. She had one brief bout of postoperative depression, but she never lapsed into self-pity. Instead, she decided to be completely candid about what had happened to her. She was warmed by the news that cancer clinics around the country were reporting a significant increase in the number of women who came in for physical examinations. She knew the publicity about her mastectomy was a factor and that it could help save lives. I was enormously proud of her.

That whole period of her absence was difficult for us all. Although I tried to concentrate all my energies on the job of being President, I was feeling pretty low, and I guess it showed. That's when Susan and David Kennerly decided to spring a surprise on me. Soon after we moved into our home in Alexandria, Betty and I had been given a golden retriever named Brown Sugar. She was a gift from Ed Landwehr of Holland, Michigan, a roommate of mine in college and our son Jack's godfather. She was with us for thirteen years before she died in 1968. Then we bought another retriever—also named Sugar—who died just before I became Vice President. So our family didn't have a dog when we moved into the White House. Susan and David thought that situation should be rectified before Betty came home from the hospital.

Without telling me his intention, David did some research and discovered that a fine retriever had recently given birth to a litter in Minneapolis. David called the kennel's owner and said he wanted to buy a puppy for a friend of his.

That was fine, the owner said, but what was the name of David's friend?

David said it was a surprise; he wanted to keep the name secret.

"We don't sell dogs that way," the owner replied. "We have to know if the dog is going to a good home."

"The couple is friendly," David said. "They're middle-aged, and they live in a white house with a big yard and a fence around it. It's a lovely place."

"Do they own or rent?" the owner asked.

David thought for a minute. "I guess you might call it public housing," he said.

The owner said the dog was healthy; she was going to eat a lot. Did his friend have a steady job? David could play the game no longer. He hinted that his friend was a very important person and finally the owner agreed to fly the dog to Washington. I was in the Oval Office the day before Betty came back from the hospital when Susan walked in. "Daddy," she asked, "if we ever get another dog, what kind are we going to get?"

"A female golden retriever about six months old," I said.

At that moment, David entered with a copper-colored pup who raced around the Oval Office yelping excitedly. "Whose dog is that?" I asked.

"It's yours." Susan and David laughed. "Her name was Streaker, but we've changed it to Liberty."

Delighted, I grabbed the pup, put her on my lap, then got down on my hands and knees and played with her on the rug. That was a joyous experience, and I knew that Betty would be just as thrilled as I was to welcome the new addition to our family.

Betty's convalescence went well, and even before her return from the hospital, I was able to devote full attention to the economy again. Almost everyone who had participated in the economic summit conference agreed that inflation was public enemy number one and that our paramount objective was to whip it. One day early in October, Hartmann came into the Oval Office to say that Paul Theis, a member of his staff, had come up with an intriguing suggestion. The best way to implement a voluntary citizens' program to combat inflation, Theis had reasoned, was to have a campaign with a symbol. The name of that campaign should be Whip Inflation Now and the symbol a button marked with the letters WIN. Hartmann thought it was a great idea, and it didn't take him long to convince me. Once you had 213 million Americans recognizing that inflation was a problem and joining in the effort to do something about it, positive results would have to follow. If both the government and the people tightened their belts voluntarily and spent less than they had before, that would reduce demand, and the inflation rate would start going down. Some of my economic advisers were skeptical about the program, but most agreed WIN was worth a try.

On October 8, I addressed a joint session of Congress and identified ten areas where the executive and legislative branches of government could take action together to solve the problem. Recent hikes in the prices of food and petroleum, I pointed out, were key factors in the spiraling inflation rate. If farmers could produce more food, supermarket prices would drop. But farmers couldn't do it all by themselves, so I asked Congress to remove all remaining acreage limitations on cotton, peanuts and rice. Turning to oil imports, I said we were paying $16 billion more for petroleum than we had just a year ago. Currently, our imports stood at six million barrels a day, and I mentioned my goal of reducing that figure by at least one million barrels before the end of 1975.

In almost every industry, costly and restrictive practices—many made mandatory by government—were decreasing productivity while contributing to the rise in prices. I asked Congress to put an end to them. To help create more jobs in the private sector, I proposed a 10 percent investment tax credit. At the same time, I called for the creation of more public service jobs and for an increase in unemployment benefits. I said I wanted to stimulate the housing industry—unemployment in the construction trades was running about double the figure for the economy as a whole—and to do something to help thrift institutions, which were suffering from tightening monetary restrictions and high interest rates. All these programs, I knew, would be costly—as much as $5 billion—so I asked for a one-year temporary tax surcharge of 5 percent on corporations and individuals earning more than $15,000 per year. For a family of four with a gross income of $20,000, the extra tax would amount to $42 per year, and that, I thought, was not too heavy a price to pay.

"Only two of my predecessors have come here in person to call upon Congress for a declaration of war, and I shall not do that," I concluded. "But I say to you that our inflation, our public enemy number one, will, unless whipped, destroy our country, our homes, our liberties, our property and finally our national pride as surely as will any well-armed wartime enemy. I concede there will be no sudden Pearl Harbor to shock us into unity and to sacrifice, but I think we have had enough early warnings. The time to intercept is right now . . . my friends and fellow Americans, will you enlist now?"

The press reaction to that speech, and to one I gave a week later at the annual convention of the Future Farmers of America in Kansas City, Missouri, was frustrating. Even members of my staff dubbed my Kansas City address the "lick-your-plate-clean speech." The *Wall Street Journal* called my proposals "neither surprising nor bold." The New York *Times*, in a series of editorials, was even more critical. "The overall impact of Mr. Ford's speech was weak, flaccid and disappointing. While some of his measures are good and some are questionable, they in no sense add up to a program for an emergency, and it is an emergency that confronts the nation and the world. . . . In his message to Congress, President Ford showed he is deeply reluctant to recommend the uncomfortable for fear it may prove to be unpopular. There is almost certainly a misjudgment of the public mood. . . . Of all the many weaknesses in President Ford's anti-inflation program, the most glaring is the absence of any direct pressure for moderation on the wage-price front, much less any mechanism for enforcing restraint."

The knocks were unfair. The proposals I made were a direct outgrowth of the economic summit conference and represented the consensus of its delegates. To say that I was afraid to "recommend the uncomfortable" was to ignore my call for a *tax increase* less than a month before the November elections, and to complain about the lack of a "mechanism for enforcing restraint" was to overlook the fact that wage and price controls had always failed in the past. Far closer to the mark was the comment of David Broder in the Washington *Post:* "Mr. Ford's mistake was in pitching his speech not to the people but to the Congressional politicians before him whose pettiness and short-sightedness know no bounds. The Congressional response, like the Congressional performance on the economy these past ten months, was a disgrace."

In the weeks that had elapsed since the Nixon pardon, the public outcry had begun to subside. In Congress, however, a number of liberal Democrats wanted to reopen the issue "to see if there was any deal." Soon after I granted the pardon, they filed a number of privileged resolutions in the House asking me to respond to their inquiries. In most instances, what the President does with a privileged resolution is direct it to the Cabinet officer who has jurisdiction over the matter in dispute. The Cabinet officer then reports back on the President's behalf. In the case of the pardon, however, I couldn't delegate authority because I was the only official in the country who had any jurisdiction.

The chairman of the Subcommittee on Criminal Justice of the House Judiciary Committee, Democrat William Hungate of Missouri, wasn't especially interested in pursuing the matter, but Representatives John Conyers, Bella Abzug and Elizabeth Holtzman were pressing him. They requested specific answers to their questions. Someone on the White House staff tried to mollify them by sending up a passel of Presidential statements together with the transcripts of my news conferences. That infuriated them. Next we tried to draft a letter that would answer the questions Conyers, Abzug and Holtzman had raised. One of those questions was: "Did you ever discuss the pardon with any member of the Nixon staff prior to the time you became President?"

Even at that point, the only people who knew what had been discussed during my meeting with Haig on Thursday, August 1, were Hartmann, Marsh and Harlow. Buchen drafted the letter and in response to this question said no. He showed the draft to Marsh. "Look," Marsh said to me, "you can't send the letter up to the Hill this way because the answer is wrong." Then he left the office to find Buchen. "Phil," he said, "there's something I have to tell you," and he proceeded to fill him in on the meeting during which the pardon had been one of the options discussed. Phil was shaken by that.

"You know," I said finally, "I'll bet you that the best thing for me to do is just go up to Capitol Hill, testify and spell it all out."

Buchen opposed the idea. Except for Marsh and Hartmann, so did others on my staff, who felt that such an appearance would be dangerous and ill-advised. The lack of a precedent was their chief concern. To the best of their knowledge, not since the days of George Washington had a Chief Executive gone up to testify before Congress. (There were unsubstantiated reports that Lincoln had done so informally in order to deny reports that his wife was a Confederate spy.) I should "stonewall" the committee requests, they said. No one could force me to testify.

Marsh prepared a memorandum of facts and showed it to key officials of the Congress. Republican Whip Les Arends said I shouldn't come. So did Lew Deschler, the parliamentarian of the House. Senate Majority Leader Mansfield was cautious. "I think it would be a good thing for him to do," he said, "but I hope he won't make a habit of it." Then Marsh discussed the situation with Speaker Albert. "There's nothing more important to this country than the success of Jerry Ford as President," Albert observed. "He has a reputation for honesty, and he ought to lay it all out. Some of the things that might have to be disclosed might hurt, but they're not going to hurt that much, and what's to be gained is so much greater."

I decided Albert was right. I had nothing whatsoever to hide, and a personal appearance would be far better than a letter from which committee members could quote excerpts out of context. If I didn't testify, the controversy would continue; all kind of bizarre inferences could be drawn. The only way to eliminate, once and for all, the lingering suspicion that there had been a deal was to let the committee question me. It was an enormous gamble, but one I had to take.

During the first two weeks of October, we worked almost every day on preparing my testimony. Then, on October 15, Leon Jaworski gave a newspaper interview which deflected some of the hostile questions I expected to receive. Having just stepped down as Special Prosecutor, he announced that he approved of the pardon: "It's a mistake to believe there would have been more evidence [about Watergate] for the public if Nixon had been tried," he said. "If he had been pardoned after indictment, the public would have no new information. If he had gone to trial, we wouldn't have learned any new details."

Two days later, on October 17, I rode up to Capitol Hill and stepped into Room 2141 of the Rayburn House Office Building. That was the same room in which I'd appeared during my confirmation hearings nearly a year before, and I felt comfortable there because at that time I had persuaded a substantial majority of the committee that my record was clean and that I was qualified to be Vice President. I was confident of responding fully to whatever questions committee members asked, though I was, of course, aware of how delicate and difficult the situation was.

Taking my seat, I told committee members: "[The] purpose [of the pardon] was to change our national focus. I wanted to do all I could to shift our attentions from the pursuit of a fallen President to the pursuit of the urgent needs of a rising nation."° I mentioned my meeting with Haig, but stressed that, according to him, the pardon had been only one of the several options that had been considered by people in the White House at the time, and I had neither said nor done a thing to imply that I was even favorable to that idea or any other. Then I waited for the questions to begin.

The committee's members were polite, thanking me for my decision to appear before them personally and expressing the hope that my testimony that morning would clear up any doubts about the pardon that still remained. The only exception was Representative Holtzman, a cynical and highly partisan Democrat from Brooklyn, New York. Soon it became obvious that nothing I could say would ever satisfy her. After expressing her "dismay" that "the format of this hearing will not be able to provide to the American people the full truth" about the pardon and after commenting that her questions stemmed from "very dark suspicions that have been created in the public's mind," she said everyone wondered whether or not there was a deal.

°"Pardon of Richard M. Nixon and Related Matters, Hearings before the Subcommittee on Criminal Justice of the Committee on the Judiciary, House of Representatives, 93rd Congress, Second Session, September 24th, October 1st and 17th, 1974." Serial No. 60.

"There was no deal, period, under no circumstances," I managed to interject.

Obviously, she didn't believe me, for she proceeded to confront me with nine accusatory questions in a row and didn't even extend me the courtesy of pausing long enough for me to answer her. Other committee members—even her fellow Democrats—bridled at her rudeness. At the end of the two-hour session, I was convinced that my appearance had accomplished its objective. "I hope that I have at least cleared the air," I said, "so that most Americans will understand what was done and why it was done. And again I trust that all of us can get back to the job of trying to solve our problems both at home and abroad."

In the area of foreign policy, several of those problems in fact appeared to be diminishing. One of the most troublesome was the Congressional reaction to the simmering dispute between Greece and Turkey over the future of Cyprus. Ignoring the objections of their own leadership, both the House and the Senate had amended the Continuing Appropriations Resolution—which provided funds to run departments and agencies as well as money for foreign aid—by tacking on a provision calling for an immediate cessation of military assistance to Turkey. Because I was convinced that such a cutoff would, in the long run, damage Greece, preclude the possibility of a Cyprus settlement and undermine NATO's eastern flank, I vetoed the measure on October 14. The House sustained my veto. The next day, Congress passed a similar resolution. I vetoed it again. Finally, on October 17, Congress suggested a compromise. It required a cutoff of military aid to the Turks but permitted me to delay the ban until December 10. Despite Kissinger's objections, I agreed to sign the bill. If it wasn't a victory, it was at least a respite, and I was hopeful that between October 18 and December 10, Congress would come to its senses and reverse its foolish ban on aid to a valued ally.

Although Kissinger's week-long trip to seven nations in the Middle East hadn't resulted in any spectacular breakthroughs, it had kept the momentum going in the search for peace and lessened the likelihood that the parties involved would resort to war. Late in October he took off again—this time for Moscow—to pick up the discussions he'd had with Gromyko in September in Washington.

The Soviets, I suspected, would adhere to their hard line on a new SALT agreement. The Jackson amendment to the Trade Reform bill, which was cosponsored in the House by Ohio Democrat Charles Vanik, was still pending in Congress. That irritated them; so did Adlai Stevenson's proposed amendment to the Export-Import Bank bill. Equally upsetting to them, and to American farmers as well, was a temporary embargo I'd placed on the overseas shipments of millions of tons of wheat and corn. (Such shipments, I decided early in October, coming at a time when the Department of Agriculture was forecasting a 12 to 15 percent drop in U.S. production of corn, would wreak havoc with our economy and push the inflation rate even higher.) So I was pleasantly surprised when Kissinger discerned a new moderation in the Soviet stand on SALT. I had already accepted invitations to visit Japan and South Korea at the end of November. If the Soviets were willing to meet us halfway on SALT, I could extend that trip and discuss with Brezhnev the issues that still divided us. Kissinger said he would see what could be arranged, and on October 26 it was announced that I would travel to the Siberian port city of Vladivostok on November 23.

But first we had to get through the fall election campaign. Republicans held only 42 seats in the Senate and 187 in the House. GOP governors held sway in the capitols of only eighteen states. Watergate, the Nixon resignation and my pardon of the former President all combined with the deteriorating economy to make our chances of scoring any gains remote. The only thing we could do was fight a holding action and try to cut our losses as much as possible. During the last three weeks of October I visited fifteen states—some of them more than once—and spoke on behalf of scores of Republicans. I wasn't as strident as some of my former colleagues in the House wanted me to be, but I feared an overdose of partisanship might disrupt the healing process which was still continuing. As the campaign neared its end, I traveled to Grand Rapids and appeared at a rally at Calvin College. When I entered the field house, the band struck up the "Michigan Fight Song." Then there was a pause. The master of ceremonies asked the band to play another number, a tune befitting the honored guest. As I walked on stage, the band obliged with "Nobody Knows the Trouble I've Seen."

Late in October, Richard Nixon's health took a turn for the worse. The phlebitis in his left leg created blood clots that threatened his life, and doctors decided to operate. After the operation he went into shock, and doctors said his condition was critical. On October 31, I flew to Los Angeles to speak at a dinner for Republican candidates at the Century Plaza Hotel. My staff debated whether or not I ought to visit Nixon at the Long Beach Hospital, only half an hour away. If I made the trip, it would remind everyone of Watergate and the pardon. If I didn't, people would say I lacked compassion. I ended their debate as soon as I found out that it had begun. Of course I would go. Before dinner that evening, I telephoned Pat and asked how her husband was doing. "I don't want to push it," I said, "but would it help if I came down there?"

"Oh, there's nothing he'd like more," she replied.

Next morning, November 1, we helicoptered to the Long Beach airport, then drove to the hospital, where I talked to Nixon's physician, Dr. John Lungren. The former President, Lungren said, was a very sick man. I could see him, but I had to be very quiet, and I couldn't say anything that might upset him.

The hospital had just opened a new wing, and Nixon was the only patient there. I took the elevator to the seventh floor, where Pat, Julie and Tricia greeted me effusively. Then, with Lungren, I stepped toward Nixon's room. An attendant tried to open the door. He couldn't. Incredibly, the lock was jammed. It wouldn't respond to our frantic efforts and we had to wait five minutes while someone fetched an expert. I shuddered to think what might have happened had Nixon suddenly needed medical attention.

When I stepped into the room and saw Nixon's condition, I was even more shocked than I had been by the delay in opening that door. He was stretched out flat on his back. There were tubes in his nose and mouth, and wires led from his arms, chest and legs to machines with orange lights that blinked on and off. His face was ashen, and I thought I had never seen anyone closer to death. He opened his eyes and said, "Hi, Jerry," in a barely audible voice. We talked about generalities and the fall campaign. I told him the party had a good chance on election day. I wanted to tell him more, but I realized how difficult it was for him to respond to me. He couldn't keep his eyes

open, and his voice was as soft as a whisper. "My own situation . . ." he said very slowly. "I'm not feeling too well, but I'm going
to make it." I reached over and took his hand. Then, as I prepared to
leave, he said, "Mr. President, this has meant a lot to me. I'm deeply
grateful."

When I left the room, I held Pat Nixon's hand and told her that she
and her husband had the nation's prayers. She was profoundly grateful. I had never thought of her as a particularly outgoing person, but
there was no mistaking the glow of love in her expression nor the
warmth of her words. Privately, I wondered if I'd ever see Nixon
alive again. I thought his chances of surviving were less than fifty-fif-
ty, and I knew that I had done the right thing. If he died and I had
passed up the chance to visit him, I wouldn't have been able to for-
give myself.

For Republicans, the results of the November 5 election were disastrous. We lost forty seats in the House and four in the Senate. The
Democrats may not have achieved their stated goal of a "veto-proof
Congress," but they had come very close, and my hands were going
to be full when the Ninety-fourth Congress convened in January. But
even more upsetting than the party's defeat was the still-plummeting
economy. During the last three weeks, while politicians everywhere
had concentrated on their campaigns, the economic indicators had
accelerated their downhill plunge.

An economist, someone once remarked to me, is a person who tells
you that there is definitely not going to be a hurricane. Then, shortly
thereafter, he volunteers to repair and rebuild your roof. In the fall of
1974, that definition seemed apt. Conventional economic theory held
that when you had high inflation, unemployment was low. That may
have been true in the past, but it wasn't true any longer. Inflation still
was running at a double-digit pace; unemployment figures were
worsening rapidly, and the gross national product—a measure of the
total output of goods and services—was declining precipitously. At
the economic summit meeting in Washington six weeks earlier, not
one of the assembled experts warned me that unemployment would
become an even more serious problem than inflation in just sixty days
time. (The only people who even hinted at that possibility were the
labor leaders, and this was a standard refrain from them.) Yet the

trend was unmistakable. The August unemployment rate was 5.4 percent, which meant that nearly six million Americans were out of work. In September the figure jumped to 5.8 percent. In October it rose again, to 6 percent, and it looked as if it would exceed 7 percent before long. (Ironically, one of the reasons for this was the tremendous influx of new people into the labor market. More workers were seeking jobs than ever before in American history.)

But statistics didn't suffice to tell the story of hardship and deprivation. Expecting a good year in 1975, businesses all across America had loaded up with inventory. Then something seemed to snap. Because of soaring inflation, confidence began to evaporate. Instead of ordering new supplies, businesses decided to get rid of the goods in their inventories first. The automobile industry was particularly hard hit. Along with everyone else, it had anticipated a good 1975 model year. Then, abruptly, Ford, Chrysler and General Motors began closing plants, readjusting production schedules and laying off tens of thousands of employees. On November 5, GM Chairman Dick Gerstenberg came to see me in the Oval Office. I agreed with him that the news was grim, but I expressed the opinion that the situation had bottomed out and that the economy would improve soon. "No, Mr. President," he said. "The worst is still to come."

For the past several weeks my economic advisers—Greenspan, Simon and Seidman—had expressed the view that we might in fact be heading into a recession. Inflation, they pointed out, was fueling this recession. It was pushing people into higher tax brackets, but it wasn't letting them catch up in real wages. Because they had less spendable income, they couldn't purchase the goods and services that manufacturers wanted to sell. Faced with dwindling sales, those manufacturers had to begin laying off employees. The nub of the problem, they said, was figuring out some way to combat this recession without adding to the inflationary pressures that already beset the economy.

While I had recognized that the economy was in trouble, I thought its illness temporary. I didn't think it would be wise for me as President to stand up and say, "Yes, we're in a recession." But after talking with Gerstenberg and meeting with my economic advisers again, I decided that it would be irresponsible to ignore the developing re-

ality. On November 12, at my instructions, Nessen told reporters:
"When the statistics come in for November and are analyzed, it will
probably appear that this month we are moving into a recession."
What we couldn't know then was that it would be the worst recession
to hit the country in more than forty years.

Admitting the truth is one thing. Coming up with plans to deal
with it is another. What we had to do was reverse completely the economic strategy developed from the economic summit meeting and
adopted during the first three months of my Presidency. The reason
was obvious. Traditional economic theory says the way to beat inflation is to reduce demand by restraining federal spending. The way to
throttle back unemployment is to stimulate demand by increasing
government expenditures. Instead of asking Congress for a tax increase, as I had on October 8, I would have to plead for a tax cut. The
WIN portion of the program would also have to be scrapped. I didn't
mind abandoning the symbol, which was probably too gimmicky.
But the rationale to reduce both private and public spending to attack inflation was a proper approach in the fall of 1974. Two months
later, however, new, unforeseen economic conditions had developed,
and our previous policies were not the right medicine for them.

The easiest solution to the unemployment problem would be for
the federal government to go on a massive spending spree. Which
was precisely what the New York *Times*, influential labor leaders
and some liberal Democrats on Capitol Hill wanted us to do. This
would result in short-term benefits—a dramatic reduction in the unemployment rate, for example—but Greenspan convinced me that it
would cause a catastrophe further down the road that would make
the present recession look like a brush fire. The budget I inherited
from Nixon anticipated a deficit of $9.4 billion. Because of the reces-
sion-caused drop in federal revenues and the need to increase unemployment compensation payments—which were mandated by law—
I realized that my efforts to keep the budget at or under $300 billion
would fail. The deficit would climb to $25 billion or $30 billion. A
new federal spending spree would send it soaring even higher than
that. Massive federal borrowing would push up interest rates and
tighten the money supply in the private sector, making it harder for
consumers and businesses to borrow the money needed to survive.

And this would create a much broader inflation, with severe consequences for employment and social stability. At some point, Greenspan said, both the President and the Congress would have to realize that we needed to pull in our belts now in order to enjoy a better life in the future. That point, he insisted, was already at hand. I realized then, as never before, that in the months ahead I'd be spending a lot of time on the economy.

The Presidency is "but a splendid misery," Thomas Jefferson once wrote. William Howard Taft called the White House "the loneliest place in the world," and Warren G. Harding termed it "a prison." I didn't feel that way at all. People were always asking me, "Aren't the burdens so heavy that you can't get any sleep?" Or, "Doesn't the job give you ulcers?" Or, "Isn't the pressure enough to cloud your mind?" I would reply, "Absolutely not." I never felt better physically. I never had a clearer mind. I never enjoyed an experience more. The truth is that I couldn't wait to start the day.

One of the reasons I liked the White House so much was the superior caliber of the permanent staff—the ushers, stewards, cooks, cleaners, maids and marvelous telephone operators who stay on from one administration to another. (We wanted a genuine family atmosphere in the residence. So from the very beginning, Betty made a point of saying "Hello" or "Goodbye" or, more often, "Thank you" to the White House personnel. She was warm and friendly, and she was puzzled by the fact that they didn't respond to her overtures. Then she discovered that during the Nixon years they had been instructed never to reply to such remarks when the President or the First Lady spoke to them. We changed that and, almost overnight, the atmosphere turned cheerful again.) A second reason was the sense of history that enveloped the place. The Oval Office is large, comfortable and inspiring. I knew there were many far-reaching things that I as President could do, but I never sat in the chair behind my desk and said, "I'm a powerful man. I can press a button or pull a switch and such and such will happen." Instead, I thought of the Presidents who had been there before me and of the decisions they had had to make. I tried to relate those to the ones confronting me. Occasionally, at night, I'd step into the Lincoln Cabinet Room on the second floor. Lincoln used to hold his Cabinet meetings there, and history permeates the room. I would sit alone and gaze at the paintings and photographs of another time, and I could almost hear the voices of 110 years before. When I left that room, I always felt revived.

As a place to live, the White House was far more pleasant than I had ever expected it to be. The "creature comforts" were all there. And then there were the extra "perks." I'd had a government limousine since 1965, when I became Minority Leader of the House, so I was used to being chauffeured around. What I hadn't expected were the little touches that so often brightened my day. The crew of *Air Force One* quickly discovered that I love strawberries. So when I flew somewhere, they usually had a bowl for me. They knew that I like to smoke a pipe, and they made sure the tobacco tin was always full. And best of all, the White House gave me the opportunity to spend more time with Betty and the family than I had ever had as a Congressman. We all took pleasure in that.

What Betty really enjoyed was the chance to plan dinners for visiting heads of state. She selected the food and entertainment and went over the guest lists very carefully. Thirty-odd years before, she had been a professional dancer with the Martha Graham troupe, and she wanted to make sure that people in the arts and humanities knew that they were welcome in the White House once again. During the first three months of my Presidency, we had several state dinners, and our guests included Jordan's King Hussein, Poland's Communist Party Chief Edward Gierek and Italy's President Giovanni Leone. The dinner I recall most vividly, however, was in honor of Austrian Chancellor Bruno Kreisky.

I had made it a point to invite Supreme Court Justice Douglas as one of our honored guests. He went through the receiving line in a wheelchair. He was gaunt. His limbs were frail and thin, but his eyes still burned with a bright intensity. Even in his poor health and at his advanced age, he was a handsome man. I welcomed him and told him how delighted I was to have him there. We had had differences in the past, but I wanted to stress that bygones were bygones.

Our featured entertainer that mid-November night was singer

Vicki Carr. She is of Mexican descent, and when I congratulated her on her performance, she offered to invite me to her home in Los Angeles for dinner sometime soon. "What Mexican dish do you like?" she asked me. I looked at her and cracked, "I like *you*." Betty overheard the exchange, and needless to say, she wasn't wild about it.

Traditionally, Washington reporters give a new President a grace period of about a hundred days to set forth and explain his policies before they start zeroing in on him. By the end of my first hundred days on November 16, I felt that I had made some progress in healing the nation's wounds, cooling the passions of the times and letting the American people know that we were going to approach things in a sensible, pragmatic way. To be sure, the jury was still out on my performance as President. The pardon had upset a lot of people. We still had horrendous economic problems, and I hadn't yet succeeded in persuading the Congress either to confirm Nelson Rockefeller as Vice President or to hold the line on federal spending. Still, I thought the American people had faith that I was working at the job, that my Administration was turning things around and that we were moving forward openly and constructively.

Commenting in the New York *Times* upon my first hundred days, James Reston observed: "Not since Ike have we had a more decent man in the White House or anyone so open and relaxed. But by his candor, he gives the impression that we are not living in a revolutionary age, and don't have to make fundamental changes in the lives of our families and nations, but that we must merely be patient and sensible, and all will be well in the end. It is a lovely dream, and he is an honest and refreshing man, but Washington wonders."

Reston didn't quite understand that we had to consolidate and pull things together before we could begin to make those "fundamental changes" he was talking about, but still, I thought his column was fair. What struck the mark even more was the analysis the *Wall Street Journal* provided. "Beyond a repeated commitment to economy in government," the *Journal* observed, my Administration had yet to develop a central theme except the one suggested by a member of my staff: "It seems there was this immigrant taking his citizenship examination before a judge. The judge was calling out famous names, and the immigrant was trying to identify their places in American history. 'Abraham Lincoln,' said the judge.

" 'President of the United States,' said the immigrant.

" 'But what did Lincoln do?' the judge persisted, waiting, of course, for 'He freed the slaves' or 'He preserved the Union.'

" 'He do the best he can,' the immigrant replied."

That, I thought, was no small accomplishment, and if the immigrant in the story had wanted to say the same thing about my first hundred days, I wouldn't have minded at all.

4

Problems Multiply

"Being a President is like riding a tiger. A man has to keep on riding or be swallowed."

— Harry S Truman

Nearly a year before his resignation as President, Richard Nixon had accepted an invitation to visit Japan. The date had not been set, Watergate had occupied increasing amounts of the President's time, and he had never made the trip. I felt—and Henry Kissinger agreed—that it was important to keep our commitment to the Japanese. Shortly after I became President, I notified the Japanese ambassador that the third week of November would be a convenient time for me to go.

The timing couldn't have been worse. Congress hadn't yet confirmed Nelson Rockefeller as Vice President. Inflation and unemployment were worsening, and there was a new threat of war in the Middle East. "Jerry, stay home," one newspaper implored. Still, I thought the trip was important. I would be the first President ever to set foot on Japanese soil, and it was about time. The Japanese had been shocked by Nixon's failure to inform them of his overtures to the People's Republic of China in 1971 and 1972. They had been equally upset by his subsequent devaluation of the dollar, and for some months afterward their attitude toward the U.S. had been tinged by suspicion and doubt. But all that was in the past, and even though the Japanese leg of the trip was more ceremonial than substantive—I would deal with weightier matters when I continued on to South Korea and Vladivostok—I looked forward to a visit that would symbolize the special relationship that existed between our two countries.

On the afternoon of November 18, after a flight that included some of the worst air turbulence I'd ever encountered, *Air Force One* touched down at Tokyo's Haneda International Airport. Helicopters whisked us to the Akasaka Palace, an elegant guesthouse near the Imperial Palace in downtown Tokyo. Even though we'd been warned that my arrival might spark violence, there was hardly a demonstrator in sight. I was due to meet Emperor Hirohito the next morning, and precisely at 9:30 A.M., he appeared in the courtyard of the palace. A shy, frail, white-haired man, he seemed delighted to welcome me to his country. We stood at attention as bands played the United States and Japanese national anthems. At the conclusion of the ceremony, I met with Prime Minister Kakuei Tanaka. A burly, aggressive man whose nickname was "Tiger," Tanaka never let diplomatic niceties stand in the way of blunt speech. Although our relations were formal and correct, he was not the kind of man to whom I could warm up easily. Even before our arrival, Japanese newspapers had carried reports that he was involved in questionable financial activities. Kissinger and I had concluded that Tanaka probably would have to resign soon, but in our discussions with him the matter never came up. The subjects we had to talk about included U.S. assurances to sell its agricultural commodities, the pooling of energy resources, the strategies both countries were using to combat recession, plus how the Japanese could contribute to the economic stability of South Vietnam.

Both of us agreed on the need to reconvene the GATT—General Agreement on Tariffs and Trade—talks in Geneva as soon as possible and to bring them to a successful conclusion by 1976. Then Tanaka brought up the touchy issue of exports. He was concerned that Congress or the Executive Branch might impose new quotas upon a variety of Japanese goods. He seemed very relieved when I assured him that I had always been a proponent of free trade and that I wasn't about to alter these convictions despite obvious political pressures to which I would be subjected during a period of high unemployment at home.

That evening, Emperor Hirohito and Empress Nagako hosted a state dinner at the Imperial Palace. The Emperor is head of state in name only; he does not discuss politics or substantive issues, and I had been told that it would be difficult to carry on an extended conversation with him. But we got along fine. A noted marine biologist, the Emperor had just completed his fourth book on the subject. He enjoyed talking about it, and I think he appreciated the fact that I'd done some homework in the area myself. When I hosted a return dinner the next evening, the subject was baseball and I discovered that he was an avid student of the game. To further strengthen the ties between our nations, I invited the Emperor and the Empress to visit the U.S. in 1976.

The next day, I flew to the ancient capital of Kyoto for a full round of sightseeing. I visited the old Imperial Palace of Flowers, the Nijo Castle—which had served as a residence for the Shogun rulers—and a Buddhist pagoda called the Golden Pavilion. Then I set out to enjoy a Japanese dinner at the Tsuruya Restaurant.

Whenever a President travels abroad, aides try to make sure that he is aware of local customs and is prepared for all eventualities. Attached to my daily schedule that November 22 was the following advice:

7:10 P.M. Dinner begins.

You will be served on a very low chair or cushion at floor level with a small back. It is customary to cross your legs, and you may stretch your legs out and change your position frequently if you desire. Chopsticks will be used exclusively during the dinner, and it is customary when you have a piece of meat or fish to eat, rather than cut it, you lift the entire piece and take a small bite, returning the remainder to your plate. Chopsticks should never be left in the plate or bowl but returned to the resting block in front of your service.

There will be Geisha girls at the meal who will come in and out and at times sit next to you in the serving of the meal. It is appropriate for you to talk to them. They will dance at the conclusion of the meal. This is a ten-course dinner served in traditional Japanese style.

Custom provides that no one should ever pour his own cup of sake.
To do so is a sign of sadness. You may, however, pour someone else's
cup, which is a sign of friendship. Whenever a Geisha girl or another
guest fills your cup, you should lift the cup while it is being filled and
take a sip before putting the cup back on the table. Whenever the
cup is empty, it will be refilled, so it is advisable not to "bottom up"
on each occasion.

Everything went according to plan. The meal—which featured
such delicacies as dried fish soup, seaweed and skewered sparrow—
was delicious, the company convivial. I even became fairly adept in
handling the chopsticks in my left hand. I was enjoying myself thoroughly. Suddenly, without warning, photographers appeared. Wait
until Betty sees the pictures of me sitting with those Geisha girls, I
thought.

Next morning we flew to the South Korean capital of Seoul. President Park Chung Hee met me at the airport and, later that day, after
lunch with troops of the U.S. Army's Second Infantry Division at
Camp Casey near the DMZ, I had a two-hour meeting with Park at
the Blue House. A trim, poker-faced man who doesn't mince words,
Park got down to business right away. There were 38,000 well-led,
highly motivated American troops in South Korea at the time. He
wanted a commitment that we keep our forces there and increase our
military aid, including more modern weapons. In 1972, after we had
withdrawn 20,000 troops from the country, we had promised to mod-
ernize the South Korean forces, at a cost of $1.5 billion, over a five-
year period. Because of technical problems and some Congressional
foot dragging, we were nearly a year behind in keeping that commitment, and Park wanted to know what he could expect.

Our troops would stay where they were, I assured him. Assuming
Congress approved, the military aid we had promised would be delivered as soon as possible, and there would be no future slowdowns
in the modernization program. Kissinger, Scowcroft, Assistant Secretary of State Philip Habib and U.S. Ambassador Richard L. Sneider
were sitting in on my talks with Park. As our meeting drew to a close,
I asked them to leave so I could chat with Park alone about the sensitive issue of human rights. While enjoying our support since 1972,
Park had disbanded the National Assembly, set aside the South Kore-

an constitution and adopted one-man rule. A former presidential candidate was under house arrest; the press had been gagged; church and student leaders had been jailed for criticizing Park's dictatorship. Congressional support, I said, would erode very quickly unless he took a more reasonable approach toward his opponents.

He understood that, he said, but he couldn't tolerate certain things the dissidents were doing. Widespread domestic unrest would undermine his ability to withstand a military attack by North Korea and prevent his own economy from growing at its programmed pace. In 1953, his country had been ravaged by war. Its economic progress since then had been remarkable, and he was not going to let those accomplishments go down the drain just to satisfy his political opponents. I told him I understood his problems, but urged him once again to be more lenient. Although he didn't commit himself to any specifics, I was led to believe that he would modify some of his more repressive policies.

The third stop on my Far Eastern tour was the Siberian port city of Vladivostok. Brezhnev, accompanied by Foreign Minister Andrei Gromyko, had come by train from Moscow—four thousand miles across seven time zones—to meet me at the airport on the morning of November 23, and from the moment we met, we got along well. "I understand you are quite an expert on soccer," I said as we shook hands for the first time.

"Yes, I play the left side," Brezhnev replied, "but I haven't played in a long time."

"I haven't played football for a long time, either," I told him. "I wasn't very fast, but I could hold the line."

The bantering continued as we boarded a train that would take us to the site of our conference, the small resort town of Okeanskaya. Looking out the dining car window at the snow-covered terrain, I mentioned the difficulty we had clearing snow from the streets of Washington and how snarled the traffic became when the weather turned sour. Brezhnev's bushy eyebrows arched, and he leaned forward across the table that separated us. "Well, that will be our first deal," he said. "We'll send you Soviet snowplows."

Gromyko, normally a dour man, joined in. "Yes, snowplows," he said, "at a good low price."

The train ride took an hour and a half, and as our talks continued, I had a fine opportunity not only to size up Brezhnev as a world leader but also to observe a special penchant of Henry Kissinger's. Soviet stewards had piled cookies, pastries and mints on the table in the dining car, and Henry simply couldn't resist them. At first he would check to see if anyone was looking before he reached out to pluck a morsel from the plate. Then, aware that everyone knew what he was doing—the Soviets thought his antics were hilarious—he no longer tried to conceal his addiction. In that ninety-minute period he must have finished off three plates.

The site of the talks was the Okeanskaya Sanatorium, a health spa used by vacationing personnel from local military bases. Although the Soviets had labored for ten days to spruce up the place and apply a fresh coat of paint to the main building, it still looked like an abandoned YMCA camp in the Catskills. The spartan surroundings didn't bother Brezhnev at all. He was still in an ebullient mood as he escorted us to our dacha. "Why did you have to bring Henry Kissinger here?" he asked with mock solemnity.

"Well, it's just very hard to go anywhere without him," I answered.

Brezhnev pretended a scowl. "Kissinger is such a scoundrel," he said.

But Henry was ready for that. "It takes one to know one," he replied.

Soon the joking stopped. We had come to this remote Siberian site hoping to reach an agreement that would put a cap on the arms race and further the chances for a lasting peace. Our two countries had first reached an agreement on strategic arms limitations in May 1972. That accord put a freeze on the numbers of land- and sea-based ballistic missiles on each side, both those in existence and those under construction. The Soviets could deploy 2,360 and the United States 1,710. There was no limitation on the number of heavy bombers each side could keep ready for combat. Nor was there a limitation on the number of missiles each side could equip with multiple warheads (MIRVs). And this is where the pact worked to our advantage. Even though the Soviets had built and were thereby permitted more missiles, we already had a far larger number of long-range bombers which compensated for the disparity. Additionally, we had MIRVed almost half our missiles. The Soviets were far behind us technologically and hadn't deployed any MIRVs of their own. On the other hand, the Soviet missiles had bigger warheads and greater megatonnage. (In the 1960s, U.S. military strategists had opted for smaller warheads, less megatonnage, for greater accuracy.)

That first SALT agreement would expire in October 1977. Long before that date, both sides endeavored to reach a permanent—and more encompassing—accord. Hoping to achieve such an agreement, Nixon had flown to Moscow in June. But his efforts to bring MIRVs into the new agreement had failed. The United States then decided to work for a more comprehensive approach and a longer time period—ten years rather than five. When he met with me in Washington, Gromyko suggested that a summit meeting could resolve our differences. Initially, my reaction was cool. I saw no reason to travel halfway around the world just to hear a restatement of known Soviet views. The Soviets responded by pushing harder and hinting that they would make new concessions. Kissinger returned from Moscow in October convinced that the Soviets were sincere in their desire to reach a new accord. Even before I arrived at Okeanskaya, we had agreed on the general framework of a SALT II pact. We still had to button down two things: the numbers of launchers and MIRVs permitted each side, and whether to specify equal numbers of these for each country or allow a differential—with the Soviets to have more launchers and the United States more MIRVs. Defense Secretary Schlesinger and the Joint Chiefs of Staff urged me to hold out for numerical equivalency of ballistic missiles. They didn't think the Soviets would ever agree and said that I'd probably have to accept a compromise. Kissinger didn't want that. "Hang tough," he said in effect, "and they'll come around."

Before my meeting with Brezhnev, Kissinger and I had talked at length about the Soviet leader's personality and negotiating techniques. Brezhnev, Henry said, would dominate the Soviet side of the discussions, but on technical points he would confer with his advisers. Invariably, Henry continued, he would lead off with an angry, blustery diatribe accusing the U.S. of sabotaging the chances for lasting peace. He would, for example, blame us for not working with the Soviets in the Middle East. But this would be primarily for home consumption. It would give him a chance to score points with the Soviet hierarchy. It would also be his way of testing my resolve. He would be curious to see if I would bend or fight back. And so, Henry maintained, we should not retreat from our position. We should be polite but firm. If they really wanted an agreement, they would be the ones to bend.

Which is precisely what transpired. No sooner had Brezhnev and I made our opening statements in the austere conference hall at Okeanskaya than we began to focus on the specific force levels that each side could have. After initially proposing different numbers—with the Soviets pushing for higher figures—we compromised at 2,400 ballistic missiles for each country. That meant they would have to reduce their launchers by about 300. Next we agreed that each side be allowed 1,320 MIRVs. We maintained our position from previous negotiations that our Forward Base System of F-4s, F-111s and FB-111s as well as the nuclear weapons we had deployed in Western Europe not be counted in our agreed-upon total of strategic weapons. Brezhnev frowned behind his wire-rimmed glasses. Chain-smoking, sipping from a glass of mineral water, he suggested a pause while he conferred with his aides. Minutes later, he returned to the conference table. Agreed, he said. That meant we had prevailed.

Now Brezhnev wanted something in return. We should stop production of the Trident submarine and cancel our plans to build the B-1 bomber. Our national security, I replied, demanded that we push forward with both. We simply couldn't rely on our aging B-52s.

Then we turned to questions of a more general nature. I assured Brezhnev that although we had economic difficulties at home, he should not assume that the U.S. was weak and getting weaker all the time. Brezhnev countered that some members of his Politburo didn't believe détente was a good idea. If he made too many concessions in his attempt to reach an accord, he would lose their support and be in trouble at home. I said I understood his predicament. Then, displaying a surprising grasp of the way our political system worked, he began talking about Congress. The Soviets had learned during Nixon's years in office that the future of their relations with the United States didn't depend solely on the decisions of the American President.

Congress was a force to be reckoned with, and Brezhnev wasn't happy about that. Congress, he said, had fouled up the progress we thought we were going to make with the expansion of trade. And now it was insisting that it had the right to pass judgment on Soviet emigration policies. "You just had elections in your country," he said. "What kind of a Congress will you be dealing with for the next two years?"

"Mr. General Secretary," I replied, "I can only say that my fingers are crossed."

Initially, we had planned to meet at six o'clock, talk for two hours, break for dinner and then resume the next morning. But we had made so much progress that both of us decided to cancel dinner and just keep going. We did take three short breaks to relax, walk outside in the snow and talk privately with our aides—without the possibility of our conversations being bugged.

During one of these breaks, Brezhnev walked up and gave me a wood portrait of myself. It was a marvelous work, although it didn't look much like me; the artist had worked from a picture in some Russian magazine. Kennerly, Hartmann and Scowcroft were standing with a group of English-speaking Russians when I stepped outside. I held the portrait up while Kennerly began reeling off his photographs. The Russians crowded in, and I said, "Isn't this nice? Just look at it. I think it's a great likeness." Kennerly paused from his picture-taking and said, "Hey now, would you look at that? They gave you a picture of Frank Sinatra." That was one time I didn't appreciate his wise-guy humor.

We didn't wind up our talks until after midnight, and I was famished. The Soviet chefs assigned to our quarters were preparing a late snack, and as I waited for the food to arrive, I remembered that back home in the U.S., Michigan was scheduled to play Ohio State. I told Bob Barrett, my military aide, to wake me at six o'clock with the score of the football game.

Precisely at six, Barrett entered my room. "Mr. President, time to wake up," he said.

"How did the game turn out? What was the score?"

"Twelve to ten," Barrett replied, and turned to leave the room.

"Wait a minute. Who had the twelve, and who had the ten?"

"I was afraid you'd ask me that." From the look on his face, I knew Michigan had lost. "Yeah," Barrett continued, "the same poor kid who missed the field goal last year missed another one seconds before the end of the game."

I knew how heartbroken that Michigan player must have been, and I found myself wishing that I were somewhere where I could easily pick up a telephone and try to brighten his day.

Shortly after ten o'clock, I returned to the conference hall for our second session. This meeting was devoted to the situation in the Middle East and the progress that both sides hoped to make in reducing our military forces in Europe. Although our discussions were candid, there were no breakthroughs. But our meeting the night before had far exceeded my expectations, and I was euphoric. As soon as technicians had ironed out the few remaining problems, we would sign a SALT II accord.

Brezhnev shared my enthusiasm. Impulsively, after a late lunch, he invited me to accompany him on a tour of Vladivostok. We climbed into the back seat of a long black limousine and headed toward the city, thirteen miles away. The local commissar, a large, dark-complexioned man wearing a thick wool coat, sat in the jump seat in front of Brezhnev, and the interpreter, Victor Sukhodrev, sat in front of me. Our conversation was natural and uninhibited. How many people lived in Vladivostok? What was the main industry? And was it always this cold? Twenty minutes later, we drove down a steep hill, entered the city and swung around the main square. A small crowd was there, and even though it was dusk, they recognized the car and applauded. The city itself reminded me of San Francisco, and I wished that I'd had more time to explore the place. But it was starting to get dark and we headed back toward Okeanskaya.

And that's when the strangest thing happened. Brezhnev reached over and grabbed my left hand with his right hand. He began by telling me how much his people had suffered during World War II. "I do not want to inflict that upon my people again," he said.

"Mr. General Secretary, I believe we made very significant progress," I said. "I hope the momentum of our meeting will continue and that next year we can finalize what we have accomplished here."

His grip on my hand tightened, and he turned to look me in the eye. "We have accomplished something very significant, and it's our responsibility, yours and mine, on behalf of our countries, to achieve the finalization of the document."

"I am optimistic that we can," I said. "We have made so much headway. This is a big step forward to prevent a nuclear holocaust."

"I agree with you," he said. "This is an opportunity to protect not only the people of our two countries but, really, all mankind. We have to do something."

I don't remember what else was said. I do remember that he held on to my hand until the car pulled up in front of my dacha at Okeanskaya.

On our departure, a train took us back to the airport. *Air Force One* was waiting and Brezhnev walked with me to the ramp. On the first leg of our trip, we had stopped to refuel in Anchorage, Alaska. A local furrier and personal friend, Jack Kim, had presented me with a heavy Alaskan wolf coat. A warm and comfortable garment, it had served me well in Siberia. I saw Brezhnev eyeing it enviously. So just before I mounted the steps, I took off the coat and gave it to him. He put it on, and he seemed truly overwhelmed. We waved goodbye, and taxied down the runway. In another few hours we would be home. The American people would be delighted to hear that my meeting with Brezhnev had gone so well, and Congress, with some exceptions, would probably endorse the new accord. But what, I wondered, would I tell my old friend Jack Kim about his Alaskan wolf coat?

Vladivostok had been an appropriate ending to a journey designed to strengthen ties with old friends and expand areas of agreement with potential adversaries. The results of the trip had exceeded my expectations. There was, of course, no way for me to know at the time that this would be a high-water mark and that the next five and a half months would be the most difficult of my Presidency—if not my life. It was a period during which Murphy's Law prevailed. Everything that could go wrong did go wrong, and on almost every front the nation took quite a battering.

The recession was deepening. Back on October 8, I had submitted to Congress a detailed program to deal with the problems of inflation. Lawmakers had sat on their hands, and most of my proposals were still pending. What upset me even more was the refusal of Congress to heed my calls to hold the budget for fiscal year 1975 below $305 billion.

Shortly after I became President, I had asked Congress to defer for three months a scheduled federal pay increase. Congress flatly refused, a decision that would cost taxpayers $700 million. Equally discouraging was the passage by Congress—over my veto—of the Railroad Retirement Act. That would cost $285 million in 1974 and $7 billion over the next twenty-five years. Then there was a bill to increase and liberalize veterans' education and training benefits. I had always felt that veterans' benefits should be improved, and I had asked for an increase of 18 percent. But Congress upped the ante to 23 percent and overrode my veto.

The economic crisis kept worsening. The gross national product (GNP) had declined for three consecutive quarters and wasn't likely to improve in the fourth quarter of the year. As Alan Greenspan, the chairman of the Council of Economic Advisers, warned me in a memo on November 26: "It is difficult to envision an economy that would be strong enough in the second half of 1975 to reduce the rate of unemployment."

On several occasions during that final week in November, I met with Greenspan and my budget advisers to discuss potential spending cuts. If the Executive Branch could set an example of fiscal restraint by trimming its own proposals, the Congress might be persuaded to follow suit. Our reductions totaled $4.6 billion, and I urged the Congress to accept them. I wasn't optimistic. Unemployment compensation payments were mandated by law, and the experts told me that payment totals would run $12 billion to $15 billion higher than we had anticipated. The figures—and their implications—were frightening.

Other heads of state of the Western democracies faced problems very similar to mine. Canada's Pierre Elliott Trudeau, for example, visited me in Washington on December 4, and when he described his country's economic plight, it sounded grimmer than our own. The next visitor was West German Chancellor Helmut Schmidt, who arrived for two days of talks on December 5. A blue-eyed, solidly built, handsome man, he spoke perfect English and enjoyed smoking a pipe. Schmidt projected natural self-confidence and personal warmth. As a former minister of both finance and defense in the West German government, he had a firm grasp of the complexities of international economic policy, yet he made his points without displaying the slightest hint of arrogance. Confronted by recessionary pressures themselves, the Germans had instituted an economic plan that coupled a tax reduction with moderate spending increases by the government. At the same time, we had decided to fight inflation by first increasing taxes and cutting back on spending. Naturally, Schmidt was concerned about the apparent contradiction in our two approaches. In October, in fact, he had expressed fears that we might adopt too strong an anti-inflation policy, which could touch off a world depression. But by the time of his arrival in Washington, we had changed our game plan, allaying his concerns.

Schmidt's policies, I discovered, were now close to mine. Both of us understood the necessity of controlling inflation. Politically, we couldn't tolerate high unemployment, yet we recognized that if we accelerated our economies precipitously to reduce the jobless rate, we would just rekindle the fires of inflation. We might get by for a year or two, but catastrophe would be inevitable down the road. The unemployment rate would spurt up again, and we would have to confront a serious depression. The course both countries were following now wasn't glamorous, but it was the only path to real recovery.

After a state dinner on the evening of December 5, I invited Schmidt to come upstairs to the residence, and we talked until 2 A.M.—not just matters of state, but our personal beliefs, hopes and disappointments. This underscores a point often overlooked in discussions of foreign policy—the importance of personality. Relations between the U.S. and West Germany were excellent throughout my Administration, primarily because Schmidt and I got along so well. As we became better acquainted, we called each other by our first names, we joked with each other, and saw eye to eye on almost everything.

To a degree that at first surprised and then delighted me, the same was true of my relations with French President Valéry Giscard d'Estaing. Photographs showed him to be a tall, balding, elegantly attired man with sharp eyes, a prominent nose and an aristocratic bearing, and he had a reputation for aloofness. There didn't appear to be much that we had in common. But Kissinger kept stressing how very important it was that we attempt to improve our relations with the French, so on December 14 I flew to meet Giscard for two days of talks on the French West Indian island of Martinique.

Although he had been in office only since May 1974, Giscard was also a former finance minister, and he was as well versed as Schmidt in discussing what had to be done to further economic recovery. And any fears I might have had that he would be aloof vanished the moment we met. We liked each other immediately and, as the New York *Times* expressed it, got along "swimmingly." (On the second day of our talks, Giscard, Kissinger, French Foreign Minister Jean Sauvagnargues and I helicoptered to a mountain resort overlooking the ocean and went swimming in the pool. Undoubtedly, that short dip contributed to the informality. I have to admit, seeing Henry in blue bathing trunks was a novel experience.)

Substantively, Giscard and I had a lot to talk about: energy, the recovery of the Western economies, détente, the prospects for a new SALT accord and, finally, the amount of money the French would agree to pay to compensate us for having moved our bases out of France—at de Gaulle's insistence—in 1967.

Some weeks earlier, the OPEC states had suggested a dialogue with the world's oil-consuming nations in order to stabilize the price of oil and to work out a system for recycling funds. Giscard favored the idea and urged us to attend the conference that he had recently proposed. I saw no problem, provided there were preliminary meetings of consumer nations to develop a common approach. The French had a hang-up about belonging to international organizations. For some time we had been trying to persuade them to join the fledgling International Energy Agency. I told Giscard we would abandon our efforts to bring France into the IEA. He responded by promising that France would work with us in seeking alternative sources of energy. He agreed on the plan to create a $25 billion emergency fund in the framework of the Organization for Economic Cooperation and Development (OECD). Like an insurance policy, this was a financial safety net designed to protect a member nation's currency against a sudden, and potentially disastrous, draw on it.

After discussing the strengths and weaknesses of our nations' economies, we focused on détente. Giscard had met Brezhnev, and he seemed convinced that the Soviet leader wanted only to consolidate good relations between East and West before retiring. Brezhnev wanted to go down in the history books as a peacemaker, Giscard said, so now was the time to move toward a new SALT accord because the Soviets would be more flexible. And Brezhnev's health really was poor, Giscard told me. He had heard rumors about an East German oral surgeon flying to Moscow to examine the Soviet leader. Apparently, Brezhnev suffered recurring infections in his lower jaw which antibiotics couldn't cure.

Finally, Giscard proposed that the French pay $100 million to settle the long dispute over the forced relocation of U.S. bases. Initially, we had wanted a payment four times the amount the French were offering. But Bill Simon and I agreed that any settlement, after so many years of deadlock, was more important for the future course of our bilateral relations than the sum involved. We told the French they had a deal.

Back in Washington, I was burned up over Congress's failure to move quickly on my nomination of Nelson Rockefeller as Vice President. Both the Senate Rules Committee and the House Judiciary Committee insisted on dragging their feet. I was not comfortable with the thought that House Speaker Carl Albert would become President automatically should something happen to me, nor was Carl happy to have that possibility hanging over his head. What upset me even more was the arrogant and at times insulting way that both Congressional committees had treated Rockefeller.

In the nearly four months since I had nominated him, he had responded fully to every question of the Senate Rules Committee, the House Judiciary Committee, the FBI, the General Accounting Office, the IRS and the Joint Committee on Internal Revenue Taxation. He had supplied his personal income tax returns for the past seven years and gift tax returns for the past seventeen years. He had made

public all his assets and trusts, his gifts and loans to his family and his
friends, his donations to charitable, educational or other tax-exempt
organizations and the political contributions he and his wife had
made since 1957. And still his critics wanted more—the last pound of
flesh.

That was reprehensible. And when I heard that some Congressional leaders were talking about not confirming Rockefeller until the
new Congress convened in January, I was furious. I telephoned Albert and Mansfield and said, "You just can't do that to the country.
You can't do it to Nelson Rockefeller, and you can't do it to me. It's
in the national interest that you confirm Rockefeller, and I'm asking
you to move as soon as possible." Finally, the Congressional leadership took the initiative. The Senate approved the nomination on December 10. On December 19, just one day before the Congress adjourned, the House followed suit. That evening, Betty and I
accompanied Nelson and Happy Rockefeller to the Senate chamber
where Nelson was sworn in as the forty-first Vice President of the
United States. It was good to have him on the team.

But why the long delay—approaching four months—in his confirmation? Partisan politics, I suppose, was the basic reason. The Democrats didn't want the new Vice President to be confirmed before the
November elections. They feared that, once in office, he would be
stumping the hustings for Republican candidates. Undoubtedly, that
is what he would have done. Still, I thought that the Democrats had
behaved irresponsibly. Partisan politics had taken precedence over
the national interest.

Another concern of mine in the waning days of 1974 was the status
of the trade bill. The House had already passed the bill, and on December 13 the Senate did too. Although I thought the bill—the most
significant trade legislation in the last forty years—would strengthen
our economy and further our hopes for peace, I was concerned by its
inclusion of language that could only be viewed as objectionable and
discriminatory by other nations, primarily the Jackson-Vanik
Amendment, which linked our granting of most-favored-nation status to the Soviets to a relaxation of their emigration policies. The
amendment had passed the Senate 88 to 0. On December 19, the day

that House-Senate conferees reached agreement on the bill, the Soviets reacted predictably. They issued a formal statement denying that they had ever given us specific assurances that they would ease their emigration policies in return for U.S. concessions on trade. Ominously, Gromyko said the Soviet Union expected a decrease—rather than an increase—in the number of Jewish citizens permitted to leave the country in 1975.

But that still didn't give pause to our lawmakers. On December 20, both houses of Congress approved the conference report and sent the bill to the White House. Although I knew that its enactment would damage the good relations my Administration had achieved with the Soviets, I decided reluctantly to sign the measure into law. A veto would have been overridden by an overwhelming majority. I could only hope that when members of Congress saw the damage they had done to the cause of furthering the emigration of Soviet Jews, they would change their minds in the next session and vote to soften or delete the amendment from the bill. But I wasn't going to hold my breath. As James Reston pointed out in the New York *Times*: "In the aftermath of Vietnam and Watergate, the Congress is reasserting itself in many positive ways, but it still has not found the line between effective and destructive intervention. It can and should influence the objectives and instruments of foreign policy, but when it intervenes in negotiations, it invariably gets into trouble." In this instance, Congressional intervention was counterproductive. Jewish emigration from the U.S.S.R. dropped precipitously, and the Soviets canceled their 1972 trade agreement with us. They also reneged on their promise to settle a World War II lend-lease debt. In a world of 150 nations and fast-moving change, diplomacy is a continuing process. It must not be frozen in a statute.

On December 22, Betty, Susan and I flew to Vail for what I hoped would be a Christmas vacation with plenty of time to enjoy the slopes. The weather and snow, as it turned out, were almost ideal. But even though I was far from Washington, the pressures of the Presidency were never far behind. In just a few days' time, I knew, I would have to make final decisions on the budget for fiscal year 1976. I would have to submit to Congress new proposals to deal with the economy and the energy crisis. So almost every day, after skiing for an hour or two, I huddled with my advisers. Gradually, our programs took shape. They would need refinement, of course, but I could worry about that after my return to the capital. Meanwhile, I had important decisions to make about four pieces of legislation that the Congress had passed in its final days.

The first bill that came to my desk was the Foreign Assistance Act of 1974. Although it reduced economic and military aid to both South Vietnam and Cambodia to levels that endangered their ability to survive as free nations, it did contain a clause that enabled us—temporarily, at least—to continue arms shipments to the Turks. Despite reservations about some provisions, I decided to sign the bill. Next I pocket-vetoed—by simply withholding my approval—two measures that would have had serious inflationary impacts on the economy. The first of these, the Surface Mining Control and Reclamation Act of 1974, would have reduced our domestic production of coal by a minimum of 48 million tons per year and would have meant the loss of thousands of jobs in the coal fields. I had to balance these losses against the gains of "protecting the environment." With our economy faltering, jobs were crucial. Since coal was the most abundant energy source this country had, I thought the environmental price tag was too high.

I had slightly different objections to the Energy Transportation Security Act of 1974, otherwise known as the "cargo preference" bill. It stipulated that 20 percent of all the foreign oil coming into the U.S. had to be carried on U.S. flag tankers. The figure would rise to 30 percent in 1977. Not only would that bill have increased the cost of oil and gas to the American consumer; it also would have hiked the prices of all products and services that depend on oil. Additionally, it would have served as a precedent for other countries to increase protection of their industries, and that would have posed a threat to free trade. But there was powerful support for the measure, including that of Senator Russell Long, the Senate Finance Committee chairman. Organized labor was also pressuring me, especially Paul Hall, the president of the Seafarers International Union of North America. He was a long-time personal friend and the Seafarers had supported me politically. But every department of the government urged me to veto the bill and their arguments were irrefutable. I knew that my decision would come as a blow to Hall and when I telephoned him from Vail, our conversation was strained. He was terribly disappointed, but took the news like a gentleman. I was learning that one of my most unpleasant responsibilities as President was telling friends that I couldn't agree with them, that the national interest was paramount.

Finally, as my last official function of 1974, I signed the Emergency Jobs and Unemployment Assistance Act and the Emergency Unemployment Compensation Act. Together, they provided 100,000 new public sector jobs and extended by an additional thirteen weeks the period that the jobless could continue to receive financial help from the government. Although the cost was high—an estimated $2.75 billion—the legislation I approved had been scaled down significantly from what Congress had originally proposed, and I was satisfied with the compromise.

During the first two weeks of January I concentrated on the decisions I'd have to make on the budget for fiscal year 1976. The Joint Economic Committee of the Congress had just reported that the budget deficit for fiscal year 1975 would be $22.8 billion and that for fiscal year 1976 it would soar to $36.4 billion. There could now be no doubt. The economy was worsening. The latest statistics painted a grim picture. Automobile plants were closing all over the country, causing massive layoffs. The gross national product had declined in the fourth quarter of 1974 by an ominous 8 percent. Now it appeared that the budget deficit for fiscal year 1975 might climb as high as $35 billion, a peacetime record. The unemployment rate in December had risen above 7 percent. Some experts were saying it would top 8 percent soon. That would mean that more than seven million Americans were out of work, the largest number since the Depression.

Until the middle of December, the recession had followed a pattern that economists had noted before. They had assured me that the slide would be V-shaped, with a rapid and sharp recovery. But their crystal ball had been cloudy. I began to fear that the recession might resemble the letter L. If that was true, we wouldn't be able to forecast when the recovery might begin. The public shared my growing concern. According to the results of a Harris poll released in January, 86 percent of the respondents expressed no confidence in my ability to turn the economy around. I felt pretty low about that.

Nor was I cheered by the way the country was facing up to an energy crisis that was growing more acute every day. Until 1950, the U.S. had been self-sufficient in energy. Then demand exceeded our domestic supply of crude oil, and the situation started to deteriorate. In 1952, President Eisenhower appointed a commission to assess the nation's future energy needs. Unless action was taken to stimulate the domestic production of energy, that commission concluded, we would face severe shortages within twenty years. The warning went unheeded. Even after the Arab oil embargo of 1973, Congress refused to believe that a crisis was at hand. The lawmakers failed to see the need for a comprehensive energy policy, and the results of their neglect were painfully obvious to me not long after I became President. Domestic production of coal was below the levels of the 1940s. Oil production had been declining every year since 1970. (Foreign oil—most of it imported from the Middle East—accounted for 37 percent of domestic petroleum consumption. The cost of that foreign oil, only $3 billion in 1970, had skyrocketed past $25 billion by 1974 and was expected to top $30 billion soon. That outflow of our national wealth was not just in dollars; it was also in jobs.) Natural gas production was starting to decline. Nuclear power programs were plagued by technical problems, government-caused delays and legal challenges. Finally, the growth of our domestic energy demand, while slowed by the recession, was sure to resume its rapid rate of increase by 1976.

There seemed to be only three broad options available to meet this serious threat to our economic stability. The first was to increase our domestic supply of energy. The second was to conserve and manage energy demand. The third was to establish standby emergency programs similar to the gas rationing that we adopted during World War II. It would be difficult to persuade Congress to move on any of these fronts. Further complicating the issue was a problem of personnel. When I became President, the head of the Federal Energy Administration was John Sawhill, a wiry young Ph.D. A likable and very talented man, Sawhill believed that one of the "obvious" solutions to the energy problem was an increase in the gasoline excise tax of about twenty cents per gallon, and he said so repeatedly. When reporters asked me if I agreed with him, I replied that I thought it was the wrong approach. Not only was the idea impractical—Congress would never pass such a tax—it was also inequitable, because it would place the full burden of conservation on the purchasers of gasoline. So it was not Administration policy, I said; it was not going to be included in the energy package that I was going to recommend.

But even after I made this clear, Sawhill kept advocating an increase in the gasoline tax. Reluctantly, because I liked him personally, I called him into the Oval Office and said that if he found it impossible to support the position that the Administration was going to take, then he might be happier in another job. He agreed to leave. To replace him at the FEA, I nominated Frank Zarb. An investment banker from New York, he was Associate Director of OMB for Science, Energy and Natural Resources. His aggressive, no-nonsense approach gained him respect on Capitol Hill; he won confirmation quickly.

While I was wrestling with the twin problems of the economy and energy, a new crisis suddenly arose. According to an article by Seymour Hersh in the New York *Times*, the CIA had, over a long period of years, exceeded its statutory authority by listening in on the telephone conversations of U.S. citizens, breaking into their homes and offices, keeping them under surveillance and committing other illegal activities. CIA Director Bill Colby had warned me that Hersh was working on the story. He predicted that its publication would be embarrassing; but at the same time, he assured me that while the agency might have broken the law in the past, it had long since abandoned such practices. As firmly as I could, I told him that I simply wouldn't tolerate any violations of the law in my Administration. The agency's charter clearly prohibited operations within U.S. borders, and I expected that charter to be upheld.

But the problem didn't die away. Sniffing a potential Watergate, reporters bore down hard on the story, and there was pressure in Congress to establish committees to investigate the agency's misdeeds. On January 3, I met with Colby in the Oval Office and learned—for the first time—about what agency executives referred to as the "family jewels." These were highly classified documents that provided details about unsavory and illegal CIA practices. In the 1950s and 1960s, the CIA had plotted to assassinate foreign leaders, including Fidel Castro. Although none of these assassinations had been carried out, the fact that government officials had even considered them was distressing.

In the aftermath of Watergate, it was important that we be totally aboveboard about these past abuses and avoid giving any substance to charges that we were engaging in a "cover-up." At the same time, I realized that unnecessary disclosures could cripple the agency's effectiveness, lower its morale and make foreign governments extremely wary about sharing vital information with us. Such unnecessary disclosures would almost certainly result if I let Congress dominate the investigation. I decided to take the initiative. On January 4, I announced that I was establishing a blue-ribbon Commission on CIA Activities within the United States to look into the allegations, determine the extent to which the agency had exceeded its authority and make recommendations to prevent such abuses in the future. "It is essential," I declared, "that we meet our security requirements and at the same time avoid impairing our democratic institutions and fundamental freedoms. Intelligence activities must be conducted consistently with both objectives."

Who should head the commission? Kissinger, Rumsfeld, Scowcroft and I struggled over this before concluding that the best candidate was Nelson Rockefeller. There was no question he was qualified. I told him I saw the investigation as part of the healing process that I had begun in August. The sores of discontent would break out again if we didn't treat them quickly. He promised to find out what he could and give me a full report within six months.

Now I turned my attention once again to the speeches I was scheduled to give on the economy and the energy crisis. The first, on January 13, was to be an informal address to the American people. The second, two days later, was the annual State of the Union speech. By January 10, I had pretty well decided to recommend a $16 billion tax cut. (Twelve billion dollars would go to individuals as a rebate of up to $1,000 per person for their 1974 tax payments, and the remaining $4 billion would reward industries that decided to expand and thus create more jobs.) That would counter the recession by increasing the amount of money consumers had to spend. Secondly, I would urge the imposition of higher taxes on both imported and domestic oil and natural gas to encourage the conservation of fuel. The levies would reduce our projected oil imports by about one million barrels a day by the end of 1975 and two million barrels a day by the end of 1977. The revenues from these new taxes would flow back into the economy in the form of additional tax cuts and credits and payments to the poor. Next I was going to propose a one-year moratorium on all new federal spending programs with the exception of crucial defense and energy producing measures. I would veto everything else. I would recommend a limit of 5 percent on federal pay increases in 1975, and I would propose that the same ceiling apply to automatic cost-of-living increases that are tacked onto social security payments as well as government and military retirement checks. Finally, I would encourage Congress to offer new incentives to spur the production of more domestic coal and oil and speed the development of both nuclear and solar energy.

I was well aware that this five-point plan contained risks. My proposed tax cut, for example, would raise the budget deficit so high that instead of restoring the public's confidence in the economy, it might frighten people out of their wits. That deficit could spur a new round of inflation. Government borrowing to finance the deficit might drive up interest rates and worsen the recession. And the increased taxes on energy could boost inflation by hiking the cost of oil and could deflate the economy by leaving industry with less money to spend in other areas.

But I would have to accept these risks. I knew much depended on the way I delivered those two speeches. If I came across as a Chief Executive fully in command of the situation, I could win the support I needed to push my programs through the Congress. If, on the other hand, the public viewed me as weak and indecisive, I would decline in their esteem to a point from which I could not hope to recover, and the legislation that the country needed wouldn't stand a chance of passage.

My advisers had suggested that I deliver the January 13 speech from the Lincoln Library, on the ground floor of the White House. The room was small and fairly cluttered, but the setting was informal. At nine o'clock on that Monday night, the little red light on the TV camera flashed on, and I looked directly into the lens. "Without wasting words," I began, "I want to talk to you tonight about putting our domestic house in order. We must turn America in a new direction. We must reverse the current recession, reduce unemployment and create new jobs. We must restore the confidence of consumers and investors alike. We must continue an effective plan to curb inflation. We must, without any delay, take firm control of our progress as a free people.

"Together we can and will do the job. Our national character is strong on self-discipline and the will to win. Americans are at their very best when the going is rough. Right now the going *is* rough, and it may get rougher. But if we do what must be done, we will be on our way to better days."

For the next fifteen minutes, I explained my programs in some detail. "We know what must be done," I concluded. "The time to act is now. We have our nation to preserve and our future to protect. Let us act together."

Even before I finished the speech, I knew that I'd done well. Reporters seemed to agree. "Mr. Ford now has his second wind and his second chance," said CBS-TV commentator Eric Sevareid. "He is seizing a chance with the vigor and decisiveness he has not shown before. He is in motion at last."

Now all that remained was the State of the Union address. Twenty-six years before, as a freshman Congressman, I had stood in the rear of the House chamber and listened to President Truman report that "the state of the Union is good." I told Hartmann I wanted to say just the opposite. The state of the Union was *not* good, and any attempt to gloss over the problems all of us faced would have destroyed my credibility. Additionally, I told Bob to insert a line saying that I didn't expect much, if any, applause. Ever since Roosevelt, I knew, American Presidents had responded to economic challenges by trying to come up with crash programs that carried short-term benefits. My programs were designed to foster a long-term recovery even at the cost of short-term suffering. Such proposals aren't likely to elicit cheers.

Hartmann's draft arrived on my desk after dinner on the night of January 14. It was short on specifics and long on rhetoric; worse, it didn't have a clear and central theme. Unbeknownst to me, Rumsfeld and some of my other aides had tried to produce a draft of their own. Those two drafts converged in my office at nine o'clock that evening, and I was scheduled to make my address at one o'clock the next afternoon. "Go back and give me *one* speech, not two speeches," I said. Unfortunately, the two factions couldn't seem to agree. Hartmann was insisting that section X or paragraph Y had to be in the final version just as he had written it, and Rumsfeld was equally adamant about his contributions. As a result, I had to be the editor, and I didn't approve the final version until nearly 4 A.M. It was a long, disagreeable night and a waste of my time, but it did teach me a lesson. In the future, I told Hartmann, important speeches had to be submitted to me well in advance of the scheduled delivery date. I simply couldn't tolerate any more performances like that.

Yet with less than three hours' sleep, I didn't do so badly. I elaborated on the economic proposals I had made two days earlier. Then I turned to other pressing concerns. "If our foreign policy is to be successful," I said, "we cannot rigidly restrict in legislation the ability of the President to act. The conduct of negotiations is ill suited to such limitations. Legislative restrictions, intended for the best motives and purposes, can have the opposite result, as we have seen most recently in our trade relations with the Soviet Union.

"America needs a new direction," I concluded, "a change of course which will put the unemployed back to work, increase real income and production, restrain the growth of federal government spending, achieve energy independence and advance the cause of world understanding. We have the ability. We have the know-how. In partnership with the American people, we will achieve these objectives."

Reaction to the speech was mixed. A Gallup poll gave my proposals a "no" vote by a margin of five to four. The *Wall Street Journal* said the speech had been one of my "most effective to date." The Congress, however, was negative. Massachusetts Democrat James A. Burke, chairman of the House Social Security Subcommittee, declared that he wouldn't even hold hearings on my request to limit benefit hikes to 5 percent a year. House Ways and Means Committee Chairman Al Ullman said that he opposed a cut in the corporate tax rate and that my proposal was not worth talking about. Maine's

Democratic Senator Ed Muskie said that he didn't like my energy ideas. Their reactions frustrated me. What I had proposed were reasonable recommendations for the improvement of our economy and the solution of our energy problem. What they were engaging in was partisan politics.

January was the deadline that Rumsfeld and I had set for the changes we wanted to make on the White House staff and in the Cabinet. Most of the people involved resigned voluntarily. Actually, the Nixon-appointed men and women who left the West Wing to return to private life were, with a few exceptions, people of high quality and personal integrity who had had nothing to do with Watergate. Counselors Anne Armstrong and Dean Burch were typical. Dean would be one of my representatives in the 1976 election debate negotiations and I appointed Anne as our ambassador to the United Kingdom. So were legislative liaison man Bill Timmons, counsel Len Garment and the executive director of the Domestic Council, Kenneth R. Cole, Jr. I was sorry to see them go because I knew they would be hard to replace.

Some, in fact, we never did replace, in line with my desire to trim the White House staff. But others had performed functions that had to be continued. When I asked Nelson Rockefeller to be Vice President, I told him that he would be given major responsibility for the formulation of domestic policy, and I intended to keep that promise. Understandably, Nelson wanted James M. Cannon III, a long-time aide, to be executive director of the Domestic Council. He also wanted to organize the council as an autonomous unit that reported directly to him. Rumsfeld opposed that. He didn't feel that there was enough time in the day for Rockefeller to do all the things that he had signed on to do. The Vice President, Don pointed out, had to preside over the Senate. He had the CIA investigation to worry about, meetings of the Cabinet and the NSC to attend and trips abroad as my personal representative. He wouldn't have time to come to the morning staff meetings where the day-to-day decisions on domestic policy were made. Similarly, Rumsfeld argued that it would be a serious mistake to allow the council to operate as an autonomous unit outside the organization that he had set up and that he controlled. Rumsfeld bore no animosity toward Rockefeller or

Cannon personally. He simply opposed what they wanted to do organizationally. Unfortunately, the end result was that tension developed between Nelson and Don.

I could see both sides of the argument. Nelson felt that he knew more about domestic policy and politics than Don, and he was probably right. On the other hand, Don was the man responsible for organizing and managing the West Wing. To do so effectively, he had to have control. Finally, after three or four unhappy meetings, I made the decision to go along with Nelson. The paper would have to flow through Don as chief of staff, but Nelson would be in charge of domestic policy. To his credit, Don didn't complain. I'm sure he was disappointed, but the only comment he made was: "Fine, we'll try to make it work."

Making changes in the Cabinet presented problems of a different sort. Normally, a President has little difficulty finding qualified people to head key departments and agencies. But this was not a normal situation, and two factors complicated my search. The first was time. My Administration had just twenty-four months left, and unless I was elected in 1976, I could offer job security only until January 20, 1977. Second was the fact that morale in some departments still hadn't bounced back after the trauma of Watergate. Despite my efforts to restore confidence in the Presidency, the press and Congress still viewed top officials of the government with a suspicious eye. The people I might want to nominate for important Cabinet posts would surely ask themselves: "Why should I go to Washington and let Congress kick me around, embarrass me publicly and then send me off bleeding from a job that I can only hold for two years?"

And nowhere did Watergate leave more lasting scars than at the Department of Justice. In less than three years, it had had three Attorneys General—Richard Kleindienst, Elliot Richardson and William Saxbe—and what it needed most now was a firm and continuing presence at the top. Initially, I didn't plan to replace Saxbe, and he didn't tell me that he wanted to leave. Then I heard indirectly that he wanted to climax his career as our ambassador to India. Our man in New Delhi at the time was Daniel Patrick Moynihan, and as luck would have it, he wanted to return to his teaching post at Harvard. I called Saxbe into the Oval Office. "Bill, I'm not asking you to resign," I said, "but I have been told by reliable sources that you'd like to be ambassador to India, and if that is true, I'll nominate you, and I'm sure you'll be confirmed." Bill was enthusiastic, and now I could select my own man to replace him.

For the past fifty years, the Department of Justice had been heavily politicized. The Attorney General's job had gone either to a political crony (James P. McGranery under Truman), a member of the President's immediate family (Robert F. Kennedy under JFK) or a former campaign manager (John Mitchell under Nixon), and the department's credibility had suffered as a result. So it was important to select someone nonpolitical, and because the issues the department was considering were so very complex, it was essential that my nominee have a superior intellect. Rumsfeld suggested that I talk to Dr. Edward H. Levi, president of the University of Chicago and a noted legal scholar.

Before talking to Levi, I made a thorough study of his background and came away extremely impressed by his qualifications. An authority on antitrust law, he held degrees from both the University of Chicago and Yale. Years earlier, he had joined the staff of the House Judiciary Committee, and people there still remembered him with affection and respect. Between 1940 and 1945, he had served as a special assistant to the Attorney General, and then, at the end of the war, he had returned to Chicago, where he had become, first, dean of the law school, then provost of the university and finally its president. And it was his cool performance as president that intrigued me. In 1968, campuses around the country were ablaze with student protests against the Vietnam War. Several hundred students occupied the University of Chicago's administration building for a sit-in that lasted fifteen days. Levi didn't panic. He didn't call the police or provoke a confrontation. He simply told the students that he would be happy to talk to them about legitimate grievances, but *not* about amnesty for them, and when the sit-in ended, some forty of its ringleaders were tossed out of school.

Everything I read convinced me that the man was both firm and fair. He was an excellent administrator. He was also unflappable. Several years earlier, he and his wife had taken a vacation trip to the Caribbean and South America. A fire broke out aboard their ocean liner, and some passengers thought they'd have to abandon ship. People started running toward the lifeboats. Levi just sat there puffing on his pipe. He was convinced that the crew would extinguish the fire, which is what happened.

Levi is not much for small talk, so when he came into the Oval Office, I got right to the point and asked him what the Department of Justice needed most. A nonpolitical head, he replied; nothing was more important than restoring public confidence in the equitable administration of justice.

"Well, something has to be done about the department," I agreed, "and we've decided that we have to start at the top. Would you be willing to serve as Attorney General?"

Levi hadn't expected this. I went on to assure him that he could be totally nonpolitical, calling the shots as he saw them. But the university had just launched an important fund drive, he said. He felt obligated to make sure that it was a success.

I knew within minutes after meeting him that Levi was the man for the job, so I decided to put the pressure on. "With the administration of justice in such difficulty," I asked, "how could you possibly turn your back on this opportunity?"

Several days later, he accepted the challenge. Then it became our job to steer his nomination through the Senate. Initially, we encountered unexpected flak. Mississippi Democrat James Eastland was the chairman of the Senate Judiciary Committee; Nebraska's Roman Hruska was the ranking Republican, and they went through the roof. Levi was an academician; he was "obviously" a liberal, and "he hasn't been in the real world." The nomination "won't fly," Hruska said. It was as simple as that.

Calling both Senators into the Oval Office, I told them that Levi was a law-and-order man. I cited the way that he had handled the student disturbances on his campus. Turning to Eastland, I said, "Jim, I assure you he is not a bushy-haired liberal. He is not another Ramsey Clark. He is not a liberal academic who is going to give the store away. I want both of you to know that when we asked, 'What's wrong with Levi?' we were told, 'He's too tough. He's too hard-headed.'"

That did it. After meeting with Levi, both Senators gave him their support. That freed me to think about other changes in the Cabinet. Bill Simon at Treasury and Earl Butz at Agriculture were anxious to return to private life, and the newspapers were full of reports that they would leave soon. I could not afford to let either man go. I needed Simon to help push my economic and energy proposals through the Congress, and I thought that Butz, despite his reputation for making earthy—and occasionally tasteless—remarks, had been very effective in his post. He had turned farmers around from supporting old and discredited programs, and he had convinced them to back more freedom for agriculture. I told them I wanted them to stay. Simon wasn't hard to persuade. I suspect that his spirits were down because of all the newspaper hints that he was on his way out. I assured him that I retained full confidence in him, and I told Nessen to read reporters a statement to that effect. Simon's spirits soared, and he said he would stay on the team.

Butz was harder to convince. He thought he'd done the job that he'd set out to do. He was tired physically, and he had some opportunities in the private sector. If he didn't accept them, he wouldn't be asked again. I had to twist his arm. "Earl," I said, "the country needs you. Agriculture needs you, and I need you. You simply cannot leave." Finally, reluctantly, he agreed to stay.

For the past several months Claude Brinegar had expressed a desire to leave the Department of Transportation and return to the oil business in California. The first name on the list that Rumsfeld gave me as his replacement was that of a Philadelphia lawyer named William T. Coleman, Jr. I had known Bill Coleman for years—he had served as a top staff attorney on the Warren Commission—and I'd always been impressed with him. First in his class at the Harvard Law School, he had clerked for Supreme Court Justice Felix Frankfurter. Before joining the Warren Commission, he had coauthored a brief in the 1954 case that resulted in the Supreme Court's ban on racial discrimination in public schools. Then he had gone on to head the NAACP's Legal Defense Fund, Inc. The fact that he had specialized in transportation law while in private practice only deepened my conviction that he would turn out to be an outstanding Secretary, and I was delighted when he said he would take the job.

Following his reelection in 1972, Nixon had named Peter J. Brennan as Secretary of Labor. The choice was understandable. Brennan had led the Building and Construction Trades Council in New York and members of his unions had vigorously supported the President's policies on Vietnam. But for a number of reasons, Brennan had not been all that effective in Washington, mainly because he didn't get along with George Meany and other top officials of the AFL-CIO. They hadn't been in contact for months. I thought that the man whose job it was to communicate labor's views ought to be able to have a rapport with labor's top echelon, so when Brennan decided to leave, I accepted his resignation. (I talked with him about the possibility of becoming ambassador to Ireland, but he wanted to return to New York City.) Then I set about finding someone who could reestablish that crucial dialogue.

John T. Dunlop, a Harvard economics professor, was the ideal candidate. I had known him in 1973 and 1974, when he had directed the Cost of Living Council. He had a delightful sense of humor, and I respected his ability to master a subject and to attract talented people to work for him. As a result of his service in Washington plus his record as an outstanding mediator, both labor and management thought very highly of him. He'd have no trouble at all being confirmed. I also sweetened the pot. In addition to his job as Secretary, I told him he'd have a position on the Economic Policy Board—after all, he was an economist—and that seemed to heighten his interest in returning to the capital. He agreed to join the Cabinet.

Given the special pressures that his job entailed, Roy Ash had done very well as director of the Office of Management and Budget, but he was Washington weary now, so we shopped around for a replacement. Rumsfeld and I agreed that we would approach James T. Lynn, Secretary of HUD. Lynn was a feisty little guy, and we hadn't always been on the best of terms. One night while I was Vice President, he and I had a big argument at a birthday party to honor Tip O'Neill. The host was South Korean lobbyist Tongsun Park. I had never even heard of Park. I just knew that Tip was the guest of honor, so Betty and I decided to attend. Lynn and his wife were seated at our table, and we got into a heated discussion over what I thought was an unnecessary delay in the naming of a Michigan man to fill a top regional job at HUD. The man was qualified, but Lynn and his people had held the nomination in limbo for months and then turned around and given the nod to some fellow from Wisconsin. At the party that night, Jim and I wound up in a shouting match. But we got over it, and later laughed about it.

I thought he had done a remarkable job at HUD. (One of the first bills that I signed as President was the Housing and Community Development Act of 1974. Inasmuch as it called for block grants to replace the far more costly and cumbersome system of categorical grants, it was landmark legislation, and Lynn had turned in a masterful performance steering the measure through Congress.) He was smart and articulate, and I liked his aggressiveness. The OMB directorship is one of the more crucial jobs in government. Instead of dealing with just one department, the director has to deal with every agency of the federal establishment, and he exerts a huge influence on spending practices. Despite the fact that he would be making a personal sacrifice (as a member of the Cabinet, he earned $60,000 per year; the OMB chief made $42,500), Jim said he would be happy to serve wherever he could do the most good.

Lynn's departure from HUD, of course, gave me another Cabinet post to fill. From the first day of my Administration, Betty had been pressing me to pick a woman for a top job, so when I saw the name of Carla A. Hills on the list of potential candidates drawn up by Rumsfeld, I decided to review her credentials carefully. I knew her husband, Rod Hills, who later came to work with Phil Buchen in the legal counsel's office, but all I knew about Carla was that she had been serving for the past year as Assistant Attorney General in charge of the Justice Department's Civil Division. It didn't take me long, however, to conclude that she would make an excellent contribution to the Cabinet. Graduating from Stanford with honors, she had gone on to Oxford and then Yale Law School, where she ranked near the top of her class. An authority on antitrust law—friends called her "Aunty Trust"—she had served as an assistant U.S. Attorney in Los Angeles and had been a partner in a prestigious firm there. Everyone to whom I talked said that she was tough, hard-working and articulate—an opinion I quickly shared when I interviewed her in the Oval Office. She didn't pretend to know much about the housing industry, but the questions she asked about the job were bright and to the point.

Her nomination, however, caused an immediate howl of protest from the interest groups over which HUD had jurisdiction. They complained about Carla's lack of expertise in the industry and urged me to select a realtor, home builder or city planner. I saw her lack of expertise as a plus. It was far better to pick someone from outside who would assimilate the necessary information and then decide the issues on their merits. Despite their disappointment, none of the interest groups opposed the nomination. With only five dissenting votes, the Senate confirmed her, and the Cabinet took on a new, more independent look.

At the end of January, I submitted to Congress my detailed proposals on the economy and energy. Additionally, I proposed a total of forty-nine new recisions and deferrals that would reduce federal spending by $2.6 billion in fiscal year 1975. That was necessary because in the two weeks since my State of the Union address, the economy had deteriorated even further. In January, unemployment had increased by seven-tenths of a point—to 7.9 percent—the highest rate since 1949. Plants were closing, layoffs were continuing, and no one could predict when the recession would "bottom out." If Congress would only act on my proposals, I thought, the turnaround could start soon. Unfortunately, Congress didn't seem disposed to move, and delay followed delay. The only part of my package that lawmakers wanted to approve was the proposal to cut taxes by $16 billion. Ignoring the inflationary impact that their action would have on the budget deficit—without spending reductions—they said they wanted to fatten that cut by $8.8 billion.

It was significant that at the same time I was asking the Congress to show some fiscal discipline, Democratic governors in some of our larger, more liberal states, such as New York and California, were submitting restrictive budgets to their legislatures along with tough messages that would have been unthinkable a few years earlier. But the Democratic lawmakers in Washington were still on the same old binge.

On February 1, acting under existing law, I issued a proclamation hiking import fees on petroleum products by one dollar per barrel. That fee would increase to two dollars per barrel on March 1 and—in the absence of Congressional passage of my energy proposals—to three dollars per barrel one month later. Then I proposed a two-dollar-per-barrel excise tax on domestic crude oil and a levy on natural gas. I also asked for a windfall profits tax on domestic petroleum coupled with price decontrol. Added together, my advisers said, these new taxes would generate between $28 billion and $30 billion in additional revenues. My plan was to return *all* this money to the economy. Some would go to individual taxpayers and some to industry; at least $2 billion was earmarked for the poor. (They, too, faced added energy costs for heating their homes and driving their cars, and to exclude them from any tax relief would have been unfair.) The only practical and effective way to achieve energy independence, I knew, would be to allow the prices of oil and gas to move higher—high enough to discourage wasteful consumption and encourage the development of new energy sources. But those prices were stuck because two-thirds of the crude oil—and most of the natural gas—that we produced domestically were under federal controls. In my message to Congress on January 30, I called for the "earliest possible" deregulation of both oil and natural gas. "Without these measures," I said, "we face a future of shortages and dependency which the nation cannot tolerate and the American people will not accept."

Three days later, on February 3, I sent Congress a budget of $349 billion for fiscal year 1976. It projected a deficit of $52 billion, which was $5 billion more than I had anticipated only two weeks earlier. The basic reason for that higher deficit was the economic downturn; federal tax collections lag as incomes and profits slide and unemployment benefits rise very sharply. Even more alarming, unless Congress agreed to spending cuts, the deficit could shoot up another $17 billion, to nearly $70 billion, and that could undermine this country's long-term economic stability. The unemployment outlook was equally grim. There was no way to lower the jobless rate soon. Miracle cures just didn't exist.

These problems had been developing for years. The warning signs had been there for everyone to see, and at the conclusion of the budget message I called attention to them. "The tremendous growth of our domestic assistance programs in recent years has, on the whole, been commendable," I said. "These programs cannot, however, continue to expand at the rates they have experienced over the past two decades. Spending by all levels of government now makes up a third of our own national output. Were the growth of domestic assistance programs to continue for the next two decades at the same rates as in the past twenty years, total government spending would grow to more than half of our national output. Taxation of individuals and businesses to pay for such expansion would simply become insupportably heavy. This is not a matter of conservative or liberal ideology. It is hard fact. The growth of these domestic assistance programs has resulted in too many overlapping programs, lack of coordination and inequities. Some of the less needy now receive a disproportionate share of federal benefits, while some who are more needy receive less. We must redouble the efforts of the past five years to rationalize and streamline these programs."

Senator Hubert Humphrey called the budget "completely unacceptable." House Ways and Means Committee Chairman Al Ullman said my recommendations added up to "a disaster for the economy," with House Majority Leader Tip O'Neill vowing that the Democrats would reverse my "misguided priorities." His prophecy was right on the mark. Both houses of Congress voted to bar me from increasing the amount that the poor had to pay for food stamps. Then they turned their attention to passing a bill that would halt for ninety days the new tax on imported oil that I had imposed on February 1. (I vetoed the bill delaying this new tax and my veto was sustained.)

Such procrastination was in line with past performances. It had taken the Congress a full four years to pass the Alaska pipeline bill. In April 1973, Nixon had asked the Congress to deregulate new supplies of natural gas. In the twenty-two months since then, only the Senate had even bothered to hold hearings on the proposal. In the six months that I had been President, I had sent the Congress three special messages pleading for that legislation. Those requests had been ignored.

The bill that I submitted to Congress to increase our domestic energy supply and cut back on the importation of foreign oil was a bulky document, 167 pages long. Traditionally, whenever it receives a measure of that length and complexity, Congress responds by cutting up the bill into as many as a half-dozen jurisdictional pieces and then assigning each piece to a different committee. That causes long delays. In order to avoid them, I asked Speaker Albert and Majority Leader Mansfield to establish an ad hoc joint committee that would consider the package as a whole. Mansfield said my request was impractical. "You may be right, Mr. President," he went on, "but it's just not possible." Albert agreed with him. "I understand what you want to do and why you want to do it," he said, "but I'm not in any position to destroy committee jurisdiction, to interfere with the established rights of a committee. If I tried to do that, it would create horrendous internal problems in the Congress."

Congressional resistance to my proposals didn't apply only to energy. Increasingly, both houses of Congress were giving me a hard time on foreign policy. The first battleground was Cyprus. On February 5, the suspension of arms deliveries to the Turks, originally voted by Congress in October, went into effect. Not only was that action likely to impede our hopes of achieving a just settlement of the Cyprus issue, it also posed a threat to the security and political stability of the entire eastern Mediterranean, and I urged the Congress to reconsider a decision so clearly contrary to our national interests. Using quiet diplomacy, Henry Kissinger had persuaded the foreign ministers of both Greece and Turkey to meet with him in Brussels to resolve their differences. But when the Turks heard what Congress had done, they stayed home. I couldn't blame them.

Congressional irresponsibility also led to new problems in other parts of the world. Wishing to punish Arab nations that had taken part in the 1973 oil embargo against us, the sponsors of the Trade Act of 1974 had tacked on an amendment that barred me from extending routine tariff preferences to countries that belonged to OPEC. What the lawmakers overlooked was the fact that at least five of OPEC's member states—Iran, Venezuela, Ecuador, Nigeria and Indonesia—had refused to participate in the embargo. Yet because Congress hadn't thought to provide an escape clause, these friendly countries were being penalized. The Venezuelans, in particular, were outraged, and even though I reassured them that I would ask the Congress to remedy its mistake as soon as possible, they stayed angry for months afterward.

No foreign policy challenges occupied more of my time in the early months of 1975 than the deteriorating situations in both the Middle East and Indochina. Negotiations between Israel and Egypt about the return of the Sinai had reached a dangerous stalemate. For the past twenty-five years, the philosophical underpinning of U.S. policy toward Israel had been our conviction—and certainly my own—that if we gave Israel an ample supply of economic aid and weapons, she would feel strong and confident, more flexible and more willing to discuss a lasting peace. Every American President since Harry Truman had willingly supplied arms and funds to the Jewish state. The Israelis were stronger militarily than all their Arab neighbors combined, yet peace was no closer than it had ever been. So I began to question the rationale for our policy. I wanted the Israelis to recognize that there had to be some quid pro quo. If we were going to build up their military capabilities, we in turn had to see some flexibility to achieve a fair, secure and permanent peace. What we wanted most was new momentum diplomatically.

To make sure that they got the message, I gave interviews to *Time* magazine and NBC-TV. "Every day that passes [without a new accord in the Middle East] becomes more dangerous," I told *Time*. I made it clear that there was "a substantial relationship at the present time between our national security interests and those of Israel." Then I added, pointedly: "But in the final analysis, we have to judge what is in our national interest above any and all other considerations." I was equally blunt on NBC-TV. The Israelis, I knew, were adamantly opposed to a Geneva conference as a forum to settle their disputes with the Arab states. Kissinger and I agreed that Geneva was not the route to take. Our purpose at Geneva should be only to *ratify* previously negotiated bilateral agreements. If we went there to *negotiate* those agreements, the conference would be at the mercy of different radical interests and break down into volatile procedural squabbles. We would never get to real negotiation on the substantive issues. We'd fail in the attempt to ensure lasting peace, and the psychological effects of that failure would virtually guarantee another war. Yet if we saw no meaningful progress soon toward a new Israeli-Egyptian accord, I said on NBC, the U.S. would be "forced" to abandon our step-by-step approach, and we would have no alternative but to turn to a comprehensive approach via a Geneva conference.

The strategy appeared to be working. Within days, we had received signals from both sides that they were moving to a position where they would at least talk about progress. Early in February, Kissinger left Washington on a ten-day trip to the Middle East, and he achieved reasonably encouraging results. Egyptian President Anwar Sadat, he said, was trying to be flexible and to accommodate the Israelis' concerns about their security. The Israelis, however, while encouraging our efforts to push for a lasting peace, were being very tough in their demands. To make matters worse, Prime Minister Rabin's Labor Party commanded only a thin majority in the Knesset, which gave him little room to maneuver. A hard-liner, he also had proved a tough negotiator. Despite these obstacles, Henry told me that nothing was more critical than a new Sinai accord.

In March, Kissinger resumed his shuttle between Cairo and Jerusalem. Again, the Egyptians bent over backward. Again, the Israelis resisted. Henry pushed and pushed—and then pushed some more. Finally, agreement was reached on the *framework* of a new accord. Israeli forces would pull back about thirty-five miles from the eastern bank of the Suez Canal, and the new dividing line between the two adversaries would be in the vicinity of the strategic mountain passes of Gidi and Mitla in the Sinai desert. The Israelis would return the oil fields at Abu Rudeis on the Gulf of Suez, and the Egyptians would be able to use a road that linked those fields to the rest of the country. Even though Sadat and Rabin acknowledged that this was only a first step and that eventually the Israelis would have to give up more of the territory they now occupied, both leaders seemed satisfied in principle with what had been worked out.

Then the fragile agreement threatened to come apart. Once an agreement had been reached in *principle*, the Israelis insisted that they wouldn't move back past the crests of the two passes. That seemed fair enough, except that they couldn't—nor could anyone else—show us a map and say where those crests were, or precisely where the oil field road lay. As the talks dragged on, Rabin became less flexible. He fought over every kilometer. I wouldn't call it nitpicking—I didn't doubt for a minute that he really wanted peace, and I recognized that the Israelis had a fundamental reluctance about giving up any territory in return for what they saw as only promises of good will—but he didn't seem to understand that only by giving do you get something in return.

White House photo by David Hume Kennerly

Early 1975. A difficult foreign policy decision. There
were many.

White House photo by David Hume Kennerly

April 28, 1975: I met with the National Security Council to discuss evacuating
Americans from South Vietnam. On Kissinger's right: Deputy Secretary of State
Robert Ingersoll and CIA Director William Colby. To my left: Defense Secretary James
Schlesinger, Deputy Defense Secretary William Clements, Rockefeller and JCS
chairman George Brown.

White House photo by David Hume Kennerly

May 1975: Could we save the *Mayaguez* and her crew?

June 1975: Arrival in Salzburg, Austria—*not* on my feet.

UPI photo

White House photo by David Hume Kennerly

My first meeting with Egyptian President Sadat. At Salzburg he proposed a secret plan for progress toward peace.

Most days we had a staff meeting. In addition to Liberty, from left to right: Bob Hartmann, Ron Nessen, Don Rumsfeld, Jack Marsh and Max Friedersdorf.

White House photo by David Hume Kennerly

Wide World Photos, ©Elizabeth Sunflower

Jack, Betty and Steve welcomed me at the White House that night. Joy and love.

Sacramento, California, September 6, 1975: I saw the gun and ducked.

UPI photo

San Francisco, September 22, 1975: A second assassination attempt.

Wide World Photos

Susan embraces both Betty and me on our return to Washington. I was spared, but every President must live with the possibility.

White House photo by David Hume Kennerly

In Peking with Chinese Vice Premier Teng Hsiao-ping, December 1975.
Whatever the joke was, it broke us up.

Dining with Teng: I was
impressed by his straight talk
and tenacity.

UPI photo

White House photo by David Hume Kennerly

Listening to a voter at a
Keene, New Hampshire,
retirement home,
February 1976. For an
incumbent President,
winning this first primary
was a must.

White House photo by David Hume Kennerly

When we got back from dinner with President Giscard at the French embassy we heard the good news about the Michigan primary.

White House photo by David Hume Kennerly

One of our Bicentennial highlights was the visit of Great Britain's Queen Elizabeth.

White House photo by David Hume Kennerly

Leaving Reagan's hotel suite in Kansas City after my nomination. It wasn't easy to patch up our differences.

Wide World Photos

Betty and I wave to the delegates after my acceptance speech. We knew we faced a tough, uphill campaign.

White House photo by David Hume Kennerly

It was neck and neck all night, but when we lost Texas even Joe Garagiola was at a loss for words.

Official White House photo

Each of us gets ready for the concession statement that Betty had to read. (Left to right: Steve, Jack, Betty, Susan, Gayle and Mike.)

Wide World Photos

President-elect Carter visits me at the White House in November—the beginning of an effort to ensure a smooth transition.

David Hume Kennerly/*PHOTO QU*

January 20, 1977. I asked the helicopter pilot to circle the Capitol for a last look.

Andrews Air Force Base. Our farewell to Washington and the beginning of another life.

David Hume Kennerly/*PHOTO QU*

The Israelis kept stalling. Their tactics frustrated the Egyptians and made me mad as hell. Both Henry and I had received firm assurances from Rabin that a line could be drawn that would be acceptable to Israel. But Rabin now seemed afraid of his Cabinet's response. He would not—or could not—deliver on commitments he had made.

Kissinger returned from the Middle East shuttle on the evening of March 23, and I made a point of greeting him personally when his helicopter touched down on the South Lawn of the White House. Henry was deeply disappointed by the Israeli attitude. He was worried that Sadat, who had gone along with many of our suggestions, would never work with us again. He might be driven into the radical Arab camp along with hotheads like Colonel Muammar Qaddafi of Libya, and if that ever happened, it would damage not only Israel's interests but our own as well.

Next morning in the Cabinet Room we briefed Congressional leaders of both parties on the results of Kissinger's trip. Asked about this meeting later by reporters, Senator Mansfield said that the Administration had decided to "reassess" its policies in the Middle East. When Nessen asked me what I thought he should say about that, I told him that he could call Mansfield's remarks "correct" and that, in an indirect way, he could indicate that we thought the Israelis had been dragging their feet.

Predictably, our "reassessment" jolted the American Jewish community and Israel's many friends in Congress. The Israeli lobby, made up of patriotic Americans, is strong, vocal and wealthy, but many of its members have a single focus. I knew that I would come under intense pressure soon to change our policy, but I was determined to hold firm. On March 27, I met in the Oval Office with Max Fisher, a prominent Detroit businessman who was chairman of the Jewish Agency for Israel. Max was a lifelong Republican and a close friend. He had served as an unofficial ambassador between the United States and Israel for years, and his contacts at the highest levels of both governments had often helped us bridge over misunderstandings. I said I thought it was imperative that we see new momentum toward peace in the Middle East, that my comments about reassessing our policies there weren't just rhetoric. I was not going to capitulate to pressure, and if the impasse continued, I might have to go public on where we stood and why. I didn't have to ask Max to get the message back to the Israelis. Word would spread very quickly that I meant what I said.

Meanwhile, other foreign policy crises were demanding more and more of my time. Foremost among them was the stepped-up war in South Vietnam and Cambodia. From the beginning of our involvement in the area, I had always thought that we were doing the right thing. Our policy was a natural outgrowth of decisions we had made at the end of World War II. In the immediate postwar period, the U.S. mounted a foreign aid program to help rebuild the shattered economies of countries all over the world. We helped scores of nations—allies, potential allies and even potential adversaries—and those aid programs formed an integral part of America's foreign policy and national defense strategy. The basic thrust behind them was the desire to eliminate, or at least contain, Communist aggression around the globe.

In the late 1940s and early 1950s, our aid programs in Vietnam were not too different from the programs we maintained elsewhere, with the exception of the fact that the French were still a major factor there. Then Dienbienphu fell to the Communists; the French withdrew and the U.S. role began to change. Slowly we became the military backup for one of the two contending factions in the country. Even by the late 1950s, we were only providing the Saigon regime with military and economic aid plus the services of several hundred advisers. We were not committed fully to the nation's defense. Yet. A decisive change in our level of commitment came, of course, in April 1962, when JFK sent 15,000 military advisers to help the South Vietnamese in their struggle against the Viet Minh, later called the Viet Cong. From that point on, escalation followed escalation, and at one point in the mid 1960s we discovered that we had committed 550,000 Americans to save our beleaguered ally.

In retrospect, legitimate questions can be raised about our involvement in the war. Had our civilian and military leaders made a sufficient analysis of the conditions there? Had they stopped to consider that our world commitments might already be too great, and did they have a clear idea of what their military objectives were? The answer to these questions is probably no. The question can also be asked: Could we have won the war? There, I think, the answer is yes, although I'm not as sure of that today as I was in the late 1960s when, as House Minority Leader, I called upon LBJ to stop pulling our best punches in Vietnam. At that time, I felt certain—given four basic assumptions—that we would prevail.

The first assumption was that we would use our military power fully and appropriately. The second was that the South Vietnamese forces would build to a level sufficient for them to defend themselves. The third was that the people of South Vietnam would support the war effort, and the final assumption was the continuing support of the U.S. Congress. To varying degrees, none of these assumptions proved out.

The war dragged on and on, and the damage it caused this country both domestically and internationally was truly staggering. Our greatest loss, of course, was the 57,000 American dead and the more than 100,000 who suffered serious injuries. Next came the loss of U.S. prestige around the world. The conflict created deep divisions among the American people and discredited our military. Lastly, LBJ's decision to provide both guns (the war cost us $150 billion) and butter without a tax increase had resulted in a terrible disruption of our economy. It would take America a long time to recover from these wounds.

In January 1973, the U.S. finally negotiated a settlement that made it possible for us to remove our combat forces and bring home our prisoners of war. If necessary, we agreed at the time, the U.S. would back up the terms of the Paris peace accords, and we would continue to provide adequate military and economic assistance to South Vietnam. The North Vietnamese, however, never considered the Paris peace accords as the end of the conflict. They had an estimated 160,000 troops in South Vietnam at the time, and they violated the agreement flagrantly by sending an additional 300,000 men into the south. They also sent in massive amounts of modern equipment and launched offensive military operations.

In the face of this situation, the U.S. failed to respond. Watergate had so weakened the President that he was not about to take a major military action, such as renewed bombings. Moreover, by November, Congress had succeeded in passing the War Powers Act of 1973, which severely limited his ability to enforce the peace agreement. North Vietnam could violate the accords with impunity. Next, Congress reduced our economic and military assistance to the Saigon regime. Finally, Congress signaled an increasing desire to cut off all support. Unsure of any more help, President Nguyen Van Thieu ordered a quick withdrawal to more defensible positions. This maneuver, decided upon without consulting us, was executed poorly and hampered by floods of refugees. Predictably, panic ensued, making the situation worse.

In January 1975, the North Vietnamese gained control of the first province they had won in fifteen years of war. Toward the end of March, they captured thirteen additional provinces, encountering little resistance. The South Vietnamese were running short of ammunition and supplies. They thought they were being abandoned, not only by the U.S. but also by the leadership in Saigon. Trapped, they tried to get out any way they could. The situation in neighboring Cambodia was even worse. During my seven months in the Oval Office, we had tried on at least half a dozen occasions to achieve a negotiated settlement there without success. Now the Khmer Rouge had encircled the capital of Phnom Penh and were preparing for the kill.

For fiscal year 1975, I requested a total of $1.4 billion in military aid for South Vietnam and Cambodia. Congress authorized $1 billion but appropriated only $700 million. From the time I became President, I urged Congress to supply additional aid to prevent the collapse of both nations. "With adequate United States military assistance, they can hold their own," I said. "We cannot turn our backs on these embattled countries." If we did not stand up to aggression, I told the Congressional leadership, we would lose our credibility around the world. Their reaction was mixed. Mansfield and O'Neill, consistent with their long-held attitude, wanted no part of it. Speaker Albert, however, tried to be helpful. "You're right," he told me privately, adding, "I'm not sure I can get the House to go along."

Late on the afternoon of March 25, I met in the Oval Office with Kissinger, Scowcroft, U.S. Ambassador to South Vietnam Graham Martin and Army Chief of Staff General Frederick C. Weyand to discuss the situation in Southeast Asia. David Kennerly was moving about taking photographs. Everyone knew the problems in South

Vietnam were serious, but no one seemed to know just how critical they were. We needed an on-the-spot assessment. I asked Weyand to fly to Saigon as soon as possible, spend a week there and bring back a full report. After the others had left, Kennerly asked if he could go along on the trip. "Vietnam is falling to pieces," he said. "I've spent two and a half years there as a Time-Life photographer, and I've just got to go back. I have to see for myself what's going on."

I knew David wouldn't try to give me any propaganda about "enemy body counts" or "light at the end of the tunnel." He had been shot at many times by the North Vietnamese. As an American, he felt ashamed that we weren't doing more to help a loyal ally, and he thought that once I saw the photographs he took of the suffering there, I would have a better feel for what we had to do. "Fine," I said. "Do it. Tell Scowcroft to take care of the arrangements."

Weyand's plane was leaving at dawn. Both the general and Kennerly had to get packed quickly. Later that evening, Kennerly came up to the residence to say goodbye. "You be careful," I said, wrapping an arm around his shoulder. Then I asked, "You have everything you need?"

Kennerly paused, a rare gesture for him. "Well," he said, "as a matter of fact, the banks are closed and I can't get any cash. Do you have any money?"

I gave him a reproving look, then picked up my wallet. There was forty-seven dollars inside. I handed it to him, patted him on the back and watched while Betty gave him a hug. Then, as he was walking out the door, I remembered something. "Kennerly," I called out. When he turned, I reached into my pants pocket and flipped him a quarter. "Here," I said. "You might as well clean me out."

The situation in South Vietnam worsened day by day. The city of Quang Tri fell, then the ancient capital of Hué. On March 26, the State Department announced that we would begin evacuating thousands of Vietnamese refugees as well as all U.S. personnel who remained in the port city of Da Nang. Boeing 727s and 747 cargo planes proceeded to fly them south; U.S. Navy ships and contract vessels took aboard as many passengers as possible and then set out to sea. And still the exodus continued.

Under the provisions of the War Powers Act, I was required to consult with the Congress before introducing U.S. military forces into hostilities or "situations where imminent involvement in hostilities is clearly indicated by the circumstances." That law also said that military actions overseas had to be terminated within sixty days unless Congress approved them. As a member of Congress I had voted against the legislation and supported the President's veto. I questioned its practicality and constitutionality. Nevertheless, as President I tried to live up to both the letter and the spirit of the law. But Congress was enjoying its annual Easter recess. Not a single leader of either party remained in the capital. Three of them were in Greece, two in the People's Republic of China, two in Mexico, one in Europe, and another in the Middle East. The rest were in twelve widely scattered locations in the United States. Obviously, the "consultation" called for by the act was impossible. Although we went to incredible lengths to reach them and explain the situation, we did not succeed. There was simply no way that I could have drawn Congress into the decision-making process when the crisis was at hand, and I was not about to withhold the help of our forces in a humanitarian evacuation. Yet when Congress reconvened after its recess, several members accused me of violating the law.

Still the onslaught continued. We appealed to the United Nations to use its moral authority to allow innocent refugees to leave. We asked Soviet Ambassador Anatoly Dobrynin if his government would intercede with Hanoi and request time to complete an orderly evacuation of the refugees. (Dobrynin replied that the Soviets couldn't help because of the hard-line attitude in Hanoi.) Early in April, I directed that money from a $2 million special foreign aid children's fund be made available to fly two thousand South Vietnamese orphans to the United States as soon as possible. I ordered American officials in Saigon to cut through any red tape that might stand in the way of the children's escape. Then I told our Air Force to begin those mercy flights as soon as possible. Everyone suffers in a war, but no one suffers more than the children, and the airlift was the least that we could do.

There were still some six thousand Americans in and around Saigon, and in that first week of April, Defense Secretary Schlesinger asked me to start evacuating them immediately. He repeated his request almost daily. Kissinger and I opposed so precipitous a with-drawal. (Later, I learned that Schlesinger had ordered the flight of empty or near-empty planes in and out of Saigon—just to establish for the record, I suspected, that it would not be his fault if we failed to remove all our people.) We felt that a premature evacuation could have serious consequences. Even greater panic than already existed in the South Vietnamese capital could develop, and in their bitterness at being "betrayed," South Vietnamese troops could turn their guns on Americans. Then, too, I hadn't given up hope that the situation could be turned around. I wanted to hear General Weyand's report.

We met on the afternoon of April 5. The military situation, he said, was very critical, but the South Vietnamese were continuing to fight with all the resources available to them. If their efforts were to have any chance of success, they needed an additional $722 million worth of supplies, primarily ammunition. That money wouldn't en-able them to recapture the ground they had lost, but it would be enough to let them establish a strong defense perimeter around Sai-gon. If they managed to stabilize the military situation, there was still hope for a political solution to the war. If that aid was not forthcom-ing, there was no hope at all.

Kennerly, who came in separately, was grimly pessimistic. He had refused to attend official briefings in Saigon. Instead, he had broken away from the Weyand group and gone "upcountry" to see for him-self what was happening. Near Nha Trang, he had flown over a ship that had just been taken over by mutinous South Vietnamese troops, and they had fired at his helicopter. Then he had gone on to Cambo-dia. He was deeply upset by what he had seen there, and his photo-graphs—of refugees at Nha Trang, of fleeing troops, of wounded children in Phnom Penh hospitals—were more revealing than any briefing I could have received. "Cambodia is gone," he said, "and I don't care what the generals tell you; they're bullshitting you if they say that Vietnam has got more than three or four weeks left. There's no question about it. It's just not gonna last."

Based on all of this intelligence, I decided to step up our efforts to get the refugees out. We were now confronted by such ominous mili-tary and foreign policy issues that on the evening of April 10, I ad-dressed a joint session of Congress. Henry Kissinger had urged me to tell the American people that Congress was solely to blame for the debacle in Southeast Asia. In fact, Henry had written a "go down with the flags flying" speech for me to use. My instinct was that this was not the right approach to take at the time. I decided to request the $722 million—plus another $250 million for economic and humanitarian assistance—and then relay the facts as they had been given to me.

> The situation in South Vietnam and Cambodia has reached a critical phase requiring immediate and positive decisions by this government. The options before us are few, and the time is very short.
>
> Members of the Congress, my fellow Americans, this moment of tragedy for Indochina is a time of trial for us. It is a time for national resolve.
>
> It has been said that the United States is overextended, that we have too many commitments too far from home, that we must examine what our truly vital interests are and shape our strategy to conform to them. I find no fault with this as a theory, but . . . we cannot, in the meantime, abandon our friends while our adversaries support and encourage theirs. We cannot dismantle our defenses, our diplomacy or our intelligence capability while others increase and strengthen theirs. Let us put an end to self-inflicted wounds. Let us remember that our national unity is a most priceless asset. Let us deny our adversaries the satisfaction of using Vietnam to pit Americans against Americans. At this moment the United States must present to the world a united front.

Abruptly, two freshman Democrats, Toby Moffett of Connecticut and George Miller of California, turned and walked out of the chamber. As best I could recall, this had never happened before, and I thought it an appallingly rude display. Some of their colleagues in the Congress were deeply embarrassed; so were Democrats around the country. One morning shortly thereafter, I reached the Oval Office before eight o'clock and received a telephone call from Chicago Mayor Dick Daley. "I just want you to know that I'm an American first and a Democrat second," he said. "I don't like what my fellow Democrats are doing. You just keep standing strong and tall for the United States and you'll have some good Democratic support out here." His call made my day.

The euphoria was short-lived. On April 14, the Senate Foreign Relations Committee requested a meeting with me to discuss the situation in Southeast Asia. This was a rare move—the last time the committee had met with the President was during the Wilson Administration—so I had Kissinger, Schlesinger and Scowcroft sit in on the session with me. The meeting in the Cabinet Room was extremely tense. I asked Kissinger and Schlesinger to review the political and military situations in South Vietnam, then solicited the Senators' views. The message was clear: get out, *fast*. "I will give you large sums for evacuation," New York's Jacob Javits said, "but not one nickel for military aid." Idaho's Frank Church saw grave problems which "could involve us in a very large war" if we attempted to evacuate all the South Vietnamese who had been loyal to us. Delaware's Joseph Biden echoed a similar refrain. "I will vote for any amount for getting the Americans out," he said; "I don't want it mixed with getting the Vietnamese out."

The Senators, I knew, were well-meaning, yet they were incredibly short-sighted. We couldn't just cut and run. We had to consider the people of Vietnam and what might happen to them, especially those who had supported us. After an hour the meeting broke up. "Gentlemen, I respect your views," I said, "but I have to carry out the plan that in my opinion is in our nation's best interest. If we try to pull out right now, it'll lead to panic and the chaos will jeopardize the lives of untold Americans. Believe me, we need to buy time, even a few days. Thank you for coming down. We've had a good discussion but the decision is my responsibility and I'll accept the consequences."

The Senators filed out of the Cabinet Room. I knew I had to chart an exceedingly careful course to keep the situation from disintegrating virtually overnight. But with this on-the-record political pressure from the Foreign Relations Committee, the stakes were higher than ever. If it turned out my judgment was wrong, my Presidency would be in dire jeopardy. I prayed that I was right.

Khmer Rouge troops stormed into Phnom Penh and seized control of Cambodia on April 17. Under intense pressure we evacuated eighty-two Americans, mainly by helicopter to our carrier, U.S.S. *Hancock*, and the assault ship U.S.S. *Okinawa*. That was bad enough, but now the noose tightened around Saigon. Congress had refused to provide any additional funds for South Vietnam. Four days later, President Thieu resigned and fled the country. Communist forces moved closer and closer to the capital. I faced the fact that the end was near.

The final siege of Saigon began on April 25. Kissinger was on the telephone to U.S. Ambassador Graham Martin several times a day, and his reports convinced me that the country was going to collapse momentarily. In the late afternoon of April 28, I was chairing a meeting of my economic and energy advisers in the Cabinet Room when Brent Scowcroft entered and handed me a note. A message had just come in to the Situation Room downstairs. Our Air Force, it said, had been forced to halt evacuation flights from Saigon because Communist rockets and artillery shells were blasting the runways at Tan Son Nhut. A C-130 transport plane had been destroyed and several U.S. Marines killed. Nearly a thousand Americans still remained in Saigon, and we had to carry out our plans to evacuate them.

Leaving the Cabinet Room, I stepped into the Oval Office and discussed the crisis with Kissinger and Rockefeller. Then I convened a meeting of the NSC in the Roosevelt Room. It was 7:30 P.M. in Washington, almost dawn in Saigon. I decided to wait an hour or so to see if the shelling stopped. If it did, we could resume the evacuation flights. The firing did cease, but we had a new problem to solve. Refugees were streaming out onto the airport's runways, and our planes couldn't land. The situation there was clearly out of control. The only option left was to remove the remaining Americans, and as many South Vietnamese as possible, by helicopter from the roof of the U.S. embassy in Saigon. Choppers were standing by on the decks of U.S. Navy ships steaming off the coast, and just before midnight I ordered the final evacuation. Over the next sixteen hours we managed to rescue 6,500 U.S. and South Vietnamese personnel without sustaining significant casualties.

When it was all over, I felt deep satisfaction and relief that the evacuation had been a success. The problem of what to do with the refugees, however, remained. More than 120,000 of them had managed to escape, but they had nowhere to go. Thailand didn't want them. Neither did Malaysia, Indonesia nor the Philippines. The United States, I felt, had a special obligation to them, and on April 30 I asked Congress to approve a bill that would provide $507 million for their transportation and care. The House rejected my request on May 1. Unbelievable! After World War II we had opened our gates and offered a new life to 1.4 million displaced persons. In 1956 we had accepted fifty thousand Hungarians, and after Fidel Castro came to power, we had welcomed more than half a million Cubans to our shores. The South Vietnamese had fought alongside us for years. They didn't want to live under a Communist dictatorship. We had to do everything we could for them.

AFL-CIO President George Meany agreed with me. So did the American Jewish Committee and the governors of several states. (Reubin Askew of Florida, James Longley of Maine and Dan Evans of Washington were very strong in their support.) More than half the refugees were children. Congress, however, didn't want to extend a helping hand. As Senate Democratic Whip Robert C. Byrd of West Virginia explained, "There is no political support for it in this country." But that was a sentiment I was determined to overcome.

Not that I couldn't understand its roots. The recession was deepening. The overall unemployment rate stood at 9 percent; for young blacks and members of other minority groups, it was more than three times that. How could we afford to be generous to the refugees, I was asked, when our own economic problems were so very severe? I replied that it was a matter of principle. To ignore the refugees in their hour of need would be to repudiate the values we cherish as a nation of immigrants, and I was not about to let Congress do that. Under our pressure, it capitulated, and we opened up refugee camps around the country. With the help of local citizens and volunteer organizations, the 120,000 Vietnamese began a new life in America, as had other refugees before them.

Actually, at that time the economy was showing the first signs of a turnaround. Price increases were easing off, and the inflation rate had dropped from a high of 12 percent to less than 8 percent. Retail sales were holding up surprisingly well. The unemployment rate was still much too high, but in the late spring of 1975, the number of people holding jobs was rising steadily. If we kept a steady, firm and consistent course and were patient about it, the economy would continue to improve. We were on the way back. Full recovery was a matter of time.

Washington has lousy winters, but its springs are gorgeous, and 1975 was no exception. Sitting in the Oval Office wrestling with difficult decisions, I'd turn around and look out the window. Dale Haney, a White House gardener, would be running Liberty on the South Lawn; the squirrels would be darting from tree to tree, and the air would be alive with the songs of hundreds of birds returning from their long winter's rest. The roses, azaleas and forsythia in the garden would be ablaze with color. It's a beautiful spring, a time of rejuvenation, I'd say to myself; what's happening to the economy just parallels the rebirth that's taking place right outside my window. Then I'd turn back to the problems on my desk, my mood uplifted, my confidence restored.

Back in January, I had asked Congress to pass a $16 billion tax reduction to stimulate the economy and put people back to work. Late in March, Congress approved a cut of $22.8 billion. This confronted me with one of the most difficult decisions I ever had to make: should I veto the bill, or should I swallow my pride and sign it into law? Bill Simon urged me to veto it; some sections of the bill were hastily conceived, ill advised and counterproductive, he said. (I knew he was right about that. In their attempts to satisfy everyone, lawmakers had tacked on amendments that would provide a tax credit of up to $2,000 for people who purchased new homes, and would give all social security and railroad retirement benefit recipients a bonus check of fifty dollars.) Furthermore, Simon continued, the bill would send the federal budget deficit soaring out of sight, and embroil us all in a new battle against inflation.

New York Representative Barber B. Conable, an influential member of both the House Budget Committee and the House Ways and Means Committee, agreed with Simon and urged me to veto the measure. Conservative Republicans absolutely abhor huge budget deficits, he pointed out. They were miffed at me already—for my nomination of Nelson Rockefeller as Vice President, my decision to grant earned amnesty to draft dodgers and deserters from the Vietnam War, and my efforts to further détente with the Soviets—and if

I did not do something for conservatives soon, I would risk a party polarization that would damage my attempts to win the GOP nomination in 1976. Conable was chairman of the House Republican Policy Committee and a personal friend whose political judgment was very astute, so I listened to him carefully.

Meanwhile, other advisers—Arthur Burns, Alan Greenspan and Jim Lynn—were urging me just as strenuously to sign the bill. Sure, they said, it's one of the biggest tax reductions in U.S. history. Sure, the bill is shaped like a Christmas tree with expensive gifts for everyone. And sure, the enormous budget deficit that is bound to result will infuriate the Republican right wing. But, they asked, what are the realistic alternatives? You have been criticizing Congress for months for not moving quickly enough to cut taxes. Well, Congress has finally acted. Suppose you veto the bill. What's that going to do to your credibility? And if you veto the bill, might not Congress pass something even more irresponsible? You'll invite fewer problems if you sign the bill than if you veto it. You'll give the economy a shot in the arm when it's needed most, and besides, you can't please the right wing anyway.

On March 29, I decided to sign the bill. But I wanted Congress and the American people to know that my approval of it was conditional. Earlier, I had said that I could tolerate a budget deficit of $52 billion for fiscal year 1976. For a man who had opposed budget deficits all his life, that had been a bitter pill to swallow. The tax reduction bill I would sign would push that deficit even higher. Congress had ignored my requests to cut back $17 billion in existing programs; lawmakers were even considering new spending proposals that added up to another $30 billion, and this meant that the deficit could reach $100 billion. I decided to draw the line at $60 billion—and I did so on nationwide TV. "This is as far as we dare to go," I said. "I will resist every attempt by the Congress to add another dollar to the deficit. I will make no exceptions."

The question of whether to sign or to veto the bill illustrates a point about the job of the President. Almost by definition, the decisions that must be made in the Oval Office are difficult. If they're easy, they're made elsewhere in the federal bureaucracy. Invariably, those that wind up on the President's desk have an equal number of supporters and opponents, an equal number of pluses and minuses, and an equal number of people who will scream bloody murder when the decisions are announced.

Every decision that a President makes involves people in one way or another, but in "substantive" matters, such as the size of the budget, I would call in my senior advisers, solicit their recommendations without indicating my own preferences, then weigh the options carefully before making up my mind. With "people" decisions I would take an additional step. I would let my personal, gut feelings about an individual or group of individuals influence my choice. A candidate for a top job in the Administration might be eminently qualified for the position, but if I didn't feel comfortable with the person, the chances are that the job would go to someone else.

Cabinet appointments I made in the spring and early summer of 1975 illustrate this point. As Secretary of Commerce for the past two years, Fred Dent had been an excellent spokesman for the business community. Although he wanted out of Washington, he also wanted to help the Administration in any way he could. I named him as my Special Representative for Trade Negotiations and asked him to look out for our interests at the GATT (General Agreement on Tariffs and Trade) talks that were about to resume in Geneva. To replace Dent at Commerce, I selected Interior Secretary Rogers Morton, my old friend and colleague in the House, with whom I really felt comfortable. Then, to fill Morton's shoes at Interior, I nominated former Wyoming Governor Stanley K. Hathaway. The New York *Times* called my decision "indefensible," but Stan had been an excellent administrator. He came from a state whose future depended not only on the development of its huge natural resources but also on the protection of its environment; he had walked the narrow path between responsible development and conservation, and he had won the respect of his fellow governors. I thought he would make a first-class Secretary of the Interior.

My final appointment to the Cabinet in the first half of 1975 was at HEW. Cap Weinberger had wanted to leave for months. I had asked him to stay on until the end of my term, but personal considerations—his wife suffered from asthma, and Washington's climate was bad for her—required his return to private life in California.

With a 1975 budget of $110 billion, HEW was the costliest bureaucracy in the federal government. Running it well was one of the most difficult challenges in Washington, so Cap's successor had to be a good administrator. I wouldn't object at all, I told Rumsfeld, if the next HEW Secretary was a political moderate with an academic background. And it would be ideal if he or she was a younger person who represented the South.

No sooner had I described what sort of person I wanted than the name of Dr. F. David Mathews came to mind. He was president of the University of Alabama, a thirty-nine-year-old Democrat who liked to call himself independent. For the past year or so he had been serving on the advisory council of the American Revolution Bicentennial Administration, and I had been impressed with his appearance and demeanor. Every check we made on him turned out to be positive. Mathews was just the man for the job and I convinced him to take it. With these changes, my Cabinet was set.

My desire to surround myself with people whom I respected and with whom I had an easy personal relationship applied even more to the members of my "kitchen cabinet." That group included such old friends as Bryce Harlow, Mel Laird, John Byrnes, Bill Scranton, David Packard and Bill Whyte. At least once every six weeks they would troop into the Cabinet Room, roll up their shirtsleeves and tell me what they thought of the job I was doing as President. They were free to praise or criticize. When things were getting tough, they gave me encouragement and said the Administration was pursuing the right course. When things were picking up, they kept me from getting carried away with myself. Sure, the polls look good, they'd say, but don't get overly optimistic. And they reminded me I still had this or that problem to solve. Laird was the most "political" member of the group, Scranton the most liberal on social issues, Harlow and Whyte the most fiscally responsible. And they gave me blunt advice when I needed it most.

Back in January, for example, they had watched me cut a practice videotape in which I outlined the economic and energy proposals that I was about to submit to Congress. That was the first time that I'd ever used a TelePrompTer, and the group thought my performance was terrible. Not only did they criticize the content of the speech, they also lambasted the delivery. As a result, I went back and revised the speech and then revised it again. On another occasion, after I had said that I wanted to refund a flat percentage of 1974 income tax payments to every taxpayer no matter how well off that person might be, the group protested that my plan was ridiculous. Packard, a millionaire who had served as Deputy Secretary of Defense, argued that the rich didn't deserve the same break as the poor or the middle class. "For me to get a rebate is absurd," he maintained, and because of his insistence, I decided to propose an income limitation on the people who would be eligible for the rebates. When Scranton and I were discussing the collapse of South Vietnam, the value of these informal sessions was brought home to me. "Bill, you didn't favor military aid to South Vietnam," I said.

"No, I didn't," he agreed.

I looked him in the eye and mentioned other areas where we had disagreed.

"You were opposed to the Nixon pardon."

"That's right," he said.

"You weren't enthusiastic about my economic program."

"That's right," he said again.

"My food stamp decision drove you up the wall."

"It sure did," he said.

I paused, puffed on my pipe and then asked, "Why are you for me at all?"

"Because you're the first President I ever knew whom I could talk to like that."

By mid April of 1975, my Administration was eight months old. The shocks of the Nixon resignation, the pardon and the recession had subsided. We still faced trouble abroad, but the healing process had continued at home. People seemed to have more confidence in themselves and in their institutions of government. In some respects, my job for the past eight months had been akin to that of the substitute quarterback who enters the game in the fourth quarter with his team trailing by several touchdowns. He has to play "catch-up" ball and inspire his tired teammates to make an extra effort to win. I don't want to carry the football analogy too far, but the truth is that by the middle of April, I felt we had put some points on the board and that if we were not yet ahead in the game, we had at least tied the score. Instead of having to respond immediately to each new emergency, I could begin to shape my own agenda and define the goals I wanted my fellow citizens to endorse. As James M. Naughton pointed out in the New York *Times:* "They are essentially conservative goals, more a reflection of the country's past than an invitation to a utopian future." He went on to list them—correctly—as follows: less government intervention in the affairs of citizens and corporations, greater reliance on individual initiative and a free market economy, and increased local responsibility for overcoming adversities.

None of these goals sounded particularly dramatic, of course, and that's why some people had difficulty responding to them. Political pundits in the nation's capital said that my ideas were stale and that I lacked "vision" as a President. Ever since FDR, that word "vision" has been equated by the media with new federal attempts to solve new problems. The more costly these attempts, the more "vision" their backers possess—and never mind that these "visionaries" are spending money that doesn't belong to them. But I have always felt that the real purpose of government is to enhance the lives of people and that a leader can best do that by restraining government in most cases instead of enlarging it at every opportunity.

If "vision" is to be defined as inspirational rhetoric describing how this or that new government program will better the human condition in the next sixty days, then I'll have to confess I didn't have it. As President, it was my job to identify the trends that were emerging in American society—trends that were not immediately apparent to everyone and generated no headlines—and then to determine what decisions could affect those trends and put the country in better shape ten to twenty years from now. That's why I kept saying the rate of growth of federal expenditures should stay below the rate of growth of the economy as a whole. And that's why I promised to inhibit the growth of income transfer payment programs. The distribution of the nation's resources was undergoing a fast and fundamental change. I might not be able to reverse the process, but at least I could point out the dangers in the trend.

If this suffices to classify me as a "conservative," I'll be proud of the label. Conservatism has always meant more to me than simply sticking up for private property and free enterprise. It has also meant defending our heritage and preserving our values. When Sir Kenneth Clark narrated the 1970 TV series *Civilisation,* he concluded: "At this point, I reveal myself in my true colors as a stick-in-the-mud. I believe that order is better than chaos, creation better than destruction. I prefer gentleness to violence, forgiveness to vendetta. On the whole, I think knowledge is better than ignorance, and I'm sure that human sympathy is better than doctrinaire ideology. I believe that in spite of the recent triumphs of science, men have not changed that much in the last two thousand years, and in consequence, we must still try to learn from history. Above all, I believe in the God-given genius of certain individuals, and I value a society that makes their existence possible." To that I could say only "Amen."

I didn't want to promise a solution for every problem I saw encompassed in every trend, but I did want to raise some questions that needed to be asked. How should we, for example, balance our national need to collect intelligence against our constitutional obligation to preserve and protect the rights of all Americans? How should we as a society deal with criminals, and were we thinking too much about the perpetrators, rather than the victims, of crime? How much government regulation did we need, and how much was too much?

At the time I was preparing to address these issues, I was reminded once again of just how far our country had come. The occasion was my appearance on April 18 at Boston's Old North Church. Two hundred years before, patriots had hung two lanterns from the steeple of that church, sending Paul Revere on his famous ride to warn his countrymen that British troops were on the march to Lexington and Concord. (The next day, Minutemen had stood at the Old North Bridge, raised their muskets and fired "the shot heard 'round the world.") I had never been to the historic church before, and the experience was so inspiring that it gave me goose bumps. As I mounted the spiral staircase to the pulpit and then turned around to face the hushed congregation, I found myself thinking of my parents and wishing they could have lived long enough to see me there as President. At the conclusion of my speech, I would be lighting a candle in a third lantern to symbolize America's third century. My parents would have been very proud.

"Let us pray here in the Old North Church tonight," I told the congregation, "that those who follow one hundred or two hundred years from now may look back at us and say: We were a society which combined reason with liberty and hope with freedom. May it be said above all: We kept the faith, freedom flourished, liberty lived. These are the abiding principles of our past and the greatest promise of our future."

Then I left the pulpit, descended the spiral staircase, lit the candle in the third lantern and walked slowly down the center aisle. The congregation began singing "Faith of Our Fathers," one of my favorite hymns, and it was all I could do to keep my emotions in check.

In the months since I had asked Nelson Rockefeller to chair a commission that would look into the alleged misdeeds of our intelligence agencies, the panel had done a good job. What worried me most was the fact that Congress seemed determined to take over the act. Both the House and the Senate had established committees to investigate CIA activities over the past twenty-five years, and they wanted to look at *everything* in the files. Back in the 1950s and early 1960s, when I was on the House Appropriations Committee, no more than ten or twelve members of Congress were fully and regularly informed about the budget and the activities of the CIA. For eight years prior to January 1965, I was one of this group. By 1975, however, that number had swollen to between fifty and seventy-five. Inevitably, there were leaks; public embarrassment followed, and the agency was having trouble doing its job.

The chairman of the House investigation was Representative Otis Pike, a Democrat from New York. His counterpart in the Senate was Idaho Democrat Frank Church. The Church probe was sensational and irresponsible—Church made no secret of his Presidential ambitions—and it was having a devastating impact on morale at the CIA. Director Bill Colby, Kissinger and Scowcroft all told me that the agency was losing good people and that the employees who remained were increasingly inhibited in supplying opinions and analyses. The

intelligence services of other nations, they continued, were more reluctant to deal with us. If the probes, and the headlines, continued
much longer, our sources abroad would dry up. Although I thought
that agency programs should receive appropriate Congressional review, I felt that a sensationalized debate over legitimate intelligence
activities constituted a disservice to the nation. The investigation, I
urged, had to be conducted with both discretion and dispatch to
avoid crippling a vital national institution.

But soon it became clear to me that some members of Congress
wanted to dismantle the CIA. They were trying to eliminate covert
operations altogether, and if they didn't succeed in that, they wanted
to restrict those operations to such an extent that they would be
meaningless. "As Congress oversees intelligence activities, it must, of
course, organize itself to do so in a responsible way," I noted in an
April speech before a joint session of Congress. "It has been traditional for the Executive to consult with the Congress through specially
protected procedures that safeguard essential secrets. But recently,
some of those procedures have been altered in a way that makes the
protection of vital information very difficult. I will work with the
leaders of the House and the Senate to devise procedures which will
meet the needs of the Congress for review of intelligence agency
activities and the needs of the nation for an effective intelligence
service."

But Congress wasn't satisfied. The House and Senate investigations
careened along their perilous course. Interestingly, the push to continue these probes came not so much from the members of Congress
who served on the two committees as from the committee staffs, and
this fact underlines a trend that I find very troubling. To a degree
that would shock 99 percent of the American people, many decisions
that affect every aspect of their lives are made not by Congressmen
or Senators but by those members' personal or committee staffs, the
Unelected Representatives of Capitol Hill.

When I first came to Washington, I was allowed to hire three people for my House staff. Today, each member can have as many as
eighteen. A Senator's staff complement has increased from fifteen to
seventy-five or more. The cost of running Congress has spiraled accordingly—from $25 million in 1949 to $1.1 billion today. But the

really significant development has been the proliferation of committees and subcommittees in both houses of Congress. In 1949, there were 135. By 1975, that total had mushroomed to 313. Each Representative served on an average of 3.5 of these panels; each Senator on an average of ten. Understandably, Congressmen and Senators spend much of their time shuttling from one committee or subcommittee meeting to another. They must also greet and listen to constituents and spend hours on the House or Senate floor, and there aren't enough hours in the day for them to understand in any depth most of the issues being discussed. The result: they depend increasingly on their personal and committee staffs.

And these employees are more than willing to fill the gap. They submit memos on important issues for their bosses to read. They draft the legislation that their committees are considering. They schedule hearings, decide whom to call as witnesses and prepare questions for the members to ask. When the hearings conclude, they write the committee reports. They affect every decision made on Capitol Hill. Admittedly, our foreign and domestic policies are more complicated today than they were in 1949. Obviously, too, Congress *should* have a staff large enough to enable it to challenge witnesses from the Executive Branch or outside spokesmen for particular points of view. Finally, it's true that members of Congress have more constituents today than they or their predecessors had thirty years ago. The work load is much heavier. Still, the growth in the number of staff employees—a 400 percent increase since 1949—has far overshadowed the jump in the number of constituents or the magnitude and complexity of the issues.

Generalizations are always risky, yet it's possible to make some broad assumptions about these staff employees, who receive anywhere from $25,000 to $50,000-plus per year. First, they're bright, well educated and hard working. More often than not, they're not from their employer's home district or state, so they don't reflect the views of the people back home. A large number of them seem to come instead from university campuses in the Boston-Washington corridor. What concerns me is that these staffers, by virtue of their long experience on Capitol Hill, think they can speak for the members they are supposed to serve. Which, in fact, is what they do.

These staffers wield enormous power, yet they're not accountable to the voters. They can have a significant impact on legislation without having to worry about being reelected every two or six years. And that, in my opinion, is not what the Founding Fathers had in mind.

There are, of course, many outstanding, highly professional staff members on Capitol Hill who reflect the views of their bosses and do not attempt to push through their own positions on policy. But, unfortunately, there are too few of them.

On many occasions, I would ask Bill Timmons, Jack Marsh or Max Friedersdorf, my legislative liaison men, to check on the status of important bills pending before various committees of the Congress. Invariably, they would come back to me and say, "Well, we've worked out a compromise with Mr. A, who works for Congressman B." Or, "We have an agreement with Mr. C, who works for Senator D." Sometimes they'd report that committee staff employees thought so little of Administration ideas that they didn't even bother to refer them to their elected bosses. They just shot them down on their own authority.

I wish I could cite simple remedies for this situation, but they don't exist. Congress has been in the control of one party for so long that there has been little turnover in staff personnel or ideology. Certainly Congress could abolish some of its numerous committees and subcommittees, but that isn't likely to happen soon. As they continue to proliferate, members will find less and less time to do their homework. The opportunities for able staffers to expand their influence will multiply. Only when citizens begin to realize that a fourth branch of government is making decisions for them at their expense and without their control will the situation change.

After raising questions about the proper role of intelligence agencies in a democratic society—and after urging Congress not to cripple those agencies' effectiveness—the next area I wanted to throw a spotlight on was crime. Serious crime had increased by 17 percent in 1974—the biggest jump since the FBI began keeping the statistics forty-five years earlier—and the trend for the first few months of 1975 was discouraging. On the surface, the reason for this was the recession. When people are hungry and out of work, they're more likely to commit crimes. Yet in truth the crime rate had been going up for a long time.

Too often, the Nixon Administration's response to this was a lot of rhetoric about the need to maintain "law and order." In addition, the Law Enforcement Assistance Administration (LEAA), an agency of the Department of Justice, funneled billions of dollars' worth of hardware to police departments in almost every community. The result was a public perception that Washington felt the federal government—and only the federal government—could do something about crime. And still the crime rate increased. Clearly, a new approach was necessary. I felt the major responsibility for combating crime rested with state and local governments, and not with some bureaucrats in Washington, and I wanted to return it there. Equally important, I felt it was time for us as a people to change the way we *thought* about crime.

Four months after becoming President, I had had a chance to talk with Harvard Professor James Q. Wilson. After our conversation, he sent me a copy of his book *Thinking About Crime*, which I read with great interest. One of his major points was that most serious crimes were committed by repeat offenders, people who had been convicted before. Another was that too many Americans had forgotten that the primary purpose of imprisonment was *not* to rehabilitate the convicted criminal so that he could return to society, but to punish him and keep him off the streets. The *certainty* of having to spend a specified time behind bars after being convicted of a serious offense, Wilson maintained, was more important as a deterrent than almost anything else. Finally, Wilson worried that the nation's opinion leaders were focusing their concerns on the criminal and not on the victims of criminal acts.

His points made a lot of sense to me. On April 25, I was scheduled to speak at the 150th birthday ceremony of the Yale Law School, my alma mater. I decided to use his arguments, not only as the skeleton for my formal address, but also as the framework for the detailed proposals that I would submit to Congress afterward. The Preamble of the Constitution contains a phrase about the responsibility of the President to ensure "domestic tranquillity." That, I decided, was a far better definition of my approach to crime than "law and order."

The audience for my address in New Haven that night included such prominent Americans as Supreme Court Justices Potter Stewart and Byron White, Secretary of HUD Carla Hills and Yale University

President Kingman Brewster, Jr. But I was even happier to see Myres McDougal, the distinguished law professor who had interviewed me before my admission to the law school some forty years before. Even facing so learned a gathering, I couldn't resist the opportunity to poke a little fun at myself. "Obviously," I began, "it's a very great privilege and pleasure to be here at the Yale Law School Sesquicentennial Convocation. And I defy anyone to say that and chew gum at the same time." The moment the laughter died down, I was into the substantive part of the speech.

"Do we provide that domestic tranquillity which the Constitution seeks? If we take the crime rates as an indication, the answer has to be no. The number of violent crimes rises steadily, and we have recently suffered the national disgrace of lawbreaking in high places. We have seen how lawbreaking by officials can be stopped by the proper functioning of our basic institutions. But [we have] been far less successful in dealing with the sort of crime that obsesses America day and night. I mean crime that invades our neighborhoods and our homes—murders, robberies, rapes, muggings, holdups, break-ins— the kind of brutal violence that makes us fearful of strangers and afraid to go out at night.

"In thinking about this problem, I do not seek vindictive punishment of the criminal but protection of the innocent victim. The victims are my primary concern." Then I listed my specific proposals with this new emphasis. Not all people convicted of crimes go to jail, I pointed out. According to one report I had read, 50 percent of all convicted felons in New York served no time at all. Sometimes repeat offenders fared even better than that. When Rand Corporation researchers studied the records of one major jurisdiction, they discovered that only 27 percent of robbers with *multiple* convictions were actually sent to prison. And this, I said, had to stop. People convicted of violent crimes should have to go to jail. I urged the imposition of mandatory sentences for them and for "career" criminals as well. Second, I suggested less delay in bringing those arrested to trial, less plea bargaining and more courtroom determination of guilt or innocence. Increasing caseloads were overcrowding the nation's courts, and the changes I was recommending would cost money. I was aware of that. But under the Constitution the states were primarily responsible for crime control. So as my third proposal, I said that we in Washington could provide leadership by amending the Federal Code to make more sentences mandatory. We could also supply funds to add judges, prosecutors and public defenders to the federal system. "This federal model," I continued, "should encourage states to adopt similar priorities for the use of their own funds and those provided by the LEAA." Summing up, I said: "The old question still remains: Can a free people restrain crime without sacrificing fundamental liberties and a heritage of compassion?

"I am confident of the American answer. Let it become a vital element on America's new agenda. Let us show that we can temper together those opposite elements of liberty and restraint into one consistent whole. Let us set an example for the world of a law-abiding America glorying in its freedom as well as its respect for law. Let us, at last, fulfill the constitutional promise of domestic tranquillity for all our law-abiding citizens."

A third priority on my agenda for the first six months of 1975 was regulatory reform. And was that reform needed! Rules and regulations churned out by federal agencies were having a damaging effect on almost every aspect of American life. They were costing taxpayers an estimated $62.9 billion per year, an average of $300 per citizen. They were increasing the cost of doing business—a cost that's always passed along to consumers—and thus contributing to inflation. They were perpetuating huge bureaucracies—more than 60,000 people were employed by the federal government for the sole purpose of writing, reviewing and enforcing regulations—to sift through pyramids of paperwork. (In 1974, Congress passed 404 new laws. The federal bureaucracy, however, produced 7,496 new rules and regulations, which accounted for some 45,000 pages of fine print in the *Federal Register*.) They were stifling American productivity, promoting inefficiency, eliminating competition and even invading personal privacy. Red tape surrounded and almost smothered us; we as a nation were about to suffocate.

How had we allowed this to happen to us? The answer stems from our own good intentions. So anxious have we been to protect our environment, improve the quality of our water and air, promote safety on the job, prevent discrimination in employment, eliminate dangerous substances in the food we eat, the clothes we wear and the products we buy, purify what we hear on radio and TV, and root out unfair business practices, that we have tended to ignore the strains these layers of legislation have placed on the American economy. We have forgotten to weigh the consequences of our acts.

In the late nineteenth and early twentieth centuries, of course, there was a real need for regulatory agencies. In 1887, the Interstate Commerce Commission was established to protect the public from railroad monopolies and to regulate the railroads' rates and practices. That was the first of these agencies. Others were to follow soon. In 1906, after Congress passed the Food and Drug Act, the Food and Drug Administration came into being to monitor laws governing food and pharmaceuticals. Then came the Federal Trade Commission, the Federal Power Commission, the Federal Communications Commission, the Securities and Exchange Commission, the Federal Maritime Commission and the Civil Aeronautics Board.

By the time Lyndon Johnson instituted his Great Society, the perception was ingrained in Washington that the solution to every problem was to create a new federal regulatory agency to write and enforce rules. Thus, we saw the creation of the Equal Employment Opportunity Commission in 1965, the Environmental Protection Agency and the Occupational Safety and Health Administration in 1970 and the Consumer Products Safety Commission two years later. By then, the regulatory itch was spreading fast. In 1975, Congress created the Federal Election Commission and the Commodity Futures Trading Commission. Pressure started to build to establish a new Consumer Protection Agency. And this was understandable. One of the enduring truths of the nation's capital is that bureaucrats *survive*. Agencies don't fold their tents and quietly fade away after their work is done. They find Something New to Do. Invariably, that Something New involves more people with more power and more paperwork—all involving more expenditures.

So by 1975, these agencies were issuing rules that were unwieldy, unnecessary, costly and contradictory. Examples of each abounded for everyone to see:

• *Unwieldy*: When an Oregon firm attempted to renew the licenses it held to manage three small TV stations, it contacted the

Federal Communications Commission and requested the appropriate forms. When completed, the applications weighed a total of forty-five pounds.

• *Unnecessary*: Presumably, the Occupational Safety and Health Administration was concerned about the presence of 22,000 different toxic substances used in American industry. Yet since its creation in 1972, it had issued regulations governing workers' exposure to fewer than twenty of them. At the same time, however, it had devoted countless hours to the proper construction of portable wooden ladders and had published twelve pages of regulations about them.

• *Costly*: Because of Interstate Commerce Commission rules, some trucks that hauled cargo on trips longer than 1,000 miles were not allowed to pick up freight at their destination and carry it back home. They had to "deadhead" back to their point of origin. Food retailers said these regulations cost $250 million per year; invariably, the shopper in the supermarket ended up paying the bill.

• *Contradictory*: Concerned about accidents at construction sites, Occupational Safety and Health Administration bureaucrats issued orders requiring the installation of alarms that sound when trucks are backing up. Then they turned around and told construction workers to wear ear plugs because of the noise.

Few sectors of the American economy were more stifled by government regulation than the transportation industry, and I thought deregulation was urgently required. If we succeeded in loosening federal control over the railroad, trucking and airline industries, we would boost competition, promote more efficient operations and lower the prices consumers had to pay. I knew that the carriers—the railroads, the airlines, the truckers and their union allies—would complain bitterly, because they liked the status quo, but the effort was worth a try. Railroad deregulation would be my number one priority. I talked to Transportation Secretary Bill Coleman at some length about this, and he enthusiastically took the lead and the bruises in those controversial areas where entrenched interests had held sway too long. Then I told staffers to get cracking on the bill that I wanted to submit to Congress before the end of May.

I realized that it would take a lot of work to push through Congress that measure and other proposals I'd made. Yet after nine months as

President, my faith in the job that my Administration was doing to "ensure domestic tranquillity" was increasing with every passing day. The American people, I felt, were more at ease with my Administration. Within a few days, however, an incident thousands of miles away would give them a chance to view another side of their President.

5

On the Move

"Difficulty is the one excuse that history never accepts."
— Edward R. Murrow

In the wake of our humiliating retreat from Cambodia and South Vietnam in the spring of 1975, our allies around the world began to question our resolve. "America—A Helpless Giant," ran the headline over a page-one editorial in the respected *Frankfurter Allgemeine Zeitung.* The British were concerned. So, too, were the French. Our friends in Asia were equally upset. In the Middle East, the Israelis began to wonder whether the U.S. would stand by them in the event of a war.

As long as I was President, I decided, the U.S. would not abandon its commitments overseas. We would not permit our setbacks to become a license for others to fish in troubled waters. Rhetoric alone, I knew, would not persuade anyone that America would stand firm. They would have to see proof of our resolve.

The opportunity to show that proof came without warning. At 7:40 on the morning of May 12, Brent Scowcroft stepped into the Oval Office to tell me that an American merchant ship, S.S. *Mayaguez,* had been seized in international waters off the coast of Cambodia. First reports from the scene were very sketchy, but there were indications that the Cambodians were towing the ship toward the port of

Kompong Som. Shortly after noon that day, I convened a meeting of the National Security Council in the Cabinet Room. CIA Director Bill Colby led off by presenting the facts as we knew them then. *Mayaguez*, carrying a crew of thirty-nine and a cargo of food, paints and chemicals, had been steaming between Hong Kong and the port of Sattahip in southern Thailand. In the vicinity of Poulo Wai island, sixty miles off the Cambodian coast, Communist gunboats had intercepted and fired upon her; troops had boarded and taken captive her civilian crew.

With these facts at hand, we could begin to deliberate policy. Kissinger leaned forward over the table and with emotion stressed the broad ramifications of the incident. The issues at stake went far beyond the seizure of the ship, he said; they extended to international perceptions of U.S. resolve and will. If we failed to respond to the challenge, it would be a serious blow to our prestige around the world. "At some point," he continued, "the United States must draw the line. This is not our idea of the best such situation. It is not our choice. But we must act upon it now, and act firmly."

Everyone agreed that we had to mount *some* response, but the military situation was discouraging. Our destroyers and the aircraft carrier U.S.S. *Coral Sea* were too far away to be of immediate help. We didn't have adequate forces on the ground in Thailand. We would have to fly in Marines from bases in Okinawa and the Philippines. They would have to use Thailand as a jumping-off point; the Thais wouldn't be very happy about that, but until *Mayaguez* and her crew were safe, I didn't give a damn about offending their sensibilities.

At the conclusion of that meeting, I decided to move forward on two fronts simultaneously. I told Kissinger to have the State Department demand the immediate release of the ship and her crew. The problem there, of course, was that State didn't know upon whom to serve the demand. We had no diplomatic relations with the new Khmer Rouge regime. Perhaps the Chinese would act as intermediaries. It was unlikely but still worth a try. At the same time, I ordered *Coral Sea* and other ships to speed toward the site of the incident. Additionally, I directed aircraft based in the Philippines to locate *Mayaguez* and keep her in view.

The diplomatic approach didn't seem promising. Summoned to the State Department, the Chinese representative in Washington refused to accept our message for the Cambodians. And all day Monday we received contradictory reports. First we heard that *Mayaguez* was steaming toward the mainland of Cambodia, then that she was anchored off Koh Tang island, thirty-four miles from shore, later that she was heading toward the mainland again. Finally, at 10:30 that night, Scowcroft called to report that a reconnaissance plane had located *Mayaguez* anchored off Poulo Wai in the company of two gunboats and that the plane had sustained damage from small-arms fire. Three hours later, he called again to say that the ship was less than an hour out of Kompong Som. At 2:30 A.M., he reported the ship was dead in the water one mile north of Koh Tang. She was preparing to anchor there, he said.

Schlesinger telephoned me at 5:52 that Tuesday morning, and we talked for more than an hour. Back in 1968, I remembered, the North Koreans had captured the intelligence ship U.S.S. *Pueblo* in international waters and forced her and her crew into the port of Wonsan. The U.S. had not been able to respond fast enough to prevent the transfer, and as a result, *Pueblo*'s crew had languished in a North Korean prison camp for nearly a year. I was determined not to allow a repetition of that incident, so I told Schlesinger to make sure that no Cambodian vessels moved between Koh Tang and the mainland.

At 10:22 that morning, I convened a second meeting of the NSC. In Bangkok, Thai Premier Kukrit Pramoj had just issued a statement warning that he would not permit us to use Thai bases for operations against Cambodia. I sensed that this was more political rhetoric than anything else; the Thais knew we had no alternative but to use the base at Utapao. Since Scowcroft's telephone call eight hours before, we suspected that at least some of the crew had been transferred from *Mayaguez* to Koh Tang. Another of our circling planes had been damaged by fire from the ground. But the orders I had given thus far had been carried out and several small boats had been turned back or sunk. To prevent the Cambodians from moving *Mayaguez* any farther, U.S. planes had fired warning shots across her bow. *Coral Sea* and several destroyers were steaming at top speed to the Gulf of Siam. Now I ordered a battalion landing team of eleven hundred

Marines airlifted from Okinawa to the base at Utapao plus two Marine platoons from the Philippines. Additionally, I issued instructions for the carrier *Hancock* to sail from the Philippines as soon as possible.

At 10:40 Tuesday night, there was a third meeting of the NSC. The news was not encouraging. An Air Force helicopter en route to Utapao had crashed in Thailand, and all twenty-three Americans on board had been killed. Our efforts to solve the crisis diplomatically had failed. The Chinese in Peking had returned the second message we had asked them to give the Cambodians. Significantly, however, a Chinese official in Paris had said that his country wouldn't do anything should we decide to use military force.

While we were debating what further steps to take, a message was hand delivered to the Cabinet Room from the Situation Room. It was from the pilot of an Air Force A-7 attack aircraft flying over the scene. A Cambodian vessel had just left Koh Tang and was headed toward Kompong Som. The pilot had made one pass. He was about to sink the ship with his 20-mm cannon when he thought he recognized Caucasians huddled on the deck below. He could not be sure, so he was radioing for further instructions. Admiral James L. Holloway III, the Chief of Naval Operations, was representing the Joint Chiefs. "You get a message to that pilot to shoot across the bow but do not sink the boat," I said. Nodding, Holloway headed for the Situation Room.

Once I've made a decision, I seldom fret about it, but this one caused me some anxiety. If the pilot had been right, crew members were on their way to the mainland where we would have a far more difficult time effecting their recovery. My concern increased during the night as new reports flowed into the Situation Room. Several other patrol craft had attempted to leave the island. When they had ignored our planes' signals to stop, they had been destroyed. Suppose those vessels had carried crew members from *Mayaguez* below their decks? There was no way to tell, and that possibility was awful to contemplate.

During that third meeting of the NSC—which didn't break up until 12:30 Wednesday morning—we decided to make one final approach diplomatically. Our ambassador to the United Nations, John Scali, would give U.N. Secretary General Kurt Waldheim a letter requesting his help in securing the release of the ship and her crew. I didn't really expect any results from that, so I determined that we would probably have to move militarily. But first we would wait and see.

At 3:52 on Wednesday afternoon, I convened the fourth and final meeting of the NSC. *Mayaguez* remained at anchor off Koh Tang and we had no new information as to the whereabouts of the crew. Some crewmen, we had to assume, remained aboard ship. Some may have been on the island, while others had been taken to the mainland. Our naval forces now were very close to the scene. The destroyer escort *Holt* was only a mile or so away. The destroyer *Wilson* was approaching fast, and *Coral Sea* would soon be close enough to launch air strikes on the mainland. Air Force General David Jones led off by reviewing the various options on his charts. They ranged all the way from a minimum use of force—helicoptering Marines to Koh Tang to rescue *Mayaguez* and her crew and then withdrawing them as soon as possible—to a maximum display: rescuing the ship and her crew and then "punishing" Cambodia by air strikes.

And this is where Kissinger and I disagreed with Schlesinger. Our first consideration, of course, was the recovery of the ship and her crew. But Henry and I felt that we had to do more. We didn't want the Cambodians to be in a position to reinforce Koh Tang once our attack began. We wanted them to know that we meant business, so we opted for air strikes against the mainland as well. Schlesinger agreed that our first priority should be to rescue the ship and her crew, but he was far less eager to use *Mayaguez* as an example for Asia and the world. He was concerned that our bombing plans were too extensive. There was a lull in the discussion. Then, from the back of the room, a new voice spoke up. It was Kennerly, who had been taking pictures of us for the past hour or so. Never before during a meeting of this kind had he entered the conversation; I knew he wouldn't have done so now unless what he had to say was important.

"Has anyone considered," he asked, "that this might be the act of a local Cambodian commander who has just taken it into his own hands to halt any ship that comes by? Has anyone stopped to think that he might not have gotten his orders from Phnom Penh? If that's what has happened, you know, you can blow the whole place away and it's not gonna make any difference. Everyone here has been talking about Cambodia as if it were a traditional government. Like France. We have trouble with France, we just pick up the telephone and call. We know who to talk to. But I was in Cambodia just two weeks ago, and it's not that kind of government at all. We don't even know who the leadership is. Has anyone considered that?"

For several seconds there was silence in the Cabinet Room. Everyone seemed stunned that this brash photographer who was not yet thirty years old would have the guts to offer an unsolicited opinion to the President, the Vice President, the Secretaries of State and Defense, the Director of the CIA and the Chairman of the Joint Chiefs of Staff. Yet I wasn't surprised, and I was glad to hear his point of view.

The discussion resumed about what our reaction should be. B-52 crews on Guam had been placed on alert in the event that carrier aircraft couldn't reach their targets on time. Rockefeller favored giving the B-52s the go-ahead. Kissinger preferred carrier strikes if the planes were available, but he was adamant about the need for a strong response. So was Scowcroft. Schlesinger didn't seem to want any bombing at all, either by the B-52s or by the Navy carrier aircraft. JCS Chairman General George S. Brown wanted to hit the mainland, but he didn't want to use the B-52s. The decision was up to me. Subjectively, I felt that what Kennerly had said made a lot of sense. Massive air strikes would constitute overkill. It would be far better to have Navy jets from *Coral Sea* make surgical strikes against specific targets in the vicinity of Kompong Som.

Slightly more than an hour after the meeting began, I started issuing the orders. *Holt* was to seize and secure *Mayaguez*. Marines were to land on Koh Tang, rescue crew members there and destroy any Cambodian units that got in the way. *Coral Sea* was to launch four air strikes against military installations near Kompong Som, including an oil depot, railroad marshaling yards and the airfield at Ream. The first of these attacks was to occur at 8:45 P.M. EDT to coincide with the estimated time of our capture of the ship.

Under the provisions of the War Powers Act, I was required to consult with Congress before sending U.S. troops into action. The afternoon before, at my direction, White House aides had contacted twenty-one Congressional leaders to inform them of my plans to prevent the ship and her crew from being transferred to the mainland. Now, at the conclusion of this final meeting of the NSC, I asked Jack Marsh to spread the word that I wanted to see the bipartisan leaders of Congress. The meeting was set for 6:30 P.M. Because of rush-hour traffic, there was a slight delay. When the members arrived and trooped into the Cabinet Room, I reviewed the events of the past three days, explained the decisions I had just made, then asked for questions. Senator Mike Mansfield wondered why I had ordered the bombing of Kompong Som. Some crew members might be there, he pointed out. Wouldn't our air strikes put them in great jeopardy? I said we just didn't know the whereabouts of the crew. Sure, it was a risk, but one that I had to take. Some 2,400 Cambodian troops were stationed in the area, and there were at least a dozen military planes at Ream airfield. Those aircraft and Cambodian forces might attack the Marines on Koh Tang, and I couldn't allow that to happen. West Virginia Senator Robert Byrd wanted an assurance from me that I would comply with the War Powers Act and give Congress a full written report on every aspect of the incident. I told him I would carry out the provisions of the act even though I seriously questioned its applicability. House Speaker Carl Albert asked if there wasn't something else we could have done before resorting to force. "We waited as long as we could," I replied.

Dutch Prime Minister Johannes den Uyl was visiting Washington at the time. I had met with him for an hour that morning and was scheduled to join him that night for a working dinner in the White House. My meeting with Congressional leaders dragged on so long, however, that we had to keep pushing the dinner back half an hour at a time. Finally, after changing into my tuxedo, I greeted den Uyl at the North Portico. We went through the formality of welcoming our other guests at a reception, but my mind was on events taking place halfway around the globe.

The Marine assault on Koh Tang was not going well. Earlier, intelligence reports had estimated that fewer than two dozen Cambodians were on the small island. Those reports were wrong. Between 150 and 200 Khmer Rouge troops were dug in there; they were ready to fight, and the eight helicopters that carried about 175 Marines flew into withering fire from the ground. Three of the choppers crashed;

two others were disabled, and only 110 Marines actually landed on the island. They pushed the Cambodians back and started looking for the crew, with no luck. Minutes later, the destroyer escort *Holt* pulled alongside *Mayaguez,* and a small force of Marines stormed aboard. They found no crew members there, either.

At eight-fifteen that night (our time), while all this was going on, Scowcroft told me that the Cambodians in Phnom Penh had just broadcast over a local radio station their willingness to return the ship. Their message, however, had said nothing about the crew. Our planes had already taken off from *Coral Sea* on their first strike against the mainland. They would be over their targets in less than half an hour. I told Brent to have Schlesinger hold up the first strike until we had a better idea of what was happening. Brent said he would. Twenty minutes later, he called me again. We decided to go ahead with the bombing because we couldn't act on the basis of a radio message that was so imprecise. And there had been no official follow-ups from Phnom Penh. In due course, Schlesinger reported, "First strike completed." I assumed the second, third and fourth bombing runs would take place as planned.

During the dinner with den Uyl, I was totally preoccupied, and on several occasions I had to leave the table and step out to the usher's office to talk to Brent by phone and find out what was being done. Den Uyl seemed irritated that I wasn't giving him my full attention. Many Dutch leaders had been carping at us for years about our involvement in Vietnam and had exhibited a smug satisfaction over the defeat of our allies there. Yet they still expected us to shoulder the major burden of Europe's—and their—defense. And here I was responding to an act of piracy by doing everything I could to save American lives. Furthermore, decisive action would reassure our allies and bluntly warn our adversaries that the U.S. was not a helpless giant. This effort, if successful, would benefit not only the United States but the Netherlands as well. Den Uyl's inability to understand that annoyed the hell out of me.

At eleven o'clock that night, after bidding farewell to den Uyl, I returned to the Oval Office. Kissinger, Scowcroft and Rumsfeld were there. So were Hartmann, Marsh, Nessen and Friedersdorf. Schlesinger telephoned from the Pentagon to say that the pilot of a reconnaissance plane had spotted a fishing vessel steaming toward Koh Tang. Caucasians were on board, and they were waving white flags. Minutes later, he telephoned again. U.S.S. *Wilson* had intercepted the fishing vessel. The men waving white flags were the crew members of *Mayaguez*. I dropped the phone into its cradle and let my emotions show. "They're all safe," I said. "We got them all out. Thank God. It went perfectly. It just went great." Kissinger, Rumsfeld and the others erupted with whoops of joy.

Immediately I gave orders that the Marines on Koh Tang should prepare to disengage as soon as possible. Then I walked to the Briefing Room (I had changed into a business suit but was still wearing my patent leather evening shoes) and read a short statement to the American people over radio and TV. Finally, before going to bed, I decided to comply with the War Powers Act by attempting to explain, in identical letters to the Speaker of the House and the president pro tem of the Senate, everything that had happened in the last sixty-five hours. It had been a long day—a long three days, in fact—so when the alarm sounded at five-fifteen Thursday morning, I turned it off and went back to sleep for another hour.

Predictably, liberals in both the press and Congress were harshly critical of my decisions. In a column entitled "Barbarous Piracy," Anthony Lewis of the New York *Times* intoned: "Once again an American government shows that the only way it knows how to deal with frustration is by force. And the world is presumably meant to be impressed." In Congress, Senator Mansfield and Representative Holtzman assailed me for my alleged failure to observe the War Powers Act. I was supposed to "consult" with lawmakers before responding to the crisis, they claimed. Instead, I had merely informed them of what I planned to do. Missouri Senator Thomas Eagleton went several steps further. He introduced three separate amendments to the War Powers Act designed to plug its "loopholes" and prevent me—or any President who followed me—from taking the steps I had taken to save American lives. Then he asked the General Accounting Office, the auditing arm of Congress, to determine whether I had ordered the bombing of Cambodia "for punitive rather than defensive purposes." Such reactions, I thought, were hopelessly naïve.

In the cold light of dawn, two aspects of the *Mayaguez* affair disturbed me a lot. The first was the number of casualties we sustained: forty-one Americans—including those lost in the chopper crash—were killed during the operation, and another fifty were wounded. This was a high toll, and I felt terrible about it. The second was some high-level bumbling at the Defense Department. The first strike never took place, although we were told it had been "completed." The Navy jets dropped their bombs into the sea. It's possible that communications problems may have contributed to the misunderstanding. It's also possible that the planes in the first wave—which I had delayed for twenty minutes—may have run low on fuel. They may have been forced to jettison their ordnance in order to return to *Coral Sea*. What is harder for me to understand is why the fourth air strike—and I had specifically ordered four—was never carried out. I hadn't told anyone to cancel that attack. Apparently, someone had, and I was anxious to find out who had contravened my authority. The explanations I received from the Pentagon were not satisfactory at all, and direct answers kept eluding me. Perhaps I should have pursued my inquiry, but since we had achieved our objective, I let the matter drop. We had recovered the ship; we had rescued the crew, and the psychological boost the incident had given us as a people was significant. As Kentucky Representative Carroll Hubbard, Jr., chairman of the House Democratic freshman caucus, said, "It's good to win one for a change."

All of a sudden, the gloomy national mood began to fade. Many people's faith in their country was restored and my standing in the polls shot up 11 points. *Mayaguez* wasn't the only reason, of course; the economy was improving at a rapid rate, but the net effect was that I felt I had regained the initiative, and I determined to do what I could with it. I had promised the country that I would keep the federal budget deficit to $60 billion or below. In the two weeks after *Mayaguez*, when Congress sent up three measures for my signature—the Surface Mining Control and Reclamation Act, a bill to authorize appropriations for tourism programs and the Emergency Employment Appropriation Act—that would have upped the deficit by more than $2.1 billion, I didn't hesitate to veto them. Then, just before leaving for the NATO summit meeting in Brussels on May 18, I tried to turn people's attention to energy again.

Back in January, I reminded viewers on nationwide TV, I had sent Congress a 167-page draft of detailed legislation and urged it to enact my program within ninety days. We were dependent upon foreign sources for 37 percent of our petroleum needs, I noted. In 1970, we had paid only $3 billion for that foreign oil; now the figure was up to $25 billion per year, and it would continue to rise so long as the lawmakers did nothing. "We are today worse off than we were in January," I said. "Domestic oil production is going down, down, down. Natural gas production is starting to dwindle. Coal production is still at the levels of the 1940s. Foreign oil suppliers are considering another price increase. We cannot continue to depend on the price and supply whims of others. The Congress cannot drift, dawdle and forever debate America's future. I will continue to press for the program I recommended in January, which is still the only total energy program there is. I cannot sit here idly while nothing is done. We must get on with the job."

Of all the problems NATO faced in the late spring of 1975, perhaps the most serious was psychological. In the wake of Vietnam, would the U.S. remain firm against Communist aggression elsewhere? Could our old allies still depend on us? Democratic Senate leader Mike Mansfield and others had been calling for us to withdraw many of our troops from Western Europe. Understandably, the leaders of the NATO countries wanted to know whether this new mood of isolationism would prevail or whether we would honor our commitments abroad. But there were specific military and political problems as well. The dispute between Greece and Turkey over Cyprus still threatened NATO's eastern flank. The new left-wing leaders of Portugal posed a danger of a different kind. Suppose Communists joined or, worse yet, dominated the Lisbon government. How could the West share military secrets with them? What would happen if the Soviets won access to Portuguese airfields or naval bases? Would we have to strip Portugal of its NATO membership?

And what should we do about Spain? The Spaniards had a role to play in the defense of the West. They recognized that and were willing to join the alliance. The problem there was that some of our more liberal NATO allies—the Dutch, Norwegians and Danes—insisted on blocking Spain's membership as long as Generalissimo Francisco Franco was alive. Finally, Italy's political and economic stability was suspect; elections were scheduled in June, and it was probable that the Communists would score heavy gains. All these were serious problems whose resolution would affect the course of our own future security. Yet they paled when compared to the ones we faced in the Middle East.

Since the collapse in March of Kissinger's tireless shuttle diplomacy, I had talked to a number of outside authorities including former Supreme Court Justice Arthur Goldberg, former Under Secretaries of State George Ball and Eugene Rostow and former Senator J. William Fulbright. Additionally, at the suggestion of my old friend Max Fisher, I met on several occasions in the Oval Office with leaders of the American Jewish community. What bothered me most was the claim by some of those leaders that inasmuch as I was suggesting the possibility of a reassessment of our policy toward Israel, I must be anti-Israel or even anti-Semitic. That was just not true; and I told these groups:

> In all my public life, I have never wavered in my support for a free and secure Israel. There was never one vote or one speech that could be interpreted otherwise. All of my life, I have had great respect for the Jewish people. I feel that way today, and anyone who says I don't doesn't know me at all.
>
> It is *because* of my affection and admiration for the Jewish people and the state of Israel that I'm so concerned about the lack of progress toward peace in that part of the world. We *must* have progress soon if we are to avoid another war, the fifth in thirty years. Quite frankly, Israel's leaders have not been as quick to recognize this as I had hoped they would be. They have not been as forthcoming as I wanted them to be. Now, I have always believed in maintaining the national integrity of Israel, but always within the context of maintaining world peace and—above everything else—within the context of protecting the national interests of the United States. What this means is that the leaders of Israel and the American Jewish community here simply can't hold up a legitimate settlement and expect me as President to tolerate it.

In mid April, Foreign Minister Yigal Allon flew to Washington for lengthy talks with Kissinger. Henry had wanted to see if there had been any "give" in the Israeli position since the collapse of the talks in March. Even Allon, one of the more moderate members of his country's cabinet, was not about to show any give. I decided to increase the pressure a bit.

For the past several weeks, the Israelis had been engaged in a not very subtle campaign to discredit Kissinger. He had been their hero after the 1973 war; now, all of a sudden, he was their adversary. Because Henry was a Jew, the Israeli hard-liners said, he was bending over backward to be "fair" to the Arabs. He was "out-Gentiling the Gentiles"; he was "sabotaging" Israel's interests. The charges were utterly false, of course. No one had worked harder to achieve a just and lasting peace in the Middle East than Henry Kissinger, and to see him attacked that way was reprehensible.

The high-stakes poker game continued. Early in May, we announced that I would be meeting Egyptian President Sadat in Salzburg, Austria, during the first week of June. Only after I'd talked with him would I meet with Rabin. Always before, American Presidents had met with the Israelis first. The fact that I had said I wanted to establish a personal relationship with Sadat seemed to worry the Israelis, and they decided to launch a counterattack. On May 21, I received a letter signed by seventy-six Senators urging me to "be responsive" to Israel's request for $2.59 billion in military and economic aid. Although I said publicly that I welcomed the letter as an expression of Senate sentiment, in truth it really bugged me. The Senators claimed the letter was "spontaneous," but there was no doubt in my mind that it was inspired by Israel. We had given vast amounts of military and economic assistance to Israel over the years, and we had never asked for anything in return.

Quite apart from that, the letter—especially its tone—jeopardized any chance for peace in the Middle East. For the past several weeks, Kissinger and I had been urging the Israelis to come up with new ideas for a just settlement of the Sinai dispute, ideas that I could present to Sadat when I met him in June. At that meeting I planned to make the same request of the Egyptian president. Once I had *his* ideas, I could relay them to Rabin, and we could get the negotiations back on track again. Because of the letter, however, the Israelis didn't want to budge. So confident were they that those seventy-six Senators would support them no matter what they did, they refused to suggest any new ideas for peace. "Concessions will have to be made," they were saying in effect, "but we will make none of them. Sadat will have to make them all. And if Ford disagrees, we will show him who's boss." I thought they were overplaying their hand. For me, that kind of pressure has always been counterproductive. I was not going to capitulate to it.

From the perspective of our European allies, I'm sure that the NATO meeting loomed as a very significant opportunity. They would have a chance to talk with the new American President, whom many of them had not met before. Shortly after eight o'clock on May 28, *Air Force One* touched down at Zavantem Airport outside Brussels. The next morning, in an effort to see what progress we could make toward reaching a settlement of the Cyprus dispute, Kissinger, Scowcroft and I met with the prime ministers of Greece and Turkey. We had a working lunch with West German Chancellor Helmut Schmidt; we visited with Danish officials, then sat down with Portugal's new Prime Minister Vasco dos Santos Goncalves.

In my speech to the NATO conference later that afternoon, I was candid about the challenges we faced. "Because of the United States' long involvement in Indochina," I said, "[recent] events [there] have led some to question our strength and reliability. I believe that our strength speaks for itself: Our military power remains and will continue to remain second to none—of this let there be no doubt; our economy remains fundamentally sound and productive, and our political system has emerged from the shocks of the past year stronger for the way in which it met a severe internal test. Our actions will continue to confirm the durability of our commitments."

I listed areas where we as NATO allies still had work to do. Obviously, we had to maintain a strong and credible defense. We had to improve the process of political consultation between member states, and we had to develop a realistic agenda for bolstering our alliance. In the future, Spain could make an important contribution to our mutual security. We had to consider ways to integrate her forces with others in the West. Then I got to the heart of the matter: "We must preserve the quality and integrity of this Alliance on the basis of unqualified participation," I said, "not on the basis of partial membership or special arrangements. The commitment to collective defense must be complete if it is to be credible. It must be unqualified if it is to be reliable."

On May 31, I flew to Spain to discuss the status of negotiations governing continued U.S. use of four military bases there. The U.S. recognized Spain's contribution to Europe's defense; even though our NATO allies had just rebuffed our suggestion that the Alliance consider Spanish membership, it was far from the final vote on the question. Less than twenty-four hours after arriving in Madrid, I was airborne again—this time to Salzburg and my meeting with Sadat. The weather in Spain had been fair; rain clouds hung low over the Salzburg airport, however, and when *Air Force One* taxied to a stop, I tumbled down the ramp. Literally. What happened was this: Betty and I were descending the steps. I had my right arm around her waist to help her, and I was carrying an umbrella in my left hand. Two or three steps from the bottom of the ramp, the heel of my shoe caught on something. I had no free hand to grab the rail, so I took a tumble to the tarmac below.

I jumped to my feet, unhurt, and thought nothing of the fall. So I was quite surprised when Ron Nessen told me later that reporters covering my trip were bombarding him with questions about my "missteps." Had I been off balance because I was exhausted? Had Dr. Lukash examined me? Had I misgauged distances? Ron asked me how I thought he should handle such questions. I told him not to worry about them. There was no doubt in my mind that I was the most athletic President to occupy the White House in years. "I'm an activist," I said. "Activists are more prone to stumble than anyone else. If you don't let their questions get under your skin, they'll realize that they're just wasting time, and they'll start to focus on something else."

I was wrong. From that moment on, every time I stumbled or bumped my head or fell in the snow, reporters zeroed in on that to the exclusion of almost everything else. The news coverage was harmful, but even more damaging was the fact that Johnny Carson and Chevy Chase used my "missteps" for their jokes. Their antics— and I'll admit that I laughed at them myself—helped create the public perception of me as a stumbler. And that wasn't funny.

On June 1, the Egyptian president and I met three times—first when he hosted a working luncheon in a beautiful resort overlooking Lake Fuschl, then later that afternoon at a famous old ornate government building called the Residenz, and finally in the evening, when Austrian Chancellor Bruno Kreisky held a state dinner in our honor. Sadat, a slim, baldish man who combined a professional soldier's erect posture with an aristocratic air of elegance, had deep-set eyes and a quiet, thoughtful voice. But he was very precise in everything he said. He told me how bitter he was at the Soviets. They had mistreated him and tried to bludgeon him by threatening to take away all military aid. He described with pride how he had thrown them out of his country and forced them to stop using the naval base at Alexandria. Under no circumstances, he said, would he let them back.

Their departure, of course, had caused problems for him. The Soviets had stopped sending him arms. He needed spare parts for his planes and tanks. His generals had told him that if he couldn't get those parts, they couldn't do their job. Sadat didn't know how he could satisfy them. His economy was in terrible shape. He couldn't feed, house and arm his people simultaneously. That's why he desperately wanted peace.

Now he came to the point and asked what new ideas I had brought from Israel for him to consider. I had to admit that I had none, because the Israelis said they had none to give. Sadat's expression didn't change. He puffed on his pipe and was silent for a while. Then he looked me in the eye. "All right," he said. "We are willing to go as far as you think we should go. We trust you, and we trust the United States."

I told him that Kissinger and I were in complete agreement on one point: If there was no new movement toward peace, if we couldn't find some new formula over the course of the next few days, then the prospects for war would increase. Sadat nodded. Something, he said, had to be done to avoid a confrontation between Egypt and Israel in the Sinai Peninsula. Then he came up with an idea. Why couldn't there be a buffer zone around the Gidi and Mitla passes, in which the United States could keep a limited number of nonmilitary personnel? These individuals, he went on, would be responsible for surveillance. They would monitor troop movements and warn either side of an impending attack. That way, both countries would have protection. He thought a force of about two hundred civilians should suffice to do the job.

Henry and I agreed that this idea made sense. The Israelis would have to approve it, of course; so would Congress, but I felt confident that implementation of this plan would break the diplomatic deadlock and start a new movement toward a lasting peace. Finally, Sadat and I talked about his country's need for military and economic assistance. Because of the strong objections of the Israelis, I said, we couldn't supply him with offensive weapons. We might, however, be able to provide some C-130 transport planes. I told him I'd ask Congress for $800 million to help his economy. Additionally, I said we'd talk to other Arab states and try to persuade them to be more generous to him in view of the risks that Egypt was taking for peace.

If the Israelis had discovered that the proposal to station civilian technicians in a Sinai buffer zone had come originally from Sadat, they might have rejected it out of hand, so when I returned from Europe and briefed the Cabinet on the afternoon of June 4, I was purposely vague about the specifics of the Salzburg talks. Sooner or later, those specifics would surface in the press. Both Henry and I recognized that. Yet if Sadat's proposal could be perceived as an American—or even better, an Israeli—plan, it would have a far greater chance of acceptance. Much depended upon the press. If some alert reporter sniffed out what had happened at Salzburg, everything could come unstuck. In order to retain "face" in the Arab world, Sadat would have to deny that he had offered any peace plan to the Israelis.

Fortunately, the press didn't ferret out the news, and on June 11, Israeli Prime Minister Rabin arrived in Washington. For the first time since the collapse of the Kissinger mission in March, I sensed that we were about to make progress. Clearly, Rabin had been shaken by our decision to "reassess" our policies in the Middle East. Instead of arguing over which country was to blame for the breakdown of the talks in March, he wanted to move forward. He asked if I had any ideas as to how peace could be achieved. I replied that "one suggestion we have been considering" involved stationing civilian technicians in a Sinai buffer zone. We'd have to get the Egyptians to agree, I said, and we'd also have to gain the backing of the Congress. Still, it was an idea that might break the current impasse. Rabin seemed intrigued. He said he'd take the idea back to Israel and let me know his government's response.

Nearly two months earlier, in a speech at Yale Law School, I had outlined my thoughts about crime. And I had promised my audience then that I would give Congress proposals to deal with the problem. On June 19, I sent a special message up to Capitol Hill. "For too long," I said, "the law has centered its attention more on the rights of the criminal than on the victim of crime. It is high time that we reverse this trend."

I suggested mandatory prison terms for federal offenses committed with firearms or other dangerous weapons, and the same for hijackers, kidnapers and traffickers in hard drugs. Fines or prison terms, I added, should relate directly to the gravity of the offense. Fines were woefully low and did nothing to deter offenders whose *business* was crime. For antitrust legislation I recommended that maximum fines be increased to $100,000 for individuals and to $500,000 for an organization, to make the penalty commensurate with the crime.

I had always opposed federal registration of guns or the licensing of gun owners, and as President, I hadn't changed my views. At the same time, I recognized that handguns had played a key role in the increase of violent crime. Not *all* handguns—just those that hadn't been designed for sporting purposes. I asked Congress to ban the manufacture and sale of these "Saturday night specials." Turning to white collar crime, which in 1974 had cost Americans an estimated $40 billion, I said that Attorney General Levi would undertake new initiatives to coordinate all federal enforcement and prosecutorial efforts in that area.

By the end of the third week in June, the economy appeared to be well on the road to a balanced recovery. Over the past six months the inflation rate had been cut in half—from 12 percent per year to 6 percent—and my advisers were saying that it might drop to 4 percent by 1980. The unemployment rate for May had been an unacceptably high 9.2 percent, but that figure, too, was beginning to decline. Virtually every economic indicator was pointing up instead of down. If this trend continued, my advisers maintained, we could actually have a budget surplus of $22 billion by 1980.

In ten and a half months as President, I'd done everything I could to force Congress to hold the line on federal spending. And considering the fact that Republicans constituted a minority in both houses of Congress, I'd been more successful than anyone had expected. Since August 1974, I had vetoed thirty-three bills. Congress had overridden me on only four of those occasions, and the net result was a $6.35 billion savings. The Democrats had complained, of course, that I was "thwarting the will of the majority"; they had accused me of "obstructionism" when I had used the veto to block some of their irresponsible spending schemes. But the truth is that I had no other tool to use. The veto was the single most powerful weapon at my disposal to force Congress to recognize fiscal restraint and to keep the economy on track.

Early in 1975, for example, I had asked Congress to pass legislation that would extend public service jobs and provide summer employment for thousands of young people. An appropriation of $1.9 billion, I thought, would be sufficient. Congress labored and brought forth an elephant. The legislation it passed was $3.3 billion *above* my budget request. On May 28, I vetoed the bill. One week later, the House sustained my veto. Then Congressional leaders sought a reasonable compromise. They began to slice away the pork barrel provisions of the earlier bill and produced legislation that extended 310,000 public service jobs and created 840,000 summer jobs at a total cost of $2.07 billion. That was slightly higher than the figure I had originally proposed, but it was far less expensive than the "Christmas tree" measure that I had been forced to veto earlier.

Another case in point was the Emergency Housing Act of 1975. I had asked Congress to give the housing industry a necessary shot in the arm. In addition, I'd called for a bill that would protect citizens who were threatened by mortgage foreclosure on their homes because of the recession. Congress responded with a bill that was much too expensive. Believing that it would damage not only the housing industry but also the entire economy, I vetoed it and the House sustained my veto. The executive and legislative branches then bargained in good faith, and the result was a less costly and far more responsible bill which I was happy to sign early in July.

Back in 1973, while still a member of Congress, I had promised Betty that I would quit politics in January 1977. I fully intended to honor that pledge, but Betty released me from it. She knew how I felt about being President. She thought the country needed me, and she said she wanted me to run. Mike, Jack, Steve and Susan all agreed with her. So on July 8, 1975, I made the decision official. "I expect to work hard, campaign forthrightly and do the very best I can to finish the job I have begun," I said. Reporters were curious. Did I expect to face opposition in the primaries? I said something to the effect that I thought competition was healthy and that I'd welcome it. Actually, I expected to win the Republican nomination for President in a breeze.

Some of my closest advisers—Marsh and Hartmann in particular— had been warning me for months to prepare for a difficult challenge from Ronald Reagan. I hadn't taken those warnings seriously because I didn't take Reagan seriously. During the years that Nixon was President, I had seen Reagan only occasionally. The two of us sometimes appeared at the same Republican functions, and while we were always polite to one another, the chemistry wasn't right. He was one of the few political leaders I have ever met whose public speeches revealed more than his private conversations. I have always been able to get to know people pretty easily. I tried to get to know Reagan, but I failed. He was pleasant and congenial, yet at the same time formal and reserved with me. I never knew what he was really thinking behind that winning smile.

Which is not to say that I didn't respect his unique talents or the record he had compiled in his eight years as governor of California. He was an extraordinarily effective public speaker who had a superb knack of exploiting a punch line. He was far more knowledgeable about a wide range of issues than many people thought, and he held deep convictions. But several of his characteristics seemed to rule him out as a serious challenger. One was his penchant for offering simplistic solutions to hideously complex problems. A second was his conviction that he was always right in every argument; he seemed unable to acknowledge that he might have made a mistake. Finally, I'd heard from people who knew him well that he liked to conserve his energy.

From every campaign I'd witnessed, I knew that you can't run for President and expect to work only from nine to five.

I was aware that the more conservative members of our party were pretty upset with me. My decision to grant earned amnesty to draft dodgers and deserters from the Vietnam War, my selection of Rockefeller as Vice President and the unprecedented federal budget deficit—all these things drove them up the wall. But I recognized that these right-wingers would *always* be on my back. I had to call the shots as I saw them from the nation's point of view, and I knew from my own experience that trying to satisfy these zealots would doom any general election hopes in 1976. I kept reading in the press that I was the most conservative President since Herbert Hoover. If that was true, I reasoned, then what I was doing should satisfy most Republicans. And I didn't think Republican voters would want to change their Presidential candidate and risk putting the Democrats back in power again.

What I failed to understand at the time was that several different factors would come together in the summer of 1975 to make a Reagan challenge inevitable. The first was the new federal election law and a conflict it created in my own ranks. The second was the presence in the United States of a noted Soviet author. Third was my decision to attend a thirty-five-nation conference in the Finnish capital of Helsinki. Finally, there was the public reaction to an interview that Betty gave to *60 Minutes* reporter Morley Safer on CBS-TV.

In March 1974, as Vice President, I had delivered a speech criticizing "CREEP"—Nixon's Committee to Reelect the President—and suggesting that all future national campaigns be run under the aegis of the Republican and Democratic National Committees. I had hoped to have the RNC manage my 1976 campaign, but that was impossible. New legislation that Congress had passed in the wake of Watergate said that RNC could handle only the campaign of the party's nominee for President; it couldn't involve itself in the primaries. If I was going to run in the primaries, I had to set up a separate political committee. So on June 19, I authorized the President Ford Committee (PFC) to start raising funds in my behalf.

The question then became who should manage the campaign. My first choice was Mel Laird. But Mel had business commitments he simply had to fulfill. Rumsfeld and I discussed other candidates and quickly agreed that Howard H. ("Bo") Callaway would be a splendid choice. A graduate of West Point, he had served with distinction during the Korean War. He had managed Callaway Gardens in Pine Mountain, Georgia, and turned it into a thriving enterprise. In 1964, he had won election to the House and two years later had nearly become Georgia's first Republican governor. As Secretary of the Army in 1973, Callaway had boosted enlistments and done a first-class job of presiding over the switch to an all-volunteer force. He was attractive and articulate, and he possessed great personal integrity. I thought his selection would give me a boost not only in the South but with conservatives everywhere.

Calling Callaway into the Oval Office, I told him that I wanted my 1976 campaign to emphasize my dedication to five central themes: increased freedom for all our citizens from the encroachments of an ever-expanding federal government, the preservation of our free enterprise system, continued fiscal responsibility, a strong national defense, and affirmation of the rights and responsibilities of state and local governments. When Bo said that he could subscribe to each of those goals, I asked him to run the campaign.

That's when the trouble began. Back on June 16, I had endorsed Rockefeller as my 1976 running mate. We had worked extremely well together, and I thought we'd make an even more effective team in the years ahead. But under the provisions of the new election law, Nelson and I couldn't run as a team; we had to run separate campaigns. On July 9, one day after I had announced my candidacy, Callaway held a press conference and commented on this procedure. "The Ford and Rockefeller campaigns are not one and the same," he said. That was accurate as far as it went. But then Callaway went on to imply that Rockefeller was a liability.

I met with a troubled Nelson Rockefeller the next afternoon and assured him that he still had my full support. I still thought that he was doing a fine job, and I deeply appreciated it. Callaway, I explained, had *had* to say that our two campaigns were separate entities. But then he had got carried away. One reason was his desire to extend an olive branch to conservatives; he sincerely believed that the way to win delegates in the South was to imply that I hadn't made up my mind about a running mate and that Reagan therefore was a strong possibility. Another reason was his inexperience in dealing with the national press. By nature, Callaway always said exactly what was on his mind. He didn't know how to deflect probing questions. I told Nelson that the problem was only temporary and would soon be forgotten.

I let Callaway know how I felt, but he didn't get the message. On July 24, he met with reporters again and ventured the opinion that I might select a younger man—Rockefeller was sixty-seven—for Vice President or someone who could provide a better balance to the ticket. Rockefeller, he told the press, was "the number one problem. You and I both know that if Rockefeller took himself out, it would help with the nomination."

I was furious. Rockefeller was placed in an almost untenable position. He had never had a high opinion of Callaway's political skills, and he seemed convinced that Callaway was getting his marching orders from Don Rumsfeld, that Rumsfeld was orchestrating a plot to get rid of him so he could become Vice President himself. That wasn't the case at all. Rumsfeld was just as upset as I was by Callaway's remarks, and he sat in the Oval Office when I told Callaway that I wouldn't tolerate any more comments like that. I didn't pound the table or shout or read the riot act to him, but I did emphasize my personal loyalty to Nelson, and I said I couldn't allow anyone to downgrade him. "Bo," I went on, "the Vice President is very sensitive to the kinds of things you are saying. He is important to us in getting the nomination. I personally have a great fondness for him and a strong allegiance to him. You just can't do this any more."

"Mr. President," he replied, "I'm sorry. I really am. I got caught. The press was after me."

Finally, toward the end of July, he began to change his tune. "The Vice President is an asset," he told reporters. "He has a great many attributes to bring to any ticket." Unfortunately, by that time, the damage had been done.

About a month earlier, my aides had received word that exiled Soviet author Aleksandr Solzhenitsyn wanted to visit me in the Oval Office. The information had come in a letter from North Carolina Republican Senator Jesse Helms. On July 2, Marsh, Scowcroft and I discussed the problem. Kissinger was out of town, but he and Brent had talked about the issue earlier. Brent said that both he and Henry thought my seeing Solzhenitsyn would be unwise. I was due to meet with Brezhnev at the end of the month to discuss matters of vital importance to both nations. Why run the unnecessary risk of sabotaging those talks before they even began? Marsh presented both sides of the coin. If I saw Solzhenitsyn, I might improve my standing with conservatives. But Jack also recognized the foreign policy implications. I might jeopardize chances of achieving a SALT II accord. In the end, I decided to subordinate political gains to foreign policy considerations. I asked Jack to get word to Helms that my schedule was too tight to allow a meeting with Solzhenitsyn before I left on my European trip at the end of July.

Then someone on Capitol Hill leaked the story to the press, and the furor began. Solzhenitsyn made no secret of the fact that he thought my policy toward the Soviet Union was wrong. As soon as I saw the damage that my "snub" was causing me among conservatives, I told Marsh to tell Helms that I'd be glad to see Solzhenitsyn when I returned from Helsinki. The Soviet author had an "open" invitation. And this was the curious aspect of the whole affair. As soon as I issued the invitation, everyone seemed to lose interest in arranging the meeting. Helms never pushed it again, and Solzhenitsyn himself was reported to be too busy to come to Washington.

Ever since 1954, the Soviets had wanted us to attend a thirty-five-nation Conference on Security and Cooperation in Europe. Initially, the United States had been cool to the idea because we didn't see any advantages to be gained. Then the Soviets had offered concessions. One was an East-West agreement on the status of West Berlin. A second was their stated willingness to begin mutual and balanced force reduction (MBFR) talks in Vienna so that the armies of the NATO and Warsaw Pact nations could be reduced in numbers and the imbalance between them lessened. In 1973, negotiators for both sides started planning the European Security Conference which was to be held in Helsinki. It was to be the largest gathering of European heads of state since the Congress of Vienna in 1815, and on the face of it, there were a number of good reasons for me to attend.

The summit's purpose was to have thirty-five nations sign documents that spelled out what their commitments were in three significant areas: security, economic and cultural cooperation, and the very important issue of freedom of movement of people and ideas. In exchange for our agreement that "legitimate" postwar boundaries were inviolable, the Soviets had conceded that national borders could be changed by peaceful means, and this, I felt, represented a real victory for our foreign policy. After all, it was not the Western countries that might be tempted to alter existing boundaries by force. The Russian tanks that had rolled into Prague in 1968 were implementing the Brezhnev doctrine that said the Soviets had the right to intervene militarily to keep their client states in line. At Helsinki they would be *renouncing* that policy. In addition, they had agreed to sign a document that pledged them to observe the basic principles of human rights. They had never recognized such international standards before. If the nations attending the conference failed to live up to their agreements, Europe would be no worse off than it had been previously, but if they made good on their promises, the cause of freedom behind the Iron Curtain would advance. That was a worthwhile goal.

Before flying to Helsinki, I'd be stopping off in West Germany and Poland; after leaving the Finnish capital, I'd be going to Romania and Yugoslavia. There were solid reasons for these visits. By touching down in West Germany first, I could emphasize the U.S. commitment to that country's defense. I could also discuss joint economic strategy with Chancellor Helmut Schmidt. Poland, Romania and Yugoslavia were the three Eastern European countries least subservient to Moscow; it was proper for us to encourage their independent course. Finally, the trip to Helsinki would give me a chance to see what progress we could make toward reaching a SALT II accord. Since my meeting with Brezhnev in 1974, technicians on both sides had tried to resolve our differences. They had achieved success in some areas but had encountered new problems in others, and as a result, we had to postpone Brezhnev's visit to the U.S. three times. The sticking points were our new cruise missile and their "Backfire" bomber.

In return for conceding our right to keep long-range bombers in Western Europe, the Soviets expected us to classify the Backfire bomber as a nonstrategic weapon. That was something we didn't want to do. Although it lacked the range of our B-52, the Backfire could fly from the Soviet Union to Cuba without refueling. Additionally, it boasted a nuclear weapons delivery capability.

We would also be discussing the cruise missile, a subsonic but highly maneuverable weapon that possesses a fantastic degree of accuracy. The cruise can be fired from manned aircraft, submarines and surface ships as well as from land-based launching pads, and it is almost impossible to detect and destroy because it flies in under the radar screen. That was what worried the Soviets. They wanted range limitations placed on the cruise. (The very fact that we had the potential of a cruise in our weapons arsenal represents something of a minor miracle. In 1972 and 1973, the Department of Defense was unenthusiastic about the missile's capabilities. Secretary Schlesinger, in fact, had opposed funding the necessary research and development. That's when Kissinger intervened. He thought the weapon was essential for our own security and persuaded Nixon to overrule the Secretary of Defense.)

Now Schlesinger and the Joint Chiefs of Staff were hardening their opposition to any limitations on the cruise. Indeed, Schlesinger had become the missile's greatest advocate. This seemed certain to complicate our hopes for a compromise. I believed, and I knew that Brezhnev agreed with me, that a SALT II accord was vital to the interests of both countries. I hoped the two of us could get together at Helsinki, level with each other as we had at Vladivostok, and wind up with a deal.

So for all these reasons, the European trip was likely to advance our hopes for peace. Yet no journey I made during my Presidency was so widely misunderstood. "Jerry, don't go," the *Wall Street Journal* implored, and the New York *Times* called the trip "misguided and empty." The responses from politicians were more predictable. Washington Senator Scoop Jackson accused me of "taking us backward, not forward, in the search for a genuine peace." And Ronald Reagan said, "I am against it [the Helsinki conference], and I think all Americans should be against it." Jackson was obviously running for President himself, and Reagan, it appeared, was gearing up for his own race.

I expected comments like these, but what I didn't expect was the outrage that the trip would provoke among Americans of Eastern European descent. A sampling of my White House mail showed 558 letters against the Helsinki agreement and only thirty-two in favor of it. Lithuanian, Latvian and Estonian groups scheduled a vigil in front of the White House to protest Administration policy. On July 25, the day before my departure, I invited seven members of Congress, together with representatives of Eastern European ethnic groups, to meet with me in the Cabinet Room. When they took their seats around the long oval table, I told them I understood their doubts. I knew why they were suspicious of promises from Marxist regimes which had not proved to be reliable in the past.

Now, however, I stressed, we had an opportunity to make good use of the European Security Conference to get a commitment from leaders of closed and controlled countries to permit greater freedom of movement for individuals and freer flow of information and ideas. The conference also promised to set a standard by which the world could measure progress.

At the same time, I explained, we continued to support the Eastern European peoples in their aspirations for more freedom. The United States had never recognized the Soviet incorporation of Lithuania, Latvia and Estonia and was not doing so now. No territory acquired in violation of international law would be recognized as legal, and the United States would not compromise this long-standing principle.

My audience, if not converted, was receptive, and I felt I had stated the case for Helsinki honestly and effectively. The trouble was that some members of the White House staff didn't view Helsinki as a significant accomplishment. In their comments to the press, they were defensive about it. They should have lauded the accord as a victory. Instead, they intimated that it was "another Kissinger deal that was forced down the President's throat"; they started making excuses for it, and this furthered speculation that the journey was ill-conceived. In terms of domestic politics they may have been correct. But I have always thought that the responsibility of a leader was to lead. If any journey anywhere offered the chance of strengthening prospects for peace and bettering America's position in the world, I would embark upon it.

Just before I left, Congress slapped me in the face by refusing to lift its embargo on the shipment of arms to Turkey. I considered this the single most irresponsible, short-sighted foreign policy decision Congress had made in all the years I'd been in Washington. In predictable retaliation, the Turks closed all but one of the roughly two dozen bases we had in their country. I had hoped to persuade Turkish Premier Suleyman Demirel to sit down with Greek Premier Constantine Karamanlis in Helsinki in order to hammer out an agreement about Cyprus. Both men had given me a positive response. Now Demirel was so angry at the Congressional vote that he changed his mind. I urged Congress to reverse itself.

Betty and our son Jack accompanied me on the trip. Our first stop, on the evening of July 26, was the West German capital of Bonn. During the next day and a half, I met twice with Chancellor Schmidt, attended a picnic with troops of the U.S. Third Armored Division and their families and enjoyed a state dinner aboard the cruise ship *Drachenfels* as it motored down the Rhine to the ancient city of Linz. On July 28 we flew to Warsaw, Poland. After laying a wreath at the Tomb of the Unknown Soldier, I met with First Secretary Gierek to discuss expansion of our bilateral trade, détente and the prospects for a SALT II accord. Our views on each issue were reasonably similar. There was a state dinner at Wilanow Palace that night, and next morning we flew south to Krakow. Then we helicoptered to Auschwitz, the infamous World War II death camp where four million civilians had been killed. I had read about the holocaust, but this couldn't have prepared me for the horror of the place. The Poles had preserved the camp as a memorial, and I could see the railroad terminal where prisoners arrived in boxcars, the brick barracks where they lived until they were too feeble to work, and the concrete ruins of the gas chambers where millions of them died. After placing a wreath at the base of a stone monument, I stepped back to observe a moment of silent prayer. I signed the visitors book, then entered one of the barracks. I saw the crowded tiers of bunks, and I could visualize the way the Nazis had tortured their victims. How long, I asked our guide, could a prisoner survive? Six months, he replied. Earlier, Henry had told me that members of his immediate family had perished at Auschwitz. He could scarcely talk about the tragedy, and as we stood by the barracks, there was little we could say without losing control. I shall never forget the unbelievable horror of that place.

Later that afternoon, we flew on to Helsinki. The next morning, after a working breakfast with Prime Minister Harold Wilson of Great Britain, Kissinger and I held the first of two lengthy sessions with Brezhnev and Gromyko. The General Secretary seemed thinner and paler than he had at Vladivostok. He occasionally slurred his speech, which appeared to confirm reports I'd heard that he had recently been ill. Once again, as they had the first time we met, the Soviets led off with a verbal attack against us. "We don't like the way you're handling the situation in the Middle East," Gromyko said. "We understood that you were going to include us in the peace process and that our two countries would work together. Here you are, going off on a tangent. That is contrary to the spirit of détente, and it's upsetting us."

We responded in kind. Once these obligatory opening statements were out of the way, we got down to business. Picking up where we had left off at Vladivostok, we discussed verification of underground nuclear tests that each side could conduct, and also the rules for counting MIRVs—how to tell whether a missile had a single or a multiple warhead. There the Soviets granted a concession. If they placed a MIRV in a certain location, then we had the right to assume that *every* missile in that field had a MIRV capability. Our talks went well until we began to address the issues that had separated us before. The Soviets concentrated on the various versions of the cruise missile and urged us to accept restrictions on their range and means of delivery.

Tentatively, we agreed to a limitation of 1,850 miles for the airborne cruise and a range of 375 miles for its submarine-carried counterpart. But how could they make sure that we were living up to the agreement? A cruise will fly as far as its fuel tank will permit. If you want to double its range, you add an extra tank. It is as simple as that. I had to agree that verification was a sticky issue and the Soviets had reasonable cause for concern. Brezhnev and I decided to leave the problem to the technical experts in the hope that they could find a solution.

Next we turned to the Backfire bomber. Brezhnev himself described the plane's capabilities and kept insisting that it was not a strategic weapon. His figures didn't coincide with the ones our own Air Force had given me. Finally, I said, "Well, Mr. General Secretary, here is what our people tell me that Backfire can do," and I began to reel off the statistics. He seemed surprised, almost shocked, by what I was telling him. He asked for a short recess so he could consult with his technical advisers. Ten minutes later, he returned, and he was angry. He didn't shout, but he raised his voice and punctuated his remarks with gestures. "Our figures are right," he said. "We know what the plane can do. Your figures are wrong."

"I have to depend on the information given me," I replied. "Our people have been right in most instances in the past. I have to use our figures in negotiating with you."

We looked each other in the eye. Neither of us was going to give ground, so we agreed to disagree about Backfire and then moved on to other things. Nearly two hours later, we recessed our talks and agreed to another meeting before leaving Helsinki.

An hour or so after Brezhnev's departure, I hosted an embassy luncheon for Greek Prime Minister Karamanlis. Despite the Congressional vote, it was vital, I said, that he and Demirel, his Turkish counterpart, get together to explore possible solutions to the Cyprus dispute. Karamanlis agreed to a meeting on August 2. So did Demirel. Then on the night of July 31, the House of Representatives reconsidered its decision to embargo military aid to the Turks. Once again emotion triumphed over common sense. The House let the ban stand. Demirel canceled his meeting with Karamanlis and returned to Ankara.

Because the roster of nations at the Helsinki conference was in English, I was among the last of the thirty-five heads of state to address the gathering. For three long days prior to my speech, I sat through every session in the elegant Finlandia House. President Giscard and Prime Minister Wilson spoke eloquently from the background of their countries' great libertarian traditions. General Secretary Brezhnev, in what struck me as a conciliatory address, observed: "The special political importance and moral force of the [Helsinki] understandings reside in the fact that they are to be certified by the signatures of the top leaders of the participating states. We assume that all countries represented will implement the understandings reached. As regards the Soviet Union, it will act precisely in that manner."

At the end of the afternoon session on August 1, it was my turn to speak. "The goals we are stating today are the yardstick by which our performance will be measured," I said. "The people of all Europe and the people of North America are thoroughly tired of having their hopes raised and then shattered by empty words and unfulfilled pledges.

"Peace is not a piece of paper. But lasting peace is at least possible today because we have learned from the experience of the last thirty years that peace is a process requiring mutual restraint and practical arrangements. This conference is a part of that process—a challenge, not a conclusion. We face unresolved problems of military security in Europe; we face them with very real differences in values and aims. But if we deal with them with careful preparation, if we focus on concrete issues, if we maintain forward movement, we have the right to expect real progress."

I paused and looked directly at Brezhnev. "To my country," I went on, "these principles are not clichés or empty phrases. We take this work and these words very seriously. We will spare no effort to ease tensions and to solve problems between us, but it is important that you realize the deep devotion of the American people and their government to human rights and fundamental freedoms and thus to the pledges that this conference has made regarding the freer movement of people, ideas, information. History will judge this conference," I concluded, "not by what we say here today but by what we do tomorrow—not by the promises we make but by the promises we keep. Our people want a better future. Our presence here offers them further hope. We must not let them down."

Press reaction to the speech was uniformly generous. The Los Angeles *Times* said it was "probably Mr. Ford's most impressive speech" as President. The Chicago *Tribune* highlighted my warning not to underestimate the devotion of the American people to the cause of human rights. I felt my message to Europe—that America still cared—had come through loud and clear.

Next morning just prior to my departure from Helsinki, I met with Brezhnev again to see if we could break our deadlock on SALT. The cruise missile and the Backfire bomber, however, remained stumbling blocks. Reluctantly, after a three-hour conversation, we concluded that we weren't going to reach agreement soon. Gromyko would be coming to Washington in September. Kissinger was scheduled to fly to Moscow in December. Perhaps by that time both sides could agree on a compromise.

After visiting Romania and Yugoslavia, we flew back to the United States. The failure to reach a SALT accord was disturbing, but on balance I felt the Helsinki trip had been a great success. As José A. Cabranes, an authority on international law and vice president of the International League for Human Rights, has said: "Careful reading of the Helsinki [documents] will confirm that the Soviet Union did not achieve its principal objectives. The Soviet bloc did *not* obtain a surrogate World War II peace treaty. It did *not* obtain renunciation of territorial claims or a commitment to the immutability of present frontiers. The Helsinki accord did *not* endorse the Brezhnev doctrine on intervention in 'fraternal countries.' The United States, Britain and France did *not* waive any four-power rights in Germany."

What the Soviets *did* achieve, Cabranes went on to say, was a propaganda victory: "The rage of American citizens of Baltic extraction—the outcry that they had been 'sold out' by President Ford and Secretary Kissinger—was a testament to the Soviets' successful public opinion campaign." No sooner had I returned to Washington than I saw evidence of this. The first sampling of White House mail showed 122 letters condemning the accords; only eleven letters approved of what I had done, and I dropped several percentage points in the polls. The well-meaning ethnic groups in this country simply didn't understand our accomplishment. This was not a failure in substance. It was a failure in public relations, and I will have to accept a large share of the blame.

Further compounding my problems was an interview that Betty gave to CBS reporter Morley Safer which was telecast on *60 Minutes* the night of August 10. "What if Susan Ford came to you and said, 'Mother, I'm having an affair'?" Betty was asked. And she replied, "Well, I wouldn't be surprised. I think she's a perfectly normal human being like all young girls. I would certainly counsel her and advise her on the subject, and I'd want to know pretty much about the young man—whether it was a worthwhile encounter or whether it was going to be one of those . . ." Betty stopped, then added, "She's pretty young to start affairs."

But Safer pressed on. "Nevertheless, old enough?"

"Oh, yes, she's a big girl," Betty replied.

She went on to discuss other subjects that First Ladies usually avoid. Had our children tried marijuana? "Probably," she said. Might she have tried it herself had it been in vogue when she was growing up? "Probably," again. Finally, what did she think of the Supreme Court's ruling to allow abortions? It was "the best thing in the world," she replied, "a great, great decision."

Betty has always been forthright in expressing her views—I had admired her candor from the moment we met and had always encouraged her to speak her mind—and we had few disagreements, but when we differed, we respected the other's opinion. Yet I was under no illusions as to what the reaction to her remarks would be. Letters, phone calls and telegrams deluged the White House, and two-thirds of them were critical. Some religious leaders said they were "appalled," and there were harsh newspaper editorials. "Coming from the First Lady in the White House," said the arch-conservative Manchester, New Hampshire, *Union Leader,* the interview "disgraces the nation itself. President Ford showed his own lack of guts by saying he had long ago given up commenting on Mrs. Ford's interviews. What kind of business is that?"

Conservatives grumbled; their grumbles swelled to a roar. My selection of Nelson Rockefeller still rankled, I had declined to meet with Solzhenitsyn, and I had "sold out" the nations of Eastern Europe at Helsinki. Now there was the *60 Minutes* interview—further evidence that Betty and I "condoned immorality." In retrospect, given the anger that my stands and statements had provoked, I should have *known* that a primary challenge was inevitable—and prepared for it. But at the time I didn't recognize the threat. After one year in office we had turned the economy around. We had begun to restore public faith in government. We had cemented old alliances abroad, and now we were moving closer in our efforts to secure peace in the Middle East. Those were solid accomplishments, I thought; they would impress voters and frighten off would-be candidates.

Since Kissinger's unsuccessful mission to the Middle East in March, we had been engaged in a war of nerves with Israel. Perhaps "test of wills" would be a better phrase because Israel was—and is—a valued ally. But even friends disagree, and that's what had happened to us. When Rabin and his colleagues saw that I wasn't about to bow to any home-front political pressure they could exert, they were ready to resume serious bargaining. Their reaction to Sadat's proposal to station American civilian technicians in a Sinai buffer zone was positive. So positive, in fact, that Henry thought he should return to the area soon. I gave him my okay, and on August 20 he left for Israel, Egypt, Syria, Jordan and Saudi Arabia.

Over the next ten days he shuttled from one capital to the other in fervent pursuit of our goal. If Henry could eventually persuade the Israelis to withdraw not only from parts of the occupied Sinai but also from parts of the Golan Heights and the West Bank of the Jordan River, then it was likely that he could convince Arab leaders that Israel *really* wanted peace. If he failed in this first step, both of us realized, the prospects for another war would increase.

The Israelis wanted to address each occupied area separately, and even before they would discuss a new Sinai pact, they demanded two concessions from us. The first was a written promise—a memorandum of understanding—that before the U.S. moved in any direction affecting the future of the region, we would notify them. I had no problem agreeing to that. The second concession was more troublesome. The Israelis were always insisting that we supply them more military equipment than our own experts thought they needed and far more than I thought we could afford. Initially, we had agreed to provide them $1.5 billion worth of arms. They would have to pay us back half that amount; the rest would be a loan with an understood forgiveness feature. The Israelis, however, wanted more. Their shopping list included sophisticated weaponry that even our own forces hadn't received yet. Pentagon officials urged me to refuse this new request. Israel, they pointed out, already had the third-largest air force in the world. She could destroy all her neighbors. It was a tough call. Nothing was more important to the Israelis than their own military security. If we provided the hardware, we could convince the Israelis that they were secure. Then they might be willing to accept some risks in the search for peace. In the end, I decided to approve a larger initial increment than the Pentagon recommended.

Now the talks focused on the most minute details. The Israelis had long insisted that their forces couldn't pull back beyond the crests of the mountains that overlooked the Gidi and Mitla passes. Eventually we came up with charts pinpointing the location of the crests that both sides accepted. That's when we began to make real progress. The Israelis made some concessions; so did the Egyptians. A force of between 100 and 150 U.S. civilian technicians, it was agreed by both sides, would be stationed in the buffer zone between the Israeli and Egyptian armies. They would not be there as "policemen"; their role would be to monitor activity in the vicinity of the passes. Finally, on the morning of September 1, Kissinger telephoned me from Jerusalem. He had achieved success at last, and he was jubilant. He and Rabin were about to initial the peace documents. He was going to fly to Cairo, where he and Sadat would repeat the ceremony. I telephoned both leaders, congratulated them personally and urged them to keep the peace process moving. But first I called Henry back. "This is a great achievement," I said. "And I know that the American people will be most grateful for the successful efforts that you made."

On September 4, after briefing bipartisan Congressional leaders on the Middle East accords, I flew to the West Coast to give speeches in Washington, Oregon and California. One of the most important was an address before a joint session of the California legislature on the subject of crime. Next morning, after breakfast in Sacramento, I left the Senator Hotel and walked across the capitol grounds toward the office of Governor Jerry Brown. I wanted to talk to him about the crime bill that I had submitted to Congress and also about federal-state differences on welfare and the drilling of offshore oil. Because I had never met him before, I also wanted to size him up as a potential Presidential candidate.

The weather that morning was clear; the sun was shining brightly, and there were several rows of people standing behind a rope that lined the sidewalk to my left. They were applauding and saying nice things; I was in a good mood, so I started shaking hands. That's when I spotted a woman wearing a bright red dress. She was in the second or third row, moving right along with me as if she wanted to shake my hand. When I slowed down, I noticed immediately that she thrust her hand under the arms of the other spectators. I reached down to shake it—and looked into the barrel of a .45 caliber pistol pointed directly at me.

I ducked.

"This country is in a mess. This man is not your President," the woman was reported to have yelled, but I didn't hear her. I do remember seeing Secret Service Agent Larry Buendorf reach for the woman's hand and wrestle her to the ground. Ernie Luzania and other agents grabbed me immediately from the rear and hustled me along the sidewalk into the capitol. It was important, I thought, to avoid panic, so when I saw that the danger had passed, I told the agents to slow down. "Everything is all right," I said. Governor Brown was waiting for me in his office; members of our respective staffs were there, and we concluded our business without my mentioning the incident, which he learned about after I left.

Following my meeting with Brown and a speech to the legislature, I returned to the hotel, where I telephoned Betty and told her that I was fine. The Secret Service agents had assured her that everything was all right, but she sounded concerned. Every President receives threats—I was getting about a hundred per month—but I had never worried about them because of my confidence in the professionalism of the agents guarding me. That confidence, I told Betty, had not been misplaced; Buendorf and the other agents had done a superb job.

Only after my return to Washington did I receive a full report on the woman who had tried to murder me—Lynette Alice ("Squeaky") Fromme, a twenty-six-year-old disciple of mass killer Charles Manson. (On November 26, she was convicted in federal court of trying to assassinate me and was sentenced to spend the rest of her life in prison.)

Squeaky Fromme, I thought, was an aberration. There had been misfits and kooks in every society since the beginning of time. I didn't think California harbored a larger number of these people than any other part of the country, so I wasn't overly concerned about my personal safety when I returned to the state on September

19. My schedule was crowded for the next three days. I gave interviews to groups of reporters, participated in ceremonies at Pepperdine University and the Stanford University School of Law, spoke at an insurance convention in Anaheim, then flew north again to San Francisco. There, on September 22, I addressed the annual meeting of the AFL-CIO Building and Construction Trades unions and attended a luncheon of the World Affairs Council of Northern California.

Shortly before three-thirty that afternoon, I stepped out of the hotel entrance and walked toward the armored Lincoln Continental that would whisk me to the airport. Groups of people stood on both sides of the entrance and there was an even larger crowd of three thousand or more across the street in Union Square. Dick Keiser, the head of the Secret Service detail, had advised me not to cross the street and shake hands in the crowd. I waved once or twice as I walked toward the car.

Bang! I recognized the sound of a shot, and I froze. There was a hushed silence for a split second. Then pandemonium broke out.

Agents Jack Merchant and Ron Pontius forced me down behind the car. Then they opened the door and pushed me inside. Rumsfeld and the agents piled in on top of me; somebody shouted, "Go," and the car took off. I don't think anyone ever drove to the airport faster than we did that afternoon, but I wasn't worried about setting a new speed record. What did bother me after we had traveled several blocks was that the agents were still on top of me in the back of the car, and they were heavy as hell. "Hey," I said finally, "will you guys get off? You're going to smother me."

Air Force One was waiting at the airport. Kennerly, cameras slung around his neck, was standing at the top of the ramp as the agents hustled me up the steps. "Other than that, Mr. President," he asked with a smile on his face, "how did you like San Francisco?"

That broke the tension of the moment. I grinned and stepped inside to my compartment. Kennerly followed me there. So did Rumsfeld, Hartmann, Nessen and Dr. Lukash. Stewards appeared with drinks, and we began to relax. Betty had been visiting friends in Monterey for the past several days. She was flying north to meet me at the airport so we could return to Washington together. Not knowing what had happened, she entered the cabin of *Air Force One* and asked breezily, "Well, how did they treat you in San Francisco?"

During the long flight back to the capital, Secret Service agents gave me a report on the incident. My assailant this time had been a forty-five-year-old matron named Sara Jane Moore, who had ties to radical groups in the San Francisco Bay area. Her weapon had been a .38 caliber revolver which she had fired from a distance of about forty feet. The slug passed a few feet to my left, hit the front of the hotel, then ricocheted off to the right. An alert bystander, Oliver Sipple, had noticed the gun in her hand and reached out to deflect her aim. Moore was in police custody. (Later, she pleaded guilty to an attempted murder charge and was sentenced to life imprisonment.)

I was determined not to let the second near miss intimidate me, and when we returned to the White House later that night, I told reporters: "I don't think any person as President ought to cower in the face of a limited number of people who want to take the law into their own hands. The American people want a dialogue between them and their President and their other public officials. And if we can't have that opportunity of talking with one another, seeing one another, shaking hands with one another, something has gone wrong in our society. I think it's important that we as a people don't capitulate to the wrong element, an infinitesimal number of people who want to destroy everything that's best about America."

Midway between the two assassination attempts, I made a decision that infuriated millions of American farmers. Over the past five years, Soviet purchases of wheat and seed grains from this country had been highly erratic, fluctuating from 1.8 million metric tons in one year to 13.7 million metric tons in another. Because the purchases had been so unpredictable—as opposed to the steadier demands for grain from our traditional customers, Western Europe and Japan—they had disrupted the market and contributed to price instability. Further complicating the situation, a longshoreman's strike at Gulf ports in September held up shipments of grain. Trainloads were backed up and elevators were filled. In desperation, farm organizations filed suit to force the loading of the grain onto the waiting ships. Backed by George Meany of the AFL-CIO, the longshoremen refused to budge. They wanted a Soviet commitment to use a larger number of American ships. The Soviets objected because they'd have to pay higher shipping costs.

At this point, I decided to act. Reluctantly, I suspended the Soviet grain sales and on September 9 announced that this moratorium would continue for at least another month. My Administration had urged farmers to increase their production in 1975 and they had responded with a record yield. Here we were telling them not to sell what they had produced. They were outraged, but I didn't feel that I had any alternative. The American farmer would be far better off if we could reach a long-term understanding with the Soviets governing the amount of grain they could purchase in the open market every year. That would guarantee sales of at least 6 million metric tons in each of the next five years. At least one third of that tonnage should be carried in American ships. In mid September, I sent a State Department delegation to Moscow to see if it could negotiate such an agreement. Shortly thereafter, we agreed on both points and the terms were favorable to us. I lifted the grain embargo and the longshoremen loaded grain again.

Then I turned my attention to the economy. Our recovery from the "stagflation" of the spring of 1975 was moving in the right direction, but my advisers saw new storm clouds ahead. Even without costly new programs, federal spending was continuing to increase. Estimates as to the size of the budget for fiscal year 1976 hovered around $368 billion, and for the year after that, they shot up to $423 billion. It was mandatory that we keep the budget below $400 billion, and on the evening of October 6 I addressed the nation on TV.

"For several years America has been approaching a crossroads in our history. Today we are there," I said. "To put it simply, we must decide whether we shall continue in the direction of recent years— the path toward bigger government, higher taxes and higher inflation—or whether we shall now take a new direction, bringing to a halt the momentous growth of government, restoring our prosperity and allowing each of you a greater voice in your own future. Tonight I will set forth two proposals that, taken together as they must be, represent the answer I believe we must choose. First, I propose that we make a substantial and permanent reduction in our federal taxes, and second that we make a substantial reduction in the growth of federal spending."

Quickly, I listed the specifics. Several months earlier, Congress had passed and I had signed a temporary $18 billion tax cut for calendar year 1975. That temporary law was due to expire at the end of the year, at which time taxes would increase again. So I told viewers that I would ask Congress to sweep away that law and replace it with a permanent tax reduction—the biggest in our history—of $28 billion. But there was a catch. I would not sign the tax reduction legislation unless Congress pledged to cut anticipated federal spending by an equivalent $28 billion. That would bring the federal budget down to $395 billion in fiscal year 1977. "If we cut only taxes but do not cut the growth of government spending," I explained, "budget deficits will continue to climb, we will have more inflation, and ultimately we will have more unemployment. Substantial cuts in your taxes must be tied to substantial cuts in the growth of government spending."

Reaction was overwhelmingly favorable. As the *Wall Street Journal* pointed out: "President Ford is in fact explicitly telling the nation that it can have more government spending or it can have lower taxes but that it cannot have both."

Perhaps predictably, Democrats assailed my plan as "totally preposterous." In order to keep spending to $395 billion, they pointed out, Congress would have to trim the rate of growth of such programs as food stamps, welfare payments, veterans' pensions and social security. Those transfer payment programs were the fastest-growing part of the budget. In 1965, they had amounted to $37 billion. Ten years later, they had ballooned to an annual rate of $176 billion—nearly half the entire budget. Unless we got them under firm control, they would send the budget soaring through the roof.

Still, the Democrats resisted my plan. "We're not gonna let you have it," House Majority Leader Tip O'Neill told me. "There's no way you're gonna get it through." And then, with a twinkle in his eye: "How's your golf game, Mr. President?"

I expected that from Tip, a fierce partisan but also a valued friend. He could be scathingly critical of my policies—and often was—but there was never anything *personal* in his attacks. Unfortunately, I can't say the same for other Democrats who lambasted my stands on certain issues. Take, for example, my position on providing federal funds to bail out a nearly bankrupt New York City. When I announced that I was dead set against supplying such aid on an open-spigot basis, my critics really let the brickbats fly. Washington Senator Scoop Jackson said that I had declared "civil war" on the city. New York Representative Bella Abzug was sure that I had "branded New York as diseased, and now he wants to pull the plug." New York Representative Edward I. Koch called my decision "immoral. We are a city surrounded by the Mongol hordes," he continued, "and I look out the window and the faces aren't those of barbarians; they are those of the White House."

Such complaints made colorful copy, but they didn't tell New Yorkers how to solve their problems. Nor did they bear the slightest resemblance to my personal views. I had had good times in the city; I admired the people and respected the unique contribution they had made to American life. But the city's politicians, Democrats and Republicans alike, had behaved so irresponsibly for so many years that a fiscal Armageddon was almost inevitable.

The crisis had not arisen overnight. Early in May 1975, Mayor Abraham D. Beame and Governor Hugh Carey had written requesting my support of federal legislation that would give New York City $1 billion in credit for a ninety-day term. They needed the money and time, they said, in order to persuade the New York State legislature to increase the city's taxing authority and to let the City Council adopt a balanced budget for the fiscal year beginning July 1. Unfortunately, a federal bail-out for ninety days would only postpone the day of reckoning. Additionally, it would set a dangerous precedent. If we "rescued" New York, officials from every city in America would come knocking on our door. What New York had to do was to get its own house in order. The longer it waited to do that, the tougher the job was going to be.

Since 1965, the city's budget had tripled. Expenses had increased by an average of 12 percent per year while revenues had risen by less than 5 percent. The federal government already contributed an annual $3.5 billion—or 25 percent of the city's budget—to help fund its Medicaid, welfare, food stamp and other programs. To ask us to pay any more simply wasn't fair. No longer could New York's officials offer high school graduates free tuition at the city university and expect taxpayers elsewhere to pick up the tab. No longer could they promise extravagant wage settlements and pension benefits without knowing how they would cover the costs. They had to start cutting back on nonessential services, and in my letter to Mayor Beame that's what I suggested he do.

The crisis deepened during the summer months. Early in September, Beame and Carey came to see me. He had inherited the city's problems from his predecessor, former Mayor John Lindsay, Beame asserted. He was a victim of Lindsay's many mistakes. I was aware that Beame and Lindsay had never gotten along well, but I also knew that Beame had been New York City comptroller for many years before becoming mayor, and I didn't think he could escape some responsibility for the mess. "What are you going to do?" I kept asking him. "Are you going to cut down your retirement benefits and your overhead? Are you going to stop giving free tuition to students at the city university?" Beame and Carey had no answers. Nor did they have a plan. And their demands were ridiculous. Apparently, they thought they could come down to Washington, employ scare tactics and roll over us. If the city went bankrupt, they warned, the effect on the banking community in the United States would be catastrophic. The city's collapse would trigger a long line of falling dominoes. Federal Reserve Board Chairman Arthur Burns never agreed with that. "Don't let them sell you a bill of goods," he kept cautioning me.

When Beame and Carey saw that they couldn't overpower me, they shifted their focus to Capitol Hill. Congress, they thought, would force the Administration to guarantee city bonds. Then they found they didn't have that many friends on the Hill. A majority of the Congress was attuned to the national mood, which said that inasmuch as New York had got into this jam by itself, it ought to find its own way out.

As the city's woes multiplied, I maintained a tough line against aid for New York in all my public remarks. New York officials, I said, would have to present a specific plan to solve their own problems themselves. The role was hard for me because I'm not a Scrooge by nature, and I knew full well that the reforms the city would have to make would entail sacrifices on the part of the *people* of New York. Would the cutbacks leave them with adequate fire and police protection? Would they have enough doctors for their hospitals and teachers for their schools? Wasn't there something—short of a cash handout—that the federal government could provide? In the Oval Office, I asked these questions of my advisers all the time. Later, lying in bed just before drifting off to sleep, I would ask the same questions of myself.

That's what I had been doing the night that I took Liberty, our golden retriever, out for a stroll on the South Lawn. Our veterinarian, Dr. Joel Knipling, had predicted that she would give birth to a large litter of puppies around the middle of September. Normally, we kept Liberty in the kennel on the ground floor, but because she might have her pups any time, we decided to shift her to a room on the third floor. Her trainer could watch her there. That evening the trainer had to go out, so I volunteered to keep Liberty in our bedroom with us. "Mr. President," the trainer said, "she's no trouble at all. If she wants to go to the bathroom, she'll just come and lick your face."

About three o'clock next morning, I was awakened from a sound sleep by a very wet kiss. I opened my eyes. Liberty was wagging her tail, and I knew what *that* meant. Groggily, I slipped on my robe and my slippers, took the elevator to the ground floor and walked outside. There I waited until Liberty was ready to return. We stepped inside again, and I pressed the button for the elevator. Nothing happened. Someone had just cut back the power, I figured, so I said, "Liberty, let's walk." I opened the door to my left, and we climbed the stairs to the second floor. At the top of the stairwell was a door that led to our family quarters. I turned the knob, but it was locked. Liberty and I walked back down to the first floor, and I tried to open the door there. It was locked too. I must have walked up and down those stairs several times. This is ridiculous, I thought, so I started pounding on the walls. All of a sudden the place came alive. Lights flicked on, and Secret Service agents appeared. When they found out what the problem was, they were chagrined. I told them not to worry. All I had missed, I said, was a few minutes' sleep.

While my embarrassment at being "lost" in the White House

faded, New York's problems took on a more alarming dimension. The city's financial position had been bad for a long time, and now the state was facing similar problems. If both city and state had to default on their obligations, the consequences could be serious. Governor Carey finally realized what had to be done, and the state began to pull itself out of the hole. But Mayor Beame was still trying to find a political solution that didn't require him to show leadership or political courage.

I decided to put the pressure on. At a press conference in Washington, I said: "I do not think it is a healthy thing for the federal government to bail out a city, and I mean any city that has handled its fiscal affairs as irresponsibly over a long period of time as New York City has." Shortly after midnight on October 17, Beame telephoned to say that default was imminent. Yet later that day, officials of the New York City teachers' pension fund came up with $150 million, which was enough to stave off default for a while. That relief, I knew, would only be temporary. The city still had not submitted a realistic plan to extend its financial obligations over a longer period of time, persuade trustees of other union pension funds to invest in its securities, freeze pay increases for its workers, readjust retirement benefits and let go thousands of employees. Until city officials did that—and I was sure they would once they realized that I was serious—I was determined to keep their feet to the fire.

On October 29, I discussed the city's problems in a speech at the National Press Club:

> The time has come to sort facts and figures from fiction and fear-mongering. One week ago, New York City tottered on the brink of financial default which was deferred only at the eleventh hour. The next day, Mayor Beame testified here in Washington that the financial resources of the city and the state of New York were exhausted. Governor Carey agreed. They said it was now up to Washington. The message was clear: responsibility for New York City's financial problems was being left on the front doorstep of the federal government—unwanted and abandoned by its real parents. . . . And when New York City now asks the rest of the country to guarantee its bills, it can be no surprise that many Americans ask why.
>
> I can tell you now that I am prepared to veto any bill that has as its purpose a federal bail-out of New York City to prevent a default.

And I will tell you why. Basically it is a mirage. By giving a federal guarantee, we would be reducing rather than increasing the prospect that the city's budget will ever be balanced. New York City's officials have proved in the past that they will not face up to the city's massive network of pressure groups as long as any other alternative is available. If they can scare the whole country into providing that alternative now, why shouldn't they be confident they can scare us again three years from now?

Such a step would be a terrible precedent for the rest of the nation. What restraint would be left on the spending of other local and state governments once it becomes clear that there is a federal rescue squad that will always arrive in the nick of time? Other cities, other states, as well as the federal government, are not immune to the insidious disease from which New York City is suffering. This sickness is brought on by years and years of higher spending, higher deficits, and so on, and so on. It is a progressive disease, and there is no painless cure.

Those who have been treating New York's financial sickness have been prescribing larger and larger doses of the same political stimulant that has proved so popular and so successful in Washington for so many years. None of us can point a completely guiltless finger at New York City. None of us should now derive comfort from New York's anguish. But neither can we let that contagion spread. If we go on spending more than we have, providing more benefits and more services than we can pay for, then a day of reckoning will come to Washington and the whole country just as it has to New York City. And so, let me conclude with one question of my own: When that day of reckoning comes, who will bail out the United States of America?

This Dutch uncle approach, I thought, might shock New York's officials into coming to grips with their plight before it was too late. I had not understated the city's problems. Nor had I exaggerated them. I had simply told the truth. And what was the result of that? A New York *Daily News* headline that read: "Ford to City: Drop Dead."

This was a minor controversy, however, compared to the one that would be sparked by a decision I was about to make involving the Cabinet, the CIA, the composition of my senior staff and the Vice President. At a meeting with members of my kitchen cabinet on October 16, I asked why my approval rating in the Gallup poll had lev-

eled off at 47 percent despite the economy's turnaround and some
successes in foreign policy. That's when Bryce Harlow said that
"public divisions" within the Administration were creating the impression that I was not fully in command. There was a growing feud
between Kissinger and Schlesinger, he went on, and it was undermining everything that I was trying to do.

I had been aware of the feud for some time and viewed it with increasing concern. Not long after my return from Helsinki, we decided to submit new proposals to the Soviets to see if we could reach a
strategic arms accord. Kissinger and I were in complete agreement as
to what these proposals should be. But Schlesinger disagreed. Someone at the Pentagon leaked the story that he thought we were willing
to give up too much. That upset conservatives.

Then there was the problem of the defense budget for fiscal 1976.
By mid October, the House Appropriations Committee had completed its review of the DOD's funding. Initially, I had requested a sum
of $104.7 billion in spending authority. Committee Chairman George
Mahon and his colleagues had trimmed that back to $97.6 billion. Al-
though I strongly opposed the reduction, I concluded that I could enlist some help in the Senate to restore the cuts. But Schlesinger
promptly complained about "deep, savage and arbitrary" cuts that
Mahon had just made and took his case to the media. Sounding off
like that about a respected committee chairman was not the way to
win friends on Capitol Hill. I was sure that Mahon would resent what
Schlesinger had said, and I resented it myself. "This is where I came
in," I thought.

My first brush with Schlesinger had occurred in March 1974, when
I was Vice President. The occasion was an argument over which Congressional committee should determine the amount of military assistance that the United States would provide our allies in South Vietnam. F. Edward Hébert, chairman of the House Armed Services
Committee, said that his committee had the proper jurisdiction and
proposed a figure of $1.4 billion. House Appropriations Committee
Chairman Mahon insisted that the jurisdiction belonged to him.
Aware that the full House would never accept so large an amount, he
suggested $1.1 billion. As the Administration's spokesman, Schlesing-

er, of course, pushed for adoption of the $1.4 billion package. But instead of lobbying members of Congress individually, he dealt only with the chairmen. In this instance, his approach was to side with Hébert and try to run roughshod over Mahon. You don't win the war by beating one of the chairmen over the head publicly. His tactics weren't working at all, and the Administration seemed sure to suffer defeat.

Finally, I talked to Hébert and Mahon myself and a compromise was reached at the last minute. Soon after, I had a casual conversation with John Osborne of the *New Republic* magazine. In it I described what I considered to be the inadequacies of Schlesinger's approach to Capitol Hill. Although Osborne, a first-rate reporter, didn't attribute the material to me, there was little doubt who his source had been. I was giving a speech in Kansas City when news stories appeared quoting the Osborne article and saying that Schlesinger was very upset.

I called Schlesinger, said I was sorry that the piece had created such a stir and apologized for the adverse publicity. Then I said I thought it was accurate. "Jim, that's the way I feel," I said, "and I don't think we should argue about this in public. I want you to know that if you're going to get your budget through—and as Vice President I want to help you with that—you're going to have to broaden the base of your Congressional support." Our conversation was pretty disagreeable, and when I hung up, I sensed that I hadn't succeeded in getting my message across.

Our personal relationship, which had never been good, slid downhill after I became President. Schlesinger didn't get along with William P. Clements, the Deputy Secretary of Defense; in effect, he kept telling me that I should get rid of Clements. What disturbed me most was the strange way he pushed that request. Clements, a successful and self-made Texas oil drilling contractor, had testified before his confirmation by the Senate that he would never involve himself in decisions affecting his own company while serving in the Pentagon. But Schlesinger kept indicating to me that Clements' involvement with Pentagon matters related to the Middle East oil-producing nations could blow up into a scandal, and in my "best interests" I should ask him to resign. I looked into the question and discovered that Schlesinger's assertions lacked substance, which didn't exactly enhance my confidence in him.

Soon after I became President, I had had to admonish Schlesinger about newspaper stories suggesting that he had put our armed forces on alert just prior to Nixon's resignation. Schlesinger never admitted to me that he had been the source of these reports, and right after our conversation, I released a statement that "I have been assured that no measures of this nature were actually undertaken." When the story died, I let the matter drop. Now, months later, I found out the story's origin. On August 23, 1974, Schlesinger had attended a lunch with Pentagon reporters. Soon afterward, newspaper headlines proclaimed: "Pentagon Kept Tight Rein in Last Days of Nixon Rule"; "Schlesinger Kept Eye on Nixon, Military"; "Military Reined in Nixon Crisis." The Defense Secretary, as one reporter put it, left the distinct impression that he had taken "precautions to prevent an unwarranted military action by President Nixon or by a subordinate commander acting on Nixon's behalf." He had done this, Schlesinger went on to say, "to avoid any going around of the chain of command. We wanted to be sure no idiot commander somewhere [was] misled." Then Schlesinger explained: "Many Air Force officers had a strong emotional attachment to Richard Nixon as a human being. He got those POW's out of Indochina. This applied to some naval aviators, too."

Newspapers and radio reports implied that, fearing a possible coup, Schlesinger had ordered some kind of alert. Clements was in California at the time. His telephone began to ring about 4 A.M., Pacific Daylight Time. What was going on? Everyone wanted to know. Clements canceled his appointments, flew back to Washington immediately and huddled with Air Force General George Brown, chairman of the Joint Chiefs of Staff. "What in the hell is this all about?" he asked.

"Nothing," Brown replied. "There was no alert."

"Are you sure?"

"Absolutely. I have checked at headquarters. There are no recorded messages coming out of the Secretary of Defense's office. Furthermore, if there had been a call, it would have been referred back to the National Military Command Center here at the Pentagon. We have no record of that. I've checked every record, and it's all pure fabrication."

"You've checked it yourself, George?"

"Yes. There's no question."

Shaken, Clements walked upstairs and entered Schlesinger's office. He mentioned the "scare" stories in the press, said that they had obviously emanated from Schlesinger's lunch with reporters, then asked, "Why did you say all this?"

At first Schlesinger didn't reply. Finally, he looked up and said, "I don't know."

For the Secretary of Defense to speculate to the press that our military commanders—men who are controlled by civilians under the Constitution—might take some unilateral and illegal action at a moment of grave national crisis was to stab our armed forces in the back. And that, in my opinion, was inexcusable. At the time I took the oath of office, I had thought it important to keep key people in their jobs in order to emphasize to allies and adversaries alike the continuity of our foreign and military policies. Had I not felt that way, I would have found a new Secretary of Defense as quickly as possible. Now, fifteen months later, I concluded that I had been remiss in not getting rid of him. I don't enjoy firing people, but I didn't see any alternative.

Schlesinger's peculiar behavior was only one of several reasons why he would have to go. Under Nixon, he had fought acceleration of research and development on the cruise missile. During my Presidency, he opposed outfitting with nuclear weapons-firing capability the F-15 fighters we were sending to our NATO allies and he urged me repeatedly to withdraw significant numbers of our nuclear weapons from Western Europe. The argument could be made that many of those weapons were obsolete and that they constituted an unnecessary financial drain. Kissinger and I were aware of that. But we wanted to use those weapons as bargaining chips in our discussions of SALT and the mutual reduction of forces in Europe. We wanted to get something in return from the Soviets before we took them away. Schlesinger wanted to remove them unilaterally.

Somehow Schlesinger had succeeded in projecting the public image of a hawk. In reality, the reverse was true. His views often were much more dovish than mine. He was obviously unsuccessful in dealing with Congress, and his rivalry with Kissinger was making me increasingly uncomfortable. But I must also admit that his aloof, frequently arrogant manner put me off. I never could be sure he was leveling with me. I decided to sever my relationship with him at the earliest opportunity.

But who could take his place? Don Rumsfeld came to mind immediately. Although he was only forty-three, he had already served with distinction as a member of Congress, director of the Office of Economic Opportunity, head of the Cost of Living Council and as ambassador to NATO. For nearly fifteen months he had been the senior member of my White House staff, with Cabinet rank. I knew he had the necessary experience, toughness and skill to help the country maintain a defense capability strong enough to preserve peace by meeting any military threat. I also knew that as a former Congressman, he had the expertise to win approval of our budget requests on Capitol Hill.

Throughout his public life, Rumsfeld had always believed in the principle of selecting, training and then giving lots of responsibility to strong deputies. Never one to hog credit for himself, he gloried in his aides' success. His chief deputy on the White House staff was a bright young political scientist named Richard B. Cheney. Cheney was still in his early thirties, a native of Nebraska who had earned bachelor's and master's degrees at the University of Wyoming, worked on Capitol Hill and then served under Rumsfeld in a number of posts. They had made a fine team. If their personalities differed— Cheney was very low-key, Rumsfeld rather intense—their approaches to the job were remarkably alike. Both were pragmatic "problem solvers"; both worked eighteen-hour days and were absolutely loyal to me. I knew that I could ask Cheney to step into Rumsfeld's shoes and that the White House would function just as efficiently.

Next I thought about other changes that I wanted to make. Bill Colby had been director of the CIA at a traumatic period in the agency's history. He had gone through hell and, in my opinion, done a splendid job. In the fall of 1975, many people felt that I was angry at him for disclosing too much about CIA activities in his appearances before Congressional committees. That was not the case. He was on a hot seat before one committee after another. I supported his decision to tell the truth about past agency misdeeds even though both of us recognized that his testimony would be embarrassing. Colby was smart; he possessed both integrity and guts, and I liked and respected him very much. Yet this did not alter my conviction that the agency needed a change at the top. Colby had completed his exhaustive Capitol Hill testimony about past CIA activities. Drawing essentially on the excellent recommendations of the Rockefeller commission, we had proceeded with plans to reorganize and reform the agency. If that reorganization was to have the substance as well as the image of a significant change, we had to appoint a new man to preside over it.

Attorney Edward Bennett Williams was my first choice. He was a brilliant lawyer, a savvy Washingtonian with an interest in intelligence matters, and a Democrat, which meant that he'd probably win Senate confirmation easily. But he decided that business commitments would prevent him from taking the job. Not long after, I thought of George Bush, who had been the United States representative in Peking for more than a year. He had written to say that he'd like to return home soon. The CIA directorship, I thought, would be the right spot for George. He was an able administrator, and in other posts he had held—member of Congress, ambassador to the United Nations and chairman of the Republican National Committee—he had succeeded splendidly.

One of the recommendations that the transition team gave me after I became President was that Henry Kissinger should wear only one hat; to expect him to function effectively both as Secretary of State and as National Security Adviser to the President was to ask too much of any one man. At the time, I hadn't gone along with that view. Henry wanted to keep both positions, and I didn't want to make any changes that might be misunderstood overseas. Over the next fifteen months, however, I became convinced that Henry ought to concentrate on the Department of State and foreign policy; he shouldn't have to worry about the mechanics of the NSC.

Those concerns, I thought, belonged rightfully to Air Force Lieu-

tenant General Brent Scowcroft, who for nearly three years had
served as deputy national security adviser to the President. Although
he was a West Point graduate, Scowcroft hardly fit the Hollywood
stereotype of a fighting man. He was thin, short and balding. Unfail-
ingly polite, he never raised his voice. If he was really upset about
something, he might say, "Gosh," but that was the strongest four-letter word I had ever heard him use. He didn't smoke or drink. Yet his
unremarkable appearance and mild manner belied a fine service
record and a first-rate intellect. He had worn a fighter pilot's wings
since 1948; he had earned a master's degree and a Ph.D. in international relations at Columbia. He had taught Soviet history at West
Point, and he spoke both Russian and Serbian. He and Henry thought
alike. I knew that their excellent relationship would continue even
after I asked Brent to wear Henry's second hat.

On Saturday afternoon, October 25, I called Kissinger and Rumsfeld into the Oval Office and explained what I wanted to do. The
only way I could feel comfortable with my own team, I said, was to
fire Schlesinger, ask Colby to submit his resignation, bring Bush back
to be director of the CIA, send Rumsfeld over to Defense, take away
one of Kissinger's two hats and upgrade both Cheney and Scowcroft.

Kissinger and Rumsfeld were stunned by the sweeping nature of
these changes. Both expressed doubts. Critics would charge that I was
firing Schlesinger only because of my personal animosity toward
him, Henry said. The political price that I would have to pay would
be exorbitant. Therefore, it would be wiser to keep him on for another year. He didn't object to losing his job as National Security Adviser to the President, but he did think it might be misunderstood in
foreign capitals. If other countries thought I was downgrading him, it
would jeopardize his ability to function effectively as my Secretary of
State.

Rumsfeld expressed similar reservations about the many changes.
My own credibility was at stake, he pointed out. I had said publicly
that my Cabinet was set. Now here I was, about to fire Schlesinger.
He was equally unhappy about my decision to send him over to Defense.

I replied affirmatively to each of these objections. Defense, I told
Rumsfeld, was the place he ought to go. With his experience and

ability, he could convince Congress to appropriate necessary funds for the military. At the end of the meeting, Henry said he would accept my decisions. Rumsfeld wanted to think it over and talk with me the next day.

On the afternoon of October 28, Rockefeller came in for his weekly meeting with me. He was a proud man, and Bo Callaway's comments about him as a political liability had lingered. In the nearly eleven months that he had served as Vice President, he had done an outstanding job, and our personal relationship was a source of great satisfaction. The two of us would get together in the Oval Office at least once a week. He would sit down, stir his coffee with the stem of his horn-rimmed glasses and fidget in his chair as he leaped from one subject to another. What an active and imaginative mind he had. Our talks would range from the need to redesign the Vice President's official flag all the way to his plan to create a $100 billion Energy Independence Authority. No detail was too small to escape his attention; nothing was too grandiose for him to propose. And always, after we had covered the substantive matters on his list, we would talk about national politics.

Nelson was deeply hurt by the fact that his contributions to the Administration had not been recognized. In mid September, 55 percent of the respondents to a Harris poll gave him a negative job performance rating. Only 27 percent thought he'd done a good job, and the rest said they weren't sure. Even more ominous, 25 percent of the Republicans polled said they wouldn't vote for me if Rockefeller remained on the ticket. I was sorely disappointed by those results, which were completely unwarranted. I couldn't believe they stemmed from anything he had done as Vice President. Rather, I thought they derived from things he'd said and stands he'd taken earlier in his political career. In his past Presidential campaigns, he'd established a reputation as a liberal, and he had outraged many ultraconservative Republicans. Apparently, their antagonism wasn't going to fade away.

All of which brought me back to square one and the need to make a decision about 1976. Nelson was absolutely loyal to me, and he would do anything I asked him to do. He had talent, experience and unlimited drive. Should something happen to me, he was supremely qualified to step into my shoes. Yet I recognized that he was nearly seventy years old. Moreover, I didn't believe he'd be happy serving four more years as Vice President. He was too active and dynamic a man, too full of new ideas.

Now, as Rockefeller and I talked on October 28, we discussed the growing strength of the GOP's right wing. Perhaps, he said, the best thing he could do would be to withdraw from consideration as my running mate. He would rather do that voluntarily than as the direct result of pressure from conservatives. "Mr. President," he said, "I'll do anything you want me to do. I'll be on the ticket or I'll be off the ticket. You just say the word."

As we talked, I didn't try to gloss over the fact that conservative opposition to him might jeopardize my own nomination. "There are serious problems," I said, "and to be brutally frank, some of these difficulties might be eliminated if you were to indicate that you didn't want to be on the ticket in 1976. I'm not *asking* you to do that, I'm just stating the facts."

"I understand," he said. "Well, it's probably better that I withdraw. If I take myself out of the picture, that will clear the air. I'll give you a letter saying that I don't want to be considered as a Vice Presidential nominee."

I knew how he felt, and that bothered me. He had suffered so many setbacks in his political life, and this was one more. I was very sad because I could not find the words to express the depth of my feeling for him.

"You've been very loyal," I said. "We've had a fine relationship, and I hope that despite this, that loyalty and friendship will endure."

Nelson assured me it would. As I walked him to the door, I put my arm around his shoulder. I was grateful for his expression of unselfishness, his willingness to do what was in the best interests of the party and the country—and me. At the same time, I was angry with myself for showing cowardice in not saying to the ultraconservatives, "It's going to be Ford and Rockefeller, whatever the consequences."

The initial plan had been to announce Rockefeller's withdrawal from the 1976 ticket on Monday, November 3, and to postpone disclosure of the shifts in the Cabinet, the CIA and the senior staff until

later that week. Then on Saturday, November 1, I learned that someone had leaked part of the story to *Newsweek*, and that it would appear two days later. That really complicated matters because I was
scheduled to fly to Jacksonville, Florida, on Sunday morning to meet
with Egyptian President Sadat. I had to talk to Colby and Schlesinger
before I left town. They should get the word directly from me and
not learn about it in the press. I asked Jack Marsh to have both men
come to the Oval Office the first thing Sunday morning.

Colby arrived shortly after eight, and I got right to the point. "We
are going to do some reorganizing of the national security structure,"
I said. I went on to describe the personnel changes I wanted to make,
and I expressed my appreciation for the job he'd done at the CIA under the most difficult of circumstances. Our ambassador to NATO,
David K. E. Bruce, had indicated that he wanted to step down. I told
Colby I'd be happy to send him there, or appoint him our ambassador to Norway. Colby replied that he would get back to me soon.
(Later, he telephoned to decline both posts—with great appreciation.) Our session was brief, only fifteen minutes, and given its circumstances, not unpleasant at all.

My discussion with Schlesinger was quite different. He and Marsh
entered the Oval Office at eight twenty-five. As I had with Colby, I
listed the personnel changes I had decided to make and explained
why I thought they would strengthen the Administration. I said he
shouldn't feel that he was being singled out; others were changing
jobs too. I needed my own team, I went on, and I referred to his resignation.

Schlesinger was upset. "I haven't resigned, sir," he said. "You're
firing me."

"Well, Jim, you could put it that way, but that's not the way I'd
like to have it understood. I think a change is necessary—that is my
prerogative—and I'd like your resignation. However, I believe we
can find an important place for you in the Administration."

Helpfully, Marsh picked up on that theme. "The President wants
you to stay where you're available as a resource," he said. "You can
continue to render valuable assistance in other areas."

The directorship of the Export-Import Bank was vacant, I pointed out. Schlesinger was an economist; he was knowledgeable about international finance. Perhaps he would like to assume that post.

His face tensed, and he rejected the offer disdainfully. He still wanted to argue about his dismissal from the Pentagon. Our session dragged on for nearly an hour. The more he talked, the angrier I got and the surer I was that my decision had been right. Finally, at nine twenty-three, after one of the most disagreeable conversations I have ever had, he got up to leave. My problems with him, I thought, haven't ended; it's likely that I'll hear from him again.

There was one final shift I wanted to make in the Cabinet in order to broaden its philosophical base. So after arriving in Jacksonville to meet with Sadat, I called Ambassador Elliot Richardson through the embassy in London and offered him the Secretary of Commerce post, which Rogers Morton was leaving because of poor health. Richardson said he would let me know the next day. He telephoned later to accept on the condition that he would have a significant role to play on my team. I agreed.

At seven-thirty Monday night, I entered the East Room to announce to reporters waiting there the personnel shifts I had made. Throughout my public life, I had always tried to be aboveboard in talking to the press. But now, because it was important to play down the fact that personality clashes between Schlesinger, Kissinger and me had triggered Schlesinger's dismissal, I was less than candid in explaining the reasons for my decision. The inquiry that got me in trouble came from John Osborne of the *New Republic*: "Are you saying that neither personal nor policy differences between Dr. Kissinger and Mr. Schlesinger contributed to this change?"

"That is correct," I replied.

Several days later, appearing on *Meet the Press*, I conceded that "a growing tension" between the two men had been a factor and that "I was uncomfortable in the situation." But by the time I said that, the damage had been done. Conservatives screamed about my dismissal of the supposedly "hard-line" Schlesinger. Liberals were upset by Rockefeller's withdrawal as my 1976 running mate. And the press had a field day. "Why now," asked the Washington *Post*, "and why in such an abrupt and clumsy manner?" Conservative columnist George F. Will called the Schlesinger ouster "a foolish thing, done in a foolish way." Liberal pundit Joseph Kraft said the personnel shifts had "stimulated new doubts as to whether [Ford] has the brains to be President." Reporters everywhere called the events of the past few days the "Halloween Massacre." Before I'd announced the changes, a Gallup poll showed me leading Ronald Reagan in the race for the GOP nomination by a margin of 58 to 36. Once the news was out, my popularity plummeted, and Reagan actually edged ahead of me in the polls.

Yet I still was not overly concerned about a challenge from the right. One reason was political. After a shaky start, the President Ford Committee was beginning to function effectively. Funds were coming in for my 1976 campaign, and significantly, my supporters had succeeded in recruiting a number of long-time Reagan backers in California. If Reagan were deprived of his financial angels, I thought, he wouldn't even try to make the race. But there were other reasons I figured I would have no opposition. As a result of my tough stand, New York City officials had finally adopted budget-cutting measures and a financial plan that would prevent default. The federal government had provided aid, to be sure, but the terms of that agreement constituted a plus for the American taxpayer. (We agreed to lend funds to the city when its cash flow was down, providing that at the end of each fiscal year New York would repay all the money it had borrowed at an interest rate 1 percent higher than the prevailing rate.)

In mid November, I had journeyed to Rambouillet, France, to attend an international economic summit conference. My sessions with President Giscard, West German Chancellor Schmidt, British Prime Minister Wilson and other leaders had been very productive, and all our countries would benefit from our agreements on monetary policy, trade and our relations with the developing world. Now that the grain embargo had been lifted, hopefully, most American farmers were happier. Negotiations aiming toward a SALT agreement were progressing at a slower pace, but Kissinger was scheduled to fly to Moscow in December; I felt confident that we would resolve all our differences and sign the accord soon.

So as Thanksgiving Day approached, I concluded that I had a lot to be thankful for. The country was at peace, and our future seemed very promising. Then, on the afternoon of November 19, a telephone call came in to the White House. I was conferring with Rockefeller and several of his aides when Terry O'Donnell entered the Oval Office and placed a message on my desk. "Governor Reagan is on the line," it read. "Would you like to speak to him?"

6

Challenge from the Right

"All your strength is in your union. All your danger is in discord."
—Henry Wadsworth Longfellow

"Hello, Mr. President," Reagan said, and then he came right to the point. "I am going to make an announcement, and I want to tell you about it ahead of time. I am going to run for President. I trust we can have a good contest, and I hope that it won't be divisive."

"Well, Governor, I'm very disappointed," I replied. "I'm sorry you're getting into this. I believe I've done a good job and that I can be elected. Regardless of your good intentions, your bid is bound to be divisive. It will take a lot of money, a lot of effort, and it will leave a lot of scars. It won't be helpful, no matter which of us wins the nomination."

"I don't think it will be divisive," he repeated. "I don't think it will harm the party."

"Well, I think it will," I said.

Neither of us is the type of person to waste words, and we concluded the conversation quickly. I think he really believed that his candidacy wouldn't be divisive, but I knew he was wrong. How can you challenge an incumbent President of your own party and *not* be divisive?

The challenge was serious. I recognized that now, and I thought ruefully·about all the time we had frittered away trying to convince ourselves that Reagan wouldn't enter the race. My supporters had been crisscrossing America lining up endorsements from prominent Republicans. We had most of the generals on our side. But Reagan had many of the troops. His volunteers were already out ringing doorbells. The first test would come in New Hampshire on February 24. Reagan had recruited former Governor Hugh Gregg, a moderate Republican, to head his effort there, and he had secured the only computerized list of registered voters in the state. His people were holding meetings, mapping strategy. By contrast, my own effort seemed in disarray. Representative James Cleveland was in charge of my New Hampshire drive, but he was about to begin a three-week vacation trip, and little would happen until his return. A defeat in New Hampshire, I knew, would render a crippling blow to my entire campaign.

Yet at the time I couldn't afford to worry about politics. I was due to leave on a trip to the People's Republic of China, Indonesia and the Philippines at the end of November, and before my departure, I wanted to make several key decisions. The most important of these involved a nomination to the Supreme Court.

Associate Justice William O. Douglas had been ill for months, unable to perform his judicial duties. On November 12, he sent me a letter saying that he wanted to step down from the bench. Although I didn't agree with many of the Justice's legal opinions, I felt no rancor toward him personally, and I responded immediately, concluding: "May I express on behalf of all our countrymen this nation's great gratitude for your more than thirty-six years as a member of the Supreme Court. Your distinguished years of service are unequaled in all the history of the Court."

That afternoon I met with Attorney General Levi and Counselor Phil Buchen to discuss a replacement. Few appointments a President makes can have as much impact on the future of the country as those to the Supreme Court. The opinions of those selected affect the course of our society and the lives of our citizens for generations to come. Under Chief Justice Warren, the Court had begun legislating by judicial decree instead of simply interpreting the law. Chief Justice Burger had tried to limit federal jurisdiction and let state courts make more final judgments themselves. I thought his course was correct, and I sought someone who would agree with that view. "Survey the field," I told Levi, "and don't exclude women from your list."

The Attorney General gave me a dozen suggestions. We asked legal scholars to read the candidates' opinions as jurists or their writings as members of the bar. Soon the list was down to five or six names, including HUD Secretary Carla Hills and Detroit Federal District Court Judge Cornelia Kennedy. The final choice was between two men: Judge Arlin M. Adams of the U.S. Circuit Court of Appeals in Philadelphia and Judge John Paul Stevens of the U.S. Circuit Court of Appeals in Chicago. Both had received excellent ratings from the American Bar Association; both had had distinguished careers. I pored over their legal opinions myself. Stevens's opinions were concise, persuasive and legally sound. It was a close call, but after talking to Levi and Buchen, I selected Stevens in December. And the Senate confirmed him by a vote of 98 to 0.

Early on the morning of November 29, *Air Force One* took off, and Betty, Susan and I were on our way to the People's Republic of China. I had never met Communist Party Chairman Mao Tse-tung or the newly designated Vice Premier, Teng Hsiao-ping; we had substantive matters to discuss, and I wanted to do everything possible to implement the Shanghai Communiqué of 1972. I was not about to abandon our commitment to Taiwan, but it was important to expand upon the dialogue that Nixon had begun nearly four years earlier. We landed in Peking on the afternoon of December 1. That night I was the guest of honor at a nine-course dinner in the Great Hall of the People. I listened as Vice Premier Teng underlined his country's concern about Soviet intentions. "Today, it is the country which most zealously preaches peace that is the most dangerous source of war," he said. "Rhetoric about détente cannot cover up the stark reality of the growing danger of war."

Henry Kissinger, who had visited the PRC in October to make arrangements for my trip, had told me that Premier Chou En-lai, reportedly dying of cancer, lay in a Peking hospital, and I would not be seeing him this time. Chairman Mao, Henry said, would receive me, but at nearly eighty-two, he was fading fast; our meeting would be very brief. It turned out to be far more than a courtesy call. When Betty, Susan and I entered the living room of Mao's residence, he was sitting in a large armchair; two female interpreters and a nurse were standing behind him. The moment he recognized us, he managed to shuffle halfway across the room to shake hands. Greeting Susan, who was then eighteen, he smiled warmly; his eyes sparkled, and he seemed more interested in her than in anything either of her parents might say.

Soon the photographers had their pictures. Betty and Susan left, and Mao sat down with Henry, Brent Scowcroft, George Bush and me for a discussion that was to last an hour and a half. He spoke in what sounded almost like a low growl. Each of his interpreters would write down what she thought he had said. At regular intervals they would stop, confer among themselves and then show him the version they had agreed upon. After he had approved or revised the text, one of the interpreters would read the statement to me. When it was my turn to speak, only one interpreter was needed to write down and translate what I said. Mao may have been weak; his hands may have been gnarled, but it was apparent that he was still mentally alert, held strong convictions and conveyed a certain mystique.

Our talks that afternoon focused upon the Soviet Union. The Soviets, Mao said, wanted world domination, and if their drive was ever to be stopped, the United States would have to stand up to them. That was why the U.S. would have to remain strong in the Pacific basin, why we'd have to be willing to challenge the Soviets everywhere. Mao seemed fully aware of the restrictions that Congress was placing on my ability to conduct foreign policy. Clearly, these restrictions upset him. Would we do anything to challenge the Soviet-Cuban thrust in Africa? When was the United States going to strengthen ties with its NATO allies? Were we going to continue helping our traditional friends in Asia? Or, in the wake of our setbacks in Cambodia and South Vietnam, would the United States turn inward again?

Kissinger had told me that Mao was no ordinary politician; rather, he was a world statesman, a brilliant poet who thought in conceptual

terms. At the end of our meeting, I came away convinced that the Soviet Union had an implacable enemy in the PRC. That enmity, I felt,
would continue even after Mao was gone, for the other Chinese leaders I met seemed to fear and distrust the Soviets just as much as Mao
did.

During the days that followed, I had several sessions with Vice Premier Teng to discuss how we could build on the foundation of the
Shanghai Communiqué and find a formula for eventual normaliza-
tion of diplomatic relations. Teng was cordial but firm, and seemed
in no hurry to press for full diplomatic recognition or the termination
of our long-standing commitments to Taiwan. I was impressed with
his vigor and directness. He was obviously a doer—more pragmatic
than theoretical. And I was amazed by his grasp of world affairs.

Finally, on the morning of December 5, we left Peking and flew
first to Indonesia and then on to the Philippines. It was important for
me to convey U.S. support for our Pacific friends. The Indonesians
wanted to know how much military and economic aid they would receive from the U.S. next year, and the Filipinos wanted new agreements to govern the status of our military bases there. The U.S. had
no irreconcilable differences with either country. They seemed reassured by our regional commitments despite the loss of Vietnam. After
less than twenty-four hours in each capital, we headed back to the
United States on Sunday, December 7, stopping for a memorial service at Pearl Harbor. As I told reporters on the plane, the trip had
been a success, "no minuses and a lot of pluses."

Back in Washington, several problems required immediate decisions, each fraught with danger politically. When I nominated Bush
as CIA director, I had hoped that Congress would put political considerations aside in this crucial appointment, and judge him on his
merits and impressive experience. But the Democrats didn't want to
play the game that way. They had no problem with his qualifications. They conceded that he would do a fine job. But with Rockefeller out of the political picture, they were fearful that Bush might get
the nod to be my running mate in 1976.

As the hearings continued, the Democrats demanded that Bush
pledge that he would not be on the ticket. "If I wanted to be Vice

President," Bush replied, "I wouldn't be here asking you to confirm me for CIA." Then he added, "I don't think that an American should be asked to forswear his political birthright."

But the Democrats persisted. Unless I promised to exclude him from Vice Presidential consideration, they would vote against his confirmation. This was blatant partisanship. And even though Congress held all the cards, I was tempted to fight. But Bush himself urged me to accept the Democrats' demand. "I know it's unfair," he said, "but you don't have much of a choice if we are to get on with the job of rebuilding and strengthening the agency." Reluctantly I agreed, and on December 18, I sent a letter to Mississippi's John Stennis, chairman of the Senate Armed Services Committee, saying we would go along with the Democrats.

Fiscal and energy matters were still pending as the year's end approached, and the outcome would affect the pocketbooks of every American. Ever since the first week of October, I had been warning Congress that I would veto a tax cut if the lawmakers failed to trim federal spending at the same time. I had called for a tax cut of $28 billion. My budget for fiscal year 1977 would total $395 billion—a reduction of $28 billion in the growth of federal spending. The tax cut and the spending slowdown were tied together. Unless Congress recognized this link, we would risk a new round of double-digit inflation and a recession worse than anything we had seen before.

Apparently, Congress didn't think that I was serious. On December 17, it lowered taxes only $9 billion by extending for just six months the $18 billion annual reduction then in effect. The lawmakers said nothing about any spending cuts. I knew that if I vetoed the bill, I would be courting political disaster, for on January 1, the withholding rates for every wage earner in America would go up an additional three or four dollars a week. With less money to spend, people would purchase less, and that would slow our economic recovery. Then, too, workers would be furious about those smaller pay checks. They wouldn't think that Congress was at fault; they'd blame me.

Yet I realized that failure to veto the bill would undermine the economy. "The American people want tax relief, need tax relief and deserve tax relief," I said on December 17. "But they also want uncontrolled federal spending to stop. The government has been cutting federal taxes with one law and raising federal benefits with another, knowing full well that those benefits have to be paid for by future taxpayers or by the merciless tax of constant inflation, which even taxes the poor. I am returning this halfway legislation and asking [Congress] to send me a bill that takes the honest and responsible first step toward a balanced federal budget, a stable economy, lower taxes and reduced rates of government spending."

To my surprise and delight, the House sustained my veto the next afternoon. All Congress had to do for me to sign the bill, I said, was to commit itself to adopt spending cuts. Less than one week later, Congress passed the Revenue Adjustment Act of 1975 and sent the measure to the White House for my signature. The tax cut was much smaller than I had asked for—$9 billion for a six-month period as opposed to $28 billion—but the important thing was that the lawmakers had committed themselves to trim spending simultaneously with any further extensions of the tax cut measure after next June 30. Treasury Secretary Bill Simon thought the legislation didn't go far enough and urged a veto, but OMB Director Jim Lynn said that it was about as much as we could hope to get. He said I should sign the bill, then ask Congress to pass an additional $10 billion tax cut. Lynn, I decided, was right. And if the Democrats tried to push the budget over the $395 billion limit—as I knew they would—I could make an issue of their broken promises by frequent use of the veto.

Back in January, I had sent the Congress a comprehensive 167-page proposal to deal with the nation's energy crisis. To avoid dependence on foreign energy sources, I urged that we take these steps: reduce the rate of growth of our energy consumption from near 4 percent a year back to 2 or 2.5 percent; double our output of coal and the electric power that we generated from our nuclear plants; maximize production of domestic oil and gas by deregulation; stockpile a billion barrels of oil in order to keep the country running in the event of another embargo. Finally, we had to allocate sufficient funds for continued energy research and development. But instead of addressing these needs directly, lawmakers did next to nothing.

Nearly a year later, nothing substantive had been done. One reason for this was political. The Democratic Congress was looking forward to the 1976 election. House Majority Leader O'Neill knew that Speaker Albert would step down soon and that O'Neill himself would become Speaker of the House. Tip wanted to elect a Democratic President. In order to do that, he had to make me look bad. Stalling my energy proposals was one way to achieve that goal, especially when there was little public concern. People still didn't believe that the energy crisis was real. In an attempt to break the deadlock, I did everything I could to convince Congress that it had to move. For nearly a year, I'd been giving speeches about the problem; I sent formal messages up to Capitol Hill, and I met with key lawmakers on at least thirty-three separate occasions. In less than three years, I warned, our petroleum imports would grow to nine million barrels a day, and we would be twice as vulnerable to an oil embargo as we had been in 1973.

Finally, in December, Congress passed the Energy Policy and Conservation Act of 1975. This was an inadequate measure, and my economic advisers urged me to veto it. What upset Bill Simon and Alan Greenspan most was the fact that the bill provided for the gradual phasing out—over a forty-month period—of government price controls on domestic oil. Both men had wanted those controls to be lifted immediately, as I had myself. Furthermore, the bill rolled back the price of domestic crude by about 12 percent per barrel, then stipulated that it could rise gradually; I could recommend a higher price every ninety days, and Congress had thirty days to review my decision. That provision, Simon and Greenspan maintained, was counter to my strategy of saving energy by *raising* prices. Additionally, it would prevent the oil companies from acquiring—at least initially— funds they needed to expand their search for new sources of energy, thus stifling domestic production and increasing our imports from abroad.

My political advisers were just as emphatic in urging me to sign the bill, and they acquired an important ally in Federal Energy Administrator Frank Zarb. With every step in the forty-month process, Zarb pointed out, prices would rise, and the oil companies would have new incentives to produce. Phased deregulation over a long period was far better than no deregulation at all. If I vetoed the bill, it wasn't likely that Congress would give me everything I wanted in an election year. The oil people were kidding themselves if they thought they could persuade lawmakers to remove all government controls on the industry overnight. Deregulation was a volatile issue politically. If we carried it over into 1976, we would be fighting a very divisive battle with Congress and taking the risk of coming away with nothing to show for it.

Additionally, Zarb continued, the bill was a first step toward the adoption of a national energy policy. It would allow the U.S. to meet some of our midterm goals for energy independence although it would not achieve what I had set forth in my first State of the Union address. The bill contained, for example, authority to establish a strategic storage system. It encouraged oil- and gas-fired utility and industrial plants to convert to coal. It listed provisions for energy efficiency labeling and new emergency powers for the President to use in the event of another foreign oil embargo. The measure was a compromise, but half a loaf was better than none, and I decided to sign it on December 22, just before leaving for Vail. Simon, however, kept pushing for a veto, and he didn't give up easily. Shortly before midnight on December 21, my telephone rang in the residence. "Hi, Mr. President," Bill began. "I'm sorry to bother you this late, but I know you're going to be announcing the decision tomorrow, and I wanted to talk to you about it." And talk he did—and talk and talk some more.

Finally, after about half an hour, he realized that I had made up my mind. "Well, I'm really sorry to have done this to you at midnight," he said. "I'll hang up now and let you get some sleep, and I'll see you in the morning." Next morning, he came in with a smile on his face. "My wife, Carol, was sitting next to me when I called you last night," he said. "At the end of our conversation, she heard you shouting into the receiver, 'Thanks a million, Bill, for calling.' Carol just looked at me when I hung up the phone. Then she asked, 'How can you get mad at a man like that?'" By the time he finished the story, I was smiling too. We might argue like cats and dogs, but once I'd made a decision, Simon would support it 100 percent, and that was nice to know.

My next decision involved the Common Situs Picketing bill that Congress had just passed, and it had me walking a tightrope for days.

Back in 1951, the Supreme Court had ruled that the throwing up of picket lines around an entire construction site—even though the striking union might have a dispute with only one contractor or sub-contractor—constituted an illegal secondary boycott. Every Administration since then had tried to push legislation through Congress that would satisfy both organized labor and the construction industry, but no one had made much headway. In the spring of 1975, shortly after he took over as Secretary of Labor, John Dunlop came to me and said he thought he could draft a bill that both sides would support. "If you can do that," I replied, "it'll clear a problem off the agenda that's been there for years. Furthermore, I'll support the bill openly."

Dunlop produced a bill that labor complained about but finally decided to accept. It allowed secondary boycotts at construction sites but it included a few sweeteners for management. Wildcat strikes, the bill said, would be illegal. A local union couldn't strike unless it had received permission from the international, the theory being that the international would have a broader perspective and would not endorse exorbitant local wage demands. Finally, a crucial provision created a labor-management panel to preside over the collective bargaining process in the industry. Dunlop persuaded Robert A. Georgine, president of the Building and Construction Trades Department of the AFL-CIO, and AFL-CIO President George Meany to accept the idea. Then he won similar approval from the top industry representatives.

Congress passed the measure, and the stage was set for settlement of this contentious issue once and for all. Suddenly, the agreement came unstuck. The problem was that the executive board of the Associated General Contractors of America, which had endorsed the legislation, reversed its position due to fierce opposition from its members. More than 700,000 letters, telegrams and telephone calls poured into the White House. An overwhelming majority urged me to veto the bill. I felt caught between a rock and a hard place. If I vetoed the bill, I would appear to be going back on my word. Never mind that the reason for my turnabout would be the AGC membership's refusal to honor an agreement that their own executive board had made.

Dunlop had known all along that my approval of the bill had been conditional, and I thought he understood my view that management's decision to jump ship freed me from having to honor my original commitment. That is not to say that he agreed with me. Indeed, he warned me that if I vetoed the bill he'd probably have to resign because he'd lose all credibility with the labor movement and the people in his department.

His resignation would be a bitter blow, and I urged him not to do anything precipitous. He was too valuable a member of my team. After he had left the Oval Office, I weighed the pluses and minuses of a veto. With the exception of Dunlop himself, every member of my Cabinet had expressed reservations about the bill. Bill Simon and Jim Lynn were vigorously opposed. So was Alan Greenspan. Other members of my Economic Policy Board didn't like the measure either. All argued that it would lead to more—not fewer—conflicts in the construction industry, with the risk of higher unemployment and slowdowns at building sites.

My veto of the Common Situs Picketing bill was one of my most difficult decisions, but in the end I concluded I simply had no choice. The bill "has become the subject of such heated controversy," I explained in announcing my veto, "that its enactment under present economic conditions could lead to more idleness for workers, higher costs for the public and further slowdown in a basic industry that is already severely depressed."

Once the tough decisions about the tax cut, the energy bill and the Common Situs Picketing measure were safely behind me, I flew to Vail with the family for a one-week Christmas holiday. I was looking forward to relaxing and skiing with my family and friends. I spent three hours on the slopes on Christmas Day and skied every day of my vacation after that. Some of my aides warned me that I was taking a risk. My public image, they pointed out, was that of an amiable bumbler who was sitting in the White House just waiting until a "real" President came along. If I fell on the slopes, the press would seize on that, and my image problems would intensify.

I told them their concerns were ridiculous. I had skied for most of my life, and I wasn't about to stop doing something I loved to do just because reporters and photographers might be there. *Every* skier falls, I said. Surely, the press would understand that. But I was wrong.

One day I took a tumble in the snow and footage of my fall was on the network news that night. Photographs appeared on the front pages of newspapers everywhere, and editorial cartoonists had a field day. I remember one cartoon in the Denver *Post*. There I was skiing, backward, down a hill; a bystander was explaining: "I understand his ski instructor is also his campaign manager."

The photographs and cartoons didn't bother me as much as they upset my family and staff, but that particular cartoon in the Denver *Post* hit uncomfortably close to home. My campaign, in fact, did seem to be sliding downhill.

Lee Nunn had resigned as director of organization at the President Ford Committee. So had David Packard, the former Deputy Secretary of Defense, who had been in charge of my fund-raising drive. Neither man got along well with Bo Callaway. Our finance committee had raised only $900,000 of a projected $10 million—and virtually all of that had come in large contributions. A few national columnists wrote that I was a "caretaker" and another asked: "Is it possible that his political illness is incurable? That he is a terminal case?"

All this was reflected in the polls. In mid October I had led Reagan by a margin of 58 to 36. By December, however, a new Gallup poll showed that 40 percent of all Republicans and 27 percent of independents would vote for Reagan. I won the support of only 32 percent of Republicans and 25 percent of the independents. Furthermore—and this revelation came in a new Harris poll—even if I won the GOP nomination for President, I would lose to Hubert Humphrey in the November election by a margin of 52 to 41.

In many respects I had all the liabilities of an incumbent President—and few advantages. No other President, while serving in the Oval Office, had ever had to go out and build a political organization from scratch. But I had entered the White House under unique circumstances. And in the sixteen months that I had been President, several of my decisions had antagonized special interest groups. I had used the veto forty-two times. Occasionally, in making up my mind whether to sign or to veto a bill, I had appeared to be indecisive. The Common Situs Picketing bill was a perfect example. I had hesitated because it was such a close call. That hesitation was combined with the news media play-ups of my falls on the ski slopes, and the result was that comedians began to ridicule me even more. Chevy Chase impersonated me by staggering into a microphone.

Then there were the political mistakes. In mid December, the Southern Republican state chairmen had convened in Houston. Some of my aides persuaded me not to go, saying I should be "Presidential" by staying in Washington. Reagan, however, went to the meeting. He delivered a hard-hitting speech and received a rousing ovation. "Reagan's rhetoric is great," Bo Callaway said, "but his record is poor." That angered Southern Republicans. So did an outburst by Nelson Rockefeller. Urging the chairmen to work harder for me, he shouted, "You got me out, you sons of bitches. Now get off your ass." Nelson's bluntness was to the point and I was proud of him, but unfortunately, his candor probably cost me some support.

Initially, Henry Kissinger had been scheduled to fly to Moscow in December to see if we could reach a new SALT agreement with the Soviets. The accord had been eluding us for more than a year, and it was vital that we make a final attempt to bridge our differences over the Backfire bomber and the cruise missile. Success with SALT would be in the best interests of the United States militarily, and it would go a long way toward ensuring my election in 1976. But Kissinger had to postpone his trip because of the deteriorating situation in Angola. Using $100 million worth of Soviet-supplied weapons and assisted by some five thousand Cuban combat troops, the pro-Communist Popular Movement for the Liberation of Angola (MPLA) was winning control of the country. For the past several months, we had been providing limited amounts of military assistance to forces sympathetic to the West. So had the French. But by the middle of December, it had become clear that our aid was insufficient. We would have to supply more. We had no intention of sending any U.S. military personnel to Angola, but about $25 million worth of arms might give the pro-West forces there a chance. The French agreed to work in conjunction with us.

That's when Congress pulled the plug. On December 19, by a vote of 54 to 22, the Senate blocked me from sending any further aid to Angola. The French backed off, unwilling to act alone. "How can the United States," I asked, "the greatest power in the world, take the position that the Soviet Union can operate with impunity many thousands of miles away with Cuban troops and massive amounts of military equipment, while we refuse any assistance to the majority of the local people who ask only for military equipment to defend themselves? This abdication of responsibility by a majority of the Senate will have the gravest consequences for the long-term position of the United States and for international order in general. A great nation cannot escape its responsibilities. Responsibilities abandoned today will return as more acute crises tomorrow."

Instead of getting mad at the Senate, people tended to blame me. Angola was going down the drain, they said, and as President, Ford was responsible. All this led to new questions. Was détente worthwhile, or just another Soviet trick? The public quite understandably found it hard to comprehend why we should have any dealings with the Russians when they were stealing a march on us in Africa.

My low standing among Republicans had less to do with any personal antipathy they might have felt toward me than with the emotions that Reagan aroused in their hearts. He would go from place to place and deliver variations on The Speech. He would talk about the New Jersey man who stopped receiving veteran's benefits because the Veterans Administration had notified him that he was dead, the "welfare queen" in Chicago who was ripping off $150,000 a year from the taxpayers, the subsidized housing project in New York City that had a doorman and a parking garage. Reporters looked into his allegations and found them to be exaggerations, but Reagan kept on telling the same tales.

And he made some ridiculous new charges. I had fired Schlesinger as Secretary of Defense, he said, because I was afraid to tell the American people "the truth about our military status." Henry Kissinger was the sole architect of our foreign policy, and he was telling me what to do. I was part of the "buddy system" in Washington, and he, Reagan, was the fresh face that the country was looking for. He was a master at oversimplifying complex issues, reducing them to one-line quips, and that was very effective politically, especially among grass roots conservatives.

All of the problems that confronted me were serious, but I made up my mind that I wasn't going to let them get me down. Despite some setbacks, 1975 was nothing to be ashamed about. We had healed the wounds of Watergate, moved the economy from the depths of the recession to more jobs and less inflation, and our basic strengths remained intact. We could look forward to the future with renewed confidence.

As the new year began, the polls provided more bad news. A new Gallup survey, released on January 8, revealed that 46 percent of the respondents disapproved of my performance as President; 39 percent approved of the way I was doing the job, and the remaining 15 percent hadn't made up their minds. Because I felt that this reflected an "image" and not a "substance" problem—we simply hadn't done a good job of communicating what I had done and why over the last seventeen months—I resolved to remain on the course I had set. We were extremely fortunate in being able to sign up Stuart Spencer, an astute political strategist, as deputy chairman of the President Ford Committee. Spencer and his partner, Bill Roberts, had handled Rockefeller's campaign against Goldwater in the 1964 California GOP primary. Their man had lost by a whisker. Then Spencer and Roberts directed Reagan's victorious 1966 and 1970 gubernatorial campaigns. Along the way, Spencer and Reagan had had a falling out. I never did find out why.

In January, as the first primaries drew near, I began meeting with Spencer at least once a week. He always let my other political advisers speak first. Only after they'd made their points would he offer his opinions. Quickly, I discovered that he was well organized and knew precisely what he wanted to say. My respect for him grew accordingly. In order for the PFC to function more efficiently, we needed someone to give it a better liaison with the White House staff. Rogers Morton, who had just stepped down as Secretary of Commerce, seemed ideal and the administrative burdens would be much lighter for him. On January 13, we announced his appointment to the White House staff.

Other talented people surfaced to play key roles in the campaign. Robert Mosbacher, a blunt-spoken Texas oilman, assumed Packard's old job as chief fund-raiser for the PFC. A California newsman, Peter Kaye, became the committee's liaison with the press. F. Clifton

White, a conservative who had headed Goldwater's search for delegates in 1964, signed on to perform a similar function for us, and I was delighted to have him on our side. Finally, Robert Teeter, a Detroit analyst, was put in charge of polling.

With personnel in place, we considered our campaign strategy. According to Teeter's polls, the public viewed me as a "nice guy" who wasn't quite up to the Oval Office's demands. Therefore, I should project an image of quiet competence and firm determination. The campaign poster we selected had me looking belligerent as hell. I would have preferred a smiling, more congenial photograph, but my advisers convinced me that my appearance had to be strong and affirmative, even combative, in the early months of 1976. Teeter's polls also disclosed that all my traveling in 1975 had hurt my standing with the voters. Therefore, I should remain in the capital and be as "Presidential" as possible. I couldn't argue with that. I had to give the State of the Union address on January 19, and I was wrapping up the budget.

One key political strategy question remained. Exactly what should I say about my challenger? Spencer wanted me to go on the offensive and attack Reagan personally. There I drew the line. I had never criticized a political opponent in that manner, but Spencer didn't give up easily. Despite Reagan's conservative rhetoric, he said, the fact remained that Reagan had taken in more taxes and spent more money than any governor in California history. Why not point that out? I demurred. Reagan was proud of his accomplishments in Sacramento. If I attacked his record, I'd have a hard time going back to him and asking for his help after I'd won the nomination. That would split the party at a time when we needed unity most. Reagan and I should keep our contest on a high plane, I concluded, and discuss the issues that mattered to Americans. I thought his knowledge of the way the federal government worked was superficial at best. Inevitably he would slip, and once he made a mistake, we could pounce on that.

What we didn't recognize then was that Reagan had *already* made a near-fatal mistake; all we had to do was draw attention to it. Back in September, in a Chicago speech, he had proposed "a systematic transfer of authority and resources to the states"— programs such as welfare, education, housing, food stamps, Medicaid, community and regional development and revenue sharing. Then he declared, "Transfer of authority in whole or part in all these areas would reduce the outlay of the federal government by more than $90 billion, using the spending levels of fiscal 1976. With such savings, it would be possible to balance the federal budget, make an initial $5 billion payment on the national debt and cut the federal personal income tax burden of every American by an average of 23 percent."

The proposal sounded good, but it was impractical, and the press didn't take it seriously. Spencer, however, asked the research people at the PFC to figure out what would happen if Reagan's plan went into effect. The conclusion: If the federal government turned these programs over to the states, the states would have to come up with massive amounts of funds to administer them. That would mean hefty hikes in state sales and income taxes. New Hampshire, as it turned out, had neither a sales nor an income tax. People there, Spencer argued, wouldn't be happy when they discovered that they might have to pay these levies soon. We should go on the attack, he said. If we mentioned the $90 billion proposal often enough, Reagan would have to spend all his time explaining what he had meant to say. He wouldn't be able to launch an offensive against me.

For the past several months, I had been thinking about my State of the Union address. The nation had sailed through rough seas, but now, as we embarked upon our Bicentennial year, we were approaching calmer waters, and the speech would give me an opportunity to point out the direction in which I wanted to steer the government, not just in 1976 but for the next four years.

My thinking was influenced by a memo I had received from William J. Baroody, Jr., director of the White House Office of Public Liaison. "I believe this is the time to make explicit what has been implicit in virtually all of your programs and speeches," Baroody wrote. "I strongly suggest that now is the appropriate time frame for laying out boldly your conception of how we can rebuild the free society this nation was intended to be."

Bob Hartmann assembled a strong team to help prepare the draft. (Among them: Baroody, OMB Director Jim Lynn, Domestic Council

Executive Director Jim Cannon, CEA Chairman Alan Greenspan, resident intellectual Robert Goldwin and political counselor Stuart Spencer.) But the group had difficulty agreeing on the substance of the speech. The first draft I saw was much too long, its thrust confused. I made some additions and deletions, then asked Hartmann to try again.

What I didn't know at the time was that I would be receiving *two* speeches instead of one. So upset was Dick Cheney with the quality of Hartmann's draft that he had asked one of his aides, a talented writer named David Gergen, to prepare a separate version. On January 15, Hartmann's revision arrived on my desk along with Gergen's effort. Neither constituted exactly what I wanted to say, but each included passages I liked. If I took the best from each, I would have a pretty good speech. That's what I did. On Saturday afternoon, January 17, I convened a meeting in the Cabinet Room of everyone who had worked on the speech. The disagreements continued. Finally, after about three hours of this, I had heard enough. "Damn it," I said, slamming my hand on the table, "we've got to stop bickering over these little details. I want a final draft by noon tomorrow."

That was one of the few times I lost my temper during a meeting of this kind, but I was determined to avoid working over the speech right up to the last minute, as had happened the year before. My outburst had the right effect. The final Hartmann version, which I received the next day, was very close to what I wanted to say. I made a few corrections, and on the evening of January 19 addressed a joint session of the Congress.

> Government . . . thought [it] could transform the country through massive national programs, but often the programs did not work. Too often they only made things worse. In our rush to accomplish great deeds quickly, we trampled on sound principles of restraint and endangered the rights of individuals. We unbalanced our economic system by the huge and unprecedented growth of federal expenditures and borrowing. And we were not totally honest with ourselves about how much these programs would cost and how we would pay for them. Finally, we shifted our emphasis from defense to domestic problems while our adversaries continued a massive buildup of arms.
>
> The time has now come for a fundamentally different approach—

for a new realism that is true to the great principles upon which this nation was founded. We must introduce a new balance to our economy—a balance that favors not only sound, active government but also a much more vigorous, healthy economy that can create new jobs and hold down prices. We must introduce a new balance in the relationship between the individual and the government—a balance that favors greater individual freedom and self-reliance.

Then I got into the specifics. In the past decade, I said, the federal budget had been growing at an average rate of more than 10 percent per year. The budget that I would submit, $394.2 billion, would slice that annual rate of growth in half. That would enable us to reduce taxes by $10 billion more than lawmakers had agreed to cut in December. Government, I went on, could not create jobs for all Americans who wanted to work. I told Congress that I would soon be submitting legislation detailing incentives to help private industry expand. I urged lawmakers to untangle the "petty tyranny" of massive government regulation, and I predicted that we could have neither sustained economic growth nor an adequate number of jobs unless we had an assured supply of energy.

On foreign policy, I criticized recent legislation that tied my hands as President and made it difficult for me to respond to challenges overseas. Then I warned my audience that "the crippling of our foreign intelligence services increases the danger of American involvement in direct armed conflict. Our adversaries are encouraged to attempt new adventures while our own ability to monitor and influence events—short of military action—is undermined. Without [an] effective intelligence capability, the United States stands blindfolded and hobbled. In the near future," I continued, "I will take actions to reform and strengthen our intelligence community. I ask for your positive cooperation. It is time to go beyond sensationalism and ensure an effective, responsible and responsive intelligence capability."

Press reaction was mixed, and some observers pointed out that I was taking an economic and political risk by recommending a slowdown in federal spending. At the time, the only risk that I was thinking about was of a different kind. Twenty-three years earlier, Harry Truman had called reporters into the Executive Office Building to brief them on the federal budget for fiscal 1953. What a change since then! Truman's budget called for expenditures of $43 billion, mine $394.2 billion. Truman's budget was eighty pages long; mine ran on 955 pages. None of Truman's successors—Eisenhower, Kennedy, Johnson or Nixon—had shown much interest in the budget process; none had briefed the press personally, and for nearly a quarter century, Washington reporters had assumed that they would have to get their facts and figures from budget officials.

I decided to change the procedure and brief reporters myself. Some of my aides were aghast. If I tried to respond to specific questions about complex items in the budget, they said, I'd slip. *Anyone* would. And if I had to refer questions to my assistants, it would appear to the public that I didn't know what the budget was all about. I'd reinforce the image of an amiable bumbler not quite up to the job. I recognized those risks, yet I was determined to proceed. The potential benefits of a personal briefing, I felt, far outweighed the risks.

A President controls his Administration through the budget. The document reflects his basic priorities. Some recent Presidents had only worried about total dollar amounts and left the fiscal details to their subordinates. Johnson, *Time* magazine's Hugh Sidey pointed out, "used to glaze over as his budget was discussed, reviving only to query bizarre items like the crotch size in the Air Force uniform trousers." Nixon was bored by the whole process. On the fiscal year 1977 budget that I was about to submit, I had made at least 150 crucial choices myself.

Discussions of the '77 budget had begun for me in June 1975, when OMB Director Jim Lynn first sat down to review not only an overall spending ceiling but also the general allocation of funds. Throughout most of the summer and fall, he had monitored the budget's preparation, coordinating the figures with the White House Council of Economic Advisers. Invariably, from every agency came the complaint: "You didn't give us enough money." In some cases, Lynn and his chief deputy, Paul O'Neill, agreed that the cuts had been too deep and moved to restore some funds. In others, they rejected appeals. The departments and agencies, they said, would learn to live with the reductions.

Heads of the departments and agencies could appeal to me—and they almost always did. (HUD Secretary Carla Hills was particularly adept at this, and she won three of every four appeals. She marshaled facts and figures to support her positions most effectively.) In November and December, I had spent two or three hours every day just deciding those appeals. The White House logs for those two months, in fact, revealed that the budget had occupied roughly one hundred hours of my time. I was fully prepared to brief reporters myself on the budget's details.

On the morning of January 20, I entered the huge State Department auditorium and faced several hundred members of the press. Vice President Rockefeller, my Cabinet and heads of other federal agencies sat at a table beside me. In a brief opening statement, I quoted from the budget message that I was going to submit to Congress the next day. " 'The combination of tax and spending programs I propose,' " I said, " 'will set us on a course that not only leads to a balanced budget within three years but also improves the prospects for the economy to stay on a growth path *that we can sustain.*' This is not a quick fix. It does not hold out the hollow promise that we can wipe out inflation and unemployment overnight. Instead, it is an honest, realistic policy; a policy that says we can steadily reduce inflation and unemployment if we maintain a prudent, balanced approach."

The questions came in a rush, fifty-six of them over the next hour and a half. Was there any "gimmickry" in my budget? Was I "really and truly" seeking Congressional help in controlling government spending? Why did I oppose a federal guarantee of a job for everyone who wanted to work? How much money was I providing for medical research? How much for the CIA? When the session ended, I felt that my appearance had done more to convince members of the press of my competence to be President than almost anything else I'd done since August 1974.

While I was defending the budget, Henry Kissinger was in Moscow making another attempt to reach agreement on SALT II. (We were also seeking to get the Soviets to reduce their involvement in the Angolan civil war.) Both of us were aware that this would probably be our last chance to achieve an arms accord in 1976. As the nomination and election approached, partisanship would flourish, making it impossible to discuss complex issues like SALT in a rational way. So Henry really wanted the Moscow talks to succeed. For a variety of reasons, most of them unfair, he had been going through exceedingly difficult times. Early in January, in fact, he had come into the Oval Office and handed me a "draft" of his letter of resignation as Secretary of State. His motivation, he explained, was political. Conservatives still blamed him for my dismissal of Schlesinger, although he had had nothing to do with it. That made him a liability to me in the primary fight. Unselfishly, in order not to embarrass me, he would step aside. Pointing to the letter, he said, "This is what I'll send you if my resignation will help."

I was shocked by the idea. His resignation was something I simply couldn't accept. The country needed him—*I* needed him—to implement our foreign policy at this difficult time.

Later, after he had left the Oval Office, I reflected upon the problems Henry faced. In the early days of the Nixon Administration, he had misjudged the political situation, which was understandable for a person not familiar with partisan politics. Because of his steadfast views on Vietnam, he assumed that he would have the support of such staunch conservatives as Senators Barry Goldwater, Strom Thurmond and John Tower whenever he needed it. So he ignored the hard-liners of the party. He did too little to educate them about what he was doing and why. Instead, he concentrated on trying to build up support among liberals in Congress. He also wooed the press, and in turn, many reporters idolized him. His face appeared on magazine covers, his name and accounts of his "romantic entanglements" in gossip columns everywhere. He was "Superman," "Henry the K," the "secret swinger" who was about to end the war in Vietnam. He could do no wrong.

The first jolt to Henry's reputation had come in May 1970, when U.S. forces had moved into Cambodia. Just before the action took place, Henry had briefed me as Minority Leader, explaining that several hundred thousand Communist troops were operating against us from "safe" bases inside Cambodia. Then he had asked my opinion as to what the Congressional response would be. "Difficult but manageable," I had replied, and my judgment was correct. What neither of us had foreseen was the furor that the incursion would provoke outside Congress. Liberals pounced upon him savagely, the first in a long line of attacks still to come.

In 1972, Nixon and Kissinger had negotiated an interim SALT accord with the Soviets. Conservatives had been suspicious of the role Henry had played and they had expressed their doubts vocally. After the Yom Kippur War of 1973, Henry had made a valiant attempt to bring peace to the Middle East. Somehow, the idea got around that he was leaning too hard on Israel, and that had cost him support in the American Jewish community. A former assistant of his on the NSC staff, Morton H. Halperin, had filed a civil suit against him (and others), claiming that he had been responsible for approving wiretaps the FBI had placed on the telephones of seventeen individuals—including Halperin—during the Nixon years. Press reports about this had cast shadows upon his personal integrity and damaged his credibility.

Nor did the attacks cease when I became President. Simply because Nixon had appointed him, Henry remained a target for Nixon-haters who didn't have the former President to revile any more. Inside my Administration, he became a target as well. In a well-meaning but misguided attempt to establish my credentials as a President who was knowledgeable about foreign policy, some members of my staff leaked stories to the effect that I had overruled Kissinger on several decisions. Reading such nonsense in the press upset me enormously. The stories were totally inaccurate—there never was a conflict of any significance between us—yet I'm sure that some of them were believed. And this hurt a proud and sensitive man.

Finally, Kissinger remained the favorite target of liberal Democrats on Capitol Hill. In the wake of war and Watergate, Congress had passed bill after bill restricting the President's power to conduct foreign policy. When Henry tried to warn doubting lawmakers that their actions could imperil the nation's security, his admonitions were dismissed. Congress knew better, Congress explained, and Congress would decide what to do without any help from him.

So during the fall of 1975, Kissinger's relations with Congress had deteriorated. That wasn't his fault. Congress simply was more rebellious, more assertive of its rights and privileges—and also more irresponsible—than it had been for years. Proof of this had come in November, when the House Select Committee on Intelligence approved three resolutions which said that Henry was in contempt of Congress because he had failed to comply with three subpoenas that the committee had served on him.

Throughout that committee's existence, I had bent over backward to cooperate. I had instructed officials to turn over documents relevant to the committee's probe of the CIA and other intelligence agencies. I had also taken steps to make sure that the sort of abuses which had occurred in the past would not happen during my Administration. Yet the committee, which was determined to stick it to Kissinger, wasn't satisfied. On November 7, it issued seven subpoenas on the Executive Branch for additional documents, demanding all that material in just four days. We decided to comply with four of those subpoenas, but not the remaining three. The first, addressed to Kissinger by name, called upon him to provide "all documents relating to [the] State Department recommending covert action . . . to the National Security Council and its predecessor committees from January 30, 1961, to [the] present." I knew that the State Department had made no such recommendations during my time in office, so those documents wouldn't embarrass me. Clearly, however, they contained highly sensitive military and foreign affairs assessments and evaluations. Also, they revealed the consultation processes that Presidents Kennedy, Johnson and Nixon had employed before making key decisions in the Oval Office. After checking with Attorney General Levi, I determined that these were the sort of documents that I could withhold on the grounds of Executive privilege, and I told Henry not to honor that subpoena. The other subpoenas demanded papers dating back to January 1965. We had already turned over some of the documents covered by these subpoenas, and we were doing our best to review the others as quickly as possible.

On November 19, I wrote the committee chairman, New York Democrat Otis G. Pike. "This issue," I said, "involves grave matters affecting our conduct of foreign policy and raises questions which go to the ability of our Republic to govern itself effectively."

After reviewing the facts of the case and stressing once again that I had done everything I could to cooperate with the committee, I urged Pike to reconsider the resolutions his committee had approved. I offered to send officials from the Executive Branch down to Capitol Hill to elaborate on the points I had made. "I believe that the national interest is best served through our cooperation," I concluded, "and adoption of a spirit of mutual trust and respect."

Fortunately, Pike backed off and on December 11, the committee withdrew its recommendation that Kissinger be cited for contempt. Thus he and I were spared what would have been a catastrophic confrontation with the Congress.

But another rebuff quickly followed, this time involving the U.S. position on SALT which Henry had prepared. The opposition came from Secretary of Defense Don Rumsfeld and the Joint Chiefs of Staff, and I recognized that they held the trump card. The Senate would have to ratify the new accord. If Rumsfeld or the Joint Chiefs testified against it, there was no way that the Senate would ever go along with it.

After several intensive NSC meetings, I told Henry to take two proposals to Moscow on January 20. The first tried to build on the agreement that Brezhnev and I had reached at Vladivostok. It proposed incorporating the Backfire bomber into the treaty—with the exception of the 120 aircraft that had already rolled off Soviet production lines—and counting it as a strategic weapon. Cruise missiles on our bombers were to be counted as MIRVs, as were those on our surface ships and submarines. The Soviets, Henry and I agreed, were likely to reject this, so I approved an acceptable alternative that still satisfied our own security needs. In this second proposal we said we would limit the Soviets to 275 Backfire bombers by 1981, with specific restrictions on their deployment and operations. We proposed banning long-range cruise missiles from our submarines—although we insisted on our right to keep adequate numbers of the short- and medium-range variety—and we suggested deploying these missiles on up to twenty-five of our surface ships. Then we recommended that both sides cut their agreed-upon total of 2,400 ballistic missiles by roughly 10 percent.

Not surprisingly, the Soviets rejected the first proposal. But they seemed interested in the second. Brezhnev, in fact, hinted that he might be willing to accept a cut of more than 10 percent. Agreement, it seemed, was very near. But when Henry returned to Washington, Rumsfeld and the Joint Chiefs had growing reservations. Most of their objections were highly technical, and I hoped that with some give from the Soviets, we could allay the Pentagon's concerns. Brezhnev wouldn't budge, however, and our Defense officials maintained their doubts, so we came up with a plan that I thought would satisfy everyone. We would ratify the Vladivostok agreement of 1974 and put both Backfire and the cruise missile into a separate package that we would continue to negotiate. While these talks were going on, we said, the Soviets could not increase Backfire production rates. In return we would agree not to deploy cruise missiles before January 1979. The Soviets reacted angrily. What we were suggesting was a "step backward," Brezhnev said, and there was no "give" in their position at all. Reluctantly, I concluded we would not be able to achieve a SALT agreement in 1976.

Meanwhile, we had other foreign policy concerns. Foremost was the widening war in Angola. Since the Senate's vote in December to cut off U.S. assistance to the pro-West forces there, the military situation had worsened considerably and the pro-Communist MPLA seemed on the verge of winning a major victory. There was no doubt in my mind that the Cuban troops, with Russian weapons, were acting as proxies for the Soviets and I called in Soviet Ambassador Anatoly Dobrynin to tell him that his country's involvement in the conflict was very damaging to our overall relations. Dobrynin, a skillful diplomat, insisted that the Cubans were mounting only a minor operation. I liked Dobrynin, but I knew he was not laying the cards on the table. In fact, at a meeting of the Organization of African Unity (OAU), a majority of the nations represented deplored the Soviet-Cuban intervention and urged the U.S. to lend a hand to the Angolan nationalists who were resisting it. The House was considering a measure—an amendment to the Defense Appropriations bill—that would enable us to do just that, and on January 27, I addressed a personal appeal to Speaker Albert. "Resistance to Soviet expansion by military means must be a fundamental element of U.S. foreign policy," I reminded him. "There must be no question in Angola or elsewhere in the world of American resolve in this regard. The failure of the U.S. to take a stand would inevitably lead our friends and supporters to conclusions about our steadfastness and resolve. It could lead to a future Soviet miscalculation [and] it would make Cuba the mercenaries of upheavals everywhere."

Albert and others in the House leadership wanted to help. But so worried were liberal Democrats about our becoming involved in "another Vietnam" that they defeated the amendment. I was absolutely convinced that a favorable vote would have given us the tools to nip Castro's adventure on this crucial continent. But Congress had lost its nerve and, as a result, we were bound to see further Cuban involvement in Africa.

Domestic politics now began to occupy my time more and more. The federal election law enacted because of Watergate would make me the first President to campaign under its new rules. The law limited to $1,000 the amount wealthy contributors could give to a Congressional or Presidential candidate in each primary, runoff or general election. (Political Action Committees—or PACs—could donate no more than $5,000 to a single individual.) It required that candidates disclose promptly the sums they had received, and in the race for President, it provided for federal financing—on a matching funds basis—of primary campaigns. Finally, it imposed spending restrictions on the candidates themselves. Before the GOP convention in Kansas City, still six months away, I could spend some $13 million on primary campaigns. After Kansas City, I could spend $21.8 million in federal election funds.

In theory, it's possible to label a trip to Chicago as "Presidential" and one to New York "political." But because almost every trip a President makes in an election year can be described as political, it's hard to draw the line. Nonetheless, we tried. If I was going somewhere to ask for votes, then the visit was political and the expenses would be shouldered by the PFC. So when Nessen announced that I would be making a trip to New Hampshire on February 7 and 8, he stressed that it would be political.

But even before I arrived, two factors complicated my campaign. One was a tactless remark, the second a trip that Nixon was planning to take. During an Oval Office talk with veteran newsman Lowell Thomas, the conversation turned to skiing and Thomas asked me if I planned to hit the slopes during my visit. I said I didn't think so. In the late 1930s, as a student at Yale Law School, I had skied in New Hampshire. The slopes were often fairly icy and you rarely found the kind of powder that usually blanketed Vail. Nessen sat in on my meeting with the broadcaster, and when reporters asked him later that afternoon if I planned to ski, he repeated my remark. The reaction in New Hampshire was immediate—and unfavorable. I was "slurring" one of the state's major industries, and that, I knew, wasn't going to help me at the polls.

Nor was Nixon's trip. On the morning of February 5, an official at the liaison office of the People's Republic of China in Washington handed Brent Scowcroft the text of an announcement that was going to be released in Peking the next day. Nixon had accepted an invitation to visit the PRC. A Chinese jet would pick him up on February 21 and he would arrive in Peking on the twenty-second. That would be the fourth anniversary of his first trip there and only two days before the New Hampshire primary.

Early in 1976, Nixon had telephoned me to say that he was going to stay out of the public eye for the rest of the year. So when Scowcroft and Cheney brought me news of his trip, I was astounded. His timing could not have been worse. The media, I knew, would carry accounts of his trip and those stories would remind New Hampshire voters of the links between Nixon and me just before they went to the polls. Inevitably, the pardon would become an issue in the campaign.

My aides couldn't believe Nixon would do such a thing. Perhaps because he suspected that this would be the case, the former President telephoned Kissinger and said that he had received just 36 hours advance notice from the PRC. Henry doubted this explanation because he knew the Chinese didn't do business that way. And Scowcroft was so angry that for once in his life he let loose with some sizzling swear words. The question now became: What should my public reaction be? The best thing I could do was downplay the former President's trip. Accordingly, I told Nessen to say that Nixon was going as a private citizen, which he had every right to do; that I was delighted his health had improved and that I hoped he would extend my best wishes to the Chinese leadership.

Next morning, Betty, Susan and I flew to New Hampshire for a weekend full of campaign activities. For a state with only twenty-one convention delegates, New Hampshire wields an enormous influence in the Presidential candidate selection process. Its primary is the nation's first and a defeat for me there would be a near-fatal blow. I was well aware that Reagan had a head start in New Hampshire. He was planning to spend several weeks campaigning in the state and his supporters had done a superior job of organizing at the grass roots. The only way I could overtake his lead was to try to put him on the defensive and hope that he would make a mistake.

Reagan's plan to cut the budget $90 billion by transferring federal programs to the states had aroused a lot of controversy in New Hampshire and my people had pounced on it. The Reagan proposal, they told local officials, would force them to come up with new taxes for everyone. Reagan did everything he could to wiggle off the hook. "Well, I wasn't talking about details," he protested. "I was just using this [the $90 billion figure] as a target." But even a target of that magnitude was irresponsible and I decided to capitalize on his mistake by showing that I was fully conversant with budget realities. Since 1972, I stated, the federal government had transferred $23 billion to the states and localities with no strings attached. Reagan's $90 billion plan would have eliminated these funds. New Hampshire had received its fair share—and would continue to do so unless Reagan's scheme were adopted—and I pointed to a series of charts that contained the facts and figures. "By the end of this calendar year," I said, "some $96 million will have been paid to New Hampshire, to its ten counties, to its thirteen cities and 221 townships." The audience seemed impressed.

What turned out to be the weekend's most successful event was a Sunday night question-and-answer session with students at the University of New Hampshire in Durham. Some 3,500 students, faculty members and guests were crowded into Lundholm Gymnasium. Many of the questions were tough. I answered them, then signaled recognition of a young man who was dressed like an ape. "Mr. President, sir," he said, "my name is Bonzo and I am an escapee from an old Ronald Reagan flick. I have been challenging him all over the country as the candidate of big business, as the fat cat's candidate. The way you talk about freedom for the giant corporations, I will be forced to challenge you as well. Why should you not be called the big business candidate?"

I couldn't help but smile. More than forty years had passed since I'd left Ann Arbor, but college students hadn't changed that much. Some years they'd tried to see how many could crowd into a telephone booth or a VW Beetle; other years they had staged panty raids. Now, apparently, the "in" thing to do was to dress up like a gorilla and interrogate the President of the United States. Well, all right; let him have his fun. "I think if you look at my voting record for twenty-five-plus years in the House of Representatives, where I voted over four thousand times," I replied, "you will find that it could not be categorized as [belonging to] a candidate of big labor *or* big business. It was a voting record that called them as I saw them for the overall benefit of the United States, and as President I have carried out precisely the same policy." The audience cheered.

Next day, I ordered the release of a report on my annual physical examination. I was in excellent health; people had a right to know that and I expressed the hope that other candidates would follow suit. It was only fair to the American people. But Reagan didn't follow my example. He didn't disclose his medical history.

So on February 12, I decided to raise the ante by releasing a personal financial statement. My net worth, the statement showed, was $323,000, and the bulk of that, more than $210,000, was in real estate. Betty and I had not yet filed our joint income tax return for 1975. For 1974, however, we had reported a taxable income after deductions of $128,000 and on that we had paid federal, state and local taxes of more than $62,000. "I think it is generally agreed," Nessen told reporters, "that he is paying a very large percentage of his income in taxes. His own philosophy is not to find those things [tax shelters] that some people find to avoid taxes."

What I wanted to do, of course, was put pressure on Reagan to issue a complete financial statement of his own. The press had already dug up the fact that, claiming "business reverses," he had paid no California state income tax in 1970. Those "business reverses" had never been fully explained. I had heard that he was a millionaire; that since he had left office, his lecture fees, newspaper column and radio commentaries were earning him $700,000 a year. I thought as a candidate he should disclose his income and the taxes that he had paid.

Late in January, he had released a "statement of economic interests." But this was just a copy of a document that he had filed, as required by law, with the California secretary of state after stepping down as governor. It was more than a year old. It didn't show his net worth or his total income for the period 1970 through 1974. Nor did it reveal how much he had received prior to making the decision to challenge me. After I had released my financial statement, reporters asked Reagan if he planned to do the same. He was going to disclose "some additional information," he said. Whereupon the press let the matter drop. I found that hard to understand. For years the press had hounded Nixon with questions about his financial affairs. They'd pestered other politicians too, and that was their right. But in February when Reagan released a "summary" of his income tax returns, reporters seemed satisfied. His lack of full disclosure never became the issue I expected it would.

While seeking New Hampshire votes, I also had to prepare for the second major primary of 1976, in Florida on March 9. And I soon learned my campaign there was in sad shape. Nessen admitted as much to the press when he said on January 27: "If the primary election were today in Florida, we'd get clobbered. I suspect that by the time the Florida primary rolls around we will still get clobbered."

Florida was basically conservative, the sort of state that in a Republican primary would be receptive to Reagan's superficial remedies for all the ills that afflicted America. Worse, my political organization was pretty much flat on its back. Our people didn't even have enough bumper stickers, lapel buttons or campaign posters. They didn't have telephone banks and they hadn't begun to try to identify voters who would support me. The Reagan forces were outhustling and outmaneuvering us at every turn.

As soon as he discovered what was happening, Stu Spencer made a decision that, as much as anything else, kept our campaign alive. Bill Roberts, his former partner in California, was in poor health and had left politics. But Stu had worked with Roberts in directing Reagan's spectacularly successful gubernatorial campaigns and he thought that if anyone could save our effort in Florida, Roberts was the man. Rob-

erts agreed to help and at the end of January flew to Florida. Knowing that nine of the state's counties contained 70 percent of the total
Republican vote, he decided that we should concentrate on them. He
hired new workers, recruited volunteers and organized phone banks
in key areas. The missing bumper stickers, buttons and posters began
to materialize. Gradually, our campaign plans evolved from pieces of
paper to reality.

Reagan still had several advantages over me. Because of the pressures of the job, I couldn't afford to spend that much time away from
the White House. He could travel anywhere he chose and stay as
long as he desired. I wasn't even in the same league with him when it
came to movie star quality; he was a born showman and all he had to
do was smile to turn on a crowd. Finally, I couldn't begin to match
his rhetoric, his assaults on the "mess in Washington." I *could*, however, use my incumbency, and on a trip to Florida on February 13, I
decided to take full advantage of it. Orlando, I was pleased to announce, would be the site of the International Chamber of Commerce convention in 1978. That would pour an extra $1 million into
the local economy. The United States Travel Service, part of the
Commerce Department, had been instrumental in attracting the convention there. Florida had already received $900 million in general
revenue-sharing funds from the federal government, I said in Fort
Lauderdale, and under the budget proposals I'd made, the state
would receive an additional $1.25 billion by 1982. That would mean,
for Fort Lauderdale alone, $12 million to hold down taxes, help fight
crime and educate children. Yes, there would be a new Veterans Administration hospital in Bay Pines, I announced. It would upgrade
the aging, inadequate facilities and add three hundred more beds.

All political figures have to make "bird-in-the-hand" promises like
that every once in a while, and I was counting on them to improve
my fortunes in Florida. They did, I am sure, but then I received an
unexpected gift—another Reagan blooper. During a press conference
at Daytona Beach, he was asked to comment about Social Security.
"One of the failures of Social Security as a pension program," he replied, "is that the funds do not grow. They are not invested as they
could be in the industrial might of America. Certainly a portion of
this money could be invested in the economy and grow as it does in
other pension funds."

Was Reagan suggesting that the government ought to plow those funds into the stock market? If so, there was proof that he didn't understand the complicated problems that the Social Security system faced. It would be absurd to risk such huge federal sums on the ups and downs of the market. It was almost too good to be true. When reporters tried to pin him down, Reagan waffled and insisted that he'd never advocated such a step. It was just "one of the things suggested by some of the economists who are talking about this program."

With reporters paying so much attention to the primaries, people could be excused if they had the impression that I was spending all my time on politics. Actually, my battles against Reagan occupied less than 20 percent of my time in the early months of 1976. For I was deeply immersed in substantive issues.

Back in July 1975, I had convened a meeting in the East Room of the White House for the chairmen and the ranking members of ten federal regulatory agencies. They had to start reducing the burden that their regulations were placing on the American people, I said. I explained that I wanted to "relax or eliminate the federal controls over areas where the marketplace can do a better job. Government should foster rather than frustrate competition. It should seek to ensure maximum freedom for private enterprise."

The key to regulatory reform was not to take a wrecking ball and dismantle the entire regulatory scheme. Rather, it was to pick up a mallet and apply a corrective tap. Even this, I knew, would provoke strong opposition. For years, an unlikely coalition known as the Iron Triangle had battled against any change in the status quo. The coalition consisted of industry and its unions, which actually preferred excessive regulation by the government, regulatory agencies that were suspicious of free enterprise, and veteran lawmakers on Capitol Hill who received campaign contributions from donors, both union and industry, who expected them not to rock the boat. It would be difficult to break this triangle—nothing resists change more stubbornly than a comfortably entrenched bureaucracy intent upon its self-preservation—yet I was determined to try.

During my Administration, we submitted to Congress proposals to deregulate the railroads, the airlines and the trucking industry. The measure with the best chance of success was the "4 R's bill," the Railroad Revitalization and Regulatory Reform Act of 1976. It established the new Consolidated Rail Corporation—or ConRail—to operate the properties of the bankrupt Penn Central and other railroads in the Northeast and Middle West. It provided financial assistance— a hefty $1.6 billion—to help railroads improve their physical plants. It also let the railroads adjust their rates with minimal interference from the ICC. And it improved procedures for mergers and abandonments. Increased competition, I reasoned, would lower costs for consumers everywhere.

Predictably, members of the Iron Triangle screamed bloody murder and did everything they could to block passage of the bill. But we had the upper hand. The Triangle people wanted ConRail; it was the deregulation features of the bill that they didn't like. I told Transportation Secretary Bill Coleman to pass word on Capitol Hill: They couldn't have one without the other. If they stripped the measure of its deregulation provisions, I would veto it. The strategy worked. Congress passed the bill with deregulation provisions, and on February 5, I signed it into law.

At this point I began to press my plan for reorganizing the intelligence community. Already, by executive order, I had prohibited our intelligence agencies from spying on U.S. citizens in this country and I'd put an abrupt end to the contemplation of assassination plots. Now it was time for me to tell Congress what I wanted to do. On the evening of February 17, at a news conference broadcast live on radio and TV, I announced the first full-scale reorganization of the intelligence community since 1947. This reorganization, I said, had been guided by two imperatives: "As Americans we must not and will not tolerate actions by our government which will abridge the rights of our citizens. At the same time we must maintain a strong and effective intelligence capability in the United States. I will not be a party to the dismantling of the CIA or other intelligence agencies." Then I got into details. I was asking three separate units to oversee the intelligence community. The National Security Council, over which I presided, would deal with overall policy directions; a new Committee on Foreign Intelligence, chaired by George Bush, would review day-to-day management of all intelligence agencies; and a new Intelligence Oversight Board, made up of private citizens and chaired by former Under Secretary of State Robert D. Murphy, would monitor the compliance of our intelligence agencies with the reforms.

Two days later, I was back in New Hampshire. My fortunes seemed to be improving there. Reagan had been hopping from one town meeting to the next all over the state. His extensive appearances, instead of helping him, were stripping away his star quality. Voters were beginning to view him as "just another politician." Former Governor Gregg, his campaign manager in the state, had maintained from the start of the campaign that Reagan would attract between 40 and 45 percent of the vote, and that was sound strategy. When you're running against an incumbent President, a showing like that would represent a "moral" victory.

On the day of the New Hampshire primary, February 24, a photograph of Nixon in Peking appeared on the front pages of newspapers everywhere. I wondered what, if any, impact this would have upon the New Hampshire vote. After dinner that night, I watched the returns on TV. The outlook wasn't encouraging. Reagan had a lead of 52 percent to my 48 percent. Our people in New Hampshire kept telephoning Rockefeller, Morton and Cheney to say that the battle wasn't over yet. The votes from the northern part of the state remained to be counted and when they were I would pull ahead. Yet when I went to bed shortly after midnight, Reagan led by 1,500 votes. I didn't really think the sparsely settled north could save me, but I wasn't going to fret about it, and I drifted off to sleep.

Cheney woke me up with a telephone call at 5 A.M. "Mr. President," he said, "I have some good news for you. You won by approximately 1,250 votes and you got every delegate but one." (Later, the margin turned out to be 1,317 votes. I had won 17 delegates and Reagan had taken 4.)

What a shot in the arm! It proved I could win an election outside the Fifth Congressional District of Michigan and I hoped it would have a springboard effect, hurtling me all the way to a first ballot nomination in Kansas City. But it also taught us several valuable lessons. First was the importance of having a solid political organization. Second was that I should avoid—as Reagan had *not* avoided—making too many personal appearances in a primary state. Most important, we learned that we were up against a very tough competitor.

Our next key test was Florida and I returned there on February 28. The combination of Bill Roberts's rescue mission and my New Hampshire win had turned everything around. Reagan's manager in the state, L. E. ("Tommy") Thomas, had predicted that his candidate would trounce me two to one. Now he was hedging his bets and telling reporters that Reagan would capture 55 percent of the vote. Actually, the polls showed that I had surged ahead, and I decided to pour it on. Reagan had adopted a "two state [New Hampshire and Florida] strategy"; he hadn't planned on a protracted fight. If I defeated him handily in Florida, he might pull out of the race.

After two speeches in Miami, we flew up to West Palm Beach. The rain was coming down in sheets as our motorcade traveled the forty-odd miles down to Fort Lauderdale. By the time we reached the Royal Park Shopping Plaza in Boca Raton—the tenth stop of the afternoon and evening—I had shaken thousands of hands; I was soaked to the skin but the crowd's enthusiasm made my spirits soar. "I don't look very good," I said, gesturing at my wrinkled suit, "but I think I'm a darn good President."

Apparently, Florida Republicans agreed, for on primary day they gave me 53 percent of the vote, adding another 43 delegates to my column. Including Massachusetts and Vermont, that was my fourth victory in a row. Reagan told reporters that he was "delighted with the outcome" in Florida and he insisted that he would stay in the race, but I thought it would be just a matter of time before he decided to quit. The Illinois primary was next, on March 16; there were 96 delegates at stake and because I had a good organization there, I expected to win a hefty share of them. On March 5 and 6, even before the Florida returns were in, I had campaigned in Illinois. Two events during that swing stick out in my mind. The first was a Q and A session that I had with students at Bradley University in Peoria—I was "up" for the occasion and felt I handled the questions well—and the second was a practical joke that gave me new insight into the working press.

As President, I'd come to appreciate just how much the White House press corps is an institution in itself. Our professional relationship had been adversarial—which was fitting and proper—but on a personal level that relationship had been friendly and warm. This is not to say that I didn't get angry at some columnists—Tom Wicker and Anthony Lewis of the New York *Times*, Richard Reeves of *New York* magazine—when they sat in their ivory towers and wrote poppycock about me. They *did* upset me from time to time. My negative feelings about them, however, didn't carry over to the regulars on the White House beat. On the whole, I liked and respected those men and women and I hoped they felt the same way toward me. Among those whom I considered to be true professionals, and whom I enjoyed personally as well, were Helen Thomas of UPI, Frank Cormier of AP, Bonnie Angelo of *Time*, David Broder of the Washington *Post*, Dick Growald of UPI, John Osborne of the *New Republic*, Aldo Beckman of the Chicago *Tribune*, the late Peter Lisagor of the Chicago *Daily News*, Phil Jones of CBS-TV, Phil Shabecoff and Jim Naughton of the New York *Times* and Tom DeFrank of *Newsweek*. Generalizations are risky, of course, but I'd say that the best of these reporters shared the same personality traits. They were bright, inquisitive and very competitive. Although they were imaginative, they always tried to be accurate and fair. Above all else, they possessed enormous drive.

Just how imaginative and energetic they were was brought home to me on the night of March 5—just after the Bradley University Q and A—when Cheney told me about a prank that was in the works. No one enjoyed playing practical jokes more than Jim Naughton, and one of his favorite victims was Tom DeFrank. DeFrank was an apple-cheeked, roly-poly, very serious sort and Naughton loved to tease him about the fact that he had attended Texas A & M when the school was almost an all-male bastion. How did the Aggies keep warm on cold winter nights? Naughton wanted to know. Was it true that they imported sheep into their dorms? No, of course not, DeFrank replied, hoping, no doubt, that Naughton would let the matter drop. Which Naughton was not about to do. That afternoon, our motorcade had rolled through the farm country of southern Illinois and the bucolic scenery had given Naughton an idea. Why not "rent" a sheep and smuggle it into DeFrank's room at the Peoria Hilton Hotel? In order for the gag to succeed, the Secret Service agents would have to know about it ahead of time. So would the White House advance men and so, too, would Cheney and Nessen of my staff. When

Cheney outlined the caper for me, I just had to smile. "Tell Naughton I want to read a full report," I said.

A White House advance man located a farmer near Peoria who agreed to deliver the sheep to the hotel at eleven-thirty that night. When the farmer arrived in his pickup truck, someone alerted Nessen, who telephoned DeFrank in his room and asked him to come downstairs to the bar. He had a scoop of some sort to give him, Ron implied. Once DeFrank was out of his room, Naughton and his co-conspirators dragged the terrified sheep toward the service elevator. A local couple wandered out of the bar, saw what was happening and decided to join the fun. "Do you fellows do this sort of thing all the time?" the woman asked. The elevator carried them up to the eighth floor and someone produced a key to DeFrank's room. The group opened the door, pushed the sheep inside and stepped in after it. The local couple still didn't know what to make of the scene and neither did the sheep. It butted its head against the door, then relieved itself with abandon on the rug. After several minutes of this, one of the Secret Service agents radioed that DeFrank had left the bar and was on his way upstairs. The reporters tried to hide in the closet and behind the shower curtain. Finally, DeFrank opened the door. "Oh, my God," he said. At which point Naughton hustled everyone out of the room. Tom had not seen a sheep in a long time, he explained. He and the sheep would want to spend some time alone.

After a triumph like that, another reporter might have called it a night and gone straight to bed. Not Naughton. He wrote until 3 A.M. and completed a full report on the incident. I found it on my breakfast tray and it was hilarious. No sooner had I finished the meal than I spotted DeFrank near the service entrance to the hotel. "Morning, Tom," I said. "How's your friend?" For one of the few times in his life, DeFrank didn't seem to know what to say.

One week later, I was back in Illinois. I spoke at rallies in Rockford and Chicago, then prepared to fly to North Carolina, where the primary was set for March 23. That's when my campaign received a severe jolt. On March 12, the Denver *Post* and NBC-TV carried reports that while he was serving in the Pentagon as Army Secretary, Bo Callaway had intervened with the U.S. Forest Service to obtain its approval of his plans to expand a ski resort that he and his brother-in-law owned in Crested Butte, Colorado. As soon as he heard the allegations, Cheney spoke to Bo, who insisted the charges were untrue, that he had done nothing illegal. Yet the *appearance* of impropriety seemed to be there: Bo had met in his Pentagon office with two officials of the Department of Agriculture (the parent agency of the Forest Service) and discussed Crested Butte's expansion plans; in the post-Watergate atmosphere, such an appearance could be very damaging to my campaign.

The next morning, as *Air Force One* flew east to North Carolina, I asked Callaway for his side of the story. Bo and his brother-in-law had been seeking government approval of their expansion plans for the past five years, he said. But all they'd encountered was bureaucratic bungling and red tape. On his last day in the Pentagon, *after* resigning as Army Secretary, he had met with the two USDA officials, who happened to be old personal friends. He had discussed his frustrations with the Forest Service and said that he hoped the matter could be resolved without any further delay. All he wanted was a decision, one way or the other, and he didn't think it was fair for them to ask him to wait another five years. He had exerted no pressure on anyone at all; the USDA and Forest Service people would verify that.

Bo, I knew, was telling the truth. Yet at the same time I realized that keeping him as campaign director would create problems. Senator Floyd Haskell, a liberal Democrat from Colorado, had already announced that his subcommittee on the Environment and Land Resources would look into the Crested Butte affair. He thought he had a hot issue for his own reelection in 1978. Hearings were likely to drag on for months and the press coverage wouldn't help my campaign. The best thing for Bo to do would be to step aside until the matter was resolved. "Mr. President, I have done nothing wrong," he said. "But I recognize that other things are more important. I'm dedicated to achieving your nomination and election and in no way will I allow my personal problems to jeopardize those goals." When *Air Force One* touched down at Greensboro, North Carolina, Bo left the campaign "temporarily." But he did not return.

Ultimately, what happened to Bo constituted one of the most shameful episodes in the recent annals of American politics. So shameful, in fact, that when, in July 1977, *Harper's* magazine published an account of my former campaign director's fate, it entitled the article: "The Persecution and Character Assassination of Howard (Bo) Callaway as Performed by Inmates of the U.S. Senate under the Auspices of the Democratic Party." The article went on to explain that Callaway's troubles had begun when one Miles Arber, the publisher of the *Crested Butte Chronicle*, sent a memo to Senator Haskell about the ski resort. The memo contained innuendoes rather than facts; it just listed Arber's suspicions that something unusual was happening.

Haskell dispatched Senate investigators to Colorado, where they interviewed witnesses and pored over Forest Service records and documents. They found no evidence of impropriety. That didn't deter Haskell. The Senate hearings were due to begin on April 8 and he insisted on sticking to the schedule. Over the next three days, seventeen witnesses testified. Not one of them said that anything improper had occurred; not one said that any pressure had ever been applied to influence the Forest Service to approve the Callaway expansion plans. At the end of those three days, Callaway had a chance to defend his name. It's fundamental to the American system of justice that a man accused of committing a crime have a chance to review the allegations against him. He can't defend himself unless he knows what the specific charges are. To Callaway it seemed clear that Haskell was drawing his "facts" from the Arber memo, so he asked for a chance to see that memo for himself. Haskell refused his request, and adjourned the hearings until after the Senate's Easter recess.

At the end of those hearings, the subcommittee staff set out to draft its report. Ignoring the testimony of every witness that Callaway was innocent of any wrongdoing, the report did everything possible to perpetuate the smear. The Senators, it said, found "no positive evidence" of impropriety. Then it added the damning phrase: "On the other hand, this possibility cannot be excluded." Finally, the issue came down to whether or not the subcommittee would approve the report. Of the eleven Senators on the panel, seven were Democrats and three of them—Washington's Henry Jackson, Ohio's John Glenn and Idaho's Frank Church—had Presidential or Vice Presidential ambitions in 1976. Unable to sit in on the hearings,

Jackson and Glenn withdrew from the debate and did not cast a vote. Church hadn't attended the hearings, either; he hadn't read the subcommittee's report and he wasn't going to be in Washington on the day of the vote. That didn't seem to bother him. He gave his proxy to Haskell and the subcommittee voted 5 to 4 to endorse the report.

Callaway's political career was over. His reputation lay in shreds and it would have remained there had not *Harper's* come forth with the truth. Unfortunately, the rescue party—welcome though it was— arrived a little late. There is a final footnote to the story. In November 1978, Haskell was up for reelection to a second term. His Republican challenger was Colorado Representative Bill Armstrong. On election day, Armstrong won a resounding 59 percent of the vote, and I would like to think Haskell's outrageous treatment of Bo Callaway contributed to his defeat.

Although I was saddened by Bo's departure, I didn't think the setback was that serious to the campaign. I had won four primaries in a row. My prospects in Illinois were encouraging—a Chicago *Sun-Times* poll showed that I led my challenger statewide by a margin of 53 to 32 percent—and soundings in North Carolina seemed positive indeed. What I didn't suspect was that Reagan was about to seize the initiative.

His issue was American foreign policy. Campaigning in New Hampshire several weeks before, he had told students at Phillips Exeter Academy: "Let us not be satisfied with a foreign policy whose principal accomplishment seems to be our acquisition of the right to sell Pepsi-Cola in Siberia. . . . We must always remember that the Soviet Union's representatives across the table will give up as little as they have to and take as much as they can get. They have a history of being tough negotiators and we should be [tough negotiators] too." According to reporters, the audience burst into enthusiastic applause. Reagan had touched a nerve.

In Florida, Reagan stepped up his attacks. "Under Kissinger and Ford, this nation has become Number Two in a world where it is dangerous—if not fatal—to be second best. All I can see is what other nations the world over see: collapse of the American will and the retreat of American power. There is little doubt in my mind that the

Soviet Union will not stop taking advantage of détente until it sees that the American people have elected a new President and appointed a new Secretary of State."

Then he touched another nerve—the Panama Canal: "Our State Department apparently believes the hints regularly dispensed by the leftist Torrijos regime that the Canal will be sabotaged if we don't hand it over. Our government has maintained a mouselike silence as criticisms of the giveaway have increased. I don't understand how the State Department can suggest we pay blackmail to this dictator, for blackmail is what it is." Pausing, he came to his guaranteed applause line: "When it comes to the Canal, we built it, we paid for it, it's ours and we should tell Torrijos and Company that we are going to keep it."

Reagan's statements were inflammatory and irresponsible. But my advisers were split on how I should respond. Kissinger wanted me to tackle him head-on and say that his reckless rhetoric was endangering our position in the world. Morton and Cheney disagreed. Mention of his charges, they said, would give them a dignity they didn't deserve. I felt the voters were smart enough to realize that his verbal swipes were the final lunges of a desperate man. I should be affirmative, ignore my challenger and just stress my own record of accomplishments. And they made another valid point: If I criticized Reagan personally, I would infuriate conservatives whose support I would need in November. That made sense. In the interests of party unity, I would stick to the high road and hope for the best.

The results of the Illinois primary on March 16 seemed to confirm the wisdom of this approach. Reagan was a native of Illinois; he had campaigned there frequently and he had blasted away at my foreign policy. Yet the state's Republicans had given me 59 percent of the vote. At that point in the primary process I had 166 delegates; Reagan had 54 and many in both camps expected him to quit. So by the time I returned to North Carolina on March 20, I was very confident of victory. I had every reason to be. Teeter's polls gave me a lead of between 10 and 12 percentage points, and we had just received some encouraging—albeit vague—signals from John Sears, the bright young lawyer who was Reagan's national campaign manager. If we softened our attacks against Reagan in North Carolina, Sears might persuade him to drop out of the race. But it was important that we stop criticizing his $90 billion blunder and his Social Security mistake and that we say some nice things about him. That way Reagan could pull out and still retain his dignity.

That was fine with me; I believed it and passed the word to my people that we should ease up in our attacks. In North Carolina, I talked about the improving state of the economy. The cost of living in February had increased by only 0.1 percent. Meanwhile, Reagan was firing away at me with every gun in his arsenal, and he was aiming at targets calculated to arouse the emotions of his crowds: the perils of détente, the "giveaway" of the Panama Canal, the awful mess in Washington. He purchased prime-time spots on fifteen of North Carolina's seventeen TV stations for a thirty-minute attack on my policies, and the response was instantaneous.

Reagan's intensive push—he made seven or eight visits to the state—narrowed the gap between us, but according to Teeter's polls I was still ahead. Betty and I had dinner in the White House on March 23, and I was looking forward to celebrating a key victory. But when I talked to Cheney shortly after nine, I learned that Reagan had jumped out to an early lead. When all the ballots were in, Reagan had won 52 percent of the vote and 28 of the 54 delegates.

Reagan's victory was only the third time in U.S. history that a challenger had defeated an incumbent President in a primary state. (Tennessee Senator Estes Kefauver had squeaked past President Truman in New Hampshire in 1952 and Minnesota Senator Eugene McCarthy had beaten President Johnson in Wisconsin in 1968—after LBJ had formally bowed out of the race.) It was the first time in nearly thirty years that I had lost at the polls, and I'll have to admit that it was a jolting experience. Yet a nationwide Gallup poll taken after the North Carolina contest showed that I retained a commanding 56 percent to 32 percent lead over Reagan among all Republican voters. But there was now no longer *any* doubt in my mind that he would contest the nomination all the way to Kansas City.

The next primaries were in New York and Wisconsin on April 6. We had excellent organizations in both states, and I was confident of winning most of the 199 delegates at stake. But Reagan pulled a surprise. He decided to concede those states and devote his time and energy to preparing a thirty-minute fund-raising appeal for nationwide TV. Wearing a blue suit, white shirt and red tie and sporting a little American flag on his jacket lapel, he delivered the address on the night of March 31.

Most of it was a clever rehash of what he'd said before ("I don't believe that people I've met in almost every state in the union are ready to consign this, the last island of freedom, to the dustbin of history") and included numerous borderline charges. But Reagan's frontal attack was astonishingly successful. According to published reports, it earned him $1.5 million, and it convinced me that I would have to take off the gloves and respond in kind. Up to this point in the campaign, I had tried to avoid mentioning Reagan by name. I had talked about "my challenger" and about "others in the Republican Party" who burned with ambition to be President. Now in speeches and at press conferences I singled him out, and while not directly accusing him of maligning the truth, I took specific issue with his "misleading statements." Nevertheless, I had to recognize that I was in an uphill fight when it came to a contest of words with Reagan, even when he was peddling phony charges.

I did begin to polish up both my appearance and my speaking style. Don Penny, a former television writer, stand-up comedian and Korean War hero, had recently become a special consultant on the White House staff. A friend of Kennerly, he was just as irreverent— he called me "Big Red"—and we hit it off extremely well. Like Kennerly, he had a way of sensing when I was feeling low. Invariably, he would try to cheer me up. One of his favorite gambits was to walk into the Oval Office with Susan, place a ring on her finger and look up into her eyes—she was several inches taller than he—adoringly. And then he would say, "Mr. President, sorry to interrupt you when you're so busy, but we just wanted you to know that we've decided to get married." I would smile and say something like "Get out of here, you two," but they would have succeeded in brightening my day.

My wardrobe, Penny kept saying, was too conservative. Just because I was President didn't mean that I had to dress like an undertaker. What I needed were more fashionable clothes. Betty agreed with him. So did Kennerly, and they arranged for some people from Britches, a Georgetown haberdasher, to outfit me in a more relaxed and modern style. Next Penny zeroed in on my speeches. They were too long-winded and full of political jargon, he said. There I was talking about the "private sector." What was that supposed to mean—a person's private parts? What I had to do was put more punch in my delivery and use more one-liners. About Reagan, for example, I might want to say, "Governor Reagan and I do have one thing in common. [Pause.] We both played football. [Pause again.] I played for Michigan. He played for Warner Brothers."

The more I listened to his advice, the more comfortable I became with it. And when I saw the text he had prepared for the annual dinner of the Gridiron Club, I couldn't help but grin. Former Georgia Governor Jimmy Carter was on hand to speak for the Democrats, and I was there for the GOP. "The primaries are really narrowing down the candidates," I began. "The Democrats are now down to twenty-eight—and the Republicans to one and a half." I smiled, then continued: "Governor Reagan did stop in at the White House not too long ago. He wanted to take a look around. He said he couldn't stay long. I said, 'You better believe it.' He went to the bathroom to wash up and I told him to be sure he used the guest towels.

"Let me congratulate Governor Jimmy Carter on his fine speech. There's the governor over there," I said, pointing. "It's easy to see where he sits. Now if we could only figure out where he stands."

Suddenly, a telephone rang on the podium. "Excuse me, I think this could be important," I said and picked up the receiver. I listened, then replied, "Hello, Hubert."

The seconds ticked by. "Uh-huh, uh-huh, uh-huh," I said, and kept nodding my head. I put the receiver down on the lectern, picked up my pipe and stuffed it with tobacco. Then I lit the pipe. That took thirty more seconds. I picked up the receiver again and pressed it close to my ear. "Uh-huh, uh-huh, uh-huh." Thirty more seconds elapsed. "Goodbye, Hubert," I said. "Goodbye, Hubert . . . Goodbye, Hubert."

Finally, after what must have seemed an eternity, I hung up the phone and told my audience: "That was Hubert. He just wanted to say hello."

Even though he had stayed out of the primaries, I was sure Hubert Humphrey would be the Democratic nominee for President. So many Democrats had entered the race that none of them could possibly pull ahead of the pack. The result would be a brokered convention in New York City in July, and the decision-makers in their smoke-filled rooms would select the man they had turned to before. Hubert and I didn't agree on domestic policy at all, but I liked and respected him as a man of ideals and integrity. He had had lots of experience—there was nothing phony about him—and I was looking forward to our race. One reason was that I knew he would wage a high-level campaign. Another was my feeling that we would be able to give the American people an opportunity to make a clear-cut choice. On several occasions during the spring of 1976, he would come to the White House with different groups of Senators. When we'd finished our talks, I would encourage him to linger on so he'd be the last to leave. I'd wrap my arm around his shoulder and say, "Hubert, you know you're my candidate. What can I do to help?" He'd respond with a quip or say something like, "Well, I just don't think I ought to do it. But then again, maybe I should." And he would leave the office with a smile. But even then, I sensed he knew something that might be holding him back, and I wondered if it had to do with his health.

At that moment, of course, Carter had more delegates than any other Democrat, but he struck me as a flash in the pan. It was hard for me to take him seriously. He had no experience in Washington, and I didn't think the Democrats—who had not won a Presidential election since 1964—were about to rest their hopes on an outsider with little more going for him than a winning smile. What was really curious to me was that Carter was trying, with evident success, to transform his being an outsider from a liability to a virtue of some sort. The morning after the Gridiron dinner, the Washington *Post* carried a photograph of him standing with his daughter, Amy, in front of the White House gate. He was pointing to the residence and saying, "I look forward to living there." His self-confidence, I thought, came very close to arrogance.

In retrospect, I think it's clear that Reagan's decision to abort his efforts in Wisconsin and New York was a serious political mistake. Teeter's polls showed a definite correlation between how well Reagan did in an area and whether or not he campaigned there. Despite his few appearances in Wisconsin, he still won 45 percent of the vote. Had he campaigned more extensively, he might have captured a number of delegates, but as it turned out, I emerged with a clean sweep. New York Republicans had voted the same day (April 6), and when the results were in from all the primaries, I found I had an overall lead of about three to one: 251 delegates were committed to me, while Reagan had only 84. An additional 161 were uncommitted, but 154 of them came from New York. Rockefeller headed that delegation, and I expected that at the proper time, he would swing most of those votes to me. Reagan hadn't even entered the Pennsylvania primary on April 27. I anticipated picking up most of the 103 delegates there, and that, I thought, would give me an almost insurmountable lead. Then I could apply the coup de grace to my challenger in Texas on May 1. All I would have to do would be to capture about 40 of the state's 96 delegates to deflect the challenge from the right. Reagan would stay in the race until the end, of course, but he wouldn't be viewed as a "serious" contender any more, and I would have time to try to unify the GOP.

Such was my rose-colored view until, of all days, April 1, when former Texas Governor John Connally came to Washington to be sworn in as a member of the President's Foreign Intelligence Advisory Board. He and his wife, Nellie, joined Betty and me for a leisurely dinner in the White House that night, and he came right out and said I had no chance of winning Texas at all. The Reagan forces, he went on, were extremely well organized and the Californian was enormously popular in the state. We might prevail in a few Congressional districts and pick up a limited number of delegates, but we should not expect too much. It would have been nice if Connally had endorsed me then and there, but I didn't ask him to do that and he didn't volunteer.

Despite Connally's pessimistic report, I still thought Texas was up for grabs. We had decided to allocate about $500,000 to the campaign, and I had agreed to make two swings through the state. During the first trip, on April 9 and 10, I traveled to San Antonio, Dallas, El Paso and Amarillo. Reporters had a field day when they spotted me trying to eat a tamale without first removing the inedible husk.

(No one had warned me about that, and I'd never eaten a tamale before.) But that was about the only miscue on the tour, and the reception I received was friendly everywhere. "I will never promise more than I can deliver," I said at almost every stop, "and I will deliver everything I promise." That always drew applause. Yet even before my return to Texas on April 27, three factors were converging to push the state out of my reach.

First, Texas was basically conservative and receptive to the Reagan line. It was almost impossible to defuse his emotional appeals. "We should tell Panama's tinhorn dictator just what he can do with his demands for sovereignty over the Canal Zone," he thundered over and over again. Then he had the gall to charge that my Administration was preparing to recognize Communist North Vietnam.

I refuted this ridiculous claim. "It is irresponsible and a disservice to the American people," I said, "to lead them to believe that there are pat answers and simple solutions to the complex issues of national security when there are none. Superficial arguments based on incomplete knowledge are fundamentally harmful rather than helpful." Somehow, my denials of his charges and my detailed explanations of the facts never quite caught up with his allegations.

For the past several months, the situation in southern Africa had been worsening. Political stability was crumbling everywhere and it was imperative to send Henry Kissinger to the continent to see if he could head off a race war. He was due to leave on a twelve-day, seven-nation tour of the area on April 23. My political advisers warned me that the timing of the trip was poor. Here we were about to contest Reagan in several key Southern states. Did we have to remind voters—as Henry's mission would do—that we favored majority rule where whites were in the minority? That was an easy decision to make. "I cannot judge whether the political impact will be good or bad," I told them. "But we must do this because it's the right thing to do."

So Henry took off from Washington about a week before the Texas vote. He was going to tell the nations of black Africa that they could not achieve what they wanted through war, and that only with U.S. help could they hope to gain majority rule in Rhodesia, independence for Namibia and the rejection of apartheid in South Africa. In

Lusaka, Zambia, on April 27, Henry declared that the U.S. would support "self-determination, majority rule, equal rights and human dignity for all peoples of southern Africa—in the name of moral principle, international law and world peace." When he added that our policy toward continued white minority rule in Rhodesia would be one of "unrelenting opposition," conservatives hit the ceiling.

Finally, my hopes of winning a sizable number of Texas delegates were dashed by the almost total collapse of George Wallace as a Democratic candidate. Carter had beaten him in Florida; he hadn't won a single primary and his campaign was floundering. This was important in Texas because it was a "crossover" state and Democrats could vote in the GOP primary. Many of those Democrats favored Wallace, but they didn't want to waste their votes. Reagan's people appealed to them skillfully. "I've been a Democrat all my life," a Reagan commercial began. "A conservative Democrat. As much as I hate to admit it, George Wallace can't be nominated. Ronald Reagan can. He's right on the issues. So for the first time in my life I'm gonna vote in the Republican primary. I'm gonna vote for Ronald Reagan."

On the evening of May 1, Betty and I attended the sixty-second annual dinner of the White House Correspondents Association at the Washington Hilton Hotel. We didn't stay too long afterward because I wanted to get back and watch the election returns on TV. No sooner had I flicked on the set than I realized I should have remained at the reception. Reagan was leading in all twenty-four Congressional districts, and was likely to win all 96 delegates. His wipe-out was complete. Cheney, Kennerly and Nessen were in the room with me and their mood was grim. "This is just one primary," I reminded them. "We are going to be back in there. We are going to win more primaries and we are going to win the nomination."

Three days later I received more bad news. Alabama, Georgia and Indiana succumbed to the Reagan charge. I had expected to lose the two Southern states, but the Indiana defeat came as a complete surprise. It shocked me as much as anything else that happened during the campaign. Indiana, after all, was next-door to Michigan. Governor Otis Bowen and the state Republican chairman, Thomas Milligan, had declared for me; so had other public officials, and Agriculture Secretary Butz was a native Hoosier. At one point a poll had me

leading Reagan by 24 percentage points, but he'd come from behind
to win by 17,000 votes and capture 45 of Indiana's 54 delegates. Suddenly, the perception spread that the President Ford Committee was
a sinking ship. Unfortunately, Rog Morton picked up on that analogy. Asked on the night of my triple defeat if he was going to recommend a new strategy, he replied, "I'm not going to rearrange the furniture on the deck of the *Titanic*." Next morning when he appeared
for a strategy meeting in the Oval Office, I looked him straight in the
eye. "Rog," I said, "we had a real bad night and your comment
didn't help one damn bit."

"Mr. President," he replied, somewhat sheepishly, "I know it.
Please don't make me feel any worse than I do."

What concerned me even more than gaffes like Rog's was the way
my defeats would be interpreted overseas. People at home understood how our political system worked. But in the minds of world
leaders, the specter of an incumbent President failing to beat back a
challenge from within his own party had to raise all sorts of questions. Were the Republicans going to nominate me, and if so, would I
adhere to the same foreign policy? If that policy changed, how would
it affect them? Did Reagan really believe that his experience as a negotiator for the Screen Actors Guild would help him in dealing with
world affairs? Wasn't all this Republican squabbling just paving the
way for a Democratic victory in November, and what would be the
implications of that?

There was nothing I could do except try to project the basic confidence I felt. Deep within me I was absolutely sure that when the last
votes were counted, I was going to win. The next two primaries were
in West Virginia and Nebraska on May 11. Because neither state permitted crossover votes, I thought the results would be more indicative
of true Republican sentiment. According to the most recent Gallup
poll, which had been conducted between April 9 and May 3, I was
still the favorite of Republicans nationally by a margin of 60 to 35.
How I wished that opinion would be reflected in the remaining primary results.

Personal popularity, however, wasn't always the key to victory.
Sometimes the situation was far more complex. Consider West Virginia. The state had 28 delegates, and I needed every one of them.

The leader of the delegation was Governor Arch Moore, Jr., a long-time personal friend. We had served together in the House; he had helped me when I became Minority Leader, and I had campaigned for him in West Virginia. Theoretically, he should have been behind me all the way. But it wasn't as simple as that. The United States Attorney for the Southern District of West Virginia was a tough Democratic prosecutor named John A. Field III. He had been conducting an investigation of political corruption in the state, and had persuaded a federal grand jury to indict the governor on extortion charges. Moore had proclaimed his innocence all along; indeed, a federal court jury later acquitted him. But even before the verdict was in—and acting upon the recommendation of Attorney General Levi—I had announced my intention to nominate Field for another four-year term, and Moore was mighty unhappy about this departmental decision.

On the afternoon of May 9, after his own acquittal and just two days before his state's primary, Moore telephoned me at the White House and we talked for nearly an hour. He insisted that he had been the victim of a U.S. Attorney who had been waging a vendetta against him. Now, through my Attorney General, I was rewarding that U.S. Attorney by reappointing him. "What's a Republican Administration trying to do to me?" he asked.

"When Attorney General Levi accepted the job," I replied, "he got an assurance from me that I would not get involved in criminal matters. Any mention of this matter by me to Levi would be way out of line. You can't ask me—and I know you *haven't* asked me—to call the Attorney General and have him recommend someone else."

Arch completely agreed with that. And he also admitted that if Levi had not pushed for Field's reappointment after the grand jury had handed down its indictment, that would have looked bad too. The press would have charged that the Administration was engaged in a cover-up. Arch never threatened me. He never said that if the Administration reappointed Field, he'd have to withhold the delegates he controlled. But he sure wanted to get some things off his chest.

"Arch, you've got to look at the bigger picture," I said. "Do you want Reagan to win the nomination?"

"Absolutely not. You're my friend and I want to help you."

"But, Arch, we could lose the nomination if West Virginia doesn't help, doesn't support us."

"I know that," he answered.

He had made his point and I had made mine. Neither of us was about to make a "deal," so there was nothing more to say. On May 11, when West Virginia Republicans cast their ballots, I won 57 percent of the vote. What mattered most, of course, was the number of delegates, and all but a handful of them were uncommitted. Moore told our people that he could probably deliver about 20 of the 28, but he didn't want to be any more specific than that.

This was disappointing, because we needed those delegates desperately. For on the same day of the West Virginia vote, Nebraska Republicans chose Reagan by a margin of 55 percent to 45 percent. That really hurt, because Nebraska was the state of my birth. In terms of the number of delegates he won—18 of 25—my loss wasn't that significant. But what counted now was "momentum," that magical word; and Reagan, who had won five of our last six tests, seemed to have all of it. He had 468 committed delegates to my 318, as well as a good share of the 354 who said they were uncommitted. At the halfway point in the process, Republicans had selected 1,140 delegates, and 1,119 remained to be chosen. If Reagan won 662—or slightly more than half of them—he had the nomination. Confidence exuded from him and his entourage, and he was predicting a first-ballot win.

The press found many explanations for this reversal—the Nixon pardon, the furor over the Panama Canal, the presence of Henry Kissinger on my team, the anti-Washington mood of the country as a whole—and I suppose that all of them had some validity. Yet the analysis that caught my attention came, as it so often did, from David Broder of the Washington *Post*. "How," he asked, "did a palpably honest President, who has brought his party back from its worst disgrace, find himself trailing in the race for nomination?" Then Broder answered his own question: "It is the inability of Mr. Ford to define the goals, the vision and the purposes of his Presidency in a way that gives coherence to his administration and to his campaign."

Broder was close to the mark, but I wasn't sure that even he understood how difficult a task that was. When I became President, I didn't initiate sweeping new programs because it was a time to heal, and new programs, which had to mean more government, would have been divisive at that point. I could have talked about the goals I hoped to achieve between 1977 and 1981, but I wanted to save that for when our country celebrated the Bicentennial. July 4 was less than two months away. I told Hartmann to drop everything and get to work on the series of speeches I'd make on the Bicentennial day. They would be the vehicle through which I would express my vision of the years ahead.

Meanwhile, I had to confront challenges of a more immediate sort. The Maryland and Michigan primaries fell on May 18. Reagan hadn't campaigned in Maryland, so I expected to fare well there. But Michigan, my home state, was a real concern because it permitted crossovers. In 1972, Wallace had won the Democratic primary there with 51 percent of the vote. More than 800,000 Michiganders had cast their ballots for him. Now that he was no longer a viable candidate, where would those people go? If enough of them followed Reagan, I would be dealt a humiliating—probably crippling—blow. I was determined not to let that happen. The fact that I was from Michigan was not enough. I decided to refine my strategy. Thus far in the campaign, Reagan had made ample and very successful appeals for Democratic crossover votes while I had concentrated on Republicans. Now it was my turn to start targeting Democrats and independents.

"I want every person who is registered in this state who can feel confidence in what we have done to vote for me, whether they call themselves Republicans, Independents or Democrats," I said on arrival at Detroit-Wayne County Metropolitan Airport on the morning of May 12. And that was the refrain I echoed throughout the rest of that busy day. "I want to answer as many of your questions as I possibly can," I told my listeners, "but first let me answer a question I have often asked myself: 'Jerry Ford, why are you asking your fellow Americans and fellow Michiganders to let you go on being President for the next four years?'" I paused, then put conviction in my reply: "Because I have done a good job and I am proud of it. Because I have turned a lot of bad things around and we are going in the right direction. Because I want a mandate from Michigan and the American people to finish that job."

In New Hampshire and Florida, I had relied on motorcades to whisk me from place to place. But the southern part of Michigan seemed suited for a whistlestop train tour. Scores of reporters and TV technicians were aboard as the *Presidential Express* pulled out of Flint on the rainy morning of May 15; a jazz band was thumping out old-time melodies, but I wasn't in a very festive mood. Michigan had 84 delegates and I had to win the vast majority of them. My prestige and credibility were on the line, and what I was fighting for was nothing less than survival as a candidate.

"What are the results of twenty-one months of Jerry Ford as President of the United States?" I asked the depot crowd at Durand, then proceeded to tell them: "We have restored trust in the White House. We have been open. We have been candid. We have been forthright. We have talked straight to the American people. I think that deserves [your] support." At Lansing, the next stop, I reminded the crowd that in the month of April alone, 710,000 more jobs had opened up. And at Battle Creek I said: "When I took office on August 9, 1974, we had lots of things to do. We had some very difficult and formidable obstacles ahead of us."

Suddenly, someone on the station platform yelled, "You blew it."

"We blew it in the right direction, young man," I replied, angrily, "and those of you who don't agree—if you would go out and look for a job, you would get one." The crowd's loud applause was music to my ears.

So was the news I received the evening of May 18. Betty and I were having dinner at the French embassy with visiting French President Giscard d'Estaing and his wife, when aides passed me notes with the latest election returns. I had won all of Maryland's 43 delegates and was on my way to a landslide win in Michigan. At the White House later that night, I invited Cheney, Nessen, Terry O'Donnell and Bob Barrett up to the residence to watch TV. I had taken 85 percent of the vote in my old Congressional district and nearly 66 percent statewide. I had captured 55 delegates to my opponent's 29. Reagan appeared on TV to say that he was satisfied with the result. "I hope we can keep him that pleased in the other primaries," I said.

The Michigan victory was marvelous, but the tide of battle had not turned. Reagan still was ahead of me in delegates, 528 to 479; six more primaries were scheduled to be held the next Tuesday, May 25, and I was an underdog in five of them. I thought I might do well in Oregon, a moderate to liberal state, but I had no illusions about Arkansas, Nevada, Idaho, Kentucky or Tennessee. Reagan was just too strong. The psychological impact of expected defeat can be just as damaging as defeat itself. On May 20, hoping to cushion that impact, New York State GOP Chairman Richard Rosenbaum disclosed that he was throwing the support of most of the delegation's 154 members to me. Two days later, Pennsylvania delegates decided to give me 88 of their 103 votes. And on the same day I won Vermont's 18 delegates, all of whom had been formally uncommitted before. Despite these welcome boosts, my prospects for success on May 25 were not encouraging. And the fact that Senator Howard Baker, the chairman of my campaign in Tennessee, had actually invited Reagan to spend the night at his Huntsville home didn't make me any happier.

But then Reagan committed another of his gaffes. During the 1964 Presidential campaign, when Barry Goldwater suggested that the Tennessee Valley Authority could be sold to private industry, the comment had cost him countless thousands of votes. A Knoxville interviewer asked Reagan what he thought about selling TVA, and Reagan replied that, while he did not know all of the facts and details, "it would be something to look at and first of all to make sure that the citizens were the beneficiaries of anything of that kind."

"It would be something to look at"—my campaign aides seized upon that with glee. When Reagan went on the defensive and said that he had no plans to sell the TVA, my supporters pointed to the comments he'd originally made. The TVA "issue" turned things around for me in Tennessee, which I won by fewer than 2,200 votes. It probably helped me as well in Kentucky, where I won an upset victory. In Arkansas, Idaho and Nevada I lost, not unexpectedly, and the only surprise was that I had emerged from the six-state scuffle with what looked like a draw. When you're supposed to be beaten in five races out of six and you lose only three, the press interprets that as a victory.

Rhode Island, South Dakota and Montana held their primaries on June 1; 59 delegates were at stake, and although I wanted to campaign personally in those states, I simply didn't have the time. For one week later came the final, crucial contests in New Jersey, Ohio and California; the first-place winner could walk away with as many as 331 votes. At that point I had 805 delegates; I needed 1,130 to win. Reagan hadn't entered New Jersey, for him another mistake. Nor had he filed a full slate of delegates in Ohio, which turned out to be a serious error. He was concentrating on California, for whoever won the popular vote captured *all* 167 delegates. Although I had spent a busy two and a half days there toward the end of May, I didn't expect to win any more than 45 percent of the vote. Our strategy was simply to keep Reagan occupied in California and out of other states.

Unwittingly, Reagan himself helped make sure that it worked. Appearing on June 2 before the Sacramento Press Club, he said in response to a hypothetical question that he would consider sending U.S. troops to embattled Rhodesia to prevent a potential blood bath there. When I pounced on that and called his suggestion "irresponsible," he backtracked and tried to "explain" what he had meant to say. That made his predicament even worse. Politics is "hardball" sometimes, and this was one of those times. The people who were producing our TV commercials focused on his flub and came up with an ad that said: "Last Wednesday, Ronald Reagan said he would send American troops to Rhodesia. On Thursday he clarified that. He said they could be observers, or advisers. What does he think happened in Vietnam? When you vote Tuesday, remember: Governor Ronald Reagan couldn't start a war. President Ronald Reagan could."

That commercial infuriated Reagan and his people. But it kept Reagan on his home turf until the weekend before the primary, when he flew east to Ohio. And no sooner had he landed there than reporters questioned him further about his Rhodesia stand. That issue became an albatross around his neck, one that just wouldn't go away. If he had been able to defuse it and had made a major effort in Ohio, he could have upset my applecart. As the election results would show, he had a surprising amount of popular support. But I was determined to win in Ohio, and I returned to the state on June 6. Next morning, I set off on a grueling 288-mile motorcade from Cincinnati to Toledo. "There is no question in my mind whatsoever that I can be elected," I said at breakfast that day, "and I have grave reservations, very serious doubts, that any other Republican candidate can be elected." Three hours later, at Middletown, I came back to that theme: "We don't want a repetition of the debacle that took place in 1964. We want a ticket from the courthouse to the White House that can win for the kind of America that is good for all of us. I ask for your support. I have done a good job, and I want your help."

I got it. Although Ohio Republicans gave 45 percent of their vote to my challenger, I walked away with 88 of the 97 delegates. Reagan, to be sure, won California's 167 in the winner-take-all primary (with 64 percent of the vote), but I countered him with a clean sweep of New Jersey. At that point I had 992 delegates to Reagan's 886. Thirty states had held primaries; we had broken even in the twenty-four where we had battled head to head, and I had won the lion's share of delegates in states where he hadn't bothered to contest me. It was still too close to call.

Now our attention turned to phase two of the 1976 campaign, the eleven states that selected delegates in conventions. Together, they accounted for 267 delegates. We had done a terrible job organizing in those states because we hadn't thought it necessary. By the time we recognized this dire need, we had to play catch-up ball. Reagan was slightly ahead of me, and the problem was how to win a sufficient number of those delegates without impairing the unity of the GOP. My hardball tactics could so anger conservatives that they would sit on their hands during the fall campaign and the prize of the nomination wouldn't be worth a damn. So I resigned myself to one inescapable fact: over the next two months—indeed, up until the final moments of the national convention itself—I would have to hold hands with, and consider doing favors for, every one of those delegates. As Elizabeth Drew of *The New Yorker* magazine observed on June 8: "Now the President of the United States will fight it out, delegate by delegate, in the remaining state conventions and among the uncommitted delegations. This may be a nice time for an uncommitted delegate, but it's not such a nice time for the President of the United States."

The first battleground was Missouri. District conventions had already selected 30 of the state's 49 delegates. I had won 15; Reagan had captured 12, and 3 still were uncommitted. The final 19 at-large delegates would be chosen in Springfield on June 12. Missouri's fine young governor, Christopher ("Kit") Bond, insisted that my appearance could stem the Reagan tide. So I decided to go. The Reagan forces had been organizing for months. Their foot soldiers outhustled our generals, and even though I telephoned 10 of the delegates personally to plead for their support, the die had already been cast and Reagan trounced me by a margin of 18 to 1.

And that was just the beginning. Reagan caught us with our pants down in other convention states as well. Washington was a perfect example. It was a moderate state, and I expected to win a majority of its 38 delegates. Yet Reagan wound up with 31. The same thing happened in New Mexico. Senator Pete Domenici and Congressman Manuel Lujan, Jr., were strong boosters of mine, but Reagan's people went in there at the precinct level, built support from the bottom up and just wiped us out. Even in states I won, misfortunes plagued our campaign. In Iowa, for example, there were 36 delegates to be selected June 19, and I was looking forward to visiting Des Moines and rallying our troops in advance of the balloting. On June 16, however, terrorists in Lebanon assassinated U.S. Ambassador Francis E. Meloy, Jr., Counselor for Economic Affairs Robert O. Waring, and their Lebanese chauffeur. Two days later, I decided to evacuate U.S. citizens from that tormented land, and on June 19, Henry Kissinger and I flew to Andrews Air Force Base to meet the plane bearing the bodies of our slain officials. The continuing crisis in Lebanon—I stayed up until 3 A.M. one morning and until 5:30 A.M. the next to monitor the evacuation of all Americans—meant, of course, that I had to cancel my plans to fly to Iowa. Betty took my place and did a tremendous job; I felt sure that people there would understand, but not everyone did. "Ford Balks at Reagan Confrontation," one newspaper headline charged.

Betty was not the only family member to campaign for me. Mike, Steve and Susan assisted in every way they could. And our son Jack was particularly effective. On July 10, Colorado Republicans met in Fort Collins to decide which candidate their 16 at-large convention delegates would support. I had a long-standing commitment to greet members of the U.S. Olympic Team in Plattsburgh, New York, and to have dinner that Saturday night with Great Britain's visiting Queen Elizabeth II and her husband, Prince Philip; I didn't have time to fly to Colorado so Jack filled in for me. Reagan had already won 11 of the 15 delegates chosen at district meetings throughout the state. He was expected to sweep the at-large delegates, too. So by appearing at Fort Collins, Jack was walking into a lion's den. It didn't faze him one bit. He was squaring off against the most skillful orator in the party's ranks, but he didn't hesitate. "My father was able to ramrod through Congress the largest defense budget in peacetime history," he told the more than 2,000 conventioneers. Then Jack asked for "a vote of confidence" for the man who was healing the nation's wounds. When I heard how well he had done, I was very proud of him.

In the middle of these contests in the convention states came an opportunity to pause and reflect upon the qualities that had made America great. It was July 4, our Bicentennial, a very significant day. When I was a boy in Michigan, the Fourth had always been a special treat for me. For weeks before, my brothers and I would save our nickels and dimes to buy fireworks, and at the last minute my stepfather would supply a few dollars for skyrockets. We had the big flag to hang out over the front porch and the ice cream freezer to turn. There were parades, bands, patriotic speeches, picnics, softball games and the endless wait until it was dark enough for the Roman candles to light up the sky. And when, finally, we went to bed that night, we were happy because we knew the celebration would repeat itself the next year.

Never in my wildest dreams had I imagined that I would be President of the United States on its 200th birthday, and Jack Marsh, a formidable historian, had been pressing me for the past twenty-three months to honor the occasion in a dignified and appropriate way. "You have to point toward July 4," he kept reminding me. "It's going to be a momentous event." The nation's Centennial celebration in

1876, Marsh explained, had been little noticed by President Ulysses S. Grant. Indeed, returning to the capital after attending a ceremony at Concord Bridge in Massachusetts, Grant had penned a note to the proprietor of the Concord Inn: "You've got the best whiskey in town." Grant's words must have made the innkeeper proud of his stock. I hoped that my remarks that historic day—one hundred years later—would make all Americans proud of their heritage.

> Two hundred years ago we, the people of the United States of America, began a great adventure which stirred the imagination and quickened the hopes of men and women throughout the world. The date was July 4, 1776; the occasion, the signing of our Declaration of Independence. No other nation in history has ever dedicated itself more specifically nor devoted itself more completely to the proposition that all men are created equal, that they are endowed by their Creator with such unalienable rights of life, liberty and the pursuit of happiness.
>
> Two centuries later, as we celebrate our Bicentennial year of independence, the great American adventure continues. The hallmark of that adventure has always been an eagerness to explore the unknown, whether it lay across an ocean or a continent, across the vastness of space or the frontiers of human knowledge. Because we have always been ready to try new and untested enterprises in government, in commerce, in the arts and sciences and in human relations, we have made unprecedented progress in all of these fields. . . .
>
> In the space of two centuries, we have not been able to right every wrong, to correct every injustice, to reach every worthy goal. But for two hundred years we have tried and we will continue to strive to make the lives of individual men and women in this country and on this earth better lives—more hopeful and happy, more prosperous and peaceful, more fulfilling and more free. This is our common dedication and it will be our common glory as we enter the third century of the American adventure.

What a busy weekend that was! Over a five-day period, I participated in the dedication of the Smithsonian Institution's new Air and Space Museum. I spoke at the National Archives, where the Declaration of Independence, the Constitution and the Bill of Rights were on public display. I flew to Valley Forge, where George Washington and his ragged Continental Army had encamped, exhausted, outnumbered and short of everything but faith. I spoke at Independence Hall in Philadelphia, where the fifty-six framers of the Declaration of Independence had signed their names to that glorious document. Then I helicoptered to New York Harbor to watch the tall ships from thirty nations pass by majestically in Operation Sail.

As *Air Force One* returned to the capital that afternoon, aides gave me reports that millions of Americans were praying in their churches and synagogues, marching in their city squares and dancing in their streets. Rarely in the history of the world had so many people turned out so spontaneously to express the love they felt for their country. Not a single incident marred our festival. The nation's wounds had healed. We had regained our pride and rediscovered our faith and, in doing so, we had laid the foundation for a future that had to be filled with hope.

My own future, politically, at least, was up in the air. In mid July, the Democrats nominated Jimmy Carter for President and Walter Mondale as his running mate. But we Republicans still didn't know who our candidates would be. By July 18, when the last of the convention states had selected their delegates, I had a total of 1,102; Reagan had 1,063. I was 28 short of the number needed to win and he trailed me by only 39. And 94 delegates were still uncommitted.

I knew that I'd have to spend the next several weeks courting those delegates individually and in groups. There would be no quid pro quo—I circulated a memo to my strategists stressing that "no official actions on any matter . . . should be directly or indirectly offered, promised or provided" in return for a delegate's pledge of support— yet at the same time I saw nothing wrong with inviting some of the uncommitteds to the White House, answering their questions and posing for photographs.

The uncommitteds weren't the only delegates about whom we had to be concerned. My advisers warned that some of my support was "soft," that anywhere between 50 and 100 delegates already pledged to me might waver and capitulate to pressure from the other side. Making sure that these potential jumpers remained on the team was the responsibility of James A. Baker III, a Houston attorney who was serving as deputy chairman of the PFC. Baker had had little or no political experience—originally, he'd come to Washington to be Rog

Morton's deputy at the Department of Commerce—but he possessed a superb mind; he was an excellent organizer who got along with everybody and worked around the clock.

As the convention drew near, Reagan's efforts to attract new delegates seemed to be bogging down. When you're behind in the fourth quarter of a football game and you have the ball with time running out on the clock, there's only one thing you can do: Throw the bomb. We knew Reagan would pull some last-minute ploy. What we didn't know was just how desperate that ploy would be.

Wearing big smiles, Marsh and Cheney came into the Oval Office shortly after noon on July 26. "We just got the best news we've had in months," Cheney said, and he proceeded to fill me in. Reagan had just announced that he planned to select Pennsylvania Senator Richard Schweiker, a liberal Republican, as his running mate.

"Oh, come on," I said. "You guys are pulling my leg." Schweiker had told me several months earlier that he supported me, and he had given no hint that he was about to change his mind. Reagan and Schweiker were poles apart on issue after issue, from the Humphrey-Hawkins full employment bill to an attempt to delay production of the B-1 bomber. Reagan couldn't make a move like that because the True Believers would feel they'd been betrayed.

But he *had* done it, and the strategy seemed clear. Schweiker was a close friend of Drew Lewis, my top man in Pennsylvania and leader of its delegation. Presumably, Reagan thought that Schweiker could persuade anywhere between 20 and 50 delegates from Pennsylvania and its surrounding states to break their commitments to me and join the other camp. Additionally, by announcing his VP selection now, Reagan could pressure me to follow suit. If I refused, he could complain that I was not "leveling" with the convention delegates. On the other hand, if I went ahead and named my candidate, I was bound to lose support. No matter whom I chose, I couldn't please everyone. Perhaps the move wasn't so dumb after all.

Political reaction was swift—and reassuring. Drew Lewis called almost immediately from Pennsylvania. He and the delegation would hold firm for me, he said. The Schweiker ploy was a gamble that was sure to fail. Less than an hour later, John Connally telephoned from Houston. Reagan's announcement, he said, had forced him to conclude that I was "unmistakably the better choice, not only for the party but for the country." He would be in Washington the next afternoon, and if I would like him to endorse me publicly, he would be happy to oblige. I told him I would be very grateful for that.

If Reagan seriously thought that Schweiker could produce any converts for him, he had to be disappointed by the results. Six Pennsylvania delegates—previously uncommitted—declared immediately for me. And the ripples spread. Congressman John Ashbrook, an Ohio conservative who had made an abortive run for President himself in 1972, labeled the Schweiker connection "the dumbest thing I ever heard of." And Illinois Congressman Henry Hyde, another staunch conservative, said it was like "a farmer selling his last cow to buy a milking machine."

Nowhere did the Schweiker selection have a greater impact than in Mississippi, and at the time there was no other state more important to us. Initially, we didn't think we had much of a chance to win the state's 30 votes, which would be cast as a block under their traditional unit rule. Mississippi was very conservative, and Reagan was extremely popular there. After our losses in North Carolina, Georgia and Alabama, we had despaired of winning support anywhere in the Deep South. The state's "Mr. Republican" was a rangy, prematurely white-haired businessman named Clarke Reed. A fast-talking conservative, Reed had built the party up from scratch, but he had one flaw: he was a man who hated to make decisions likely to disappoint friends. And that desire to please everyone would soon give him some terrible problems.

In the spring of 1976, when Mississippi Republicans set out to select the 60 members of their delegation, each of whom would be able to cast half a vote, Reed decided to reward the young moderates who had worked so hard the year before in a tight but losing bid to elect Gil Carmichael as governor. He would let them attend the Kansas City convention as alternates (but with the same vote in determining the delegation's choice).

Then Reed made another move which, in retrospect, was entirely in character. The nomination, he seemed convinced, would never go down to the wire in Kansas City. Either Reagan or I would knock the other out long before that. In his heart Reed favored the former California governor. In his head, he probably favored me. Above all, he wanted to be on the winning team. And until he knew the winner, he wasn't going to make a commitment. After all, he rationalized, why do something that might make Reagan mad at him? And conversely, why antagonize me? If he had to, he would wait until the battle was over in the primary and the convention states. Then he would throw his support to the one candidate who had survived.

Things didn't work out the way Reed expected. By the last week of July, neither campaign had collapsed, and it appeared that Reed would finally have to make a choice. Unbeknownst to him, the delegation wasn't as pro-Reagan as he assumed. For the past several months, former Nixon aide Harry S. Dent, a South Carolinian who was coordinating my campaign in the South, had been subjecting the alternates to intensive lobbying. He reported back to Cheney that there were some "sleepers" in the Mississippi delegation and that, if approached properly, they would vote for me.

When Reed found out about this, he convened a caucus of the delegates and tried to stop the slippage in the Reagan ranks. His effort didn't succeed. Cheney flew to Jackson and appeared at the caucus himself. He talked to some of the alternates and came away convinced that we could win the state. Gil Carmichael agreed. It would be nip and tuck, but we had a better than even chance. Mississippi on my side? Frankly, I found that incredible.

What eventually tipped the scales was the Schweiker ploy. One of the reasons Reed had left the Democratic Party to become a Republican was that Democrats were always trying to balance their tickets with ideologically opposite candidates. Such as Kennedy and LBJ. Reagan was simon pure ideologically. Now this, a stunning reversal of everything Reed had always believed about the man. Cheney and Dent urged me to telephone Reed to ask him for an endorsement, and I did. Reed wanted forty-eight hours in which to make his choice, but I told him in effect that the train was pulling out from the station and if he wanted to go anywhere at all he had better climb aboard. Finally, he agreed. In a press conference, he said the Schweiker selection had been "wrong and dumb," an "act of desperation."

Two days later, I flew to Jackson and spoke to the Mississippi delegates. At that moment I had 29 sure votes in the 60-member delegation, and there were 10 more who seemed to be leaning my way. Remembering the humiliation I had suffered in Missouri several weeks before, I decided not to press my luck. I didn't ask the delegates to commit themselves. If they chose to remain uncommitted, that was fine with me. Reed had thrown me his support. Yet in the two weeks before the convention, I knew, he would equivocate and try to wiggle off the hook. He would seek some way to fend off the pressures he would feel from both sides—and he would discover that it was impossible. Then he and his delegation would go for me. It was as simple as that.

The weather was glorious the afternoon of August 15 as we arrived in Kansas City. Reagan might have outmaneuvered and outhustled us in a number of states, but here the tables were about to be turned. Bill Timmons, my convention manager, and Bob Griffin, my floor manager, had done a super job putting together a first-class organization. By Jim Baker's latest count, I had 1,135 votes, five more than I needed to win. The Reagan advisers, of course, disputed that total, insisting their man had enough support to go over the top. The tension was unbelievable.

The Reagan strategy was clear. His people wanted to force me to disclose my running mate before the balloting for President on Wednesday night. I resisted, and John Sears, Reagan's clever and tenacious manager, was under no illusion that I might change my mind. So he had drafted a proposal, called 16C, requiring that contenders for the party's Presidential nomination name their running mates in advance of the balloting, then submitted it to the rules committee of the Republican National Committee. Not surprisingly, it was voted down. Next he took 16C to the convention's rules committee, a different group with a number of Reagan backers. Once again he lost, by a tally of 59 to 44, but the vote was close enough to permit the issue to be considered again on the convention floor, and it was this pending vote that concerned me the most. We tried not to let our apprehension show. My supporters called 16C the "misery loves company" amendment. If Reagan hadn't blundered by naming Schweiker in advance of the party convention, they said, the Californian wouldn't be trying to make me follow suit. But behind these good-natured jibes was a gnawing fear that we just might lose on 16C—and perhaps with it lose the nomination.

Reagan was not going to rest his hopes of defeating me on a procedural issue. I was sure of that. He would give rule 16C a try, but what he really needed was an emotional issue to turn the convention around. Thus it came as no surprise when, on Monday, he suggested incorporating a "Morality in Foreign Policy" plank into the Republican platform. Among other things, it commended Aleksandr Solzhenitsyn for his "human courage and morality," characterized the Helsinki Agreement as "taking from those who do not have freedom the hope of one day getting it" and, finally, committed the Republicans to a foreign policy "in which secret agreements, hidden from our people, will have no part."

When I read the plank, I was furious. It added up to nothing less than a slick denunciation of Administration foreign policy. Kissinger wanted me to take on the Reaganites. They were trying to humiliate us publicly, he said, and we shouldn't let them get away with it. Scowcroft agreed with him; so did Rockefeller, and for a while I thought we'd have to fight. Cheney, Spencer and Nessen, however, argued the other way. The Reaganites *wanted* us to do battle on the foreign policy plank, they said. If we fell into their trap, accepted their challenge and then lost the vote, that could mean the nomination. What we wanted, *the only thing we wanted*, they continued, was a direct contest between Reagan and me, free of emotional issues. They were right, I concluded. The vote on the platform would follow the roll call on 16C Tuesday evening. I asked Nessen to tell reporters that I hadn't made a final decision on what I was going to do. Then, just after ten o'clock Monday night, I met with Rockefeller. When I indicated that I would go along with the plank, Nelson was extremely disappointed. But he recognized the political realities, and like the good soldier he was, he said he would support whatever I decided to do.

On Tuesday afternoon, the Mississippi delegates caucused at their hotel to consider 16C. After heavy lobbying by both sides, the vote was 31 to 28 against 16C, with one abstention. (Reed waited until he was sure my position would prevail and then cast his vote—for the

Reagan stand.) I was jubilant. Several hours later, however, that jubilation almost turned to grief. The late edition of the Birmingham *News,* describing a meeting that Rog Morton had had with reporters that morning, appeared on the convention floor with the page one headline: "Ford Would Write Off Cotton South?" Because I knew the Reagan people would seize upon this and circulate it among the Mississippi delegates as "proof" of our disinterest, I made sure that Reed and his colleagues understood the story was not accurate; it didn't reflect our strategy for the fall campaign. The Mississippi delegates held; I won all 30 of their votes on the convention floor, and 16C went down to defeat, 1,180 to 1,069. Later that evening, the convention endorsed the Reagan foreign policy plank overwhelmingly. It was an embarrassing moment for me, but it didn't matter much because, as the struggle over 16C had shown, I was going to win the nomination on the first ballot.

Around midnight Wednesday, the roll call began. Alabama: all 37 delegates for Reagan. Alaska: I won 17 to my challenger's 2. Arizona: he routed me there. Arkansas: he won again, and when California gave him all 167 votes, the convention hall exploded with applause. But slowly I recaptured the lead: Massachusetts, Michigan, New Jersey and New York. West Virginia lifted me over the top with 20 of its 28 votes, and the final tally was 1,187 to 1,070. I had been watching the proceedings on TV in the office adjacent to my hotel suite. When it was all over, my advisers congratulated me and shook my hand. I said something inane about how "tough" the battle had been and how "great" it felt to win. Then, at one-thirteen next morning, I headed for Reagan's hotel.

About a month before the convention, my aides had met with Reagan's representatives to discuss the need for party unity. And they had reached an agreement. At the end of the Presidential balloting, the winner would go to the loser's hotel suite and congratulate his opponent for waging a fine campaign. Together, they would appear at a press conference and urge all Republicans to put aside their differences and rally behind the ticket. That was the only way we could leave Kansas City with a hope of victory in November. When it appeared that I was going to win, Sears contacted Cheney and refined the scenario. He insisted on two conditions. First, I had to see Reagan alone; there could be no aides from either camp in the room. Second, under no circumstances should I offer him the VP spot. Reagan had said all along that he wasn't interested in the job. He had meant what he said. If I tried to talk him out of it, he would have to turn me down, and that would be embarrassing; it would appear that he was refusing to help the GOP. When Cheney relayed those conditions to me, I agreed to go along. I would need Reagan's assistance in the fall campaign. It would be stupid to anger him or his followers at this moment.

Much later, I was told that just before my arrival at the Californian's hotel, one of his closest advisers, businessman Justin Dart, had urged him to say yes if I asked him to be my running mate. Regardless of anything he'd said before, Dart had insisted, it was his patriotic duty to accept the number two post. Finally, according to Dart, Reagan had agreed. But at the time, no one mentioned this new development to me. Had I been aware of the Dart-Reagan conversation, would I have chosen him? I can't say for sure. I thought his challenge had been divisive, and that it would probably hurt the party in the fall campaign; additionally, I resented some of the things that he'd been saying about me and about my Administration's policies— but I certainly would have considered him.

A Reagan aide met me in the lobby of the Alameda Plaza Hotel and escorted me up to the tenth floor. "Governor, it was a great fight," I said, shaking his hand as reporters looked on. "I just wish I had some of your talents and your tremendous organization." Then we stepped into his suite and talked privately. Choosing my words carefully, I asked if there was anyone he wanted to recommend as my running mate. I tossed six names on the table—Bill Simon, John Connally, Bob Dole, Howard Baker, Elliot Richardson and Bill Ruckelshaus—and waited for his response. Dole, he replied, would be an excellent choice.

I changed the subject and stressed how much I needed his help in the fall campaign. "We're way behind," I said. "All the polls show it. The Democrats have a head start, and there has to be a maximum effort by all Republicans if we're going to win." Reagan would cooperate, he said, and he hoped his followers would do the same. He would travel around the country helping Republican candidates and speaking up for the platform, and he would try to coordinate his schedule with mine. After nearly an hour, we went downstairs and talked to the press. We smiled, congratulated each other once more and tried to project the appearance of unity. I don't know how successful we were, because the meeting in his suite had been awkward for both of us. The tension of our long contest permeated that room.

By the time I returned to my hotel, it was after 2 A.M. I was tired and wanted to go to bed. But first we had to make a decision on my running mate. Actually, we'd started considering prospective candidates several weeks before, when I asked attorney Ed Schmults, Phil Buchen's deputy, to interview half a dozen contenders and ask questions about their health and finances. In addition to the names I gave Reagan, others were on my list. Among them: Ambassador to Great Britain Anne Armstrong, Iowa Governor Robert Ray and Washington Governor Daniel Evans. The basic criteria were the same as they had been two years earlier, when Rockefeller had been my choice. The nominee had to be fully qualified to be President. He or she had to share my political philosophy, and finally, the person had to be someone with whom I felt comfortable. And in the interest of party harmony, the person we chose had to be acceptable to Reagan and his delegates.

The meeting to decide on the nominee didn't begin until 3:15 A.M. Michigan Senator Bob Griffin, my convention floor leader, was present, as were Texas Senator John Tower, Rockefeller, Laird, Marsh, Hartmann, Harlow, Cheney, Spencer and Teeter. Trying to keep my own opinions to myself, I asked for advice and listened carefully as they winnowed down the list. (At times during the evening I wished George Bush had been available.) Evans and Ray were early casualties. Although both had done excellent jobs of running their states, neither had a national name. Nor did they project experience in international affairs.

Given the conservative mood of that convention, Richardson wasn't a realistic nominee. The Reaganites would have bolted at the mere mention of his name. And Simon was too conservative. He was a tough campaigner, a Catholic from New Jersey who was both smart and principled, and he had been a fine Secretary of the Treasury. But his image of fiscal extremism would have been a liability. Many of my advisers were high on Connally, including Rockefeller, who several weeks before had confronted him over lunch with a series of direct questions about his personal and political affairs—and come away a believer. Yet Connally's unquestioned competence was not the only factor that we had to consider. Teeter's polls showed that his wheeler-dealer image just wouldn't fade away. Too much polarization, we concluded, and he was off the list.

Now we were down to four, and we considered each one very carefully. Had I been forced to disclose my nominee several weeks before the Presidential balloting, Ruckelshaus might well have been my choice. He had been head of the Environmental Protection Agency and, for a while, Acting Director of the FBI. Most people remembered him for the courage he displayed as Deputy Attorney General when he refused to fire Special Prosecutor Archibald Cox during the Saturday Night Massacre and resigned instead. Naming him would be a signal that I had severed ties with the Nixonites. He was young, he was a Catholic, and he had an attractive, articulate wife who would have been an asset on the campaign trail. But there were drawbacks to naming Ruckelshaus. He was from Indiana, next-door to Michigan, and he had never won a statewide race. Reluctantly, we put his name on the shelf.

Was the country ready for a woman as Vice President? There was no doubt in my mind that Anne Armstrong was capable. A Texas business executive and rancher, she was smart and charming. She had toiled in the trenches and risen to become vice chairman of the Republican National Committee. During the Nixon years she had served as a White House counselor, never once being tainted by Watergate, and later she had been an outstanding ambassador to Great Britain. If the Conservative Party in Britain could select Margaret Thatcher as its leader, why couldn't one of the major parties in America nominate a woman to be Vice President?

But what a gamble it would be! Spencer argued that we should take the risk anyway. In terms of her philosophy and outlook on life, she would be acceptable to the convention. Besides, this would be the sort of dramatic announcement that would electrify the country. It might reverse our party's slide in the polls. Teeter's surveys indicated that she would gain us votes from people who don't normally back

Republicans, but she would also cost us more of our traditional support than any other potential nominee. She came close. Very close. Naming her was something I really wanted to do, but I found myself drawing back every time I thought about it. (In retrospect, if given the opportunity to make that decision again, I might well have said, "Damn the torpedoes," and gambled on Anne.)

That left Baker and Dole. The Tennessean was a moderate, an engaging and articulate Senator who was acceptable to every wing of the party. He was proud of his reputation for integrity, and he had been on the right side of Watergate. His wife had once had a battle with alcohol, but everyone knew that she had conquered the problem, and it wouldn't be an issue in the campaign. That wasn't a factor in our deliberations at all. But we had to consider the minuses, and unfortunately, there were several of them. First, he came from a border state, and I didn't think that even with him on the ticket I'd be able to wrestle the region away from Carter. According to Teeter's polls, he had no great appeal either in the Northeast or in the Western states that we had to win if we were going to prevail. Finally, as a skillful legislative leader he had often worked out compromises to reach practical solutions. This reputation, however, didn't project the strength the ticket needed.

Dole, on the other hand, was a man with whom I felt very comfortable. We had been friends for years in the House. He had supported my effort to become Minority Leader, and I had returned the favor in 1971 when he wanted to be named chairman of the Republican National Committee. He had done a good job in his two years there, keeping out of intraparty feuds and working to broaden the base of Republican appeal. Because he had been wounded during World War II, he had strong links with veterans' groups and the handicapped. He had never identified with the Reaganites, but they respected him and acknowledged his skills as a campaigner. He was bright, hard-working and very loyal to me, and I knew that he would never complain about having to perform disagreeable chores. Equally important, he was the ranking Republican on the Senate Agriculture Committee. The farmers in the plains states still were mad at me. Someone had to convince them that I was their friend and that I'd ordered the grain embargo in 1975 only because I had to put the

national interest first. Someone had to make them understand. The
more I thought about this, the more I concluded that Dole might be
the man.

But once again we had to review the minuses. I wondered whether
voters would view him as "Presidential material." He had a reputation in the capital as a slashing—and very partisan—orator who loved
to let fly with sarcastic one-liners. He had a sharp, quick tongue—
and paid a price for it. Instead of judging him on his voting record,
which was moderate and responsible and, on some issues, surprisingly
liberal, Washington reporters concentrated on his rhetoric and considered him a Republican hatchet man. If I selected him and if he
took a hard-line approach to the issues of the campaign, the press
corps would crucify him, and I would be the loser in the end.

By this time, it was after 5 A.M., and I hadn't made a final decision.
"Mr. President," Rockefeller said, "we are not going to get a consensus tonight; we might as well get some sleep." I agreed and the meeting broke up. In retrospect, I can understand why some of my aides
felt at the time that the nominee was going to be Ruckelshaus, Baker,
or someone else. For the past several hours, I had heard everyone out
and hadn't signaled which way I was leaning myself. Gradually, the
choice became obvious. It was a close call, but I remember thinking,
just before dozing off, how crucial the farm states would be to my
victory. And no one could do better in those states than Dole.

At nine-twenty, we were back at it again with two new advisers,
Scowcroft and Nevada Senator Paul Laxalt, who had been one of
Reagan's chief strategists. Now, without revealing my preference for
Dole, I ran his name past the group one more time. There were no
objections. "All right, gentlemen," I said. "It's Dole." At ten thirty-
one, I telephoned Dole's suite at the Muehlebach Hotel. "We'll be a
great team," I said.

He didn't hesitate. "I'm proud to do it," he replied.

Nothing was more important than the acceptance speech that I
was to deliver that night. It just had to get the campaign off and running. I had been preparing it for the past several weeks. Hartmann
had labored hard and well on the basic draft, I had made a few revi-
sions, and then I'd rehearsed the speech time and time again. Don
Penny produced a videotape machine. After I read each paragraph,

he would play the tape to let me judge my own performance. At first, it wasn't too good. I garbled some of the words; my gestures were exaggerated, and I discovered to my amazement that I had a tendency to move from side to side, something that could be very distracting on nationwide TV. The answer was to spread my feet farther apart and simply make up my mind not to sway. Betty was helpful too. When she heard the speech, she said it was much too long. So we made some cuts. She also criticized my tendency not to smile when I was on TV. I looked as if I was ready to shoot someone, she said. As usual, she was right.

About a week before the convention began, I had mentioned something to Betty that I'd been thinking about for quite a while. When I first ran for Congress, I'd challenged my opponent to a debate. I believed in debates and had engaged in them throughout my Congressional career. According to the polls, Carter had an overwhelming lead. I had to do something dramatic and different in order to win. Furthermore, I had a visceral feeling that if I didn't seize the initiative, Carter would—and that would put me on the defensive. So why not take him on? Then the people could decide.

Betty thought that was a good idea. Several days later, I mentioned it to Hartmann. "You're the only one on the staff who knows," I said. I was encouraged by Bob's enthusiastic reaction to the plan even though it would be a big gamble. Soon it was time to solicit others' views. At five-thirty in the afternoon, the day of the speech, I asked Cheney and Marsh to come down to my suite. When they arrived, I showed them a paragraph I'd just written on a legal pad: "And I will tell you one more thing. This year the issues are on our side. I am ready, I am eager to go before the American people and debate the real issues face to face with Jimmy Carter. The American people have a right to know firsthand exactly where both of us stand."

They read the challenge, then looked up at me. "Great," they said.

"All right," I replied. "Get it typed up and put it in the speech."

After dinner with the family, I settled back in my suite to watch the first part of the evening's proceedings on TV. If Arizona Congressman John Rhodes, the convention chairman, followed the original script, I would leave the hotel soon, reach Kemper Arena a few minutes later and deliver the speech about 9 P.M. That would be prime time in most of the country. But snags developed almost immediately. Reagan's backers started cheering and chanting for their man. They wanted him to address the convention even before I arrived. And Rhodes responded to all this by inviting Reagan to the podium. He remained in his box. Whereupon Rhodes repeated the invitation. Reagan stayed where he was. "This is someone else's night," he said. But his supporters wouldn't give up. Their demonstration went on and on, and it was preventing me from giving my speech on time. "Dammit," I shouted to Cheney. "Get hold of Rhodes and tell him to get this thing under control. *Now.*" I was angry, and I used four-letter words I almost never use. Finally, the demonstration wound down, and at ten o'clock I set out for the convention hall. There was another delay—my advisers wanted to show a twenty-minute film—and it wasn't until ten-forty that night that I began my speech.

> We will wage a winning campaign in every region of this country, from the snowy banks of Minnesota to the sandy plains of Georgia. We concede not a single state. We concede not a single vote. I speak not of a Republican victory but a victory for the American people. You at home listening tonight, you are the people who pay the taxes and obey the laws. You are the people who make our system work. You are the people who make America what it is. It is from your ranks that I come and on your side that I stand. Having become Vice President and President without expecting or seeking either, I have a special feeling toward these high offices. To me the Presidency and the Vice Presidency were not prizes to be won but a duty to be done. So tonight it is not the power and the glamour of the Presidency that lead me to ask for another four years. It is something every hard-working American will understand: the challenge of a job well begun but far from finished. That is why, tonight, I turn to the American people and ask not only for your prayers but also for your strength and your support, for your voice and for your vote. I come before you with a two-year record of performance, without your mandate. I offer you a four-year pledge of greater performance with your mandate. From August of 1974 to August of 1976 the record shows steady progress upward toward prosperity, peace and public trust. My record is one of progress, not platitudes. My record is one of specifics, not smiles. My record is one of performance, not promises. It is a rec-

ord I am proud to run on. It is a record the American people—Democrats, Independents and Republicans alike—will support on November 2. From start to finish, our campaign will be credible; it will be responsible. We will come out fighting, and we will win. Yes, we have all seen the polls and the pundits who say our party is dead. I have heard that before. So did Harry Truman. I will tell you what I think. The only polls that count are the polls the American people go to on November 2. And right now I predict the American people are going to say, "Jerry, you have done a good job. Keep right on doing it."

During the thirty-eight-minute speech, the delegates applauded me an incredible sixty-five times. Ear-splitting shouts erupted at the close. The sounds of bells, whistles and horns merged with victory chants coming from every corner of the huge arena. Staring out through the haze, I could see delegates bobbing their placards and posters up and down and waving their flags. My adrenaline was flowing, and the beaming faces of my wife and children standing beside me on the podium made me feel enormously proud. Bob and Liddy Dole joined us to acknowledge the applause. Then I asked Ron and Nancy Reagan to come up to the stage. Betty was on my left. Suddenly, I felt her hand in mine, and all of us—as if by some unspoken signal—clasped our hands and raised them high above our heads. The crowd responded with a deafening roar. It was one of the most thrilling moments of my life, and as I stood there, I had to believe the affection was genuine. That was when a very pleasant thought entered my mind. Maybe party unity wasn't so ephemeral a vision after all.

7

Neck and Neck

"There is nothing I love as much as a good fight."
— Franklin D. Roosevelt

T he Reagan challenge had required an awful lot of time, money
and energy. It had forced me to take some positions that I suspected would hurt me in November and it had delayed some substantive accomplishments. There was no doubt in my mind, however,
that the challenge had improved the efficiency of the White House
staff and the PFC. It had taught all of us—for the very first time—
how to run a national campaign, and I was thankful for that. I just
hoped we hadn't learned the lesson too late.

Even before I gave my acceptance speech, I had disagreed with
my staff about where to kick off the campaign. We were planning to
leave Kansas City and fly directly to Vail for strategy discussions and
a much-needed rest. Because Bob Dole's hometown of Russell, Kansas, was on the route, I thought that stopping there for a rally would
give us a unique campaign opportunity. It was a simple gesture that
would appeal to rural Americans and make them more inclined to
vote for the ticket in the fall. Dole liked the idea, but everyone else
opposed it: we had less than thirty-six hours to plan and execute the
visit, there would be a problem attracting a sizable crowd in a town

of only five thousand, and reporters traveling with us would be annoyed at the delay in getting to Vail, where they could relax.

My intuition, however, told me that it was the right thing to do, and when Spencer, Cheney and Nessen kept resisting the idea, I put my foot down and said that was it, we were going. Then I walked out of the room. Spencer followed me into the hall. "Okay, Mr. President," he said, "if that's what you want, we'll do it."

I grabbed him by the arm. "Dammit, I know what I'm doing," I said. "I know a little bit about politics."

So the next afternoon, August 20, there we were driving along Main Street in Russell to the courthouse where Dole had served as county attorney from 1953 to 1961. A large crowd was waiting for us, and Bob was overcome by emotion when he tried to speak. "If I have done anything," he said in a choked voice, "it was because of what you did for me." And he started to explain how the community had raised funds to help him pay for the operations he needed after World War II. Then he recognized some of the faces in the crowd, the same people who had gone door to door collecting money for him, and broke down for a moment. Someone in the crowd started applauding, and I stood up to clap too. Bob quickly regained his composure and went on to introduce me as a "friend of small-town America—really one of us."

A barbecue followed the rally, and the entire reception was fantastic. I was glad that I'd overruled my advisers, because the visit got our campaign off to a solid start.

It wasn't until several days after we got to Vail that the euphoria began to give way to reality. The latest Gallup poll put Carter ahead of me by 56 to 33. The Harris survey gave him an even wider lead of 61 to 32. Our pollster, Bob Teeter, worked with his own figures, which projected that I could lose the election by 9,490,000 votes. There were seventy-three days left until November 2. All I had to do to win, Teeter pointed out, was convert 130,000 Carter supporters every day.

And that was the purpose of our week-long "working vacation" at Vail—to devise the overall campaign strategy that could somehow close the massive Carter lead. The personnel decisions were the easiest. Rog Morton had been ailing for months, and he didn't feel that his health would allow him to continue on as chairman of the PFC. Jim Baker had demonstrated an outstanding organizational capability as our chief delegate-hunter, so he would be a fine replacement to run the campaign.

Others, of course, would be helping him. Spencer would stay on as deputy to handle politics. Teeter would be in charge of research and compile polling statistics. Bill Greener, Assistant Secretary of Defense for Public Affairs, would come over from the Pentagon to be campaign spokesman, and Cheney would continue to handle liaison between the White House and the PFC. Everyone recognized that our preconvention radio and TV ads could be improved; now we brought aboard the outstanding team of Doug Bailey and John Deardourff to run our ad campaign. Finally, I asked Dean Burch and Bill Ruckelshaus to contact the Carter camp and negotiate an agreement covering the campaign debates. There should be four ninety-minute sessions, I said. The first should be on national defense, the others on domestic issues, foreign policy and the state of the economy. Time was of the essence, and I asked Dean and Bill to see if Carter would agree to hold the first debate as early as September 8.

Dole, Rockefeller and Connally arrived in Vail August 26. For the next few days, sitting around the fireplace in the basement of a rented chalet, they, my senior aides and I developed our campaign strategy. Perhaps the most important of our themes was contained in the single word "trust." The voters, in my opinion, didn't care that much about my position on this specific issue or that. What they wanted was someone in the White House who would be honest with them. I had tried to run an open Administration for the past two years, and my term had been scandal-free. I hoped this would convince people that I deserved their trust.

Under this umbrella were policies and programs that we wanted the campaign to emphasize—realistic objectives for the next four years. We wanted to spur the creation of millions of new jobs, accelerate home ownership, provide quality, affordable health care and reduce crime. We would keep inflation down, retain unquestioned military strength, guarantee the peace.

But what was the most effective way for me to project these goals? Here the options narrowed to two. In 1948, when he was behind in the polls, Truman went on the attack against a "do-nothing" Congress. That was one option. The other was to have Dole hit the hustings while I remained in Washington, prepared for the debates and tried to be "Presidential." This, my advisers said, was the "Rose Garden strategy." To which Dole remarked that he was obviously being consigned to the "brier patch."

Yet there were some compelling reasons for me to accept option number two. During the Reagan contest I had discovered that personal appearances didn't necessarily generate national popularity. When I flew, say, to Miami to make a speech, my approval rating in Dade County went up. But it declined across the country. People saw me as "just another pol," and I suffered accordingly. Frantic trips across the country in search of votes could well cause a continuing slide in the polls. Carter would be the candidate constantly on the road. The press and television would cover his appearances; yet, to be fair, they'd report on what I had done that day no matter what it was, and the contrast would be clear. I was in the White House doing my job, and he was flying from place to place making extravagant political promises.

Moreover, we had to consider our traveling costs. The new federal campaign law set a $21.8 million limit on what Presidential candidates could spend in the general election. I was planning to allocate about half of that to advertising. The rest of it would go very quickly for salaries, overhead, mailings, and telephones. Moving a President and his entourage around the country is an expensive proposition, and I wanted to have enough money available to pay for an intensive, last-minute push in key areas as we came down to the wire. As Jim Baker told reporters in Vail, "The candidate who makes the wisest use of dollars is going to win the election."

Knowing *where* to allocate our resources was important too. We focused on those states where we had the best chance to secure the magic total of 270 electoral votes. Carter's strategy was to campaign in the North as a traditional Democrat while retaining his strong Southern base. Somehow we had to find a crack in that strategy. For us the South was a long shot. Florida was touch and go; the only Southern state we felt sure we would win was Virginia. The West, with the exception of California, where we were far behind in the polls, seemed strong for us. Ohio was a question mark, but the Middle West appeared to be friendly. Our problems were in the Northeast and the Middle Atlantic states.

Then we talked about the interest groups. Nixon had done extremely well with the blue-collar vote in 1972, and some observers said at the time that organized labor was defecting from the old Democratic coalition and emerging as a force within the GOP. That was hogwash. Labor had gone for Nixon only because it feared McGovern, and any hope I might have had of attracting broad union support had been dashed by my veto of the Common Situs Picketing bill and the cargo preference legislation. With farmers I still had a chance. The Dole selection had pleased them, and Agriculture Secretary Butz was mighty effective on the stump. Veterans' organizations hadn't liked my earned amnesty plan, but I sensed that they were even more concerned about Carter's plans to cut billions of dollars from the defense budget.

Among Catholics, abortion was a major issue. It didn't deserve to be a Presidential issue, but it had started to surface, and I would have to deal with it. While I opposed abortion on demand, I also opposed a constitutional amendment that would prohibit it. I did, however, favor an amendment that would allow a majority of the voters in each state to decide which position to take. I hoped this would be more acceptable to Catholics than Carter's stand—if only we could figure out precisely what that stand was. Traditionally, Jews and Hispanics had favored Democrats overwhelmingly. Nonetheless, we agreed to try to make inroads there. Despite my conviction that I had a commendable record publicly and privately on racial matters, most blacks were unlikely to vote for me no matter what I did. Southern blacks would turn to Carter because of regional pride and a common Baptist faith. And we'd be lucky to attract 10 percent to 15 percent of the black vote in the industrial Middle West.

On one thing all my advisers agreed: it was imperative to go on the offensive and make Carter *the* issue of the campaign. If we could portray him as untested and untried, if we could tie him to the liberal spending policies of urban Democrats and say that he was taking those stands because he didn't know the facts, we might be able to provoke him into a serious mistake.

Traditionally, candidates of both parties kick off their fall campaigns on or shortly after Labor Day. The University of Michigan, my alma mater, was a natural site for my first major speech, and I arrived in Ann Arbor on the afternoon of September 15. Heavy rain had fallen earlier in the day; still, there was a crowd of about fifteen thousand in Crisler Arena.

"The question in this campaign of 1976," I said, "is not who has the better vision of America. The question is who will act to make that vision a reality. The American people are ready for the truth, simply spoken, about what government can do for them and what it cannot do and what it should not do. They will demand performance, not promises; specifics, not smiles. There are some in this political year who claim that more government, more spending, more taxes and more control [over] our lives will solve our problems. More government is not the solution. Better government is."

I discussed the programs that I intended to push when the new Congress convened in January, then I turned back to the gut issue of the campaign: "It's not enough for anyone to say, 'Trust me.' Trust must be earned. Trust is not having to guess what a candidate means. Trust is leveling with the people before the election about what you are going to do after the election. Trust is not being all things to all people but being the same thing to all people. Trust is not cleverly shading words so that each separate audience can hear what it wants to hear but saying plainly and simply what you mean—and meaning what you say."

Returning to Washington later that night, I began preparing for my face-to-face confrontations with Carter. For the past several weeks, our aides had been working out the debate details. Both sides made concessions. Carter's people, for example, went along with my wish to be standing throughout the debates. (Carter aide Barry Jagoda suggested in all seriousness that I be required to stand in a hole to offset the fact that I was the taller man.) Carter's men wanted small lecterns; mine favored larger ones because they knew I was more comfortable with them. We gave ground there. Throughout these talks, Carter's representatives feared I would take unfair advantage of my incumbency. There could be no Presidential seal in front of the lectern where I stood. Of course. Jagoda also insisted—until Dean Burch set him straight—that I not be addressed as "Mr. President." Then, facetiously, one of my people suggested that we have the band play "Hail to the Chief" the moment I walked onto the stage. Just as facetiously, Carter spokesman Jody Powell said this would be all right with him—as long as it was a Dixieland band.

Finally, we agreed that there would be three Presidential debates, each ninety minutes, and one debate between Mondale and Dole. The first, to be held in Philadelphia on September 23, would be limited to domestic issues and economic policy. The second, in San Francisco on October 6, would concern foreign policy and national defense, and the grand finale, in Williamsburg, Virginia, on October 22, would be general in scope.

These were to be the first debates between party nominees since 1960 and the first ever to involve an incumbent President. All of us knew the stakes were high—an audience of between 80 million and 100 million Americans would be watching—and all of us realized that first impressions would be critical. Millions of votes could be decided during the first half hour of the first debate. I was confident that I could win. Throughout my Congressional career, whenever my opponents had challenged me, I'd always agreed to debate—and I'd always prevailed.

At this point in the campaign, I had mixed feelings about my challenger. On the one hand, I was impressed by his quick mind and ability to articulate. On the other, he struck me as cold and arrogant, even egotistical, and I was convinced he played fast and loose with the facts.

How ironic it was, I thought, that his limited experience in government could turn out to be an advantage for him. I had been in Washington for nearly twenty-eight years, had made thousands of decisions on national issues, all on the record. Carter had never had to make a hard decision on a *national* issue, so he could be more strident in his accusations and challenges. In order to counter them, I'd have to familiarize myself with his performance as governor of Georgia.

During the week before the first debate, I studied a briefing book on his record. I reviewed positions I'd taken myself on every conceivable issue, and I watched reruns of the Nixon-Kennedy debates. Nixon had been nervous and deferential to his challenger. I wasn't going to make the same mistake. To prepare for the Philadelphia debate, my aides positioned me behind a lectern, turned on the spotlights and fired the toughest questions they could find. All this was videotaped, and at the end of every session we reviewed my performance carefully. Over a four-day period, I spent nine hours under the lights, and the grueling interrogation boosted my confidence. By nine-thirty on the evening of the twenty-third, I was as ready as I'd ever be.

Carter won the toss of the coin, and the first question, from a panel of three reporters, went to him. "Governor," said ABC's Frank Reynolds, "you have made jobs your number one priority, and you are committed to a drastic reduction in unemployment. Can you say now, Governor, in specific terms, what your first step would be next January, if you are elected, to achieve that?"

If viewers expected a reply "in specific terms," they were disappointed. We have "to recognize the tremendous economic strength of this country," Carter said, "and to set the putting back to work of our people as a top priority. This is an effort that ought to be done primarily by strong leadership in the White House, the inspiration of our people, the tapping of business, agriculture, industry, labor and government at all levels to work on this project." And he went on to say: "There is an additional factor that needs to be done and covered very succinctly, and that is to make sure that we have a good relationship between management, business on the one hand, and labor on the other."

"I don't believe that Mr. Carter has been any more specific in this case than he has been on many other instances," I said when it was my turn to respond. I noted that he hadn't even mentioned the Humphrey-Hawkins full employment bill, legislation which he had previously endorsed and which would add between $10 billion and $30 billion to the federal budget. The answer to unemployment, I said, was not costly new federal programs, but major tax cuts to spur jobs in the private sector.

For the rest of the debate, Carter and I sparred along traditional party lines. He no doubt scored some points when I was asked how I could justify pardoning Nixon while refusing a blanket pardon for all draft dodgers and deserters. I explained my reasoning and discussed the earned amnesty program. Carter jumped all over that, said he favored a full pardon for draft evaders, and declared that "what the people are concerned about is not the pardon or the amnesty of those who evaded the draft but whether or not our crime system is fair. The big shots who are rich, who are influential, very seldom go to jail. Those who are poor and who have no influence quite often are the ones who are punished."

But I hit back hard when he claimed that as governor of Georgia, he had taken some 300 agencies and eliminated 278 of them. What Carter neglected to say, I quickly pointed out, was that during his term of office, state expenditures went up over 50 percent, the number of state employees increased by 25 percent, and the state's bonded indebtedness rose more than 20 percent. His famous "reorganization" had cost Georgia taxpayers plenty.

Throughout the debate, I tied Carter to the big spending policies of the Democratic Congress. And in my summation I stressed his support for "the Democratic platform, which calls for more spending, bigger deficits, more inflation or more taxes. Governor Carter in his acceptance speech called for more and more programs, which mean more and more government. I think the real issue in this campaign is whether you should vote for his promises or my performance in two years in the White House."

The only thing that marred the evening was an audio breakdown, which held up the debate for 27 minutes. Worse, it happened just a few minutes before the end. But when it was all over, I had a tremendous upbeat feeling because it had gone well. Within just a few days, a Harris poll of 1,500 registered voters said that I had won the debate by a margin of 40 to 31 (the Gallup poll had it 38 to 25) and that I had narrowed Carter's lead in the Presidential contest from 52–39 to 50–41. The AP was even more encouraging; it reported I trailed Carter now by only two percentage points.

Then came more good news. In late September, Playboy magazine released an interview in which Carter said some remarkable things. "I've looked on a lot of women with lust," Carter confessed. "I've committed adultery in my heart many times. This is something that God recognizes I will do—and I have done it—and God forgives me for it. But that doesn't mean that I condemn someone who not only looks on a woman with lust but who leaves his wife and shacks up with somebody out of wedlock. Christ says don't consider yourself better than someone else because one guy screws a whole bunch of women while the other guy is loyal to his wife." And then he continued: "I don't think I would ever take on the same frame of mind that Nixon or Johnson did—lying, cheating, and distorting the truth."

Throughout the campaign, Carter had talked about his religious convictions in a way that I found discomfiting. I have always felt a closeness to God and have looked to a higher being for guidance and support, but I didn't think it was appropriate to advertise my religious beliefs. Carter, I was sure, had made a serious mistake. The interview would hurt him all over the South, and his comment about LBJ would be especially damaging in Texas.

Yet at the time, I had problems of my own—allegations that I had received undisclosed contributions from the Marine Engineers Beneficial Association (MEBA), a small but powerful maritime union, in my Congressional campaigns. I was absolutely innocent of any wrongdoing, but the mere suspicion that I might have done something illegal was enough to blunt the momentum of my election drive and dog the campaign for weeks. And the curious way that the allegation surfaced speaks volumes about post-Watergate "morality" in Washington.

During my years in the House, I had received MEBA's financial support, and I had disclosed every contribution. But my veto of the cargo preference bill—which would have cost consumers at least $200 million a year—had infuriated MEBA President Jesse Calhoon. And Calhoon, according to a subsequent report in the Chicago *Sun-Times*, had "determined to get" me any way he could. The article went on to say that during my primary contests against Reagan in the spring of 1976, Calhoon claimed to all who would listen to him that I had accepted cash payments from the union. Eventually, this story found its way to the FBI and reached the desk of Director Clarence M. Kelley, who brought it to the attention of Attorney General Levi. The Attorney General decided that he had no choice but to refer the matter to Charles F. C. Ruff, who was in charge of the Watergate special prosecution force. So despite the fact that hundreds of FBI

agents had already pored over all my records prior to my confirmation as Vice President, Ruff sent the FBI back to Grand Rapids. He
issued a subpoena to the Kent County Republican Committee and its
fund-raising affiliate demanding financial records and documents
dating back to 1964. He issued a similar subpoena to MEBA.

An investigation involving the President of the United States isn't
the sort of thing that can stay secret very long. The Grand Rapids
Press found out; so did the *Wall Street Journal*, and the first national
story broke on September 21. I didn't pay much attention to it because I knew I was clean, and I was busy preparing for the first debate. I failed to see how the story would build and inject the foul
aroma of Watergate into the closing weeks of the campaign.

"Possible Covert Union Gifts to Ford from '64 to '74 Called Target
of Inquiry by Watergate Prosecutor," said a headline in the New
York *Times* on September 26. "Allegations About Ford Said Serious,"
was the banner over a story by Bob Woodward and Carl Bernstein in
the Washington *Post* the next morning, and in the same paper three
days later: "Ford to Face Questions on Fund Probe." Carter must
have been enjoying the spectacle enormously. "The best way to resolve the question if there is a doubt among the American people,"
he said, "is for Mr. Ford to have a frank discussion with the American people, which so far he's failed to do."

But what was I supposed to say? Day after day, these stories appeared, linking me to possible improprieties. No one ever said specifically what it was that I was alleged to have done—all I knew was
what I read in the press or heard on the TV news—and I had no way
to defend myself. I couldn't talk to Levi about any of this because I
had given him my word that I would never interfere with an investigation. Nor could I challenge the Special Prosecutor because that
would smack of Nixon and the Saturday Night Massacre all over
again. What so frustrated me was that while serving as Special Prosecutor, Ruff was also teaching law courses at Georgetown University.
He had neither the time nor the staff to expedite the probe. That left
me hanging.

Further compounding the problem was the fact that I was traveling on the campaign trail. Jack Marsh, Phil Buchen and his deputy,
Ed Schmults, represented my interests in Washington. With my ap-

proval, they brought in two attorneys, Abe Krash and Daniel Rez-
neck, from the prestigious firm of Arnold and Porter, to help move
the matter as swiftly as possible. They were given access to all the
records. They examined every one of the charges and concluded that
they had no validity. Soon after, Schmults told Ruff, "The reason you
have to resolve this is that if the President isn't cleared soon, you will
not only have hurt him, you will have done a greater injustice to
Carter. If Carter wins, his victory will be marred and you will have
impaired his Presidency."

Finally, on September 30, I summoned reporters into the Oval Office. I told them that I had full confidence in Ruff's integrity and
that I had instructed my staff not to do anything that could impede
the ongoing probe. "I can say with complete confidence," I went on,
"that when the investigation is completed, I will be free of any allegations such as I've read about. I would add this final comment.
There is a saying that's prevalent in the law that 'justice delayed is
justice denied.'" In other words, if you think you have a case, Mr.
Prosecutor, please get on with it. If you don't, please admit it and ex-
onerate me.

At the end of the session, one of the reporters said, "Mr. President,
you look more worried than I've seen you in a long time."

"Worried?"

"Yes, sir. You haven't smiled very much in this news conference.
You really look troubled, and I've known you for ten years. Does this
bother you? Is it something that's going to hurt you badly in the campaign?"

"I am not unhappy," I replied, trying to avoid appearing pessimistic about the election. But I was worried. And my troubles were just
beginning.

Before dinner that evening, Cheney had some bad news. Former
Nixon counsel John Dean had covered the Kansas City convention for
Rolling Stone magazine and at the end of the convention had flown
to California on the same plane with an unnamed member of my
Cabinet. In his article, Dean had quoted this official as telling an ab-
solutely irresponsible anti-black "joke." Then *New Times* magazine
figured out that Dean's companion had been Agriculture Secretary
Earl Butz. The magazine would be on the newsstands soon.

Everyone who knew Earl Butz understood that he had a habit of talking too freely and telling yarns that he didn't mean to be taken as any more than rough humor. Yet those two tendencies now combined to produce a political bombshell. I was upset because I considered Butz to be a man of high moral principles, and I knew that the "joke" in no way reflected his real feelings about blacks. Then, too, he had been a loyal, effective Secretary of Agriculture, and I just didn't feel that I could fire him on the spot. I asked Cheney to have him come to the Oval Office in the morning.

Our session lasted only five minutes. I told him flatly that the language and attitudes that had been attributed to him were not acceptable in my Administration. His remarks had been offensive to me and to the American people as well. Butz said that he was sorry and that he'd issue a public apology. But as the fire storm of criticism grew, it was apparent that an apology was not enough. On October 4, Butz entered the Oval Office again. "Mr. President," he said, "I goofed. You know that I didn't intend it as a racial slur, and I should have known better than to trust a man like John Dean. But it's causing you an awful lot of trouble, and under no circumstances do I want to jeopardize your election next month. So I'm going to submit my resignation."

It was an uncomfortable moment for both of us. "Earl, you know how I feel about you personally," I said, "how close we've been as friends and how much we've agreed on farm policy. But I think your analysis of the situation is accurate, and on that basis I'll accept your resignation." As he turned to leave the office, I saw tears in his eyes, and I didn't feel any better.

Because of the press furor over the Ruff investigation and now the Butz incident, I failed to spend as much time preparing for the second debate as I should have. Foreign policy and national defense were my forte, and these would be the only two issues discussed during the confrontation that was scheduled for the evening of October 6 in San Francisco.

The first question, from Max Frankel of the New York *Times*, was addressed to Carter, and it added up to a recitation of the foreign policy gains my Administration had made.

"Governor," Frankel began, "since the Democrats last ran our foreign policy, including many of the men who are advising you, the country has been relieved of the Vietnam agony and the military draft; we've started arms control negotiations with the Russians; we've opened relations with China; we've arranged the disengagement in the Middle East; we've regained influence with the Arabs without deserting Israel. Now maybe we've even begun a process of peaceful change in Africa.

"Now, you've objected in this campaign to the style with which much of this was done, and you've mentioned some other things that you think ought to have been done. But do you really have a quarrel with this Republican record? Would you not have done any of those things?"

Carter ducked the question. "This Republican Administration has been almost all style and spectacular and not substance," he said. "We've got a chance tonight to talk about, first of all, leadership, the character of our country and a vision of the future. In every one of these instances, the Ford Administration has failed. Our country is not strong any more; we're not respected any more. We've lost, in our foreign policy, the character of the American people. We've ignored or excluded the American people and the Congress from participation in the shaping of our foreign policy. It's been one of secrecy and exclusion. In addition to that, we've had a chance to become now, contrary to our long-standing beliefs and principles, the arms merchant of the whole world. We've tried to buy success from our enemies, and at the same time, we've excluded from the process the normal friendship of our allies. I might say this in closing, and that is, that as far as foreign policy goes, Mr. Kissinger has been the President of this country. Mr. Ford has shown an absence of leadership and an absence of a grasp of what this country is and what it ought to be."

As I listened to these accusations, my resentment mounted almost to the breaking point. But I remembered my advisers' admonition: "Don't lose your cool. Stay Presidential." In retrospect, a more emotional reaction would have been better. This was a cheap shot at Kissinger and me and I should have said so. Furthermore, it wasn't true. Of course I got Henry's advice on foreign policy, but I made the decisions myself. For Carter to charge otherwise was a distortion of fact.

After some more debate, during which I tried to pin Carter down on specifics, Frankel addressed me, saying he wanted "to explore a little more deeply our relationship with the Russians. They used to brag, back in Khrushchev's day, that because of their greater patience and because of our greed for business deals, they would sooner or later get the better of us. Is it possible that, despite some setbacks in the Middle East, they've proved their point? Our allies in France and Italy are now flirting with communism; we've recognized a permanent Communist regime in East Germany; we virtually signed, in Helsinki, an agreement that the Russians have dominance in Eastern Europe; we bailed out Soviet agriculture with our huge grain sales. . . . Is that what you would call a two-way street of traffic in Europe?"

"I believe that we have negotiated with the Soviet Union since I've been President from a position of strength," I said, and I cited some examples. The Vladivostok agreement was one. The grain accord—which would prove very beneficial to American farmers—was another. Then I turned to Helsinki. "I am glad you raised it, Mr. Frankel. In the case of Helsinki, thirty-five nations signed an agreement, including the Secretary of State for the Vatican. I can't under any circumstances believe that His Holiness the Pope would agree, by signing that agreement, that the thirty-five nations have turned over to the Warsaw Pact nations the domination of Eastern Europe. It just isn't true."

Clearly, I should have stopped there. Instead, I went on: "Now, what has been accomplished by the Helsinki agreement? Number one, we have an agreement where they notify us and we notify them of any military maneuvers that are to be undertaken. They have done it in both cases where they've done so. There is no Soviet domination of Eastern Europe, and there never will be under a Ford Administration."

Frankel pressed me on that: "Did I understand you to say, sir, that the Russians are not using Eastern Europe as their own sphere of influence and occupying most of the countries there and making sure with their troops that it's a Communist zone?"

I was stepping through a minefield, but I failed to recognize it at the time. "I don't believe, Mr. Frankel," I said, "that the Yugoslavians consider themselves dominated by the Soviet Union. I don't believe that the Romanians consider themselves dominated by the Soviet Union. I don't believe that the Poles consider themselves dominated by the Soviet Union. Each of those countries is independent, autonomous; it has its own territorial integrity. And the United States does not concede that those countries are under the domination of the Soviet Union. As a matter of fact, I visited Poland, Yugoslavia and Romania to make certain that the people of those countries understood that the President of the United States and the people of the United States are dedicated to their independence, their autonomy and their freedom."

Carter jumped all over that. "I would like to see Mr. Ford convince the Polish-Americans and the Czech-Americans and the Hungarian-Americans in this country," he said, "that those countries don't live under the domination and supervision of the Soviet Union behind the Iron Curtain."

Still, when the debate was over, I felt that I had come out ahead. Teeter's initial poll showed that I had "won" by 11 percentage points. In a ninety-minute span, my aides pointed out, Carter had made fourteen distortions or misrepresentations of the facts. The first indication that *I* was the one who had some explaining to do came next morning as *Air Force One* was flying south to Los Angeles. Cheney entered my cabin and said, in effect, that I had goofed. The press was hollering about my Eastern European "mistake." Leaders of ethnic groups had expressed serious concern.

Cheney thought I should issue a clarification immediately. I told him I didn't see any need for that. If the critics didn't understand what I had meant to say, then that was their problem, not mine. And in my own mind I was sure what I had meant to say. Although the Soviet Union dominated Polish territory by stationing troops there, it didn't dominate the heart, soul and spirit of the Polish people. No, I reiterated, I wasn't going to retract what I had said. If a slip, it was not significant.

Minutes later, Cheney returned to my cabin, this time with Spencer in tow. The political fallout, Stu warned, was continuing. Teeter's latest polls showed that people who thought I had won the debate were beginning to change their minds. I couldn't afford to lose votes from ethnic groups over a verbal miscue, but I *would* lose them unless I acted fast. I can be very stubborn when I think I'm right, and I just didn't want to apologize for something that was a minor mistake. Finally, reluctantly, I agreed to try to put the issue to rest during an afternoon speech at the University of Southern California.

"Last night in the debate, I spoke of America's firm support for the aspiration for independence of the nations of Eastern Europe," I said. "The United States has never conceded—and never will concede— their domination by the Soviet Union. I admire the courage of the Polish people and have always supported the hopes of Polish-Americans for freedom of their ancestral homeland. It is our policy to use every peaceful means to assist countries in Eastern Europe in their efforts to become less dependent on the Soviet Union and to establish closer and closer ties with the West and, of course, the United States of America."

But that didn't end it. Ron Nessen told me these remarks had not gone far enough; the issue was bound to surface again. I disagreed with him. And I was anxious to put the problem out of my mind and get on with other matters. For one thing, I was planning to meet with Reagan before a fund-raising dinner in Beverly Hills the night of October 7. He had campaigned hard for the platform and individual Republicans, but I wanted him to give me a strong personal endorsement, as he had promised. The polls showed that I had just taken a three-percentage-point lead over Carter in California—where he had led me once by as much as 20 points—and I knew that a Reagan boost would keep me ahead. In addition, if he were willing to speak up for me in South Carolina, Mississippi, Louisiana and Texas, I might eke out a win in those states too.

Shortly after five o'clock that afternoon, Reagan came to my hotel suite, and we talked for nearly half an hour. He was friendly but reserved. I told him how hard Dick Schweiker, his choice for running mate, was working for my election in Pennsylvania, but he didn't pick up on this and offer to start putting out wholeheartedly for me. His speech to the GOP dinner that night was disappointing. Once again he stressed the virtues of the platform, yet his comments about me came as an afterthought and were noticeably lukewarm. Worse, during the rest of the campaign he refused to work directly for my election.

Next morning, October 8, I spoke to a breakfast of San Fernando Valley area businessmen, and in response to a question, I tried again to explain what I really meant. "I was in Poland a year ago, and I had the opportunity to talk with a number of citizens, and believe me, they are a courageous, strong people. They don't believe that they are going to be forever dominated—if they are—by the Soviet Union. They believe in the independence of that great country, and so do I. And we are going to make certain, to the best of our ability, that any allegation of domination is not fact."

Cheney and Spencer were extremely upset. What was I trying to do, self-destruct my own campaign? Reporters would seize on my phrases "if they are" and "allegation of domination" as pegs to write that I still didn't know what I was talking about. I had to put out a statement ending the issue once and for all. Most voters didn't care *that* much about my policies toward Eastern Europe, Cheney and Spencer argued, but they *did* want to elect a President who said what he meant and meant what he said. All this confusion was just reinforcing an impression that I wasn't on top of the job. They were right. I should have taken this step immediately after the second debate. Harry Truman once said, "The President hears one hundred voices telling him that he is the greatest man in the world. He must listen carefully indeed to hear the one voice that tells him he is not." Well, I hadn't listened, and I would pay the price.

"I was perhaps not as precise as I should have been," I told reporters at the Glendale city hall. "I recognize there are Soviet divisions in Poland. I regret it. And I am very proud of the courageous attitude of the Polish people who want freedom. There are several other countries in Eastern Europe that tragically have Soviet military forces. I hope and trust that my observations will put an end to a misunderstanding. It *was* a misunderstanding."

And then I was off on a whirlwind swing through Oklahoma, Texas and New York. The Reverend W. A. Criswell, pastor of the nation's largest Baptist church, endorsed me in Dallas on October 10, and I was encouraged by the results of Teeter's polls in New York. I was behind there, but closing the gap. So on October 12, with New York Senators Jacob Javits and James Buckley at my side, I campaigned through Brooklyn.

Hubert Humphrey had been operated on for cancer of the bladder four or five days before. He was recuperating at the Sloan-Kettering Institute for Cancer Research in Manhattan, and I decided to pay him a call—that irrepressible man, my political antagonist but close personal friend. He didn't look well at all but seemed overjoyed to see me that afternoon. We talked for about fifteen minutes; he wanted to know how we were doing in the campaign. Near the end of our talk, he motioned me over to his bedside. "Mr. President," he whispered with a grin, "I want to confide in you. You're going to be getting some votes from the Humphrey family."

"Hubert," I replied, "that really bucks me up. I must be doing something right." I clasped his hand, gave it an extra squeeze and left.

The Democrat who aspired to be the next Vice President, the office Hubert had once held, came from the same state and shared the same liberal philosophy, but there the similarity ended. This was brought home to me the very next afternoon. While campaigning through Westchester and Rockland counties, I received a telephone call from my son Steve, who had been campaigning for me, primarily in small towns out West. But he had come to New York to represent me in the Columbus Day parade. Mondale had been there, so Steve had walked up to him and said, "Good afternoon, Senator. I hope you enjoyed the parade as much as I did. My name is Steve Ford." Then he had stuck out his hand. Mondale had turned his back and just walked away. Hubert would never have pulled a stunt like that.

For three weeks now, Special Prosecutor Ruff's investigation had dragged on, casting a dark shadow over my election drive. Throughout this period, the press harped on the "issue" every day. (Nessen told me that CBS Evening News reporter Fred Graham had devoted thirty-two minutes to the allegations; he just kept repeating the same old story every night.) Finally, on October 13, after my return from New York and New Jersey, a letter arrived from Ruff stating that "the evidence developed has disclosed no violation of the law on the part of President Ford" and that "the matter has therefore been closed."

It was about time. I telephoned Nessen at home and told him to schedule a press conference. "When I was chosen to be Vice President," I said to the scores of reporters who crowded into the EOB the night of October 14, "I underwent the most intensive scrutiny of any man who has ever been selected for public office in the United States. My past life, my qualifications, my beliefs—all were put under a microscope. Nonetheless, all of you here tonight and many in our listening audience are aware of allegations that came forth in recent weeks involving my past political campaigns.

"As I have said, these rumors were false. I am very pleased that the Special Prosecutor has finally put this matter to rest once and for all. The one thing that means more to me than my desire for public office is my personal reputation for integrity. Today's announcement reaffirms the original findings of my Vice Presidential confirmation hearings. I hope that it will elevate the Presidential campaign to a level befitting the American people and the American political tradition."

Fat chance. Questions kept coming up about my finances plus preposterous allegations by John Dean that I had tried to block an early Watergate probe in 1972. "He's a little snake in the grass who'll say anything about anyone," I exploded, warning my advisers that I planned to blast him during my next session with the press. I was talked out of it mainly because it was a no-win situation—the entire issue reminded voters of Nixon and Watergate.

Earlier, seizing eagerly upon all these matters, Carter had struck below the belt. "I call on the American people to force Mr. Ford to tell the truth, the whole truth and nothing but the truth. I call on the American news media to insist that Mr. Ford be cross-examined in a carefully prepared, open, previously announced news conference. And I call on Mr. Ford to make sure that these discrepancies are eliminated so the American people will know who he is, what he stands for and what he means when he makes these conflicting statements."

That cheap political demagoguery got my goat, and I became strident in return. At Iowa State University on October 15, I said: "Mr. Carter does have a strange way of changing his accent as he moves about this great country. In California he tries to sound like Cesar Chavez. In Chicago he sounds like Mayor Daley. In New York he sounds like Ralph Nader. In Washington, D.C., he sounds like George Meany. Then Mr. Carter comes to the farm belt. He becomes a little old peanut farmer."

Dole was debating Mondale in Houston, Texas, that night, and I watched their confrontation on TV. "You hit hard but hit fairly," I told Dole afterward, but not all of my advisers thought he had done that well. Some said he had come off like a wisecracking hatchet man, and others objected to his mention of "Democrat wars" in this century—but my competitive juices had been aroused. I was angry at the Democrats for distorting the truth, and Dole had zeroed in on some of those distortions.

"Jimmy Carter wants to divide America," I charged next morning as Betty and I whistle-stopped through Illinois. "Jimmy Carter will say anything anywhere to be President of the United States. He wavers, he wanders, he wiggles and he waffles, and he shouldn't be President of the United States. There was a great, great President a few years ago named Teddy Roosevelt who once said, 'Speak softly and carry a big stick.' Jimmy Carter wants to speak loudly and carry a fly swatter." I used the same lines at every stop, and the crowds greeted them with laughter and applause. But then at Alton, the end of the line for the *Honest Abe*, I stumbled over the words "fly swatter." "Fly spotter . . . fly spot . . ." Finally, I got it right. It had been a long day.

And a long campaign, and now I had a new problem to worry about. Earlier in the year as we battled back from the recession of 1974–1975, my advisers had warned me that there would be a "pause" in the recovery. They didn't know when it would happen, just that it would occur and that it would be a "perfectly natural" phenomenon. To forestall this, I could have accelerated federal spending, pushed for an increase in the money supply and then tried to reduce interest rates. These actions would have stimulated the economy and postponed the pause past the election. But then I had to consider the consequences in the spring of 1977. Increased federal spending would lead to a bigger budget deficit; inflation, which we'd cut to 4.8 percent in 1976, would go on a rampage again, and we'd be back in the middle of a recession. Millions of Americans would be out of work. So I told my advisers, "I'm not going to gun the economy for short-term political benefit—it just isn't right." I decided to gamble instead that the pause wouldn't hit until after election day.

I lost. By mid October, the figures for the first three quarters of the year revealed that the growth rate of the GNP, which had soared to 9.2 percent for the first three months of 1976, had fallen back to 4 percent. Unemployment, 7.3 percent in May, had increased to 7.9 percent in August and remained at about the same level in September. The stock market averages were tumbling, down 8 percent in the last three weeks alone; wholesale prices had shot up in September, their biggest jump of the year. And Alan Greenspan was predicting that inflation would continue at an annual level of at least 6 percent. Not surprisingly, Teeter's polls now showed that uncertainty about the economy was really hurting us politically.

In the final weeks of the campaign, these polls also showed that the pardon still was a big issue—a fact that Carter exploited by his constant references to the "Nixon-Ford Administration." The issue clearly wasn't going to fade away. We had to step up our efforts to get the message across that Carter was inexperienced and was promising things he couldn't deliver.

A camera crew went out and filmed interviews with hundreds of ordinary citizens in every section of the country, and the ads that resulted from that were particularly effective. They began with someone praising me, then cut to "average citizens" expressing reservations about the former Georgia governor. "When I tell people here in Georgia that I'm going to vote for Ford," a young woman drawled, "they don't understand my reasons why." She paused, looked directly into the camera and added, "It would be good to have a President from Georgia—but not Carter."

On the afternoon of October 19, I met with my advisers to focus on our strategy for the final ten days of the race. The eight most populous states—California, New York, Pennsylvania, Illinois, Texas, Ohio, Michigan and New Jersey—accounted for 228 of the 270 electoral votes I needed to win. I decided to campaign in every one of them. The polls showed we had a chance in another nine states with 93 votes—Virginia, North Carolina, South Carolina, Washington, Oregon, Indiana, Kentucky, Wisconsin and Missouri. I made up my mind to stump in all of them too. To supplement these appearances,

Teeter urged me to appear on nationwide TV with a "nonpolitical" celebrity who would question me about the issues of the campaign. Deardourff said that Joe Garagiola would be an excellent choice.

As a sports enthusiast, I'd followed his career in major league baseball and later enjoyed watching him as a TV broadcaster. He had a down-to-earth way of describing events on the playing field, and he wasn't embarrassed to let his enthusiasm show. We had met for the first time in July 1976, when I had invited him to the All Star baseball game in Philadelphia. On the trip back to Washington that night, we had a chance to talk at length, and I felt as if he had been a friend for years. After we landed, I put my arm around his shoulder and said, "Joe, I really enjoyed this. We should do it again."

He flashed me a broad grin. "Well, I think I could work it into my schedule," he said.

So now on the morning of October 20, I telephoned him and said I needed his help. I was asking him to take quite a risk by sticking his neck out publicly—possibly jeopardizing his career as a TV personality—but Joe didn't hesitate. He was with me all the way, and I soon discovered his questions on our TV show gave me a chance to talk about the issues in an informal, conversational way. And when he teamed up with former Democratic Congresswoman Edith Green— whose credentials were so impressive—the combination was dynamite. "How would you characterize the President?" Joe asked. And Edith, a friend for nearly twenty years, replied, "He's honest, he's decent and he doesn't have a mean bone in his body."

On October 22, Carter and I met in Williamsburg, Virginia, for our third and final debate. It proved to be anticlimactic. Carter declared that I "ought to be ashamed" about my performance in dealing with the economy, and I defended that record—ending the recession, slashing inflation in half, getting the nation on the road to real prosperity. Summing up, I said: "I've been proud to be President of the United States during these very troubled times. I love America just as all of you love America. It would be the highest honor for me to have your support on November 2 and for you to say, 'Jerry Ford, you've done a good job. Keep on doing it.'"

Next morning, I was off on a grueling 15,705-mile swing through seventeen states, and I didn't return to Washington until election day.

What a *team* effort that was! Betty and the children all campaigned for me independently, and nothing we had ever done pulled us closer together as a family than that final drive. My aides worked feverishly; Garagiola and Edith Green were by my side at almost every stop, and members of my Cabinet—Treasury Secretary Simon, Commerce Secretary Richardson, HUD Secretary Hills and Transportation Secretary Coleman—traveled all over the country and did everything they could to achieve victory. And all this was having a positive effect. When the latest polls showed that we were closing fast, confidence soared. Spencer, ever the realist, kept reminding me that in order to win on November 2, we had to capture at least five of the eight largest states. Teeter's surveys showed that we led in only three of them—California, Michigan and Ohio—but everyone said a last-minute surge could push us over the top. Some of my aides called this final leg of the campaign the "Bataan Death March," but so long as we still had a chance to pull the political comeback of the century, I was determined to crowd as many events as possible into each day.

On October 23, for example, I campaigned in Virginia, North Carolina, South Carolina and California. Six days later, I had breakfast in Wisconsin, lunch in Missouri and dinner in Texas. The scenery varied from place to place, and so did the faces in the audience, but the constants remained: the motorcades with their sirens and their flashing red lights, the crowds waiting for me waving their placards and signs, the bands striking up the "Michigan Fight Song" and "Hail to the Chief." There were disappointments. I was saddened, for example, to receive a telegram from Reagan expressing his "sincere regrets" that he wouldn't be able to campaign with me in California because he had other obligations.

Yet on the whole I was buoyant about my chances. Government spending and national defense—these were the issues that voters really cared about, and at every stop I told them how my sixty-six vetoes had saved taxpayers at least $9 billion and how my Administration would keep the country strong over the next four years.

I hadn't had any real exercise for days. My eyes were puffy and I was having trouble with my voice. But then I received some astonishingly good news. The final Gallup poll—to be released November 1 —would have me leading Carter 47 to 46. This was the first time in the entire campaign that I had led, and I was so "up" that I called Dole to share the news. It was 7 A.M. and I was in Philadelphia; he was somewhere in New Mexico. "Morning, Bob," I said. "What are you doing?"

"Well, Mr. President," he replied, "it's only five o'clock out here. I'm still sleeping."

I gave him the poll results and he, too, was ecstatic. "We have the momentum now," I said, "and I just know we're going to win." What a twist, I thought, that Carter, the man who prided himself on being an outsider, had turned inside for the campaign. He was calling the old-line Democratic bosses like Chicago Mayor Dick Daley and Philadelphia's Frank Rizzo to make sure that their machines delivered for him on election day. But I couldn't let myself think about that for long. We were scheduled to fly west to Indianapolis at seven-thirty, and after that would come stops in Kentucky and Ohio. It would be go, go, go and then go some more for the next five days.

Finally, on the evening of November 1, Betty and I came home to Grand Rapids. By this time I was exhausted and my voice was shot, but there was a gigantic rally that night in front of the Pantlind Hotel. I looked into the faces of that crowd and saw countless friends who had helped me over the years. This brought back so many memories that I discarded my prepared remarks and spoke from the heart:

"Betty and I have been honored to represent this part of the country—and all America—in the White House during the last two years, and they have been troubled and they have been tough. But we kept the ship of state on the right course and I tried to keep a firm, common-sense hand on the tiller. And the net result is, things have turned around. America has made incredible progress in the last two years. But we are going to get better. We are going to make America what our forefathers said it would be. When I was sworn in I asked for your prayers, but tomorrow I ask that you confirm me with your votes and I won't let you down. I promise that."

Next morning, Betty and I got up early to vote. One final ceremony was on the schedule—the unveiling of a large mural in the Kent County airport—and that was the most special moment of the entire campaign. A local artist, Paul Collins, had painted the mural to depict my entire career. There I was with my parents as an Eagle

Scout, as a high school football player, behind the wheel of a Model T
Ford. There were Betty and I after our wedding in 1948, and finally
there was a newspaper headline from 1974: "Ford Becomes President." It was all I could do to keep myself under control.

"I guess the name will be the 'Gerald R. Ford Mural,' " I said. "It
means so much to me because of the first Gerald R. Ford and his
wife, Dorothy, my mother and father. I owe everything to them and
to the training, the love, the leadership"—the tears welled up in my
eyes and I had to pause to brush them away—"and whatever has
been done by me in any way whatsoever, it is because of Jerry Ford,
Senior, and Dorothy Ford. And that is what that mural will always
mean to me in the years ahead."

Then we flew back to Washington to await the election returns. Although we had sets tuned to each network, I spent most of the time
watching NBC, which had decided to color the states Carter won red
and the states I carried blue. Betty and the children had invited some
of their personal friends—Clara Powell, for example, and Pearl Bailey—to join us in the White House, and I had invited others—Joe
Garagiola, Edith Green and their families, Bob and Liddy Dole, Jacob Javits, who had campaigned so very hard for me. Cheney, Nessen, Kennerly, Barrett and Greg Willard represented the White
House staff. Teeter was there from the President Ford Committee.

At first we didn't have much to cheer about. Carter was sweeping
the Deep South. By the time we finished our buffet supper, he had
won about a dozen states, while I had prevailed in only two or three.
I guess I looked pretty lonesome sitting there in front of the TV. Garagiola came up and put his hand on my shoulder. "It's all right,
Prez," he said. "We've given up a couple of runs, but the ball game is
only in the top of the fourth; we got a long way to go."

Connecticut appeared to be ours. So did Virginia. As did New Jersey, and that was a surprise because we hadn't counted on those 17
electoral votes. New Hampshire and Vermont seemed to be solid for
me. Ohio was too close to call. That disappointed me, because I'd
spent a lot of time and effort there and I'd expected to win. Well, I
still had a chance. If we held on to the states where we were ahead
and if we carried Ohio, California and Hawaii, we could pull it out. I
got pretty excited about that.

At midnight, I still maintained a narrow lead in New York. Then the votes from New York City came in, and at one-twenty, NBC declared that Carter had won the state. The results in Pennsylvania weren't encouraging and Texas was doubtful, an unpleasant surprise. John Connally had insisted all along that he would deliver the state, and at one forty-five Wednesday morning, I called him to find out what was happening. "Don't count us out," John said. "We're going to win. Before the night is out you'll have Texas."

Twenty minutes later, NBC gave Carter Texas. "That hurt," I said, shaking my head. "That *really* hurt." But then North Dakota went for me. It had only three electoral votes, but the victory boosted me psychologically. "Go Blue," I yelled at the TV screen.

"Go, Big Blue," Joe kept shouting. "We're gonna pull it out."

By two-forty the election had come down to four states. Four million residents of Ohio had gone to the polls and I had a lead of 2,000 votes. In Hawaii, the situation was reversed. I was trailing by 4,000 votes. Mississippi was a possibility. And then there was Wisconsin. Although the networks had given the state to Carter, Teeter insisted that late returns could put me over the top. But no one could say when—or if—that would happen. I was bushed. It was three-twenty in the morning and there wasn't a darn thing that I could do, so I went to bed.

Kennerly gave me the bad news shortly after nine o'clock. "I'm afraid we've had it," he said, and he looked even sadder than I felt. I was so hoarse I couldn't reply. "Ohio is still out, but even if you win its 25 votes," he continued, "there's no state that's going to give you the four more you need to hit 270."

Marsh, Cheney, Spencer and Teeter confirmed that analysis when I met with them an hour later. I was terribly hurt and disappointed, but at the same time I was proud of the effort we'd made. We had run a good campaign. I'm not the sort to brood over defeat. I didn't *like* to lose, but I wasn't going to sit there and wring my hands. I told the children that I didn't want any moaning, no sour grapes. I knew how upset they were—*all* of us had worked hard—but the important thing now was to look to the future.

Some of my aides—Marsh was among them—thought that we should consider contesting the results in Wisconsin and Ohio. Apparently, there had been some illegal, on-the-spot voter registration in Wisconsin and there were allegations that Democrats had voted in West Virginia and then crossed the river to vote again in Ohio. "The election is over," I said. "We lost. I will not be a party to any recount or lawsuit in any state."

Shortly after eleven o'clock, I telephoned Carter in Georgia to congratulate him. It was a hard call to make, but something I had to do. As it turned out, he was as exhausted as I was, so our conversation was short. Then I stepped out into the briefing room, where reporters had assembled. I wanted to thank the millions of Americans who had supported me and I also wanted to read the telegram that I'd sent to the President-elect. Unfortunately, my voice was just about gone, so Betty volunteered to read it for me. I was very proud of her. Speaking slowly, struggling with her own emotions, Betty expressed my thanks to all the people who had worked so hard on my behalf. Then she read the text of the telegram. "Dear Jimmy," it began. "It is apparent now that you have won our long and intense struggle for the Presidency. I congratulate you on your victory. As one who has been honored to serve the people of this great land both in Congress and as President, I believe that we must now put the division of the campaign behind us and unite the country once again in the common pursuit of peace and prosperity. I want to assure you that you will have my complete and wholehearted support as you take the oath of office this January. I also pledge to you that I and all members of my Administration will do all that we can to ensure that you begin your term as smoothly and as effectively as possible. May God bless you and your family as you undertake your new responsibilities."

Fifteen minutes after I returned to the Oval Office, Garagiola came in with his family. We threw our arms around each other without saying a word, because nothing needed to be said. For as long as I live, I won't forget that scene. There we were, two has-been athletes, hugging each other in total silence. Then the mood broke and the tears began to flow. "Damn it, we shoulda won. We shoulda won," he said.

I tried to comfort him. "Hey," I replied, "there are more important things to worry about than what's going to happen to Jerry Ford."

"Not today, damn it," he sobbed. "Not today."

A number of my aides were just as upset as Joe, and I suppose they expected me to show my hurt more openly. But my son Jack captured the way I felt. "You know," he said, "when you come so close, it's really hard to lose. But at the same time, if you can't lose as graciously as you had planned to win, then you shouldn't have been in the thing in the first place." I couldn't have said it better myself.

8

Moving On

"If you would not be forgotten, as soon as you are dead and rotten,
either write things worth reading, or do things worth writing."

— Benjamin Franklin

What if I hadn't pardoned Nixon? How many people had voted against me because of that? What if I had kept Rockefeller on the ticket as my running mate and hadn't selected Dole? Bob, a loyal friend, had campaigned very effectively and we had won the crucial farm states. But would Nelson have made the difference in New York, Ohio or Pennsylvania? What if the economic pause hadn't hit us in September and October? What if the good news—which appeared in mid November—had come out three weeks earlier? Did pocketbook issues determine the way people decided to vote? What if we had been able to achieve a SALT II accord with the Soviets? Brezhnev would have come to the United States in 1976. Would our joint commitment to a lasting peace have tipped the scales in November? And what if Reagan had been able to put aside his own disappointment and campaign more enthusiastically for me? Would we have captured Texas?

There were other "what ifs," but I realized early on that dwelling on them would be a pointless exercise. Seventy-eight days remained until the end of my Presidency, and there was still much that I wanted to do. I had promised Carter a smooth transition. I intended to give him and his team all the help we could. I told the Cabinet to cooperate in every possible way. And I directed my old reliable, Jack Marsh, to handle our liaison with them. It went well and the country was better for it.

After an eight-day vacation in Palm Springs, I set to work on the budget for fiscal 1978. I spent nearly fifty hours on it in November and December. The Congress that had just been elected was again overwhelmingly Democratic. Its liberal orientation, I knew, probably would cause it to reject the concept of fiscal restraint. Yet the need for that restraint was just as evident now as it had been for the last two years.

Over the past three decades, federal, state and local government spending had nearly doubled from 18 percent to 34 percent of the GNP. And since 1968, federal spending had increased an average of 10 percent per year. The only way to curb that growth was to discipline ourselves to a long-range program of cutting back government's share of the GNP and giving the beleaguered taxpayer permanent relief.

But this required some radical changes in public attitudes. For beginners, we had to understand that income and wealth are not produced in Washington; they are only redistributed there. Secondly, we had to overcome the idea that members of Congress are elected primarily to bring home the federal bacon. Finally, we had to cast aside the prevalent attitude that only new programs with fancy names and multibillion-dollar price tags can solve our problems. Could we make these changes in our thinking before a massive, impersonal government engulfed us all? Frankly, I didn't expect this Congress to agree with me, but in my final budget I was certainly going to try.

As I put the finishing touches on the document, I was also preparing for my final State of the Union speech. I asked Hartmann to produce a draft that resembled in mood the remarks I'd made when I became President. Once again he did a superior job.

There was tremendous applause from both sides of the aisle as I entered the House chamber the evening of January 12. The standing ovation was as warm as any I'd ever received. "Mr. Speaker, Mr. Vice President, members of the Ninety-fifth Congress and distinguished guests," I began. "This report will be my last—maybe." Even Tip O'Neill joined in the laughter at the last word, which I had pencilled in on the way to the Capitol. "The state of the Union," I reported, "is good." I wished the President-elect "the very best in all that is good for our country," and I pointed out how marvelous it was that transitions of power in the United States could occur so naturally: "There are no soldiers marching in the streets except in the inaugural parade; no public demonstrations except for some of the dancers at the inaugural ball; the opposition party doesn't go underground, but goes on functioning; and a vigilant press goes right on probing and publishing our faults and our follies."

During World War II, FDR once asked General Douglas MacArthur where his *real* home was. MacArthur thought for a moment and replied, "The Point." My real home had always been the House, so it was difficult for me to end my remarks. "It was here that I stood twenty-eight years ago with my freshman colleagues as Speaker Sam Rayburn administered the oath. I see some of you now—and I remember those who have gone to their rest. It was here we waged many, many a lively battle—won some, lost some, but always remained friends. It was here, surrounded by such friends, that the distinguished Chief Justice swore me in as Vice President. It was here that I returned eight months later as your President to ask not for a honeymoon but for a good marriage. I will always treasure those memories and your many, many kindnesses. I thank you for them all.

"My fellow Americans, I once asked you for your prayers, and now I give you mine. May God guide this wonderful country, its people and those they have chosen to lead them. May our third century be illuminated by liberty and blessed with brotherhood so that we and all who come after us may be the humble servants of thy peace."

During the next week there were farewell breakfasts and luncheons and dinners almost every day. I signed the budget and submitted it to Congress. I presented the Medal of Freedom to Henry Kissinger and Don Rumsfeld and the National Security Medal to CIA Director George Bush. Then Betty and I flew to Camp David for a final weekend there. Betty's mood, in fact, was something that concerned me. Thinking that we would be far too busy to socialize, many of our closest friends were keeping their distance from us.

They were trying to be considerate, but Betty didn't understand and she was depressed. I talked to Kennerly about this on the morning of January 15. "Dave," I said, "I'd like to cheer her up. What do you suggest?"

"How about a surprise party?" he said. "Why don't the two of you come over to my place for dinner? She's always liked coming over, and I could invite a few people both of you know."

"That's not bad." I grinned, and began to cook up a surprise of my own.

We arrived at Kennerly's Georgetown house on the evening of January 18. Dave had asked Germaine Swanson, a fantastic Vietnamese cook, to cater the affair. He had invited another friend, photographer Bruce Dale, to put on a stunning slide show. Betty was enjoying herself enormously, and both Dave and I knew that it was going to be difficult to persuade her to leave and go back to the White House. But I had a ready excuse. The members of the Marine Band that had played at all our state dinners had assembled in the Grand Hall for a final photograph. It was the only night in their holiday schedule we could pose with them. They had done so much for us; we couldn't disappoint them now.

Reluctantly, Betty agreed. The South Portico of the White House was dark as our limousine pulled up to the entrance shortly after ten o'clock that Tuesday night. We took the family elevator to the first floor. All was quiet; only a few lights were on, but I could see the members of the band waiting for us by the foot of the grand staircase. "Well, so long as we're here," I suggested, "why don't we have a last dance?" She nodded and made a request, "Thanks for the Memory," and we began to twirl around the floor.

Suddenly, from the hallway on the right, other couples began gliding onto the floor—the Buchens, the Harlows, the Kissingers, the Lairds—more than one hundred people in all, and they were beaming with delight. But they were as quiet as mice. I was maneuvering Betty around the dance floor so that her back was to the door; she still didn't know anyone else was there. Finally, someone—I think it was Bunny Buchen—tapped her on the shoulder. She whirled around; she gave a gasp of surprise and then tears came to her eyes. Then everyone crowded around, hugging and kissing her. Seeing her so happy was one of the greatest joys of my life.

The next night was to be our last in the White House. Over the past two and a half years, Betty and I had become very fond of Nelson and Happy Rockefeller. We wanted to show our appreciation, so we invited them to have dinner with us and spend the night. We encouraged them to bring along Mark and Nelson, Jr., their two young sons. Nelson was full of enthusiasm when he arrived. He brought a camera and he proceeded to take pictures of everything. We reminisced over dinner and, later, went up to the third floor. I was due to play golf with Arnold Palmer in the Bing Crosby Tournament in California on January 21. I wanted to loosen up, so we erected a practice driving range in the hall. Nelson and I took turns whacking away at the ball, then gave the clubs to Nelson's sons. Nelson, Jr., stepped up over the ball, then swung as hard as he could. He missed. He tried again—and missed. Turning to his father, he said, "I wonder what President Ford thinks about me now." Nelson flashed me a broad grin. "Don't worry," he replied. "President Ford understands all about missing shots."

There was a final farewell breakfast with senior staff members the next morning, and I told them that they had contributed to an Administration "which I think was good and which history will treat kindly." Then I returned upstairs and waited for Betty to get ready to leave. All our photographs had been removed from the walls; all our furniture had been taken away. At ten-thirty we went down to the State Dining Room and said goodbye to the members of the White House residence staff, those marvelous men and women who had made our stay so enjoyable. Minutes later, the Carters arrived to have coffee with us in the Blue Room, and soon it was time for our motorcade to leave for the Capitol.

The weather that morning was windy and cold, but the atmosphere was full of hope and the crowd that gathered below the East Front of the Capitol reflected that. Chief Justice Burger administered the oath to the thirty-ninth President of the United States. Carter's first words were, "For myself and for our nation I want to thank my predecessor for all he has done to heal our land."

That was so unexpected, such a gracious thing for him to say. The crowd began to applaud, and I bit my lip to mask my emotions. I didn't know whether to remain seated or to stand. But when the cheers continued I decided to stand, and I reached over to clasp Carter's hand.

Then it was over. Betty and I walked through the Rotunda and down the back Capitol steps toward the helicopter that would carry us to Andrews Air Force Base. Normally, the flight takes no more than ten minutes, but I asked the pilot to circle slowly over the Capitol dome one final time. "That's my real home," I said. There was a crowd waiting for us at Andrews. All my Cabinet was there. People were waving signs that read "Good Luck" and "Thank You, Jerry." The band was playing "God Bless America." I hugged the Rockefellers and Kissingers and I shook hands all around. I waved a final goodbye. Then Betty and I walked up the ramp and stepped inside the plane.

The mood aboard that plane—a backup to *Air Force One*—was high-spirited and extremely festive at first. Dean Burch and his wife, Kennerly and Barrett were among the thirty-three passengers, and everyone was trying to crack jokes and laugh. We still were exhilarated by President Carter's comment and by the warmth of the crowd's response. Then, too, Betty and I wanted everyone to feel happy and comfortable. But halfway across the country, it was as if an invisible force had entered the plane. The merriment ceased, and people began returning to their seats. Betty and I were sitting up forward in our private compartment, and I reached out to hold her hand. My thoughts went back to the morning of August 1, 1974, when I received that first phone call from Al Haig. And I remembered how cloudy it had been in Washington that day. Now I looked out the window of the plane. The sun was shining brightly. I couldn't see a cloud anywhere, and I felt glad about that.

Index